Take the Next Step in Your IT Career

T0188630

Save
10%
on Exam Vouchers*

(up to a $35 value)

*Some restrictions apply. See web page for details.

CompTIA.

CompTIA®
Network+®
Practice Tests
Third Edition

CompTIA®
Network+®
Practice Tests
Exam N10-009
Third Edition

Craig Zacker

SYBEX®
A Wiley Brand

About the Author

Craig Zacker is the author or coauthor of dozens of books, manuals, articles, and websites on computer and networking topics. He has also been an English professor, a technical and copy editor, a network administrator, a webmaster, a corporate trainer, a technical support engineer, a minicomputer operator, a literature and philosophy student, a library clerk, a photographic darkroom technician, a shipping clerk, and a newspaper boy.

About the Technical Editor

Chris Crayton, MCSE, CISSP, CASP+, CySA+, Cloud+, S+, N+, A+, is a technical consultant, trainer, author, and industry-leading technical editor. He has worked as a computer technology and networking instructor, information security director, network administrator, network engineer, and PC specialist. Chris has served as technical editor and content contributor on numerous technical titles for several of the leading publishing companies. He has also been recognized with many professional and teaching awards.

Contents

Introduction

Welcome to *CompTIA® Network+® Practice Tests: Exam N10-009, Third Edition.* This book gives you a focused, timesaving way to review your networking knowledge and prepare to pass the Computing Technology Industry Association (CompTIA) Network+ exam. The book combines realistic exam prep questions with detailed answers and two complete practice tests to help you become familiar with the types of questions that you will encounter on the Network+ exam. By reviewing the objectives and sample questions, you can focus on the specific skills that you need to improve before taking the exam.

N10-009 Objective Map

The following table gives you the extent, by percentage, that each domain is represented on the actual examination, and where you can find questions in this book that are related to each objective.

Objective	Percentage of Exam	Chapter
1.0 Networking Concepts	23%	1
2.0 Network Implementations	20%	2
3.0 Network Operations	19%	3
4.0 Network Security	14%	4
5.0 Network Troubleshooting	24%	5

How This Book Is Organized

The first five chapters of this book are based on the five objective domains published by CompTIA for the N10-009 Network+ exam. There are approximately 200 questions for each objective domain, covering each of the suggested topics. The next two chapters each contain a 100-question practice test covering all of the objective domains. Once you have prepared each of the objective domains individually, you can take the practice tests to see how you will perform on the actual exam.

Who Should Read This Book

CompTIA recommends, but does not require, that candidates for the Network+ exam meet the following prerequisites:

- CompTIA A+ certification or equivalent knowledge
- At least 9–12 months of work experience in IT networking

CompTIA's certification program relies on exams that measure your ability to perform a specific job function or set of tasks. CompTIA develops the exams by analyzing the tasks performed by people who are currently working in the field. Therefore, the specific knowledge, skills, and abilities relating to the job are reflected in the certification exam.

Because the certification exams are based on real-world tasks, you need to gain hands-on experience with the applicable technology in order to master the exam. In a sense, you might consider hands-on experience in an organizational environment to be a prerequisite for passing the Network+ exam. Many of the questions relate directly to specific network products or technologies, so use opportunities at your school or workplace to practice using the relevant tools. Candidates for the exam are also expected to have a basic understanding of enterprise technologies, including cloud and virtualization.

Like all exams, the Network+ certification from CompTIA is updated periodically and may eventually be retired or replaced. At some point after CompTIA is no longer offering this exam, the old editions of our books and online tools will be retired. If you have purchased this book after the exam was retired, or are attempting to register in the Sybex online learning environment after the exam was retired, please know that we make no guarantees that this exam's online Sybex tools will be available once the exam is no longer available.

How to Use This Book

Although you can use this book in a number of ways, you might begin your studies by taking one of the practice exams as a pretest. After completing the exam, review your results for each objective domain and focus your studies first on the objective domains for which you received the lowest scores.

As this book contains only practice questions and answers, the best method to prepare for the Network+ exam is to use this book along with a companion book that provides more extensive explanations for the elements covered in each objective domain. Todd Lammle's *CompTIA® Network+® Study Guide: Exam N10-009, Sixth Edition,* provides complete coverage of all the technology you need to know for the exam.

After you have taken your pretest, you can use the chapters for the objective domains in which you need work to test your detailed knowledge and learn more about the technologies involved. By reviewing why the answers are correct or incorrect, you can determine if you need to study the objective topics more.

What's Next

The next step is to review the objective domains for the Network+ N10-009 exam and think about which topics you need to work on most. Then, you can turn to the appropriate chapter and get started. Good luck on the exam.

How to Become Network+ Certified

As this book goes to press, Pearson VUE is the sole Network+ exam provider. Below you will find the contact information and exam-specific details for registering. Exam pricing might vary by country or by CompTIA membership.

Vendor	Website	Phone Number
Pearson VUE	www.pearsonvue.com/comptia	US and Canada: 877-551-PLUS (7587)

How to Contact the Publisher

If you believe you have found a mistake in this book, please bring it to our attention. At John Wiley & Sons, we understand how important it is to provide our customers with accurate content, but even with our best efforts, an error may occur.

In order to submit your possible errata, please email it to our Customer Service Team at wileysupport@wiley.com with the subject line "Possible Book Errata Submission."

Chapter

1

Networking Concepts

THE COMPTIA NETWORK+ EXAM N10-009 TOPICS COVERED IN THIS CHAPTER INCLUDE THE FOLLOWING:

✓ **1.1 Explain concepts related to the Open Systems Interconnection (OSI) reference model.**

- Layer 1 – Physical
- Layer 2 – Data link
- Layer 3 – Network
- Layer 4 – Transport
- Layer 5 – Session
- Layer 6 – Presentation
- Layer 7 – Application

✓ **1.2 Compare and contrast networking appliances, applications, and functions.**

- Physical and virtual appliances
  - Router
  - Switch
  - Firewall
  - Intrusion detection system (IDS)/intrusion prevention system (IPS)
  - Load balancer
  - Proxy
  - Network-attached storage (NAS)
  - Storage area network (SAN)
  - Wireless
    - Access point (AP)
    - Controller

- Applications
    - Content delivery network (CDN)
- Functions
    - Virtual private network (VPN)
    - Quality of service (QoS)
    - Time to live (TTL)

✓ **1.3 Summarize cloud concepts and connectivity options.**

- Network functions virtualization (NFV)
- Virtual private cloud (VPC)
- Network security groups
- Network security lists
- Cloud gateways
    - Internet gateway
    - Network address translation (NAT) gateway
- Cloud connectivity options
    - VPN
    - Direct Connect
- Deployment models
    - Public
    - Private
    - Hybrid
- Service models
    - Software as a service (SaaS)
    - Infrastructure as a service (IaaS)
    - Platform as a service (PaaS)
- Scalability
- Elasticity
- Multitenancy

✓ 1.4 Explain common networking ports, protocols, services, and traffic types.

Protocols	Ports
File Transfer Protocol (FTP)	20/21
Secure File Transfer Protocol (SFTP)	22
Secure Shell (SSH)	22
Telnet	23
Simple Mail Transfer Protocol (SMTP)	25
Domain Name System (DNS)	53
Dynamic Host Configuration Protocol (DHCP)	67/68
Trivial File Transfer Protocol (TFTP)	69
Hypertext Transfer Protocol (HTTP)	80
Network Time Protocol (NTP)	123
Simple Network Management Protocol (SNMP)	161/162
Lightweight Directory Access Protocol (LDAP)	389
Hypertext Transfer Protocol Secure (HTTPS)	443
Server Message Block (SMB)	445
Syslog	514
Simple Mail Transfer Protocol Secure (SMTPS)	587
Lightweight Directory Access Protocol over SSL (LDAPS)	636
Structured Query Language (SQL) Server	1433
Remote Desktop Protocol (RDP) 3389	3389
Session Initiation Protocol (SIP)	5060/5061

- Internet Protocol (IP) types
    - Internet Control Message Protocol (ICMP)
    - Transmission Control Protocol (TCP)
    - User Datagram Protocol (UDP)
    - Generic Routing Encapsulation (GRE)

- Internet Protocol Security (IPSec)
  - Authentication Header (AH)
  - Encapsulating Security Payload (ESP)
  - Internet Key Exchange (IKE)
- Traffic types
  - Unicast
  - Multicast
  - Anycast
  - Broadcast

✓ **1.5 Compare and contrast transmission media and transceivers.**

- Wireless
  - 802.11 standards
  - Cellular
  - Satellite
- Wired
  - 802.3 standards
  - Single-mode vs. multimode fiber
  - Direct attach copper (DAC) cable
    - Twinaxial cable
  - Coaxial cable
  - Cable speeds
  - Plenum vs. non-plenum cable
- Transceivers
  - Protocol
    - Ethernet
    - Fibre Channel (FC)
  - Form factors
    - Small form-factor pluggable (SFP)
    - Quad small form-factor pluggable (QSFP)

- Connector types

  - Subscriber connector (SC)

  - Local connector (LC)

  - Straight tip (ST)

  - Multi-fiber push on (MPO)

  - Registered jack (RJ)11

  - RJ45

  - F-type

  - Bayonet Neill–Concelman (BNC)

✓ **1.6 Compare and contrast network topologies, architectures, and types.**

- Mesh

- Hybrid

- Star/hub and spoke

- Spine and leaf

- Point to point

- Three-tier hierarchical model

  - Core

  - Distribution

  - Access

- Collapsed core

- Traffic flows

  - North-south

  - East-west

✓ **1.7 Given a scenario, use appropriate IPv4 network addressing.**

- Public vs. private

  - Automatic Private IP Addressing (APIPA)

  - RFC1918

  - Loopback/localhost

- Subnetting
  - Variable Length Subnet Mask (VLSM)
  - Classless Inter-domain Routing (CIDR)
- IPv4 address classes
  - Class A
  - Class B
  - Class C
  - Class D
  - Class E

✓ **1.8 Summarize evolving use cases for modern network environments.**

- Software-defined network (SDN) and software-defined wide area network (SD-WAN)
  - Application aware
  - Zero-touch provisioning
  - Transport agnostic
  - Central policy management
- Virtual Extensible Local Area Network (VXLAN)
  - Data center interconnect (DCI)
  - Layer 2 encapsulation
- Zero trust architecture (ZTA)
  - Policy-based authentication
  - Authorization
  - Least privilege access
- Secure Access Secure Edge (SASE)/Security Service Edge (SSE)
- Infrastructure as code (IaC)
  - Automation
    - Playbooks/templates/reusable tasks
    - Configuration drift/compliance
    - Upgrades
    - Dynamic inventories

- Source control
    - Version control
    - Central repository
    - Conflict identification
    - Branching
- IPv6 addressing
    - Mitigating address exhaustion
    - Compatibility requirements
        - Tunneling
        - Dual stack
        - NAT64

1.1 Explain concepts related to the Open Systems Interconnection (OSI) reference model.

1. At which of the following layers of the Open Systems Interconnection (OSI) model do the protocols on a typical local area network (LAN) use media access control (MAC) addresses to identify other computers on the network?

    A. Physical

    B. Data link

    C. Network

    D. Transport

2. Which of the following organizations developed the Open Systems Interconnection (OSI) model?

    A. International Telecommunication Union (ITU-T)

    B. Comité Consultatif International Télégraphique et Téléphonique (CCITT)

    C. American National Standards Institute (ANSI)

    D. Institute of Electrical and Electronics Engineers (IEEE)

    E. International Organization for Standardization (ISO)

3. Which layer of the Open Systems Interconnection (OSI) model is responsible for the logical addressing of end systems and the routing of datagrams on a network?

    A. Physical

    B. Data link

    C. Network

    D. Transport

    E. Session

    F. Presentation

    G. Application

4. On a TCP/IP network, which layers of the Open Systems Interconnection (OSI) model contain protocols that are responsible for encapsulating the data generated by an application, creating the payload for a packet that will be transmitted over a network? (Choose all that apply.)

    A. Physical

    B. Data link

    C. Network

    D. Transport

    E. Session

    F. Presentation

    G. Application

5. Which layer of the Open Systems Interconnection (OSI) model is responsible for translating and formatting information?

    A. Physical

    B. Data link

    C. Network

    D. Transport

    E. Session

    F. Presentation

    G. Application

6. Which of the following devices typically operates at the Network layer of the Open Systems Interconnection (OSI) model?

    A. Proxy server

    B. Network interface adapter

    C. Hub

    D. Router

7. Which layer of the Open Systems Interconnection (OSI) model provides an entrance point to the protocol stack for applications?

    A. Physical

    B. Data link

    C. Network

    D. Transport

    E. Session

    F. Presentation

    G. Application

8. Which layer of the Open Systems Interconnection (OSI) model is responsible for dialogue control between two communicating end systems?

    A. Physical

    B. Data link

    C. Network

    D. Transport

    E. Session

    F. Presentation

    G. Application

9. Some switches can perform functions associated with two layers of the Open Systems Interconnection (OSI) model. Which two of the following layers are often associated with network switching? (Choose all that apply.)

   A. Physical

   B. Data link

   C. Network

   D. Transport

   E. Session

   F. Presentation

   G. Application

10. At which layer of the Open Systems Interconnection (OSI) model are there TCP/IP protocols that can provide either connectionless or connection-oriented services to applications?

   A. Physical

   B. Data link

   C. Network

   D. Transport

   E. Session

   F. Presentation

   G. Application

11. Which of the following layers of the Open Systems Interconnection (OSI) model typically have dedicated physical hardware devices associated with them? (Choose all that apply.)

   A. Physical

   B. Data link

   C. Network

   D. Transport

   E. Session

   F. Presentation

   G. Application

12. At which layer of the Open Systems Interconnection (OSI) model is there a protocol that adds both a header and a footer to the information that is passed down from an upper layer, thus creating a frame?

   A. Physical

   B. Data link

   C. Network

   D. Transport

   E. Session

   F. Presentation

   G. Application

13. Identify the layer of the Open Systems Interconnection (OSI) model that controls the addressing, transmission, and reception of Ethernet frames, and also identify the media access control method that Ethernet uses.

   A. Physical layer: Carrier Sense Multiple Access with Collision Detection (CSMA/CD)

   B. Physical layer: Carrier Sense Multiple Access with Collision Avoidance (CSMA/CA)

   C. Data link layer: CSMA/CD

   D. Data link layer: CSMA/CA

14. At which layer of the OSI model do you find the protocol responsible for the delivery of data to its ultimate destination on an internetwork?

   A. Data link

   B. Network

   C. Session

   D. Application

15. Which of the following is not a protocol operating at the Network layer of the OSI model?

   A. IP

   B. ICMP

   C. IGMP

   D. IMAP

16. Ed is a software developer who has been given the task of creating an application that requires guaranteed delivery of information between end systems. At which layer of the Open Systems Interconnection (OSI) model does the protocol that provides the guaranteed delivery run, and what type of protocol must Ed use?

   A. Data link layer; connectionless

   B. Network layer; connection-oriented

   C. Transport layer; connection-oriented

   D. Application layer; connectionless

17. Alice is a network administrator designing a new local area network (LAN). She needs to determine the type of cabling and the network topology to implement. Which layers of the Open Systems Interconnection (OSI) model apply to cabling and topology elements?

   A. Physical and Data link layers

   B. Data link and Network layers

   C. Network and Transport layers

   D. Transport and Application layers

18. Which layers of the Open Systems Interconnection (OSI) model do not have protocols in the TCP/IP suite exclusively dedicated to them? (Choose all that apply.)

   A. Physical

   B. Data link

   C. Network

   D. Transport

   E. Session

   F. Presentation

   G. Application

19. The protocols at which layer of the Open Systems Interconnection (OSI) model use port numbers to identify the applications that are the source and the destination of the data in the packets?

   A. Application

   B. Presentation

   C. Transport

   D. Network

20. Which of the following is a correct listing of the Open Systems Interconnection (OSI) model layers, in order, from top to bottom?

   A. Physical, Data link, Transport, Network, Session, Presentation, Application

   B. Application, Session, Presentation, Transport, Network, Data link, physical

   C. Presentation, Application, Transport, Session, Network, Physical, Data link

   D. Session, Application, Presentation, Transport, Data link, Network, Physical

   E. Application, Presentation, Session, Transport, Network, Data link, Physical

21. At which of the Open Systems Interconnection (OSI) model layers do switches and bridges perform their basic functions?

   A. Physical

   B. Data link

   C. Network

   D. Transport

22. On a TCP/IP network, flow control is a function implemented in protocols operating at which layer of the Open Systems Interconnection (OSI) model?

   A. Presentation

   B. Session

   C. Transport

   D. Network

23. Which layer of the Open Systems Interconnection (OSI) model defines the medium, network interfaces, connecting hardware, and signaling methods used on a network?

   A. Physical

   B. Data link

   C. Network

   D. Transport

   E. Session

   F. Presentation

   G. Application

24. Which of the OSI model layers is responsible for syntax translation and compression or encryption?

   A. Data link

   B. Network

   C. Session

   D. Presentation

   E. Application

25. Which layer of the Open Systems Interconnection (OSI) model is responsible for transmitting signals over the network medium?

   A. Physical

   B. Data link

   C. Network

   D. Transport

   E. Session

   F. Presentation

   G. Application

26. Specify the layer of the Open Systems Interconnection (OSI) model at which the Internet Protocol (IP) operates and whether it is connection-oriented or connectionless.

   A. Network; connection-oriented

   B. Network; connectionless

   C. Transport; connection-oriented

   D. Transport; connectionless

27. An Ethernet network interface adapter provides functions that span which two layers of the Open Systems Interconnection (OSI) model?

   A. Physical and Data link

   B. Data link and Network

   C. Network and Transport

   D. Transport and Application

28. Which of the following protocols operate at the Application layer of the Open Systems Interconnection (OSI) model? (Choose all that apply.)

A. HTTP

B. SNMP

C. ICMP

D. IGMP

E. UDP

29. Which layer of the Open Systems Interconnection (OSI) model would be responsible for converting a text file encoded using EBCDIC on the sending system into ASCII code, when required by the receiving system?

A. Application

B. Presentation

C. Session

D. Physical

30. Which of the following protocols operates at the Network layer of the OSI model but does not encapsulate data generated by an upper layer protocol for transmission over the network?

A. IP

B. UDP

C. ARP

D. ICMP

E. TCP

31. Which of the following devices run exclusively at the Physical layer of the Open Systems Interconnection (OSI) model? (Choose all that apply.)

A. Routers

B. Repeaters

C. Hubs

D. Switches

32. Which of the following devices enables two computers to communicate when they are using different protocols at each layer of the Open Systems Interconnection (OSI) reference model?

A. A router

B. A hub

C. A switch

D. A gateway

1.2 Compare and contrast networking appliances, applications, and functions.

33. Which of the following best describes the function of a firewall?

- **A.** A device located between two networks that enables administrators to restrict incoming and outgoing traffic
- **B.** A device that connects two networks together, forwarding traffic between them as needed
- **C.** A device that enables Internet network clients with private IP addresses to access the Internet
- **D.** A device that caches Internet data for subsequent use by internal network clients

34. Which of the following terms is used to describe the method by which a firewall examines the port numbers in Transport layer protocol headers?

- **A.** IP address filtering
- **B.** Service-dependent filtering
- **C.** Deep packet inspection (DPI)
- **D.** Next-generation firewall (NGFW)

35. Which of the following physical network devices can conceivably be implemented as software in a computer's operating system? (Choose all that apply.)

- **A.** Hub
- **B.** Switch
- **C.** Router
- **D.** Firewall

36. Which of the following criteria does a firewall capable of service-dependent filtering use to block traffic?

- **A.** Hardware addresses
- **B.** Protocol identifiers
- **C.** IP addresses
- **D.** Port numbers

37. Ralph is a freelance network consultant installing a three-node small business network. The computers are all in the same room and use wired Ethernet to connect to the switched ports of a multifunction device. The device also functions as a network address translation (NAT) router for a cable modem connection to the Internet. NAT provides a measure of security, but Ralph wants to be sure that the network is protected from unauthorized Internet traffic and attacks against open ports. Which of the following solutions would enable Ralph to accomplish this goal with the minimum cost to the client?

   A. Install a hardware firewall between the multifunction device and the cable modem.

   B. Install an intrusion prevention system (IPS) between the multifunction device and the cable modem.

   C. Install a personal firewall on each of the computers.

   D. Connect an intrusion detection system (IDS) to one of the switched ports in the multifunction device.

   E. Use a port scanner to monitor the traffic entering the open ports on the computers.

38. Which of the following statements about hubs and switches are true? (Choose all that apply.)

   A. Hubs operate only at the Physical layer, whereas switches operate only at the Network layer.

   B. All of the devices connected to a hub are part of a single collision domain, whereas each device connected to a switch has its own collision domain.

   C. There are switches available with Network layer functionality, but there are no hubs with that capability.

   D. Switches create a separate broadcast domain for each connected device, whereas hubs create a single broadcast domain for all of the connected devices.

39. Which of the following devices perform essentially the same function? (Choose two.)

   A. Hubs

   B. Bridges

   C. Switches

   D. Routers

40. Which of the following switch types immediately forwards frames after looking at only the destination address?

   A. Cut-through

   B. Source route

   C. Store-and-forward

   D. Destination

41. Which of the following is something that only a firewall capable of stateful packet inspection can do?

   A. Filter traffic-based port numbers

   B. Block traffic destined for specific IP addresses

   C. Scan Transport layer header fields for evidence of SYN floods

   D. Block all TCP traffic from entering a network

42. Which of the following are methods typically used by intrusion detection systems (IDSs) to analyze incoming network traffic? (Choose all that apply.)

A. Anomaly-based detection

B. Behavior-based detection

C. Signature-based detection

D. Statistic-based detection

43. Which of the following is another term for a multiport bridge?

A. Router

B. Switch

C. Hub

D. Gateway

44. Which of the following statements about switches and routers are true? (Choose all that apply.)

A. Routers operate at the Network layer, whereas switches operate at the Data link layer.

B. All of the devices connected to a switch are part of a single broadcast domain, whereas the networks connected to a router form separate broadcast domains.

C. Routers can communicate with each other and share information, but switches cannot.

D. Switches forward packets based on their hardware addresses, whereas routers forward packets based on their IP addresses.

45. Which of the following types of systems are frequently used to collect information from intrusion detection systems (IDSs)?

A. SIEM

B. NAS

C. RADIUS

D. VoIP

46. Which of the following explains why splitting a large, switched Ethernet LAN into two LANs by adding a router can help to alleviate traffic congestion and improve performance? (Choose all that apply.)

A. Adding a router reduces the amount of broadcast traffic on each of the two LANs.

B. Adding a router reduces the amount of unicast traffic on each of the two LANs.

C. Adding a router diverts traffic to an alternate path through the network.

D. Adding a router prevents computers on one LAN from communicating with computers on another LAN.

47. Which of the following statements about traditional bridges and switches is true?

   A. Bridges and switches are Network layer devices that use logical addressing to forward frames.

   B. Bridges and switches are Data link layer devices that use media access control (MAC) addresses to forward frames.

   C. Bridges and switches build their internal tables based on destination addresses and forward packets based on source addresses.

   D. Bridges and switches must support the Network layer protocol implemented on the local area network (LAN).

   E. Each port on a bridge or switch defines a separate broadcast domain.

48. Which of the following is a correct term describing the function of a traditional switch?

   A. Layer 2 router

   B. Ethernet hub

   C. Multiport bridge

   D. Layer 3 repeater

49. Which of the following is the primary reason why replacing hubs with layer 2 switches on an Ethernet local area network (LAN) improves its performance?

   A. Layer 2 switches forward packets faster than hubs.

   B. Layer 2 switches do not forward broadcast transmissions.

   C. Layer 2 switches reduce the number of collisions on the network.

   D. Layer 2 switches read the IP addresses of packets, not the hardware addresses.

50. Which of the following statements about routers are true? (Choose all that apply.)

   A. Routers are Network layer devices that use IP addresses to forward frames.

   B. Routers are Data link layer devices that use media access control (MAC) addresses to forward frames.

   C. Routers build their internal tables based on destination MAC addresses and forward frames based on source MAC addresses.

   D. Routers must support the Network layer protocol implemented on the local area network (LAN).

   E. Each port on a router defines a separate broadcast domain.

51. Which of the following statements about routers is not true?

   A. Routers can connect two or more networks with dissimilar Data link layer protocols and media.

   B. Routers can connect two or more networks with the same Data link layer protocols and media.

   C. Routers store and maintain route information in a local text file.

   D. Servers with multiple network interfaces can be configured to function as software routers.

   E. Routers can learn and populate their routing tables through static and dynamic routing.

52. The network administrator for a small business is installing a computer to function as a firewall protecting their internetwork from Internet intrusion. At which of the following locations should the administrator install the firewall system?

A. Anywhere on the private internetwork, as long as the Internet is accessible

B. Between the Internet access router and the Internet service provider's (ISP's) network

C. At the ISP's network site

D. Between the Internet access router and the rest of the private internetwork

53. Proxy servers operate at which layer of the OSI reference model?

A. Data link

B. Network

C. Transport

D. Application

54. Which of the following is a feature that is not found in a traditional firewall product, but which might be found in a next-generation firewall (NGFW)?

A. Stateful packet inspection

B. Deep packet inspection (DPI)

C. Network address translation (NAT)

D. Virtual private network (VPN) support

55. Which of the following statements about content filtering in firewalls is true?

A. Content filters examine the source IP addresses of packets to locate potential threats.

B. Content filters enable switches to direct packets out through the correct port.

C. Content filters examine the data carried within packets for potentially objectionable materials.

D. Content filters use frequently updated signatures to locate packets containing malware.

56. Which of the following is not one of the criteria typically used by load balancers to direct incoming traffic to one of a group of servers?

A. Which server has the lightest load

B. Which server has the fastest response time

C. Which server is next in an even rotation

D. Which server has the fastest processor

57. Which of the following devices enables administrators of enterprise wireless networks to manage multiple access points (APs) from a central location?

A. Hypervisor

B. Wireless controller

C. Wireless endpoint

D. Demarcation point

58. A load balancer is a type of which of the following devices?

    A. Switch

    B. Router

    C. Gateway

    D. Firewall

59. Which of the following devices expands on the capabilities of the traditional firewall by adding features like deep packet inspection (DPI) and an intrusion prevention system (IPS)?

    A. RADIUS server

    B. CSU/DSU

    C. NGFW

    D. Proxy server

60. Which of the following statements about Internet access through a proxy server accounts for the security against outside intrusion that a proxy provides?

    A. The proxy server uses a public IP address, and the client computers use private addresses.

    B. The proxy server uses a private IP address, and the client computers use public addresses.

    C. Both the proxy server and the client computers use private IP addresses.

    D. Both the proxy server and the client computers use public IP addresses.

61. Which of the following devices can an administrator use to monitor a network for abnormal or malicious traffic?

    A. IDS

    B. UPS

    C. RADIUS

    D. DoS

    E. RAS

62. Which of the following features enables an intrusion detection system (IDS) to monitor all of the traffic on a switched network?

    A. Stateful packet inspection

    B. Port mirroring

    C. Trunking

    D. Service-dependent filtering

63. Which of the following storage area network (SAN) protocols are capable of sharing a network medium with standard local area network (LAN) traffic? (Choose all that apply.)

    A. iSCSI

    B. Fibre Channel

    C. FCoE

    D. InfiniBand

64. Which of the following protocols is not used for storage area networks (SANs)?

   A. iSCSI

   B. FCoE

   C. VoIP

   D. Fibre Channel

65. Which of the following storage area network (SAN) technologies do iSCSI initiators use to locate iSCSI targets on the network?

   A. Active Directory

   B. ICMP

   C. DNS

   D. iWINS

   E. iSNS

66. What is the highest possible data transfer rate on a storage area network (SAN) using Fibre Channel?

   A. 8 Gbps

   B. 16 Gbps

   C. 32 Gbps

   D. 128 Gbps

67. In its primary functionality, a network-attached storage (NAS) device is most closely associated with which of the following devices?

   A. Failover cluster

   B. File server

   C. JBOD

   D. RAID

68. Which of the following statements about the differences between network-attached storage (NAS) and storage area networks (SANs) are true? (Choose all that apply.)

   A. NAS provides file-level storage access, whereas SAN provides block-level storage access.

   B. NAS devices typically contain integrated iSCSI targets.

   C. SAN devices have an operating system, whereas NAS devices do not.

   D. NAS devices typically provide a filesystem, whereas SAN devices do not.

69. Which of the following statements specify advantages of FCoE over the original Fibre Channel standard? (Choose all that apply.)

   A. FCoE is less expensive to implement than Fibre Channel.

   B. FCoE can share a network with standard IP traffic, whereas Fibre Channel cannot.

   C. FCoE is routable over IP networks, whereas Fibre Channel is not.

   D. FCoE uses standard Ethernet networking hardware.

70. Which of the following are Application layer protocols that network-attached storage (NAS) devices can use to serve shared files to clients on the network? (Choose all that apply.)

    A. CIFS

    B. NFS

    C. RDMA

    D. HTTP

71. Which of the following is not one of the advantages of iSCSI over Fibre Channel?

    A. iSCSI is routable, whereas Fibre Channel is not.

    B. iSCSI is less expensive to implement than Fibre Channel.

    C. iSCSI includes its own internal flow control mechanism, whereas Fibre Channel does not.

    D. iSCSI can share the same network as standard local area network traffic, whereas Fibre Channel cannot.

72. Which of the following is the term for the client that accesses an iSCSI device on a storage area network?

    A. Initiator

    B. Target

    C. Controller

    D. Adapter

73. Which of the following protocols are included in an iSCSI packet on a storage area network (SAN)? (Choose all that apply.)

    A. Ethernet

    B. IP

    C. TCP

    D. UDP

    E. None of the above

74. Which of the following protocols are included in a Fibre Channel packet?

    A. Ethernet

    B. IP

    C. TCP

    D. UDP

    E. None of the above

75. Which of the following protocol standards defines a layered implementation that does not correspond to the layers of the Open Systems Interconnection (OSI) model?

    A. iSCSI

    B. Fibre Channel

    C. PPP

    D. RDMA

76. Which of the following protocols are included in an FCoE packet?

    A. Ethernet

    B. IP

    C. TCP

    D. UDP

    E. None of the above

77. Ralph, the administrator of a 500-node private internetwork, is devising a plan to connect the network to the Internet. The primary objective of the project is to provide all of the network users with access to web and email services while keeping the client computers safe from unauthorized users on the Internet. The secondary objectives of the project are to avoid having to manually configure IP addresses on each one of the client computers individually and to provide a means of monitoring and regulating the users' access to the Internet. Ralph submits a proposal calling for the use of private IP addresses on the client computers and a series of proxy servers with public, registered IP addresses, connected to the Internet using multiple T-1 lines. Which of the following statements about Ralph's proposed Internet access solution is true?

    A. The proposal fails to satisfy both the primary and secondary objectives.

    B. The proposal satisfies the primary objective but neither of the secondary objectives.

    C. The proposal satisfies the primary objective and one of the secondary objectives.

    D. The proposal satisfies the primary objective and both of the secondary objectives.

78. Which of the following is not a mechanism for distributing incoming network traffic among multiple servers?

    A. Load balancer

    B. Round-robin DNS

    C. NLB cluster

    D. VPN headend

79. Which of the following is not a function that is typically provided by a unified threat management (UTM) appliance?

    A. Virtual private networking

    B. Network firewall

    C. Network-attached storage

    D. Antivirus/antimalware protection

80. A multilayer switch can operate at which layers of the Open Systems Interconnection (OSI) model? (Choose all that apply.)

A. Physical

B. Data link

C. Network

D. Transport

E. Session

F. Presentation

G. Application

81. Control plane policing (CPP or CoPP) is a feature on some routers and switches that limits the rate of traffic on the device's processor to prevent denial-of-service (DoS) and reconnaissance attacks, using which of the following technologies?

A. IPsec

B. 802.1X

C. RA guard

D. QoS

E. VLAN hopping

82. Which of the following is a device that switches calls between endpoints on the local IP network and provides access to external Internet lines?

A. VoIP PBX

B. VoIP gateway

C. VoIP endpoint

D. Multilayer switch

83. Which of the following is the true definition of the term *modem*?

A. A device that connects a computer to the public switched telephone network (PSTN)

B. A device that connects a local area network (LAN) to the Internet

C. A device that converts analog signals to digital signals and back again

D. A device that connects a local area network (LAN) to a wide area network (WAN)

84. Which of the following terms are used to describe the device used to place calls on a Voice over Internet Protocol (VoIP) installation? (Choose all that apply.)

A. Terminal

B. Gateway

C. Endpoint

D. PBX

85. Which of the following devices enables you to use a standard analog telephone to place calls using the Internet instead of the public switched telephone network (PSTN)?

A. Proxy server

B. VPN headend

C. VoIP gateway

D. UTM appliance

86. Which of the following prevents packets on a TCP/IP internetwork from being transmitted endlessly from router to router?

A. Open Shortest Path First (OSPF)

B. Maximum transmission unit (MTU)

C. Administrative distance

D. Time to live (TTL)

87. Which of the following is the abbreviation for a network of Internet datacenters supplying end users with localized access to their data?

A. CDN

B. QoS

C. NAS

D. SAN

1.3 Summarize cloud concepts and connectivity options.

88. Which of the following cloud service models enables you to perform a new installation of an operating system of your choice?

A. IaaS

B. PaaS

C. SaaS

D. DaaS

E. All of the above

89. When you contract with a provider to obtain email services for your company using their servers in the public cloud, which of the following service models are you using?

A. IaaS

B. PaaS

C. SaaS

D. DaaS

E. None of the above

90. Which of the following cloud service models provides the consumer with the most control over the cloud resources?

A. IaaS

B. PaaS

C. SaaS

D. DaaS

E. IaaS, PaaS, SaaS, and DaaS all provide the same degree of control.

91. Alice has just created a new Windows Server virtual machine using remote controls provided by a cloud service provider on the Internet. Which of the following cloud architectures is she using? (Choose all that apply.)

A. IaaS

B. PaaS

C. SaaS

D. Public cloud

E. Private cloud

F. Hybrid cloud

G. Virtual private cloud

92. In which of the following cloud models can a single organization function as both the provider and the consumer of all cloud services?

A. Public cloud

B. Private cloud

C. Hybrid cloud

D. Multicloud

93. Ed is the overnight manager of his company's datacenter, and he is responsible for both private and public resources in the company's hybrid cloud. Due to a new TV commercial shown that night, the company's website experiences a massive upsurge in traffic. The web server farm on the private cloud is being overwhelmed, so Ed configures some virtual machines in the public cloud to take up the slack. Which of the following is a common term for what Ed has done?

A. Cloud busting

B. Cloud bursting

C. Cloud splitting

D. Cloud migrating

94. Microsoft's `Outlook.com` email service is an example of which of the following cloud service models?

A. IaaS

B. PaaS

C. SaaS

D. DaaS

E. None of the above

95. Which of the following statements about cloud delivery models is true?

A. A public cloud is inherently insecure because anyone can access it.

B. A private cloud consists of hardware that is all located in a single datacenter.

C. A hybrid cloud enables administrators to migrate services between public and private resources.

D. Public, private, and hybrid clouds all utilize the same hardware resources.

96. Ed has just created a new Windows application for his company and wants to deploy it in the public cloud. He is looking for a provider that will furnish his company with a fully installed and configured Windows server on which he can install and run his application. Which of the following service models is he seeking to use?

A. IaaS

B. PaaS

C. SaaS

D. DaaS

E. None of the above

97. Which of the following are valid advantages or disadvantages of multitenancy in a public cloud datacenter? (Choose all that apply.)

A. Multitenancy presents a potential security risk because other tenants are utilizing the same hardware.

B. Multitenancy reduces the cost of utilities and other overhead.

C. Multitenancy introduces the possibility of competition for bandwidth with other tenants.

D. Multitenancy separates tenants by assigning each one its own virtual machine.

98. Ralph is designing a hybrid deployment for a corporate client that will require a connection between the client's private network and a public cloud provider. The client is concerned about this connection becoming a speed bottleneck at times of heavy user traffic. Which of the following options can Ralph offer the client that will best address this potential problem?

A. Use a different ISP for the cloud connection.

B. Use a VPN for the cloud connection.

C. Use a cloud direct connection for the hybrid link.

D. Use a leased line connection to the ISP.

99. Which of the following is not one of the primary components of the network functions virtualization (NFV) framework?

A. VNF

B. NFV ISG

C. NFVI

D. NFV-MANO

100. Ralph is designing the datacenter for his company's new branch office. He is considering various options, including building a new datacenter at the branch office facility, using a colocated datacenter, and creating a virtual datacenter using a public cloud provider. Which of the following statements about the differences between these options are true? (Choose all that apply.)

   A. A colocated datacenter would be less expensive to implement than a branch office or public cloud datacenter.

   B. In a branch office or colocated datacenter, Ralph's company would own the hardware.

   C. In all three datacenter options, the administrators in Ralph's company would be responsible for setting up and managing the hardware.

   D. In a branch office or colocated datacenter, Ralph's company would be responsible for all utility costs, including heating, cooling, and power.

   E. A public cloud datacenter would have greater physical security than the other two options.

   F. A public cloud datacenter is easier to expand than a colocated or branch office datacenter.

101. Alice's company regularly hires a large number of operators for its phone center. The operators require access to a customer database and an order entry system. Because this is a high-turnover position, Alice has streamlined the onboarding process by creating a security group with the appropriate permissions needed to access the necessary software. This way, she can simply add each new user to the group, rather than assigning the permissions individually. This is an example of which of the following security concepts?

   A. Least privilege

   B. Zero trust

   C. Role-based access control

   D. Defense in depth

102. Which of the following statements about the differences between network security groups and security lists is true?

   A. Security lists contain ingress and egress rules that apply to all of the virtual network interface cards (VNICs) in a subnet.

   B. Network security groups can have no more than five member VNICs.

   C. A VNIC can be added to no more than five security lists.

   D. Network security groups can only contain members from their assigned subnet.

103. Which of the following statements about the differences between a NAT gateway and an Internet gateway in a virtual cloud network (VNC) are true? (Choose all that apply.)

   A. A NAT gateway allows traffic from the VNC to reach the Internet but does not allow Internet traffic into the VNC.

   B. A NAT gateway allows VNC traffic both to and from the Internet.

   C. An Internet gateway allows traffic from the VNC to reach the Internet but does not allow Internet traffic into the VNC.

   D. An Internet gateway allows VNC traffic both to and from the Internet.

1.4 Explain common networking ports, protocols, services, and traffic types.

104. Which of the following pairs of well-known ports are the default values you would use to configure a POP3 email client?

  A. 110 and 25

  B. 143 and 25

  C. 110 and 143

  D. 80 and 110

  E. 25 and 80

105. Which of the following server applications use two well-known port numbers during a typical transaction?

  A. NTP

  B. SNMP

  C. HTTP

  D. FTP

106. Which of the following protocols does the Ping utility use to exchange messages with another system?

  A. UDP

  B. TCP

  C. ICMP

  D. IGMP

107. Which of the following components does the port number in a Transport layer protocol header identify?

  A. A Transport layer protocol

  B. An application

  C. A gateway

  D. A proxy server

108. Which of the following organizations is responsible for assigning the well-known port numbers used in Transport layer protocol headers?

  A. Institute for Electronic and Electrical Engineers (IEEE)

  B. Internet Assigned Numbers Authority (IANA)

  C. Internet Engineering Task Force (IETF)

  D. International Organization for Standardization (ISO)

109. Which of the following is the default well-known port number for the Hypertext Transfer Protocol (HTTP) used for web client/server communications?

    A. 22

    B. 20

    C. 80

    D. 443

110. The secured version of the Hypertext Transfer Protocol Secure (HTTPS) uses a different well-known port from the unsecured version. Which of the following ports is used by HTTPS by default?

    A. 25

    B. 80

    C. 110

    D. 443

111. What field in the Transmission Control Protocol (TCP) Option subheader specifies the size of the largest segment a system can receive?

    A. MSS

    B. Window

    C. MMS

    D. WinMS

112. What is the term for the combination of an IPv4 address and a port number, as in the following example: 192.168.1.3:23?

    A. Socket

    B. OUI

    C. Well-known port

    D. Network address

    E. Domain

113. Which of the following protocols generate messages that are carried directly within Internet Protocol (IPv4) datagrams, with no intervening Transport layer protocol? (Choose all that apply.)

    A. ICMP

    B. IGMP

    C. SMTP

    D. SNMP

114. Which of the following protocols is used to exchange directory service information?

    A. RDP

    B. LDAP

    C. SNMP

    D. SMB

115. Ralph is configuring a new email client on a workstation to use the Simple Mail Transfer Protocol (SMTP) and Post Office Protocol (POP3) email protocols. He wants SMTP to use encryption when communicating with the email server. Which of the following port numbers should Ralph use to create the POP3 connection and secure the SMTP connection with Transport Layer Security (TLS)? (Choose all that apply.)

A. 110

B. 25

C. 587

D. 443

116. Which of the following is not a port number used for Structured Query Language (SQL) communications?

A. 1433

B. 1521

C. 3306

D. 3389

117. Which of the following port numbers is assigned to a Unix/Linux logging services program?

A. 389

B. 514

C. 636

D. 993

118. Which of the following is the primary Application layer protocol used by web browsers to communicate with web servers?

A. HTTPS

B. HTML

C. SMTP

D. FTP

119. Which of the following protocols appears on the network as a service that client computers use to resolve names into IP addresses?

A. DHCP

B. BOOTP

C. DNS

D. SNMP

120. Which of the following protocols use the term *datagram* to describe the data transfer unit they create? (Choose all that apply.)

A. Ethernet

B. IP

C. TCP

D. UDP

121. What is the native file sharing protocol used on all Microsoft Windows operating systems?

    A. Hypertext Transfer Protocol Secure (HTTPS)

    B. Network File System (NFS)

    C. File Transfer Protocol (FTP)

    D. Server Message Block (SMB)

    E. Lightweight Directory Access Protocol (LDAP)

122. When analyzing captured TCP/IP packets, which of the following control bits must you look for in the Transmission Control Protocol (TCP) header to determine whether the receiving host has successfully received the sending host's data?

    A. ACK

    B. FIN

    C. PSH

    D. SYN

    E. URG

123. Which of the following terms describes the Transmission Control Protocol (TCP) exchange that establishes a connection prior to the transmission of any data?

    A. Synchronization

    B. Initialization exchange

    C. Connection establishment

    D. Three-way handshake

124. Alice has been instructed to install 100 Windows workstations, and she is working on automating the process by configuring the workstations to use PXE boots. Each workstation therefore must obtain an IP address from a DHCP server and download a boot image file from a TFTP server. Which of the following well-known ports must Alice open on the firewall separating the workstations from the servers? (Choose all that apply.)

    A. 65

    B. 66

    C. 67

    D. 68

    E. 69

125. Which of the following explanations best describes the function of a Transmission Control Protocol (TCP) or User Datagram Protocol (UDP) port number?

    A. The port number indicates to the receiver that the sender can activate a specific port only.

    B. The port number is used by both the sender and the receiver to identify the application that generated the information in the datagram.

C. The port number is used only by the receiver, to indicate the application process running on the sender.

D. The port number is used by both the sender and the receiver to negotiate a well-known server port for the communicating processes.

126. What is the valid range of numbers for the ephemeral client ports used by the Transmission Control Protocol (TCP) and User Datagram Protocol (UDP)?

A. 1023 through 65,534

B. 0 through 1023

C. 49,152 through 65,535

D. 1024 through 49,151

127. Which of the following statements about the User Datagram Protocol (UDP) are true? (Choose all that apply.)

A. UDP does not use packet sequencing and acknowledgments.

B. UDP uses packet sequencing and acknowledgments.

C. UDP is a connection-oriented protocol.

D. UDP is a connectionless protocol.

E. UDP has an 8-byte header.

F. UDP has a 20-byte header.

128. Which of the following port values are used by the File Transfer Protocol (FTP)? (Choose all that apply.)

A. 21

B. 23

C. 20

D. 53

E. 69

129. Which of the following protocols provides connectionless delivery service at the Transport layer of the Open Systems Interconnection (OSI) model?

A. TCP

B. HTTP

C. UDP

D. ARP

130. What is the valid range of numbers for the well-known Transmission Control Protocol (TCP) and User Datagram Protocol (UDP) ports used by servers?

A. 1024 through 49151

B. 1 through 49151

C. 49152 through 65534

D. 1 through 1023

131. Ralph is a network administrator who has just installed a new open-source email server for the users at his company. The server is configured to send and receive Internet email and create a mailbox for each user that will permanently store the user's mail on the server. Ralph next uses a protocol analyzer to examine the network traffic resulting from the new server installation. Which of the following new protocols should Ralph expect to see in his network traffic analysis? (Choose all that apply.)

A. SNMP

B. SMTP

C. POP3

D. IMAP

E. RIP

132. Which of the following values could a web client use as an ephemeral port number when communicating with a web server?

A. 1

B. 23

C. 80

D. 1024

E. 1999

F. 50134

133. Which of the following protocols provides connection-oriented service with guaranteed delivery at the Transport layer of the OSI model?

A. TCP

B. UDP

C. HTTP

D. IP

134. Which of the following protocols is limited to use on the local subnet only?

A. Address Resolution Protocol (ARP)

B. Dynamic Host Configuration Protocol (DHCP)

C. Domain Name System (DNS)

D. Simple Mail Transfer Protocol (SMTP)

E. Generic Routing Encapsulation (GRE)

135. Which of the following prefixes must you use in the URL you type into a web browser when the website you want to access has been secured with Transport Layer Security (TLS)?

A. TLS://

B. HTTPS://

C. HTTP://

D. HTLS://

136. What is the difference when you specify the HTTPS:// prefix in a Uniform Resource Locator (URL) instead of HTTP://? (Choose all that apply.)

    A. The connection between the web browser and the server is encrypted.

    B. The browser uses a different port number to connect to the server.

    C. The connection uses SSL or TLS instead of HTTP.

    D. The browser uses a different IP address to connect to the server.

137. You are a consultant installing a web server application for a client called Adatum. The domain name `Adatum.com` has been registered in the DNS, and the server has one public IP address, so the new website will be accessible to users on the Internet. You want to be able to access the web server application's administrative site from your remote office, so you configure that site to be encrypted and to use the port number 12354 instead of the default. Which of the following URLs will you have to use to access the administrative website?

    A. `www.adatum.com`

    B. `www.adatum.com:12354`

    C. `www.adatum.com:80`

    D. `www.adatum.com:12354`

138. Which of the following protocols does IPsec use to digitally encrypt packets before transmitting them over the network?

    A. ESP

    B. SSL

    C. AH

    D. IKE

139. Which of the following are the protocols that IPsec uses to secure network traffic? (Choose all that apply.)

    A. SSH

    B. AH

    C. ESP

    D. SSL

140. What is the primary shortcoming of the File Transfer Protocol (FTP) that is addressed by FTPS and SFTP?

    A. Lack of security

    B. Slow file transfers

    C. File size limitations

    D. Lack of authentication

141. Which of the following File Transfer Protocol (FTP) variants do not transmit authentication passwords over the network in cleartext?

- **A.** FTP
- **B.** FTPS
- **C.** SFTP
- **D.** TFTP

142. Which of the following File Transfer Protocol (FTP) variants is typically used to download boot image files during Preboot Execution Environment (PXE) startup sequences?

- **A.** FTP
- **B.** FTPS
- **C.** SFTP
- **D.** TFTP

143. Which of the following protocols does IPsec use to digitally sign packets before transmitting them over the network?

- **A.** ESP
- **B.** SSL
- **C.** AH
- **D.** IKE

144. Which of the following security protocols used to protect traffic exchanged by web browsers and servers was created first?

- **A.** SSL
- **B.** TLS
- **C.** SSH
- **D.** DTLS

145. Which of the following security protocols for web servers or browsers was deprecated in 2015 in favor of Transport Layer Security (TLS) and Datagram Transport Layer Security (DTLS)?

- **A.** SSH
- **B.** SSL
- **C.** RDP
- **D.** IPsec

146. What must you do to configure a firewall to admit File Transfer Protocol (FTP) traffic to the internal network using its default port settings? (Choose all that apply.)

- **A.** Open port 20
- **B.** Open port 21
- **C.** Open port 22
- **D.** Open port 23
- **E.** Open port 24

147. Which of the following protocols uses a form of flow control called the sliding window technique?

   A. UDP

   B. HTTP

   C. TCP

   D. SIP

148. Which of the following Transmission Control Protocol (TCP) control bits is set to 1 to initiate the termination of a session?

   A. SYN

   B. URG

   C. FIN

   D. END

   E. PSH

149. A client on a TCP/IP network is attempting to establish a session with a server. Which of the following correctly lists the order of the TCP flags raised in the Transmission Control Protocol (TCP) session establishment messages?

   A. SYN, ACK, SYN, ACK

   B. SYN, SYN, ACK, ACK

   C. SYN/ACK, SYN/ACK

   D. SYN, SYN/ACK, ACK

150. Which of the following traffic types is used exclusively on IPv6 networks?

   A. Unicast

   B. Broadcast

   C. Multicast

   D. Anycast

1.5 Compare and contrast transmission media and transceivers.

151. Which of the following best describes the function of the network medium?

   A. The network medium provides the physical connection between networked computers.

   B. The network medium provides the protocol used to transmit data between end systems.

   C. The network medium passes data packets between two routers.

   D. The network medium processes electrical or light signals and converts them to data.

152. Which of the following signal types is carried by copper cable?

   A. Fiber-optic

   B. Microwave

   C. Infrared

   D. Electrical

153. Identify the organizations that developed the general cable type standards for voice and data communications that are currently in use and identify their document names.

   A. ANSI/TVA, document C568

   B. TWA/ANSI/EIA, document T530-A

   C. EIA/ANSI/TWA, document 802.2

   D. TDA/EIA/TIA, document 802.11

   E. ANSI/TIA/EIA, document T568b

154. Which of the following cable types and connectors are used to attach a television set to a cable television (CATV) network?

   A. A multimode fiber-optic cable and a Straight Tip (ST) connector

   B. A coaxial cable and a Bayonet-Neill-Concelman (BNC) connector

   C. A twisted-pair cable and an RJ-45 connector

   D. A coaxial cable and an F-type connector

   E. An AUI cable and a vampire tap connector

   F. A twinaxial cable and a Bayonet-Neill-Concelman (BNC) connector

155. Which of the following cable types is used for Thick Ethernet network segments?

   A. RG-8

   B. RG-58

   C. RJ-45

   D. RJ-11

156. Which of the following cable types is used for Thin Ethernet network segments?

   A. RG-8

   B. RG-58

   C. RJ-45

   D. RJ-11

157. Which of the following coaxial cable types are still in general use? (Choose all that apply.)

   A. RG-6

   B. RG-8

   C. RG-58

   D. RG-59

158. Which of the following statements about the differences between fiber-optic Angled Physical Contact (APC) and Ultra Physical Contact (UPC) connectors are true? (Choose all that apply.)

    A. APCs should only be joined to other APCs.

    B. APCs generate more insertion loss than UPCs.

    C. UPCs generate more return loss than APCs.

    D. UPCs use a green connector boot or body.

159. Which of the following is not a type of fiber-optic connector?

    A. SC

    B. MT-RJ

    C. ST

    D. BNC

    E. LC

160. Which of the following Physical layer transceiver module standards is the oldest and therefore the most obsolete?

    A. SFP

    B. SFP+

    C. GBIC

    D. QSFP

    E. QSFP+

161. Which of the following cable types is typically configured in a star/hub and spoke topology, uses eight copper conductors arranged in four pairs, and uses RJ-45 connectors?

    A. RG-8

    B. Twisted-pair

    C. RG-58

    D. Fiber-optic

162. Which of the following statements explains the purpose of the twists in twisted-pair cabling?

    A. The twists prevent collisions.

    B. The twists completely eliminate crosstalk and electromagnetic interference (EMI) in adjacent wire pairs.

    C. The twists prevent crosstalk in adjacent wire pairs and limit the effects of EMI on the signals carried over the cable.

    D. The twists extend the bend radius allowance of the cable.

163. Which of the following combinations of attributes describes the cable used for a Thin Ethernet network?

  A. RJ-45, 50-ohm, 0.270-inch, coaxial cable with BNC connectors

  B. RG-59, 75-ohm, 0.242-inch, coaxial cable with F connectors

  C. RG-58, 50-ohm, 0.195-inch, coaxial cable with BNC connectors

  D. RG-8, 50-ohm, 0.405-inch, coaxial cable with N connectors

  E. RJ-6, 75-ohm, 0.242-inch, coaxial cable with BNC connectors

164. Which of the following connector types are typically associated with Ethernet networks? (Choose all that apply.)

  A. F-type

  B. BNC

  C. DB-9

  D. RJ-45

165. Which of the following connector types was typically associated with a T-connector attached to the computer?

  A. RJ-45

  B. MT-RJ

  C. 8P8C

  D. BNC

  E. F

166. Which of the following connector types are associated with fiber-optic cables? (Choose all that apply.)

  A. RJ-11

  B. ST

  C. F

  D. LC

  E. MT-RJ

  F. MPO

167. Which of the following types of cable, when installed, sometimes employed a device called a vampire tap?

  A. Unshielded twisted-pair

  B. Shielded twisted-pair

  C. Multimode fiber-optic

  D. Single-mode fiber-optic

  E. Coaxial

168. Which of the following statements about single-mode and multimode fiber-optic cables are true? (Choose all that apply.)

   A. Single-mode cables can span longer distances than multimode cables.

   B. Single-mode cables are more resistant to electromagnetic interference than multimode cables.

   C. Single-mode cables are more difficult to install than multimode cables.

   D. Single-mode cables have a much larger core diameter than multimode cables.

169. Which of the following components are typically used only for telephone cable installations, and not for data networking? (Choose all that apply.)

   A. 66 blocks

   B. 110 blocks

   C. 25 pair UTP cables

   D. 100 pair UTP cables

170. Which of the following statements about single-mode fiber-optic cable are true? (Choose all that apply.)

   A. Single-mode cables use an LED light source, whereas multimode cables use a laser.

   B. Single-mode cables can span longer distances than multimode cables.

   C. Single-mode cables have a smaller core filament than multimode cables.

   D. Single-mode cables have a smaller bend radius than multimode cables, making them easier to install.

   E. Single-mode fiber-optic cables require a ground, whereas multimode cables do not.

171. Which of the following tools do cable installers use to connect bulk cable runs to wall plates and patch panels?

   A. A crimper

   B. A splicer

   C. A pigtail

   D. A punchdown block tool

172. Ralph has been hired by a client to install cabling to connect two existing networks. The two networks are in different buildings approximately 1,000 feet apart. The cable type must support Gigabit Ethernet data rates of 1,000 megabits per second (Mbps) and provide a high level of resistance to electromagnetic interference (EMI). Your client wants the most economical cabling solution that meets their needs. Which of the following cable types best meets the needs of this client?

   A. Multimode fiber-optic cable

   B. Shielded twisted-pair (STP) cable

   C. Unshielded twisted-pair (UTP) cable

   D. Thin coaxial cable

   E. Single-mode fiber-optic cable

173. Which of the following are connector types used with coaxial cables? (Choose all that apply.)

A. BNC

B. F-type

C. N-type

D. ST

E. RJ-11

174. In the punchdown process for unshielded twisted-pair (UTP) cable, which of the following is the last step that you perform when connecting bulk cables to jacks in wall plates and patch panels?

A. Cut off the excess wire that protrudes past the contacts.

B. Press the bare wire down between the two metal contacts that hold it in place.

C. Strip some of the insulating sheath off the cable end to expose the wires.

D. Insert the wires into the appropriate contacts in the jack.

E. Strip a small amount of insulation off each wire.

F. Separate the twisted wire pairs at the ends.

175. Which of the following cable connector types is not used with fiber-optic cable?

A. Straight Tip (ST)

B. Subscriber Connector (SC)

C. Mechanical Transfer–Registered Jack (MT-RJ)

D. F-type

E. Fiber Local Connector (LC)

176. Which of the following cable connector types have been rendered nearly obsolete by Universal Serial Bus (USB) connections? (Choose all that apply.)

A. BNC

B. RJ-11

C. DB-9

D. DB-25

177. Which of the following cable types are typically used in newly constructed local area network (LAN) installations? (Choose all that apply.)

A. Single-mode fiber-optic

B. Multimode fiber-optic

C. Coaxial

D. Unshielded twisted-pair

178. Which of the following statements are true about coaxial cable? (Choose all that apply.)

    A. Coaxial cable has three conductors within the same sheath.

    B. Coaxial cable has two conductors within the same sheath.

    C. Coaxial cable has a copper core that carries light pulse signals.

    D. Coaxial cable has a copper core that carries electrical signals.

    E. Coaxial cable has an insulating outer sheath made of braided strands.

    F. Coaxial cable has an insulating sheath made of either PVC or Teflon.

179. Which of the following statements about fiber-optic cabling are true? (Choose all that apply.)

    A. There are two main fiber-optic cable types: single-mode and multimode.

    B. Fiber-optic cable is typically used to span long distances.

    C. Fiber-optic cables use IBM Data Connector (IDC) connectors.

    D. Fiber-optic cables often use Straight Tip (ST) and Subscriber Connector (SC) connectors.

    E. Single-mode fiber-optic cable uses a laser light source and a glass core.

    F. Multimode fiber-optic cable uses a light-emitting diode (LED) light source.

180. Which of the following are characteristics of an internal cable installation? (Choose all that apply.)

    A. An internal cable installation uses bulk spools of cabling with no connectors attached for most cable runs.

    B. An internal cable installation uses only prefabricated cables with connectors attached for all cable runs.

    C. An internal cable installation uses solid wire conductors for all cable runs, regardless of distance.

    D. An internal cable installation uses stranded wire conductors for short cable runs and solid core for longer cable runs.

    E. In an internal cable installation, cables are typically not run through walls or ceilings.

    F. In an internal cable installation, cables are typically run through walls or ceilings.

181. Which of the following IEEE 802.3 specifications calls for CAT8 UTP cable exclusively?

    A. 10GBase-T

    B. 40GBase-T

    C. 100Base-TX

    D. 1000Base-SX

182. Ralph has been hired to connect three local area networks (LANs) together with redundant paths that form a fault-tolerant backbone. The LANs reside on different floors in the same building and are approximately 600 meters apart. Each LAN is currently configured in a star/hub and spoke topology using twisted-pair cabling. Each LAN includes wall plates and rack-mounted patch panels and switches. Building and fire codes allow cables to run through existing risers, ceilings, and walls, but a 50,000-watt radio station occupies one of the floors between the LANs. Which topology, cable type, and installation method are best suited for this network?

    A. Star/hub and spoke topology, fiber-optic cabling, and internal installation

    B. Star/hub and spoke topology, coaxial cabling, and external installation

    C. Mesh topology, fiber-optic cabling, and external installation

    D. Bus topology, twisted-pair cabling, and internal installation

    E. Mesh topology, fiber-optic cabling, and internal installation

    F. Star/hub and spoke topology, twisted-pair cabling, and external installation

183. Alice is a network consultant who has been contracted to evaluate a network design created many years ago, to determine if the design is still viable. The network will support 20 workstations, scattered throughout the building, to run an inventory database application. The two most distant computers are 150 meters apart. The primary goal for the network design is to connect all 20 workstations to a single LAN running at 1 gigabit per second (Gbps). The two secondary goals are to provide sufficient fault tolerance for a single cable break to occur without affecting the entire network and to provide resistance to the electromagnetic interference (EMI) generated by machinery in the building. The earlier design calls for a CAT 6 UTP Ethernet LAN in a star/hub and spoke topology with all of the computers connected to a single switch. Which of the following statements about the old proposal is true?

    A. The solution achieves neither the primary goal nor either of the secondary goals.

    B. The solution achieves the primary goal but neither of the secondary goals.

    C. The solution achieves the primary goal and one of the secondary goals.

    D. The solution achieves the primary goal and both of the secondary goals.

184. Ed is a network consultant who has been contracted to design the network for a new manufacturing plant. The plant consists of two buildings 150 meters apart: an office with 20 computers and a manufacturing facility that has 30 computers. The two most distant computers at the site are 225 meters apart. Ed's design calls for a Gigabit Ethernet network using fiber-optic cable. On receiving the proposal, the client asks Ed to justify the additional labor and expense of installing fiber-optic cable instead of unshielded twisted-pair (UTP). Which of the following is not a valid reason for choosing fiber-optic over UTP for this project?

    A. The 225-meter distance between the two most distant computers exceeds Ethernet's maximum cable segment length for UTP.

    B. Only fiber-optic cable can keep the two buildings electrically isolated.

    C. Fiber-optic cable is completely resistant to any electromagnetic interference generated by the equipment in the manufacturing plant.

    D. Fiber-optic cable provides a greater degree of tolerance to cable breaks than UTP.

185. Which of the following 802.3 10 Gigabit Ethernet specifications calls for the use of copper cable?

A. 10GBase-LR

B. 10GBase-CX4

C. 10GBase-ER

D. 10GBase-LX4

E. 10GBase-SR

186. Alice is a network consultant who has been contracted to upgrade an existing Ethernet network to Gigabit Ethernet. The network consists of 20 workstations with integrated 100Base-TX/1000Base-T network interface adapters. The network cabling is Category 6 (CAT6) unshielded twisted-pair (UTP), installed when the building was constructed. All of the workstations are connected to a single 100Base-TX switch. Which of the following options would Alice find to be a valid upgrade path to Gigabit Ethernet?

A. Replace the CAT6 cable with at least Category 6a (CAT6a) and leave the existing network interface adapters and switch in place.

B. Install a 1000Base-T network interface card in each computer and leave the existing cables and switch in place.

C. Replace the CAT6 cable with at least CAT6a and replace the 100Base-T switch with a 1000Base-T switch.

D. Replace the 100Base-TX switch with a 1000Base-T switch and leave the existing cables and network interface adapters in place.

187. Ralph is a network consultant with a client who wants him to design the local area network (LAN) for his company's new branch office. The site consists of a building with unshielded twisted-pair (UTP) cable already installed, which the client considered a major selling point when selecting the property. He wants Ralph to install the fastest possible LAN using the existing cable. After examining the site, Ralph notes that the cable is Category 6 (CAT6), installed using a star/hub and spoke topology, and that the individual cable runs are all 90 to 100 meters long. Which of the following Ethernet Physical layer specifications can Ralph use for the new network to provide the fastest transmission speeds without replacing the cable?

A. 10GBase-T

B. 100Base-TX

C. 1000Base-T

D. 1000Base-LX

E. 1000Base-SX

188. Which Institute of Electrical and Electronics Engineers (IEEE) 802.3 standards for Ethernet support 10-megabit-per-second (Mbps) communications, and what are the correct segment limitations for each standard? (Choose all that apply.)

A. 10Base2; segment maximum is 100 meters

B. 10Base2; segment maximum is 185 meters

C. 10Base5; segment maximum is 500 meters

    D. 100Base5; segment maximum is 500 meters

    E. 10Base-T; segment maximum is 100 meters

    F. 10Base-T segment maximum is 328 meters

189. Which of the following are Ethernet cable types that must be configured in a bus topology? (Choose all that apply.)

    A. RG-8

    B. RG-10

    C. RG-14

    D. RG-58

190. Wavelength-division multiplexing is a fiber-optic technique for carrying multiple signals on a single network medium. There are several types of this technique, including coarse wavelength-division multiplexing (CWDM), dense wavelength-division multiplexing (DWDM), and bidirectional wavelength-division multiplexing (BWDM, or just WDM). Which of the following is not one of the ways in which these types of multiplexing differ?

    A. They use different wavelength spacings.

    B. They carry different numbers of channels on a single medium.

    C. They provide different amounts of signal amplification.

    D. None of the above.

191. Ralph is installing an Ethernet local area network (LAN) for a small business with two offices on opposite sides of a courtyard. Ralph plans to run a multimode fiber-optic cable across the courtyard, but the budget is limited, and he cannot use fiber for the whole network. Therefore, he installs unshielded twisted-pair (UTP) cable in the two offices, which have 10 and 12 workstations, respectively. Which of the following devices should Ralph use to join the two UTP installations together into one LAN using the fiber-optic run across the courtyard, while keeping the cost to a minimum?

    A. Media converters

    B. Hubs

    C. Switches

    D. Routers

192. Under which of the following conditions is a cable installer required to use plenum cable?

    A. When cables run close to sources of electromagnetic interference (EMI)

    B. When cables are running through building air flow spaces

    C. When data and voice traffic will be running over the same cable

    D. When cables are running through areas of low temperature

193. Which of the following wireless networking standards is capable of supporting speeds over 72 Mbps and is also backward compatible with IEEE 802.11b and 802.11g?

    A. IEEE 802.11

    B. IEEE 802.11a

    C. IEEE 802.11n

    D. IEEE 802.11ac

    E. IEEE 802.11ax

194. Which of the following is a cellular communication technology that is virtually obsolete in the United States?

    A. GSM

    B. CDMA

    C. TDMA

    D. LTE

195. Ralph is planning a wireless LAN installation for a warehouse with two offices, one at either end of the building, approximately 300 feet apart. If he installs a single access point (AP) in the center of the warehouse, equidistant from the two offices, which of the following standards should he look for when purchasing hardware so that workstations in both offices will be able to connect to the network at the best possible speed?

    A. IEEE 802.11a

    B. IEEE 802.11g

    C. IEEE 802.11n

    D. IEEE 802.11ac

    E. IEEE 802.11ax

196. Which of the following broadband WAN services provides equal amounts of upstream and downstream bandwidth?

    A. ADSL

    B. SDSL

    C. Satellite

    D. Cable

197. Ralph's company has expanded to include an additional building on the far end of the corporate campus, approximately 4 kilometers away from the building housing the datacenter. A single-mode fiber-optic cable connection has been installed between the new building and the datacenter for a 1000Base-BX10 connection, but the cable is not yet connected to a transceiver at the datacenter end. Noticing that there is a 1000Base-SX Ethernet transceiver module in the datacenter storeroom, Ralph is wondering if he could use this on the new cable run. Which of the following are reasons why this might not work? (Choose all that apply.)

    A. Transceiver mismatch

    B. Incorrect cable type

    C. Excessive cable length

    D. Wavelength mismatch

198. A Small Form-factor Pluggable (SFP) Ethernet implementation uses direct-attach copper (DAC) connections for short distance runs within the datacenter. Which of the following cable types do the DAC connections use?

    A. Unshielded twisted-pair

    B. Shielded twisted-pair

    C. Fiber-optic

    D. Coaxial

    E. Twinaxial

1.6 Compare and contrast network topologies, architectures, and types.

199. An electrician installing a new light fixture accidentally severs one of the LAN cables running through the dropped ceiling space. With which topology would the severed cable cause the greatest amount of disturbance to the network?

    A. Bus

    B. Star/hub and spoke

    C. Logical ring

    D. Mesh

200. Which of the following statements about a wired local area network (LAN) is true?

    A. Wired LANs support only the star/hub and spoke topology.

    B. Wired LANs support only the star/hub and spoke and bus topologies.

    C. Wired LANs support only the star/hub and spoke and ring topologies.

    D. Wired LANs can support ring, bus, or star/hub and spoke topologies.

201. Which of the following is an example of a hybrid LAN topology?

    A. A workstation with two network interface cards, one of which is connected to a star/hub and spoke network and one to a bus network

    B. Four Ethernet switches connected using a bus topology

    C. Four workstations, each with a separate network connection to each of the other three

    D. Four Ethernet switches, each with a separate network connection to each of the other three

202. Which type of network connects local area networks (LANs) in distant locations?

    A. WAN

    B. LAN

    C. MAN

    D. CAN

203. Which of the following topologies is used by the majority of new Ethernet networks installed today?

   A. Bus

   B. Point-to-point

   C. Mesh

   D. Star/hub and spoke

204. Alice has constructed a five-node failover cluster in which all five servers are connected to a hard disk array using a dedicated Fibre Channel network. Which of the following terms describes this network arrangement?

   A. SAN

   B. PAN

   C. WAN

   D. MAN

205. Which of the following network topologies are used by wireless local area networks (WLANs)? (Choose all that apply.)

   A. Ad hoc

   B. Bus

   C. Infrastructure

   D. Star/hub and spoke

206. On an Ethernet network using the star/hub and spoke topology, which of the following devices can function as the cabling nexus that forms the figurative center of the star?

   A. Firewall

   B. Router

   C. Switch

   D. Access point

207. Which of the following cabling topologies provides the greatest number of redundant paths through the network?

   A. Star/hub and spoke

   B. Ring

   C. Mesh

   D. Bus

208. Which of the following Ethernet Physical layer options does not use the star/hub and spoke topology?

   A. 10Base2

   B. 10Base-T

   C. 100Base-TX

   D. 1000Base-T

209. Which of the following statements is true about the differences between a peer-to-peer network and a client-server network?

   A. Peer-to-peer networks are inherently less secure than client-server networks.

   B. Peer-to-peer networks are illegal, while client-server networks are legal.

   C. On peer-to-peer networks, every workstation is capable of authenticating users.

   D. On a peer-to-peer network, all workstations must share their resources.

210. Ed has been hired by a private company to connect two remote sites with a wide area network (WAN). Each of these sites has more than 200 users, and they all need to constantly transfer files across the WAN. One of the sites has a customer database that is accessed by both sites at all hours of the day. Access to the database and other information is time sensitive and constant. The company estimates that their aggregate bandwidth needs to be approximately 40 Mbps. Management says that they need to guarantee access to this information and that money is not a factor in the WAN implementation. Which WAN technology should Ed recommend for this scenario?

   A. A standard modem-to-modem connection

   B. A T-3 dedicated leased line

   C. A cable television (CATV) connection

   D. An ADSL (asymmetrical digital subscriber line) connection

211. Ralph is an employee of a company that offers the option to telecommute from home. As a telecommuting employee, he needs to connect to the company network to access client information, transfer files, and send email through a virtual private network (VPN) connection. Ralph is investigating the different wide area network (WAN) services available for the remote connection before he implements one. His home is over 30 years old; the existing telephone wiring was not run through conduit, and the wiring seems to be deteriorating. Ralph has cable television (CATV) service, and his home is also approximately 20,000 feet from the nearest telephone central office. He wants to implement the fastest remote connection service possible, but cost is a factor in the decision. Which WAN technology should Ralph implement?

   A. A dedicated leased line (fractional T-1)

   B. A standard modem-to-modem connection

   C. A DSL (digital subscriber line) connection

   D. A broadband CATV connection

212. Which two of the following constructs provide roughly the same function? (Choose two that apply.)

   A. SIP trunk

   B. CSU/DSU

   C. VoIP gateway

   D. Smartjack

   E. VPN concentrator

213. Which of the following wide area network (WAN) services typically uses a switched fabric that was called a cloud long before the term came into general use?

    A. ATM

    B. Fractional T-1

    C. SONET

    D. Frame Relay

214. Ralph has been contracted to consult for a company that wants to update its legacy Ethernet network to Gigabit Ethernet. When examining the site, he discovers that the network is still using coaxial-based Thin Ethernet. What change in network topology must occur to upgrade the existing network to Gigabit Ethernet using unshielded twisted-pair (UTP) cable?

    A. Bus to mesh

    B. Mesh to star/hub and spoke

    C. Star/hub and spoke to bus

    D. Bus to star/hub and spoke

    E. Star/hub and spoke to mesh

215. Which of the following best describes the function of a vSwitch (or virtual switch)?

    A. A vSwitch is a software product that enables a computer with multiple network adapters to function as a switch.

    B. A vSwitch is a feature in layer 3 switches that enables VLANs on the same switch to communicate with each other.

    C. A vSwitch is a feature in layer 3 switches that enables VLANs on different switches to communicate with each other.

    D. A vSwitch enables virtual machines (VMs) running on the same hypervisor to communicate with each other internally.

216. On which of the following virtual networking components can you create VLANs?

    A. Virtual NIC

    B. Virtual switch

    C. Virtual router

    D. Virtual firewall

217. Which of the following components is responsible for providing a virtualized hardware environment and running virtual machines?

    A. Hypervisor

    B. Virtual server

    C. vSwitch (virtual switch)

    D. VPN concentrator

218. Which of the following is the proper term for a computer with a hypervisor on which you can create virtual machines and other virtual components?

A. Guest

B. NAS

C. Host

D. SAN

219. In which of the following components can a virtual firewall be implemented?

A. On a host operating system

B. On a guest operating system

C. In a dedicated virtual machine

D. In a virtual switch

E. All of the above

220. Which of the following is not a protocol that uses tunneling to establish secured links between TCP/IP systems?

A. L2TP

B. IPsec

C. MGRE

D. NAT

221. Which of the following is not the name of one of the layers in the three-tier datacenter architecture?

A. Core

B. Intermediate

C. Distribution

D. Access

222. Which of the following is not a reason why the spine and leaf datacenter topology is superior to the standard three-tier topology?

A. The spine and leaf arrangement uses a full mesh switching topology.

B. In a spine and leaf topology, all data flows require the same number of hops.

C. The spine and leaf topology is less expensive to implement than the three-tier topology.

D. The spine and leaf topology uses software-defined networking to direct traffic, rather than blocking ports using the spanning tree protocol.

223. Which of the following best describes the difference between east-west and north-south traffic in a datacenter?

A. East-west describes traffic between devices at the same layer of the OSI model, while north-south describes traffic between OSI model layers.

B. East-west is switch-to-switch traffic, while north-south is switch-to-router traffic.

   C. East-west traffic stays within the datacenter, while north-south traffic does not.

   D. East-west is backbone traffic among switches and routers, while north-south is traffic to end systems, such as servers.

224. Top-of-rack switches most commonly form which layer of the datacenter topology?

   A. Leaf

   B. Backbone

   C. Spine

   D. Core

225. Which of the following statements about switches is not true?

   A. Switches are Data link layer devices that connect network devices in a star/hub and spoke topology.

   B. Switches amplify and repeat signals received through one port out all other ports regardless of the destination.

   C. Switches use MAC addresses to identify the devices connected to specific ports.

   D. Switches provide internal crossover circuits and use uplink ports to form a hierarchical star/hub and spoke topology.

226. A collapsed core network is one in which the standard three-tier hierarchical model is compressed into two tiers. Which of the following two tiers are combined to form this architectural model?

   A. Core and distribution

   B. Distribution and access

   C. Core and access

   D. Distribution and intermediate

1.7 Given a scenario, use appropriate IPv4 network addressing.

227. Which of the following services enables computers on a private IPv4 network to access the Internet using a registered IP address?

   A. DHCP

   B. NAT

   C. DNS

   D. NTP

228. Which of the following is the most accurate description of the subnetting process on an IPv4 network?

    A. You extend the IP address by adding bits for a subnet identifier.

    B. You borrow bits from the network identifier to create a subnet identifier.

    C. You borrow bits from the host identifier to create a subnet identifier.

    D. You create a subnet identifier by borrowing half of the bits from the network identifier and half from the host identifier.

229. Which of the following IPv4 addresses are you unable to assign to a network host? (Choose all that apply.)

    A. 1.1.1.1

    B. 229.6.87.3

    C. 103.256.77.4

    D. 9.34.0.1

230. How many bits are allocated to the host identifier in an IPv4 address on the 10.72.0.0/17 network?

    A. 8

    B. 15

    C. 16

    D. 17

231. Which of the following are not valid IPv4 addresses in the private address space defined by RFC 1918? (Choose all that apply.)

    A. 10.16.225.1

    B. 172:33:19:7

    C. 192.168.254.77

    D. 10.255.255.255

    E. 172.15.2.9

232. Alice has been instructed to create an IPv4 network with 8 subnets and 30 hosts per subnet. She has been assigned a Class C network address. Which of the following subnet masks will she have to use?

    A. 255.255.255.128

    B. 255.255.255.192

    C. 255.255.255.224

    D. 255.255.255.240

    E. 255.255.255.248

    F. 255.255.255.252

233. Which of the following is the default subnet mask for an IPv4 Class A network?

- **A.** 255.0.0.0
- **B.** 255.255.0.0
- **C.** 255.255.255.0
- **D.** 255.255.255.255

234. Which of the following is the range of IPv4 addresses that Automatic Private IP Addressing (APIPA) assigns to DHCP clients that cannot access a DHCP server?

- **A.** 10.0.0.0 to 10.0.255.255
- **B.** 169.254.0.0 to 169.254.255.255
- **C.** 192.168.0.0 to 192.168.0.255
- **D.** 224.0.0.0 to 224.0.255.255

235. In which IPv4 class is the address 127.0.0.1 found?

- **A.** Class A
- **B.** Class B
- **C.** Class C
- **D.** None of the above

236. To which class does the following IPv4 address belong: 190.126.14.251?

- **A.** Class A
- **B.** Class B
- **C.** Class C
- **D.** Class D
- **E.** Class E

237. Classless Inter-Domain Routing (CIDR) is a standard for IPv4 addressing that includes the capability to create subnets using any number of IP address bits, rather than using 8-bit blocks. Which of the following terms describes this ability?

- **A.** VLSM
- **B.** APIPA
- **C.** VLAN
- **D.** EUI-64

238. Ralph has been instructed to use the network address 10.12.0.0/14 for the new network he is installing. What subnet mask value should he use when configuring his computers?

- **A.** 255.248.0.0
- **B.** 255.252.0.0
- **C.** 255.254.0.0
- **D.** 255.255.248.0
- **E.** 255.255.252.0
- **F.** 255.255.254.0

239. Ed has been hired to design a company's network. The company has an assigned Class C network address of 192.168.30.0. Ed's client wants the network to be configured with 10 subnets, each with 14 hosts. Is this configuration possible with the given address, and if so, how many subnets and hosts can Ed create on the network?

    A. Yes, this will work. By using 4 subnet bits, it is possible for Ed to create up to 16 subnets. He can then use the remaining 4 host bits to create 14 hosts on each subnet.

    B. No, this will not work. A Class C address cannot be subnetted to create 8 subnets.

    C. No, this will not work. Although there are sufficient bits available to create 10 subnets, there are not enough bits left over for Ed to create 14 hosts per subnet.

    D. Yes, this will work. Ed can create 10 subnets with 14 hosts per subnet. By using 3 subnet bits, he can create 10 subnets, which leaves 5 bits to create up to 30 hosts per subnet.

240. What is the greatest number of subnets you can create with a Class A IPv4 address if you use a 14-bit subnet identifier?

    A. 256

    B. 1,022

    C. 1,024

    D. 16,382

    E. 16,384

241. Alice has been asked to design her company's Internet Protocol (IPv4) addressing scheme. The company has been assigned a Class C network address of 192.168.30.0. Alice's director wants 4 subnets with 28 hosts per subnet. How many bits are required for subnets? How many bits are required for hosts? What will the new subnet mask be for this network?

    A. 3 subnet bits, 5 host bits, and subnet mask 255.255.255.240

    B. 4 subnet bits, 3 host bits, and subnet mask 255.255.255.248

    C. 3 subnet bits, 5 host bits, and subnet mask 255.255.255.224

    D. 5 subnet bits, 3 host bits, and subnet mask 255.255.255.192

242. The default mask for an IPv4 Class B network is 255.255.0.0. How many subnet bits do you need to create 600 subnets with 55 hosts per subnet, and what is the new subnet mask for the network?

    A. 10 subnet bits with a subnet mask of 255.255.255.192

    B. 9 subnet bits with a subnet mask of 255.255.255.128

    C. 10 subnet bits with a subnet mask of 255.255.224.0

    D. 11 subnet bits with a subnet mask of 255.255.255.192

243. What is the greatest number of host addresses you can create on a single subnet of a network with the following address: 172.16.0.0/20?

   A. 142

   B. 144

   C. 4,094

   D. 4,096

244. Ralph has an IPv4 Class B network with a subnet mask of 255.255.248.0. How many subnets can he create, and how many hosts can he create per subnet?

   A. 64 subnets and 2,046 hosts

   B. 32 subnets and 2,046 hosts

   C. 30 subnets and 1,022 hosts

   D. 62 subnets and 1,022 hosts

245. Convert the binary mask 11111111.11111111.11100000.00000000 into its equivalent decimal value. What is the decimal representation of this mask?

   A. 255.255.224.0

   B. 255.255.240.0

   C. 255.255.248.0

   D. 255.255.252.0

246. If you have an IPv4 network address of 192.168.1.32/27, what is the valid range of host addresses you can use for your workstations?

   A. 192.168.1.33 through 192.168.1.63

   B. 192.168.1.33 through 192.168.1.62

   C. 192.168.1.34 through 192.168.1.62

   D. 192.168.1.34 through 192.168.1.63

247. Alice has been assigned the IPv4 network address 172.21.0.0/22 for the creation of a new department network in her company. How many host addresses does she have available to her?

   A. 510

   B. 512

   C. 1,022

   D. 1,024

248. Automatic Private IP Addressing (APIPA) assigns IPv4 addresses from which of the following classes to Dynamic Host Configuration Protocol (DHCP) clients that cannot contact a DHCP server?

   A. Class A

   B. Class B

   C. Class C

   D. Class D

249. Which of the following Internet Protocol (IPv4) address classes identifies multicast addresses?

    A. Class A

    B. Class B

    C. Class C

    D. Class D

    E. Class E

250. Which of the following is an address that you can assign to a host on a private IPv4 network?

    A. 192.167.9.46

    B. 172.16.255.255

    C. 10.1.0.253

    D. 225.87.34.1

251. Which of the following is the correct subnet mask for an IPv4 network with the address 172.16.0.0/20?

    A. 255.255.224.0

    B. 255.255.240.0

    C. 255.255.248.0

    D. 255.255.255.224

    E. 255.255.255.240

252. Ed has been assigned the IPv4 network address 192.168.2.32/28 for the computers in his department. Which of the following ranges of addresses can Ed use to configure the TCP/IP clients on his computers?

    A. 192.168.2.32 to 192.168.2.55

    B. 192.168.2.33 to 192.168.2.46

    C. 192.168.2.33 to 192.168.2.40

    D. 192.168.2.1 to 192.168.2.254

253. Which of the following IPv4 addresses is available for use on a network device?

    A. 1.0.0.1

    B. 127.98.127.0

    C. 234.9.76.32

    D. 240.65.8.124

1.8 Summarize evolving use cases for modern network environments.

254. Which of the following are mechanisms by which IPv6 traffic can be transmitted on an IPv4 network through the use of tunneling? (Choose all that apply.)

A. Teredo

B. IPsec

C. ICMPv6

D. 6to4

E. NAT64

255. Which of the following best describes why IPv6 hosts exchange ICMPv6 Router Solicitation and Router Advertisement messages with routers?

A. To obtain the prefix needed to generate a link-local address

B. To learn the IPv6 address of the nearest router

C. To perform address conflict detection for its link-local address

D. To encapsulate IPv4 packets and transmit them over the router

256. Which of the following is the IPv6 equivalent of Automatic Private IP Addressing (APIPA)?

A. EUI-64

B. SLAAC

C. APIPAv6

D. DHCPv6

257. Which of the following IPv6 address types is the functional equivalent of an IPv4 APIPA address?

A. Link local

B. Global unicast

C. Site local

D. Anycast

258. A network interface adapter in a workstation has a hexadecimal MAC address of 001F9EF-C7AD0. Which of the following would be the adapter's IPv6 link local address based on its EUI-64 value?

A. FE80::001F:9EFF:FEFC:7AD0

B. FE80::FFFE:021F:9EFC:7AD0

C. FE80::FF00:1F9E:FC7A:D0FE

D. FE80::021F:9EFF:FEFC:7AD0

259. Which of the following is a valid IPv6 address?

    A. fe00::b491:cf79:p493:23ff

    B. 2001:0:49e6:39ff:8cf5:6812:ef56

    C. fe00::c955:c944:acdd:3fcb

    D. 2001:0:44ef68:23eb:99fe:72bec6:ea5f

260. Which of the following best defines the concept of the dual stack?

    A. A computer with two network interface adapters

    B. A computer with two installed operating systems

    C. A computer with two sets of networking protocols

    D. A computer with connections to two different network segments

261. In a software-defined network (SDN), as defined in the RFC 7426 specification, a plane is a set of resources related to a particular function. Which of the following is not one of the five planes defined in the SDN architecture?

    A. Forwarding

    B. Operational

    C. Control

    D. Management

    E. Infrastructure

    F. Application

262. Which of the following layers in a software-defined network (SDN) architecture consists of hardware devices?

    A. Application

    B. Control

    C. Infrastructure

    D. Core

263. Ralph is evaluating software products for potential deployment on his company's network. Which of the following types of searches can Ralph use to identify security issues that have been discovered in specific products?

    A. CIA

    B. CVE

    C. SKU

    D. SIEM

264. When starting her new position as a network administrator, Alice was given two user accounts. One account is intended for standard user activities, and the other has the additional permissions needed for Alice to perform administrative tasks. This is an example of which of the following security concepts?

    A. Zero day

    B. Multifactor authentication

C. Least privilege

D. Defense in depth

265. Which of the following is a practice that a zero trust architecture (ZTA) is designed to protect against?

A. Zero day vulnerabilities

B. External threats

C. Deauthentication

D. Lateral movement

266. Which of the following is not one of the advantages of infrastructure as code (IaC) deployment for cloud-based virtual machines?

A. IaC provides rapid deployment of playbooks containing virtual machine configurations.

B. IaC provides configuration drift protection for virtual machines.

C. IaC provides cost savings by automating the virtual machine configuration process.

D. IaC provides increased security by encrypting the virtual machine configuration.

E. IaC provides elasticity and scalability by simplifying the virtual machine deployment process.

F. IaC can automate the deployment of operating system and application upgrades and updates.

267. Which of the following is a benefit that the SD-WAN architecture brings when compared to a standard WAN architecture?

A. The SD-WAN architecture routes traffic based on IP addresses and access control lists.

B. The SD-WAN architecture provides routing and QoS based on the application producing the data.

C. The SD-WAN architecture routes traffic through a central datacenter to the cloud.

D. The SD-WAN architecture provides end-to-end performance guarantees.

E. The SD-WAN architecture is implemented as a virtual overlay that is entirely transport agnostic.

268. Which of the following is not one of the three core services that make up the security service edge (SSE) cloud security framework?

A. CASB

B. ZTNA

C. SASE

D. SWG

269. Which of the following are the three fundamental principles of a zero trust architecture (ZTA)? (Choose three.)

A. Use least privileges

B. Always authenticate and authorize

C. Assume a breach

D. Use the three-tier hierarchical model

270. Which of the following protocols are commonly used in zero touch provisioning (ZTP)? (Choose all that apply.)

  A. DHCP

  B. FTP

  C. TFTP

  D. HTTPS

271. Which of the following are reasons why an overlay network using a virtual extensible LAN (VXLAN) might be preferable to one using VLANs? (Choose all that apply.)

  A. VXLANs can be used for Data Center Interconnect (DCI).

  B. VXLANs use a 24-bit network identifier.

  C. VXLANs run as an overlay network.

  D. VXLANs encapsulate layer 2 frames within TCP segments.

Chapter 2

Network Implementation

THE COMPTIA NETWORK+ EXAM N10-009 TOPICS COVERED IN THIS CHAPTER INCLUDE THE FOLLOWING:

✓ **2.1 Explain characteristics of routing technologies.**

- Static routing
- Dynamic routing
  - Border Gateway Protocol (BGP)
  - Enhanced Interior Gateway Routing Protocol (EIGRP)
  - Open Shortest Path First (OSPF)
- Route selection
  - Administrative distance
  - Prefix length
  - Metric
- Address translation
  - NAT
  - Port address translation (PAT)
- First Hop Redundancy Protocol (FHRP)
- Virtual IP (VIP)
- Subinterfaces

✓ **2.2 Given a scenario, configure switching technologies and features.**

- Virtual Local Area Network (VLAN)
  - VLAN database
  - Switch Virtual Interface (SVI)

- Interface configuration
  - Native VLAN
  - Voice VLAN
  - 802.1Q tagging
  - Link aggregation
  - Speed
  - Duplex
- Spanning tree
- Maximum transmission unit (MTU)
  - Jumbo frames

✓ **2.3 Given a scenario, select and configure wireless devices and technologies.**

- Channel width
- Non-overlapping channels
- Regulatory impacts
  - 802.11h
- Frequency options
  - 2.4GHz
  - 5GHz
  - 6GHz
  - Band steering
- Service set identifier (SSID)
  - Basic service set identifier (BSSID)
  - Extended service set identifier (ESSID)
- Network types
  - Mesh networks
  - Ad hoc
  - Point to point
  - Infrastructure

- Encryption
    - Wi-Fi Protected Access 2 (WPA2)
    - WPA3
- Guest networks
    - Captive portals
- Authentication
    - Pre-shared key (PSK) vs. Enterprise
- Antennas
    - Omnidirectional vs. directional
- Autonomous vs. lightweight access point

✓ **2.4 Explain important factors of physical installations.**

- Important installation implications
    - Locations
        - Intermediate distribution frame (IDF)
        - Main distribution frame (MDF)
    - Rack size
    - Port-side exhaust/intake
    - Cabling
        - Patch panel
        - Fiber distribution panel
    - Lockable
- Power
    - Uninterruptible power supply (UPS)
    - Power distribution unit (PDU)
    - Power load
    - Voltage
- Environmental factors
    - Humidity
    - Fire suppression
    - Temperature

2.1 Explain characteristics of routing technologies.

1. Network address translation (NAT) operates at which layer of the Open Systems Interconnection (OSI) model?

   A. Data link

   B. Network

   C. Transport

   D. Application

2. Which of the following devices enable users on private networks to access the Internet by substituting a registered IP address for their private addresses? (Choose all that apply.)

   A. NAT router

   B. RADIUS server

   C. Proxy server

   D. UTM appliance

3. Which of the following routing protocols uses the packet format shown in the figure?

   1 2 3 4 5 6 7 8 1 2 3 4 5 6 7 8 1 2 3 4 5 6 7 8 1 2 3 4 5 6 7 8

Address Family Identifier	Route Tag
IP Address	
Subnet Mask	
Next Hop	
Metric	

   A. RIPv1

   B. RIPv2

   C. OSPF

   D. EIGRP

   E. BGP

4. Which of the following statements about the Enhanced Interior Gateway Routing Protocol (EIGRP) is not true?

   A. EIGRP does not support classless IPv4 addresses.

   B. EIGRP is a hybrid routing protocol.

   C. EIGRP can only transmit incremental routing table updates.

   D. EIGRP shares routes within an autonomous system.

5. Which of the following are techniques used in traffic shaping to prevent networks from being overwhelmed by data transmissions? (Choose all that apply.)

   A. Bandwidth throttling

   B. Rate limiting

   C. Broadcast storming

   D. Network address translation (NAT)

6. Which of the following terms refers to methods by which network traffic is prioritized to prevent applications from suffering faults due to network congestion?

   A. Port forwarding

   B. Dynamic routing

   C. VLANs

   D. QoS

7. Which of the following mechanisms for prioritizing network traffic uses a 6-bit classification identifier in the Internet Protocol (IP) header?

   A. Diffserv

   B. CoS

   C. Traffic shaping

   D. QoS

   E. Administrative distance

8. Which of the following elements enables routers to select the best path to a destination when there are multiple routing protocols running on the network?

   A. Metrics

   B. Administrative distance

   C. CoS

   D. MTU

9. Which of the following statements about static routing are true? (Choose all that apply.)

   A. Static routes are manually configured routes that administrators must add, modify, or delete when a change in the network occurs.

   B. Static routes are automatically added to the routing table by routing protocols when a new network path becomes available.

   C. Static routes adapt to changes in the network infrastructure automatically.

   D. Static routes are a recommended solution for large internetworks with redundant paths to each destination network.

   E. Static routes are a recommended solution for small internetworks with a single path to each destination network.

10. Which of the following terms refers to a routing protocol that does not rely on hop counts to measure the efficiency of routes?

   A. Interior gateway protocol

   B. Edge gateway protocol

   C. Distance vector protocol

   D. Link state protocol

11. What is the maximum number of routes that can be included in a single RIP broadcast packet?

   A. 20

   B. 25

   C. 32

   D. Unlimited

12. Which of the following routing protocols can you use on a TCP/IP internetwork with segments running at different speeds, making hop counts an inaccurate measure of route efficiency? (Choose all that apply.)

   A. Enhanced Interior Gateway Routing Protocol (EIGRP)

   B. Routing Information Protocol (RIP)

   C. Open Shortest Path First (OSPF)

   D. Border Gateway Protocol (BGP)

13. Which of the following statements about the Open Shortest Path First (OSPF) routing protocol is false?

   A. OSPF is an interior gateway protocol.

   B. OSPF is a link state routing protocol.

   C. OSPF does not support Classless Inter-Domain Routing (CIDR).

   D. OSPF shares routes within an autonomous system.

14. What is the term for the process by which dynamic routing protocols update other routers with routing table information?

   A. Convergence

   B. Distance vectoring

   C. Redistribution

   D. Dissemination

15. Which of the following TCP/IP routing protocols measures the efficiency of routes by the number of hops between the source and the destination?

   A. Routing Internet Protocol (RIP)

   B. Open Shortest Path First (OSPF)

   C. Border Gateway Protocol (BGP)

   D. Intermediate System to Intermediate System (IS-IS)

16. Which of the following types of routing protocols routes datagrams between autonomous systems?

    A. EGP

    B. RIP

    C. IGP

    D. OSPF

17. Which of the following command-line tools can you use to create and modify static routes on a Unix or Linux system? (Choose all that apply.)

    A. `route`

    B. `ifconfig`

    C. `traceroute`

    D. `ip`

18. Routers that use the Open Shortest Path First (OSPF) routing protocol calculate the relative costs of routes through the network by exchanging which of the following specifications for each interface with other routers?

    A. Transmission speed

    B. Data link layer protocol

    C. Network medium

    D. IP address

    E. Prefix length

    F. Metric

19. Which of the following statements about the Border Gateway Protocol (BGP) is not true?

    A. BGP is an exterior gateway protocol.

    B. BGP is a link state routing protocol.

    C. BGP supports Classless Inter-Domain Routing (CIDR).

    D. BGP shares routes among autonomous systems.

20. In an IPv4 routing table, what is the network destination address for the host system's default route?

    A. 0.0.0.0

    B. 127.0.0.0

    C. 127.255.255.255

    D. 255.255.255.255

21. Which of the following routing protocols has both interior and exterior designations, based on whether it is used for routing within an autonomous system or on the Internet?

    A. RIP

    B. OSPF

    C. EIGRP

    D. BGP

22. Which of the following Network layer protocols include a Time to Live (TTL) field? (Choose all that apply.)

    A. IPv4

    B. IPv6

    C. ICMP

    D. IGMP

23. Which of the following is not a method of traffic shaping?

    A. Rate limiting

    B. WAN optimization

    C. Bandwidth throttling

    D. Self-limiting

24. Which of the following statements about proxy servers and NAT servers are true? (Choose all that apply.)

    A. NAT servers and proxy servers can both provide Internet access to clients running any application.

    B. NAT servers and proxy servers both use public IP addresses.

    C. NAT servers and proxy servers both access Internet servers and relay the responses to network clients.

    D. NAT servers and proxy servers both cache web data for later use.

25. Which two of the following functions is the multifunction device on a small office, home office (SOHO) network known as a broadband router least likely to provide? (Choose two.)

    A. Wireless access point (WAP)

    B. Switch

    C. Proxy server

    D. DHCP server

    E. VPN headend

26. Small office, home office (SOHO) networks typically use a multifunction connectivity device that can perform all but which one of the following functions?

    A. DHCP

    B. DNS

    C. Switch

    D. Router

    E. Hub

    F. NAT router

    G. Access point (AP)

27. Review the following figure. How many collision domains and broadcast domains exist in the network diagram?

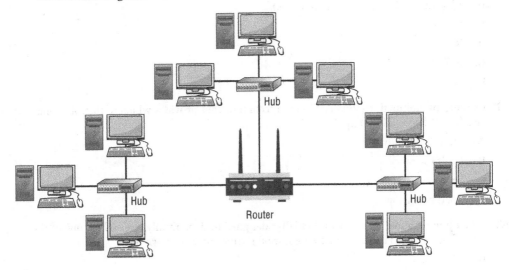

A. There are three collision domains and three broadcast domains.

B. There is one collision domain and three broadcast domains.

C. There is one broadcast domain and three collision domains.

D. There are no collision domains and only one broadcast domain.

E. There are nine collision domains and three broadcast domains.

28. Which of the following is a correct definition of a collision domain?

A. A group of local area networks (LANs) connected by routers, thus enabling any node to transmit to any other node

B. A group of computers connected so that a broadcast transmission by any one device reaches all of the other devices

C. A group of devices connected by cable segments that are longer than the maximum length stated in the physical layer specification

D. A group of devices connected so that when two devices transmit at exactly the same time, a data collision occurs

29. A VPN headend is an advanced type of which of the following devices?

A. Switch

B. Router

C. Gateway

D. Bridge

30. Routers using link states and Dijkstra's algorithm to calculate the lowest cost route to a specific destination can conceivably be running which of the following interior gateway routing protocols? (Choose all that apply.)

A. OSPF

B. RIP

C. EIGRP

D. BGP

31. Concurrent multipath routing (CMR) is a technique that provides which of the following benefits? (Choose all that apply.)

A. Increased bandwidth

B. Fault tolerance

C. Data encapsulation

D. Load balancing

32. A first hop redundancy protocol (FHRP) is designed to dynamically alter which one of the following Internet Protocol (IP) configuration settings on a network host?

A. IP address

B. Subnet mask

C. Default gateway

D. DNS server address

33. Which of the following is not a first hop redundancy protocol (FHRP)?

A. CARP

B. VRRP

C. HSRP

D. RARP

34. When two workstations access the Internet using the same port address translation (PAT) router, which of the following does the router assign to each workstation? (Choose all that apply.)

A. A common public IPv4 address

B. A unique port number

C. A common port number

D. A unique public IPv4 address

35. Which of the following are examples of virtual IP (VIP) addresses? (Choose all that apply.)

A. An IP address assigned to a host workstation by a DHCP server

B. A public IP address substituted for a host's own private IP address by a NAT router

C. An IP address assigned to a host workstation by APIPA

D. An IP address assigned to a virtual NIC

36. Which of the following is the best definition of a subinterface?

    A. A logical network interface created from a physical network interface

    B. One of the ports on a physical network interface adapter with multiple ports

    C. A physical network interface connected to a subnet

    D. One of the IP addresses associated with a network interface that has multiple IP addresses

37. When a router receives a packet destined for the address 192.168.14.73, which of the routing criteria will it use first to select from the following routing table entries?

Protocol	Administrative Distance	Prefix	Next Hop	Metric
RIP	120	192.168.14.64/26	172.16.9.1	6
OSPF	110	192.168.14.0/25	172.16.10.1	240
EIGRP	90	192.168.14.0/24	172.16.11.1	33789

    A. Administrative distance

    B. Prefix length

    C. Next hop

    D. Metric

2.2 Given a scenario, configure switching technologies and features.

38. The jumbo frame capability is associated with which layer of the Open Systems Interconnection (OSI) model?

    A. Application

    B. Transport

    C. Network

    D. Data link

39. Port security on an Ethernet switch is implemented through the use of which of the following methods?

    A. Deny listed MAC addresses

    B. Allow listed MAC addresses

    C. Port-by-port MAC address filtering

    D. Spoofed MAC addresses

40. Which of the following features helps to protect network switches from attacks related to the Spanning Tree Protocol (STP)? (Choose all that apply.)

  A. BPDU guard

  B. Root guard

  C. DHCP snooping

  D. Geofencing

41. An enterprise network has been designed with individual departmental switches because, in most cases, the devices in a specific department exchange network traffic with other devices in the same department. Each of the departmental switches is also connected to a host switch, which enables devices to communicate with other departments. Which of the following terms describes this switching architecture?

  A. Distributed switching

  B. Port forwarding

  C. Traffic shaping

  D. Neighbor discovery

  E. Flow control

42. Review the following figure. Note that each store-and-forward switch has three connected node ports and one port for switch-to-switch connections. All node ports and links are configured for half-duplex communication. The switch-to-switch links are configured for full-duplex communication. Which of the following statements about the switched network is true?

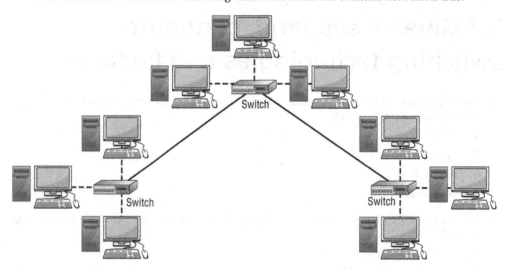

  A. There are nine collision domains, one for each half-duplex connection.

  B. There are 12 collision domains, one for each switch connection.

  C. There are three collision domains, one for each switch-to-switch connection.

  D. There is one collision domain for this network.

43. Which of the following could be a valid MAC address for a network interface adapter?

    A. 10.124.25.43

    B. FF:FF:FF:FF:FF:FF

    C. 00:1A:6B:31:9A:4E

    D. 03:AE:16:3H:5B:11

    E. fe80::89a5:9e4d:a9d0:9ed7

44. Which of the following protocols prevents network switching loops from occurring by shutting down redundant links until they are needed?

    A. RIP

    B. STP

    C. VLAN

    D. NAT

    E. ARP

45. Which of the following cable types can be used to connect an MDI port on a workstation to an Auto-MDI-X port on an Ethernet switch? (Choose all that apply.)

    A. A crossover twisted-pair cable

    B. A straight-through twisted-pair cable

    C. A coaxial cable

    D. A single-mode fiber-optic cable

    E. A multimode fiber-optic cable

46. Which of the following is a protocol that identifies VLANs by inserting a 32-bit field in the Ethernet frame?

    A. IEEE 802.1P

    B. IEEE 802.1Q

    C. IEEE 802.1X

    D. IEEE 802.1AB

    E. IEEE 802.1AX

47. Each of the following Carrier Sense Multiple Access with Collision Detection (CSMA/CD) events occurs on an Ethernet network when two stations transmit simultaneously, although not in the order listed. Which of the following events occurs immediately after the collision?

    A. The two stations observe a random backoff interval.

    B. The two stations transmit a jam signal.

    C. The two stations stop transmitting.

    D. The two stations listen to see if the channel is idle.

    E. The two stations begin retransmitting their frames.

48. For the Carrier Sense Multiple Access with Collision Detection (CSMA/CD) mechanism to function properly on an Ethernet network, host systems must be able to detect when a collision occurs so they can react to it. Which of the following cabling errors can prevent the collision detection process from functioning properly?

A. Excessively long cable segments

B. Incorrect wiring pinouts

C. Too many systems on a single network

D. An excessive number of collisions

49. When a packet collision between two systems occurs on an Ethernet network, Carrier Sense Multiple Access with Collision Detection (CSMA/CD) causes the two systems to stop transmitting and generate a jam signal. After sending the jam signal, why do the two systems wait for a randomized backoff interval before retransmitting their packets?

A. They need time to reassemble the packets.

B. To prevent another collision from occurring.

C. They need to rebuffer the packet.

D. To recalculate the packets' checksum values.

50. Which of the following devices is used to physically connect computers in the same VLAN?

A. A bridge

B. A hub

C. A switch

D. A router

51. Which of the following statements is true about an Ethernet network that uses CSMA/CD?

A. Collisions are a normal occurrence.

B. Collisions never occur unless there is a network fault.

C. Collisions cause data to be irretrievably lost.

D. Collisions are the result of duplicate IP addresses.

52. Which of the following is an abnormal occurrence on an Ethernet network?

A. Packet retransmissions

B. Collision detection

C. Jam signals

D. Late collisions

53. VLANs create the administrative boundaries on a switched network that are otherwise provided by which of the following devices?

A. Hubs

B. Routers

C. Domains

D. Bridges

54. Which of the following statements about VLANs are true? (Choose all that apply.)

   A. All of the devices in a particular VLAN must be physically connected to the same switch.

   B. A VLAN creates a limited broadcast domain on a switched network.

   C. You must have VLANs on a switched network for communication between computers on different cable segments to occur.

   D. A router is required for communication between VLANs.

55. Which of the following elements can be used to identify the devices in a particular VLAN? (Choose all that apply.)

   A. Hardware addresses

   B. IP addresses

   C. DNS names

   D. Switch port numbers

56. Alice has a network that consists of three virtual LANs (VLANs) defined on all of the network's switches. VLAN 10 is the Sales VLAN; VLAN 20 is the Marketing VLAN; and VLAN 30 is the Accounting VLAN. Users are reporting that they cannot communicate with anyone outside of their own VLANs. What is the problem, and what must Alice do?

   A. The problem is a faulty VLAN configuration on one of the switches. Alice needs to re-create the VLANs and configure each VLAN for routing.

   B. One of the VLANs is configured to filter all other VLAN traffic for security purposes. Alice needs to change the filter on this VLAN.

   C. VLANs are limited to Data link layer communication only. To allow communication between VLANs, Alice must add a router or a layer 3 switch to the network and configure it to route traffic between the VLANs.

   D. The VLANs are using different Data link layer protocols. VLANs must use the same Data link layer protocol in order to communicate.

57. Which of the following technologies would you be less likely to find on the average small office, home office (SOHO) network? (Choose all that apply.)

   A. NAT

   B. DHCP

   C. 10GBase-T

   D. VLAN

58. Which of the following modifications occurs when you configure the native virtual local area network (VLAN) on your network switches to use 802.1Q tagging?

   A. Double-tagged packets are prevented.

   B. BPDU guards are applied.

   C. Root guards are applied.

   D. Trunk traffic is routed, not switched.

59. Which of the following protocols is responsible for inserting the tags into frames that enable switches to forward them to the appropriate virtual local area network (VLAN)?

  A. IEEE 802.3x

  B. IEEE 802.1X

  C. IEEE 802.1Q

  D. IEEE 802.11ac

60. Which of the following best explains how tagging the native virtual local area network (VLAN) traffic can improve in-band switch management security?

  A. By renaming the default VLAN

  B. By preventing double-tagged packets

  C. By encrypting in-band management traffic

  D. By moving in-band management traffic off the native VLAN

61. A switch with auto-medium-dependent interface crossover (MDI-X) ports eliminates the need for which of the following?

  A. 8P8C connectors

  B. Switch-to-switch connections

  C. Straight-through cables

  D. Crossover cables

62. Which of the following cable types is needed to connect an MDI port on a workstation to an MDI-X port on an Ethernet switch?

  A. A crossover twisted-pair cable

  B. A straight-through twisted-pair cable

  C. A coaxial cable

  D. A single-mode fiber-optic cable

  E. A multimode fiber-optic cable

63. Which of the following problems is the Spanning Tree Protocol (STP) intended to prevent? (Choose all that apply.)

  A. Broadcast storms

  B. Late collisions

  C. Bridging loops

  D. Crosstalk

64. Which of the following identifiers does a switch use to forward incoming packets out through the correct ports?

  A. IP addresses

  B. MAC addresses

  C. DNS names

  D. MTU values

65. Which of the following statements about the Spanning Tree Protocol (STP) is not true?

   A. STP operates at the Data link layer of the OSI model.

   B. STP is implemented in switches.

   C. STP prevents traffic from circulating endlessly around a network.

   D. STP compiles a database containing the IP addresses of connected devices.

66. Ralph has been hired by a company to redesign its local area network (LAN). Right now, it has a single 100 Mbps Ethernet LAN with 40 users and two shared servers, all connected through three hubs. The users on the network must be able to share files with one another and also access the shared servers. The users are complaining that the network is too slow. Management states that cost is a factor that must be considered. Which of the following upgrade scenarios should Ralph recommend in this situation?

   A. Split the network into smaller segments with dedicated hubs as opposed to shared hubs.

   B. Split the network into two routed LANs with 20 users each.

   C. Replace the hubs with switches to define separate collision domains and filter unnecessary traffic from each segment.

   D. Replace the hubs with a layer 3 switch and define two virtual LANs (VLANs) with 20 users each.

67. Which of the following is the correct term for the process by which the Spanning Tree Protocol (STP) on a switch evaluates the paths through the network and places each port in the forwarding or blocking state?

   A. Assimilation

   B. Convergence

   C. Tree-building

   D. Listening

68. A multilayer switch typically functions at which layers of the OSI reference model? (Choose two.)

   A. Data link

   B. Network

   C. Transport

   D. Application

69. Five computers are connected to the same switch, but only four are able to communicate with each other. Assuming that all of the hardware is functioning properly, which of the following could be a reason for the fifth computer's communication problem?

   A. The switch has the fifth computer connected to a virtual local area network (VLAN) that is different from that of the other four.

   B. The network is experiencing a switching loop.

   C. The fifth computer is experiencing an MTU black hole, whereas the other four computers are not.

   D. There is a virtual router between the fifth computer and the other four.

70. A small business office currently has a 1000Base-T Ethernet network with a single eight-port switch. All of the switchports are populated, and the business owner wants to expand the network further. However, the switch does not have an uplink port. The owner has purchased a new switch, also with eight ports, that does have an uplink port, but he does not know how to connect them together. What must the owner do to install the new switch on the network?

   A. Use a standard patch cable to connect a standard port on the existing switch to a standard port on the new switch.

   B. Use a standard patch cable to connect a standard port on the existing switch to the uplink port on the new hub.

   C. Purchase a crossover cable and use it to connect a standard port on the existing switch to the uplink port on the new switch.

   D. Purchase a second new switch with an uplink port to replace the old one and use a standard patch cable to connect the two uplink ports together.

71. Which of the following tasks can you perform to split a large, switched local area network (LAN) into multiple broadcast domains? (Choose all that apply.)

   A. Replace one or more switches with hubs.

   B. Install a firewall to filter broadcast traffic.

   C. Enable the Spanning Tree Protocol (STP) on the switches.

   D. Create virtual local area networks (VLANs) in the switches.

   E. Install routers on the network.

72. Which of the following devices can administrators use to create multiple virtual local area networks (VLANs) and forward traffic between them?

   A. Virtual router

   B. Load balancer

   C. Broadband router

   D. Multilayer switch

73. Which of the following best explains why networks using Voice over IP (VoIP) often have separate voice and data virtual local area networks (VLANs)?

   A. To prevent voice and data packet conflicts

   B. To encrypt voice traffic

   C. To encrypt data traffic

   D. To prioritize voice traffic

74. On a network carrying both voice and data traffic, separate virtual local area networks (VLANs) enable the voice traffic to be assigned a higher priority than the data traffic. Which of the following are methods for identifying the packets carrying voice traffic, so the switches can assign them to the voice VLAN? (Choose all that apply.)

   A. MAC addresses

   B. VLAN tags

   C. IP addresses

   D. DNS names

75. Which of the following are equivalent terms for the process of combining the bandwidth of two or more network adapters to increase the overall speed of the connection and provide fault tolerance? (Choose all that apply.)

    A. Bonding

    B. Link aggregation

    C. Clustering

    D. Port aggregation

    E. NIC teaming

76. Which of the following statements about port aggregation is not true?

    A. All of the aggregated ports use the same MAC address.

    B. Port aggregation can be a fault tolerance mechanism.

    C. Aggregating ports increases network throughput.

    D. Port aggregation provides load balancing.

77. Ralph is designing a new network with the redundant switching arrangement shown in the accompanying figure. This redundancy enables every node on the network to communicate with any other node, even if one of the switches should fail. Which of the following is a potential drawback of this arrangement?

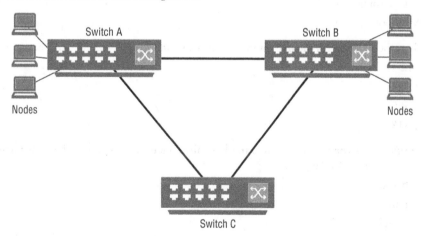

    A. Runt frames

    B. Late collisions

    C. Broadcast storms

    D. Corrupted switch lookup tables

78. Which of the following mechanisms for load balancing web servers is able to read the incoming HTTP and HTTPS requests and perform advanced functions based on the information they contain?

   A. Content switches

   B. Multilayer switches

   C. Failover clustering

   D. Round-robin DNS

79. Which of the following statements about a switch's default VLAN are true?

   A. Administrators must create a default VLAN when configuring a new switch.

   B. The default VLAN on a switch cannot be deleted.

   C. The default VLAN on most switches is designated as VLAN 0.

   D. The default VLAN on a switch cannot be renamed.

80. Which of the following bridging types has never been used on Ethernet local area networks (LANs)?

   A. Store and forward

   B. Transparent

   C. Source route

   D. Multiport

81. Which of the following is the maximum transmission unit (MTU) size for an Ethernet frame?

   A. 512

   B. 1,024

   C. 1,500

   D. 1,518

82. Which of the following devices is used to physically connect computers in the same virtual local area network (VLAN)?

   A. A bridge

   B. A hub

   C. A switch

   D. A router

83. Which of the following protocols uses jumbo frames to increase performance levels on storage area networks?

   A. Ethernet

   B. IP

   C. Fibre Channel

   D. iSCSI

2.3 Given a scenario, select and configure wireless devices and technologies.

84. Which of the following IEEE standards calls for the use of the Carrier Sense Multiple Access with Collision Avoidance (CSMA/CA) Media Access Control (MAC) mechanism?

- **A.** 802.11ac
- **B.** 802.1X
- **C.** 802.3
- **D.** All of the above

85. Which of the following topologies enables wireless devices to access resources on a wired network?

- **A.** Ad hoc
- **B.** Star/hub and spoke
- **C.** Infrastructure
- **D.** Bus
- **E.** Mesh

86. Which of the following components is required for two computers to communicate using an IEEE 802.11 wireless LAN in an ad hoc topology?

- **A.** A router connected to the Internet
- **B.** A wireless access point (WAP)
- **C.** An external antenna
- **D.** None of the above

87. Which of the following wireless networking technologies will never experience interference from a 2.4 GHz wireless phone? (Choose all that apply.)

- **A.** IEEE 802.11a
- **B.** IEEE 802.11b
- **C.** IEEE 802.11g
- **D.** IEEE 802.11n
- **E.** IEEE 802.11ac
- **F.** IEEE 802.11ax

88. Which of the following wireless LAN standards include the ability to use multiple input, multiple output (MIMO) antennas? (Choose all that apply.)

    A. IEEE 802.11a

    B. IEEE 802.11b/g

    C. IEEE 802.11n

    D. IEEE 802.11ac

    E. IEEE 802.11ax

89. Which of the following IEEE wireless LAN standards uses the direct-sequence spread spectrum (DSSS) signal modulation technique?

    A. 802.11a

    B. 802.11b

    C. 802.11g

    D. 802.11n

    E. 802.11ac

90. When designing a wireless LAN installation, which of the following are valid reasons to install a unidirectional antenna in an access point (AP), rather than an omnidirectional one? (Choose all that apply.)

    A. The AP will be located against an outside wall.

    B. There are many interior walls between the AP and the most distant workstation.

    C. A unidirectional antenna can be focused to a specific signal pattern width.

    D. All of the above.

91. How do wireless networking devices conforming to the IEEE 802.11n and 802.11ac standards achieve transmission speeds greater than 72.2 Mbps?

    A. By using direct-sequence spread spectrum (DSSS) modulation

    B. By using multiple antennas to transmit several data streams simultaneously

    C. By using frequencies in the 5 GHz band

    D. By sacrificing transmission range for speed

92. Which of the following are possible reasons why the 5 GHz frequency tends to perform better than the 2.4 GHz frequency on a wireless LAN? (Choose all that apply.)

    A. The 5 GHz frequency has more channels than the 2.4 GHz frequency.

    B. The 5 GHz frequency supports longer ranges than the 2.4 GHz frequency.

    C. The 5 GHz frequency conflicts with fewer common household devices than the 2.4 GHz frequency.

    D. The 5 GHz frequency transmits at faster speeds than the 2.4 GHz frequency.

93. Alice is attempting to deploy an IEEE 802.11b/g wireless LAN on the fifth floor of a 10-story office building that is surrounded on all sides by other office buildings, all of which seem to be running many wireless LANs. Scanning the 2.4 GHz band, she sees literally dozens of networks, spread across all of the available channels. As a result, her wireless devices have trouble connecting to their access point (AP), and when they do, they achieve only low speeds. Which of the following tasks should Alice perform to enable the wireless clients to connect to the network more reliably? (Choose two.)

   A. Upgrade all of the wireless network devices to IEEE 802.11n.

   B. Configure all of the network devices to use WPA2 encryption with AES.

   C. Configure the wireless devices to use the 5 GHz band.

   D. Configure the AP to suppress service set identifier (SSID) broadcasts.

   E. Upgrade all of the network devices to the latest firmware.

94. What is the term for the technology implemented in the IEEE 802.11ac standard that enables a wireless device to transmit multiple frames to multiple clients simultaneously?

   A. MIMO

   B. Channel bonding

   C. CSMA/CA

   D. MU-MIMO

95. On an IEEE 802.11b/g/n wireless network running at 2.4 GHz with multiple access points (APs), the traditional best practice is to use channels 1, 6, and 11, with no two adjacent APs configured to use the same channel. Which of the following is the real reason why this is a good plan?

   A. Channels 1, 6, and 11 are the only channels with frequencies that do not overlap.

   B. Channels 1, 6, and 11 have more bandwidth than the other channels.

   C. Channels 1, 6, and 11 have greater ranges than the other channels.

   D. Channels 1, 6, and 11 are the default settings on most wireless devices.

96. Which of the following terms defines a wireless LAN transmission technique in which devices use multiple antennas to increase transmission speeds?

   A. MIMO

   B. TDMA

   C. PAN

   D. Ant+

97. What is the maximum channel width possible using wireless networking equipment based on the ratified IEEE 802.11 regulatory standards?

   A. 20 MHz

   B. 40 MHz

   C. 80 MHz

   D. 160 MHz

98. Which of the following wireless networking standards are capable of using only the 5 GHz frequency? (Choose all that apply.)

   A. IEEE 802.11a

   B. IEEE 802.11b

   C. IEEE 802.11g

   D. IEEE 802.11n

   E. IEEE 802.11ac

   F. IEEE 802.11ax

99. Which of the following IEEE 802.11 wireless LAN standards is capable of supporting the 6 GHz frequency band?

   A. 802.11a

   B. 802.11b

   C. 802.11g

   D. 802.11n

   E. 802.11ac

   F. 802.11ax

100. Which of the following IEEE wireless LAN standards provides the greatest possible throughput?

   A. 802.11a

   B. 802.11ac

   C. 802.11ax

   D. 802.11b

   E. 802.11g

   F. 802.11n

101. Which of the following IEEE 802.11 wireless LAN standards are capable of supporting both the 2.4 GHz and 5 GHz frequencies? (Choose all that apply.)

   A. 802.11a

   B. 802.11b

   C. 802.11g

   D. 802.11n

   E. 802.11ac

   F. 802.11ax

102. What is the maximum number of transmit and receive antennas supported by the currently ratified IEEE 802.11 wireless LAN standards?

   A. 2

   B. 4

   C. 8

   D. 16

103. Which of the following is the term for the network name that you use to connect a client device to an access point (AP) on a wireless LAN?

    A. BSS

    B. ESS

    C. SSID

    D. BSSID

    E. ESSID

104. Which of the following IEEE wireless LAN standards define devices with a maximum aggregate channel width of 20 MHz? (Choose all that apply.)

    A. 802.11a

    B. 802.11g

    C. 802.11n

    D. 802.11ac

105. At which layer of the Open Systems Interconnection (OSI) model do wireless range extenders operate?

    A. Physical

    B. Data link

    C. Network

    D. Transport

    E. Session

    F. Presentation

    G. Application

106. Which of the following wireless security protocols provides the greatest degree of network device hardening?

    A. WEP

    B. WPA

    C. WPA2

    D. WPA3

    E. EAP

107. Which of the following encryption protocols was introduced in the Wi-Fi Protected Access (WPA) wireless security standard?

    A. CCMP-AES

    B. TKIP-RC4

    C. EAP-TLS

    D. TACACS+

108. TKIP-RC4 is an encryption protocol used with which of the following wireless network security standards?

   A. WEP

   B. WPA

   C. WPA2

   D. WPA3

   E. EAP

109. Which of the following protocols provides wireless networks with the strongest encryption?

   A. AES

   B. TKIP

   C. EAP

   D. 802.1X

110. To connect a wireless client to a wireless access point (WAP) using the Wi-Fi Protected Access 3-Personal (WPA3-Personal) security protocol, which of the following must you supply on both devices?

   A. Base key

   B. Passphrase

   C. Serial number

   D. MAC address

111. Upgrading a wireless network to the WPA3-Personal security protocol provides clients with additional protection from replay attacks. Which of the following WPA3 elements accomplish this? (Choose all that apply.)

   A. PSK

   B. NFC

   C. SAE

   D. PFS

112. Which of the following wireless security protocols use CCMP-AES for encryption? (Choose all that apply.)

   A. WEP

   B. WPA

   C. WPA2

   D. WPA3

   E. TKIP

113. Which of the following wireless LAN security protocols does not support the use of a pre-shared key (PSK) in its Personal configuration?

   A. WEP

   B. WPA

   C. WPA2

   D. WPA3

114. Which of the following did the Wi-Fi Protected Access 2 (WPA2) security protocol add to the existing WPA standard?

   A. CCMP-AES

   B. MIMO

   C. WEP

   D. TKIP

115. Alice is setting up a wireless LAN in a friend's home, using an 802.11n wireless access point and three computers with 802.11n adapters. She has installed and successfully tested the devices on an open network, and now she is ready to add security. Which of the following protocols should Alice choose to provide maximum security for the wireless network?

   A. WPA3

   B. IPsec

   C. TLS

   D. L2TP

116. CCMP-AES is an encryption protocol used with which of the following wireless network security standards? (Choose two.)

   A. WEP

   B. WPA

   C. WPA2

   D. WPA3

   E. EAP

117. Which of the following wireless security protocols can enable network users to authenticate using smart cards?

   A. WPA3

   B. WPA2

   C. EAP

   D. AES

118. Which of the following forms of the Wi-Fi Protected Access (WPA), WPA2, and WPA3 protocols require a RADIUS server? (Choose all that apply.)

   A. WPA-Personal

   B. WPA-PSK

   C. WPA-Enterprise

   D. WPA-802.1X

119. Which of the following forms of the Wi-Fi Protected Access (WPA), WPA2, and WPA3 protocols call for the use of a pre-shared key (PSK)?

   A. WPA-Personal

   B. WPA-Enterprise

   C. WPA-EAP

   D. WPA-802.1X

120. Which of the following stream ciphers does the Temporal Key Integrity Protocol (TKIP) use for encryption on a wireless network?

   A. RC4

   B. AES

   C. CCMP

   D. SHA

121. Which of the following wireless security protocols uses CCMP for encryption?

   A. WPA

   B. WPA2

   C. WPA3

   D. 802.1X

122. CCMP is based on which of the following encryption standards?

   A. TKIP

   B. RC4

   C. AES

   D. 802.1X

123. Ralph has installed a new wireless access point (WAP) on his network and configured it to use WPA3 for security and an SSID that is not broadcast. Which of the following describes what Ralph must do to configure his wireless clients?

   A. Select the SSID from a list and allow the client to automatically detect the security protocol.

   B. Select the SSID from a list and then select WPA3 from the security protocol options provided.

    C. Type the SSID manually and allow the client to automatically detect the security protocol.

    D. Type the SSID manually and then select WPA3 from the security protocol options provided.

124. Which of the following encryption protocols was introduced in the Wi-Fi Protected Access 2 (WPA2) wireless security standard?

    A. CCMP-AES

    B. TKIP-RC4

    C. EAP-TLS

    D. TACACS+

125. Which of the following wireless LAN security protocols were rendered obsolete after they were found to be extremely easy to penetrate? (Choose all that apply.)

    A. WEP

    B. WPA

    C. WPA2

    D. WPA3

    E. EAP

126. Which of the following encryption ciphers was replaced by CCMP-AES when the WPA2 wireless security protocol was introduced?

    A. EAP

    B. WEP

    C. TKIP

    D. CCMP

127. Ralph is installing a wireless LAN that includes three access points (APs) to provide coverage for a large building. Which of the following must Ralph do to ensure that users are able to roam without interruption from one AP to another using their portable devices? (Choose all that apply.)

    A. Configure each AP with the same IP address.

    B. Configure each AP with the same security passphrase.

    C. Configure each AP to use the same security protocol.

    D. Configure each AP with the same SSID.

128. Which of the following is the maximum theoretical download speed for a 5G cellular network?

    A. 42 Mbps

    B. 150 Mbps

    C. 1 Gbps

    D. 10 Gbps

    E. 100 Gbps

129. Which of the following statements about 5G cellular networks are true? (Choose all that apply.)

   A. 5G networks can operate on three frequency bands.

   B. 5G networks with the highest speeds also have a more limited range.

   C. 4G devices can connect to 5G networks at reduced speeds.

   D. On a 5G network, the lower frequency bands provide the highest speeds.

130. Which of the following IEEE standards describes an implementation of port-based access control for wireless networks?

   A. 802.11ac

   B. 802.11h

   C. 802.11n

   D. 802.1X

   E. 802.3x

131. Unauthorized users are connecting to Alice's wireless access point (WAP) and gaining access to the network. Which of the following are immediate steps Alice can take to prevent this from happening? (Choose all that apply.)

   A. Disable SSID broadcasting.

   B. Use Kerberos for authentication.

   C. Place the access point (AP) in a screened subnet.

   D. Implement MAC address filtering.

132. On a wireless access point (WAP) that uses an access control list (ACL) to specify which devices are permitted to connect to the network, which of the following is used to identify the authorized devices?

   A. Usernames

   B. IP addresses

   C. Device names

   D. MAC addresses

133. Which of the following best describes the process of allow listing on a wireless network?

   A. Using an access control list (ACL) to specify the IP addresses that are permitted to access a wireless network

   B. Using port protection to specify the well-known port numbers of applications that users are permitted to run over a wireless network

   C. Using MAC filtering to create a list of devices that are permitted to access a wireless network

   D. Using an AAA server to create a list of users that are permitted to access a wireless network

134. Which of the following protocols can be used by wireless controllers to communicate with the access points (APs) on a wireless local area network (WLAN)? (Choose all that apply.)

A. CAPWAP

B. LWAPP

C. LDAP

D. PPTP

135. On a wireless network, which of the following best describes an example of a captive portal?

A. A switch port used to connect to other switches

B. A web page with which a user must interact before being granted access to a wireless network

C. A series of two doors through which people must pass before they can enter a secured space

D. A web page stating that the user's computer has been locked and will only be unlocked after payment of a fee

136. A user attempting to connect to a Wi-Fi hotspot in a coffee shop is taken to a web page that requires her to accept an end-user license agreement (EULA) before access to the network is granted. Which of the following is the term for such an arrangement?

A. Captive portal

B. Ransomware

C. Port security

D. Root guard

137. A wireless access point (WAP) enables computers equipped with wireless network interface adapters to function in which of the following topologies?

A. Star/hub and spoke

B. Ad hoc

C. Bus

D. Infrastructure

138. A wireless network adapter that automatically chooses the best available network frequency, 2.4 GHz or 5 GHz, based on signal strength and distance from the access point, is performing which of the following functions?

A. Channel bonding

B. Band steering

C. Link aggregation

D. Traffic shaping

139. Which of the following types of wireless access point (WAP) requires the network to include a wireless LAN controller (WLC)?

   A. Lightweight access point

   B. Standalone access point

   C. Autonomous access point

   D. Traffic access point

2.4 Explain important factors of physical installations.

140. At what humidity level do electronic components become vulnerable to damage from electrostatic shock?

   A. Below 30 percent

   B. Below 50 percent

   C. Above 70 percent

   D. Above 90 percent

141. Ralph is designing the HVAC implementation for his company's new central datacenter, which will house all of the equipment for the corporate headquarters and the company's manufacturing facility. The datacenter must adhere to the Tier III standard defined by the Uptime Institute, which calls for at least 99.9 percent uptime. As part of the environmental infrastructure for the datacenter, Ralph plans to install sensors to monitor environmental factors that can affect computer equipment and generate alerts when conditions exceed accepted thresholds. Which of the following environmental factors is not one of those that Ralph should arrange to monitor to protect the equipment specific to a datacenter?

   A. Flood

   B. Humidity

   C. Radon

   D. Static electricity

   E. Temperature

142. Which of the following are places where network wiring connections are found? (Choose all that apply.)

   A. MDF

   B. MTBF

   C. IDF

   D. RDP

143. Which of the following is the term used to describe a wiring nexus—typically housed in a closet—where horizontal networks meet the backbone?

    A. MDF

    B. MTBF

    C. IDF

    D. SLA

    E. MOU

144. Your company has been acquired by another firm and, as IT director, you will have to comply with the new firm's safety policies in your datacenter and other IT workspaces. One of the new requirements states that there must be a fail closed policy for the datacenter. Which of the following best describes what this policy dictates should occur in the event of an emergency?

    A. All computers that are logged on should automatically log off.

    B. All computers that are running should automatically shut down.

    C. All doors that are normally open should lock themselves.

    D. All doors that are normally locked should open themselves.

145. Redundant power circuits can enable a server to continue running despite which of the following events?

    A. A citywide power outage

    B. A server power supply failure

    C. An uncorrected building circuit failure

    D. A failure of the server's uninterruptable power supply (UPS)

146. A server with dual power supplies must be running in which of the following modes for the system to be fault tolerant?

    A. Combined mode

    B. Redundant mode

    C. Individual mode

    D. Hot backup mode

147. Which of the following statements about the differences between online and standby uninterruptible power supplies (UPSs) are correct? (Choose all that apply.)

    A. A standby UPS runs devices using battery power all the time.

    B. An online UPS provides no gap in the power supplied to the devices during a main power failure.

    C. An online UPS switches devices to battery power only during a main power failure.

    D. A standby UPS provides only enough power for an orderly shutdown of the devices.

148. Which of the following are valid reasons why online uninterruptible power supplies (UPSs) are more expensive than standby UPSs?

A. Online UPSs enable devices to run longer when a main power failure occurs.

B. Online UPSs enable devices to run continuously when a main power failure occurs.

C. Online UPSs are managed devices that can generate alerts.

D. Online UPSs provide greater protection against power spikes and sags.

149. Which of the following is the primary function of an uninterruptible power supply (UPS) during a two-hour building power failure?

A. To keep servers running until building power is restored

B. To keep servers running until they can be powered down safely

C. To keep servers from being damaged by power spikes

D. To keep servers running in the event of a computer power supply failure

150. If you have a server with dual power supplies, one of which is plugged into a single uninterruptible power supply (UPS) and the other into a wall socket with a surge protector, and the building's power circuit is connected to a backup generator, which of the following failures can the server survive and keep running indefinitely? (Choose all that apply.)

A. Failure of one server power supply

B. Failure of the UPS

C. Failure of the building power circuit

D. Failure of the building backup generator

151. If you have a server with dual power supplies, each of which is connected to a separate uninterruptible power supply (UPS), with each UPS connected to a separate building power circuit connected to a backup generator, which of the following failures can the server survive and keep running indefinitely? (Choose all that apply.)

A. Failure of one server power supply

B. Failure of one UPS

C. Failure of one building power circuit

D. Failure of the building backup generator

152. Which of the following is the most commonly recommended fire suppression system for a datacenter?

A. Carbon Dioxide

B. Pre-action sprinklers

C. Water mist

D. Clean agents

153. Which of the following is the primary difference between the power distribution units (PDUs) used in datacenters and the standard power strips used in offices and homes?

  A. More outlets

  B. Larger power input

  C. Larger voltage output

  D. All of the above

154. Which of the following types of physical security is most likely to detect an insider threat?

  A. Smart cards

  B. Motion detection

  C. Video surveillance

  D. Biometrics

155. Which of the following is the term used to describe a wiring nexus that is typically the termination point for incoming telephone and wide area network (WAN) services?

  A. MDF

  B. MTBF

  C. IDF

  D. RDP

  E. MOU

156. Which of the following physical security mechanisms can either "fail close" or "fail open"?

  A. Motion detectors

  B. Video cameras

  C. Honeypots

  D. Door locks

157. Smart lockers are storage devices that can provide users with access to supplies, deliveries, and other items using various security mechanisms. Which of the following are technologies that smart lockers can use to authenticate users and provide secure access to their contents?

  A. PIN

  B. NFC

  C. Bluetooth

  D. Biometrics

  E. RFID

  F. All of the above

158. Which of the following are common types of cameras used for video surveillance of secured network installations? (Choose two.)

    A. IP

    B. LDAP

    C. CCTV

    D. NAC

159. Which of the following statements describes what it means when the automated lock on the door to a datacenter is configured to fail open?

    A. The door remains in its current state in the event of an emergency.

    B. The door locks in the event of an emergency.

    C. The door unlocks in the event of an emergency.

    D. The door continues to function using battery power in the event of an emergency.

160. A high security installation that requires entrants to submit to a retinal scan before the door unlocks is using which of the following types of technology?

    A. Pattern recognition

    B. Hand geometry

    C. Biometrics

    D. Tamper detection

161. Which of the following are means of preventing unauthorized individuals from entering a sensitive location, such as a datacenter? (Choose all that apply.)

    A. Biometric scans

    B. Identification badges

    C. Key fobs

    D. Motion detection

162. Which of the following security measures can monitor the specific activities of authorized individuals within sensitive areas?

    A. Video surveillance

    B. Identification badges

    C. Key fobs

    D. Motion detection

    E. Locking cabinets

163. Which of the following physical security devices can use passive RFIDs to enable an authorized user to enter a secured area? (Choose all that apply.)

    A. Key fob

    B. Keycard lock

    C. Proximity card

    D. Cypher lock

    E. Smart locker

164. Some key fobs used for authenticated entrance to a secured area have a keypad that requires the user to enter a PIN before the device is activated. Which of the following authentication factors is this device using? (Choose all that apply.)

    A. Something you do

    B. Something you have

    C. Something you are

    D. Something you know

165. Which of the following physical security devices can enable an authorized user to enter a secured area without any physical contact with the device? (Choose all that apply.)

    A. Key fob

    B. Keycard lock

    C. Proximity card

    D. Cypher lock

166. Video surveillance of sensitive areas, such as datacenters, can aid in the detection of which of the following types of attacks? (Choose all that apply.)

    A. Social engineering

    B. Evil twin

    C. Brute force

    D. Insider threats

167. Which of the following statements is true when a biometric authentication procedure results in a false positive?

    A. A user who should be authorized is denied access.

    B. A user who should not be authorized is denied access.

    C. A user who should be authorized is granted access.

    D. A user who should not be authorized is granted access.

168. In the datacenter of a company involved with sensitive government data, all servers have crimped metal tags holding the cases closed. All of the hardware racks are locked in clear-fronted cabinets. All cable runs are installed in transparent conduits. These are all examples of which of the following physical security measures?

    A. Tamper detection

    B. Asset tracking

    C. Geofencing

    D. Port security

169. A secured government building that scans the faces of incoming people and compares them to a database of authorized entrants is using which of the following types of technology?

  A. Pattern recognition

  B. Hand geometry

  C. Biometrics

  D. Tamper detection

170. Which of the following is not a means of preventing physical security breaches to a network datacenter?

  A. Badges

  B. Locks

  C. Key fobs

  D. Tailgaters

171. Identification badges, key fobs, and access control vestibules all fall into which of the following categories of security devices?

  A. Physical security

  B. Data security

  C. Asset tracking

  D. Port security

172. Which of the following are not means of detecting intruders in a network datacenter? (Choose all that apply.)

  A. Motion detection

  B. Video surveillance

  C. Biometrics

  D. Smart cards

173. Which of the following statements describes what it means when the automated lock on the door to a datacenter is configured to fail closed?

  A. The door remains in its current state in the event of an emergency.

  B. The door locks in the event of an emergency.

  C. The door unlocks in the event of an emergency.

  D. The door continues to function using battery power in the event of an emergency.

174. After an incident in which your company's datacenter was penetrated by an intruder, the management has installed a double doorway at the entrance to the datacenter. The two doors have a small area in between them, and one door must be closed before the other one can open. Which of the following terms describes this arrangement?

  A. Server closet

  B. Access control vestibule

  C. Controlled entrance

  D. Honeypot

175. In an internal UTP cable installation, each horizontal cable run connects a wall plate in the work area to a centralized cabling nexus in a telecommunications room. Which of the following is the correct term for this cabling nexus?

  A. Telepole

  B. Demarc

  C. Backbone

  D. Patch panel

  E. Fiber distribution panel

176. Datacenter equipment racks are typically ruled into vertical rack units, which are standard-sized divisions that hardware manufacturers use when manufacturing rack-mountable components. Which of the following is the standard vertical height of a single rack unit?

  A. 1.721 inches

  B. 1.75 inches

  C. 40 mm

  D. 3.5 inches

177. Ralph is evaluating switches and, in the documentation for some of the switch models, he sees an option allowing the switch to be set for port-side intake or port-side exhaust. Ralph is not sure what this option does. Which of the following best describes the function of the port side intake/exhaust setting?

  A. The setting specifies the direction that incoming signals take through the row of switch ports: left to right or right to left.

  B. The setting specifies which set of cable ports should be active: front or back.

  C. The setting specifies the direction of the airflow through the switch: front to back or back to front.

  D. All of the above.

178. Alice is designing the datacenter for her company's new facility and is attempting to calculate the total power load for the entire datacenter. Which of the following functions should Alice include in her power load calculations? (Choose all that apply.)

  A. HVAC

  B. Servers

  C. Lighting

  D. IDF

  E. Security equipment

  F. Switches and routers

Chapter
3

Network Operations

THE COMPTIA NETWORK+ EXAM N10-009 TOPICS COVERED IN THIS CHAPTER INCLUDE THE FOLLOWING:

✓ **3.1 Explain the purpose of organizational processes and procedures.**

- Documentation
    - Physical vs. logical diagrams
    - Rack diagrams
    - Cable maps and diagrams
    - Network diagrams
        - Layer 1
        - Layer 2
        - Layer 3
    - Asset inventory
        - Hardware
        - Software
        - Licensing
        - Warranty support
    - IP address management (IPAM)
    - Service-level agreement (SLA)
    - Wireless survey/heat map
- Life-cycle management
    - End-of-life (EOL)
    - End-of-support (EOS)
    - Software management
        - Patches and bug fixes
        - Operating system (OS)
        - Firmware
    - Decommissioning

- Change management
  - Request process tracking/service request
- Configuration management
  - Production configuration
  - Backup configuration
  - Baseline/golden configuration

✓ **3.2 Given a scenario, use network monitoring technologies.**

- Methods
  - SNMP
    - Traps
    - Management information base (MIB)
    - Versions
      - v2c
      - v3
    - Community strings
    - Authentication
  - Flow data
  - Packet capture
  - Baseline metrics
    - Anomaly alerting/notification
  - Log aggregation
    - Syslog collector
    - Security information and event management (SIEM)
  - Application programming interface (API) integration
  - Port mirroring
- Solutions
  - Network discovery
    - Ad hoc
    - Scheduled

- Traffic analysis
- Performance monitoring
- Availability monitoring
- Configuration monitoring

✓ **3.3 Explain disaster recovery (DR) concepts.**

- DR metrics
  - Recovery point objective (RPO)
  - Recovery time objective (RTO)
  - Mean time to repair (MTTR)
  - Mean time between failures (MTBF)
- DR sites
  - Cold site
  - Warm site
  - Hot site
- High-availability approaches
  - Active-active
  - Active-passive
- Testing
  - Tabletop exercises
  - Validation tests

✓ **3.4 Given a scenario, implement IPv4 and IPv6 network services.**

- Dynamic addressing
  - DHCP
    - Reservations
    - Scope
    - Lease time
    - Options
    - Relay/IP helper
    - Exclusions
  - Stateless address autoconfiguration (SLAAC)

- Name resolution
  - DNS
    - Domain Name Security Extensions (DNSSEC)
    - DNS over HTTPS (DoH) and DNS over TLS (DoT)
    - Record types
      - Address (A)
      - AAAA
      - Canonical name (CNAME)
      - Mail exchange (MX)
      - Text
      - Nameserver (NS)
      - Pointer
    - Zone types
      - Forward
      - Reverse
    - Authoritative vs. non-authoritative
    - Primary vs. secondary
    - Recursive
  - Hosts file
  - Time protocols
    - NTP
    - Precision Time Protocol (PTP)
    - Network Time Security (NTS)

✓ **3.5 Compare and contrast network access and management methods.**

- Site-to-site VPN
- Client-to-site VPN
  - Clientless
  - Split tunnel vs. full tunnel

- Connection methods
  - SSH
  - Graphical user interface (GUI)
  - API
  - Console
- Jump box/host
- In-band vs. out-of-band management

3.1 Explain the purpose of organizational processes and procedures.

1. Which of the following is the term usually applied to a representation of network devices, automatically compiled, and containing information such as IP addresses and connection speeds?

    A. Network map

    B. Network diagram

    C. Cable diagram

    D. Management information base

2. Which of the following types of network documentation is often overlaid on an architectural drawing or blueprint?

    A. Heat map

    B. Network map

    C. Cable diagram

    D. Network diagram

    E. Management information base

3. Which of the following is not one of the typical heights for devices mounted in IT equipment racks?

    A. 1 unit

    B. 2 units

    C. 3 units

    D. 4 units

4. The cable plant for Alice's company network was installed several years ago by an outside contractor. Now, some of the paper labels have fallen off the patch panels, and Alice does not know which wall plate is connected to each port. Assuming that she is working on a properly maintained and documented network installation, which of the following is the easiest way for Alice to determine which port is connected to which wall plate?

    A. Consult the cable diagram provided by the cabling contractor at the time of the installation.

    B. Call the cable installation contractor and see if they can remember which ports go with which wall plates.

    C. Attach a tone generator to a patch panel port and then test each wall plate with a locator until you find the correct one. Repeat this for each port that needs labeling.

    D. Use a cable certifier to locate the patch panel port associated with each wall plate port.

5. Which of the following IT asset management documents published by the International Organization for Standardization (ISO) defines a standard for Software Identification Tags (SWIDs) containing asset inventory information about the software running on a computer or other device?

    A. ISO 19770-1

    B. ISO 19770-2

    C. ISO 19770-3

    D. ISO 19770-4

    E. ISO 19770-5

6. A rack diagram is typically ruled vertically using which of the following measurements?

    A. Inches

    B. Centimeters

    C. Units

    D. Grids

7. Many network diagrams use Cisco symbols to illustrate the locations of and relationships between network components. Cisco symbols are standardized pictographs that illustrate the basic function of a network component. In a network diagram that uses Cisco symbols, what component does the symbol in the figure represent?

    A. A router

    B. A switch

    C. A hub

    D. A gateway

8. Which of the following statements are true about the differences between a diagram of a patch panel installation organized physically and one that is organized logically? (Choose two.)

    A. A physical diagram is organized according to the floors and rooms where the cable drops are located.

    B. A physical diagram is precisely scaled to represent the actual patch panel hardware.

    C. A logical diagram is organized according to the divisions within the company, such as departments and workgroups.

    D. A logical diagram uses an organization that represents company divisions but does not physically resemble the actual patch panels.

9. A diagram of a telecommunications room or intermediate distribution frame (IDF) for an office building is typically based on which of the following?

    A. A hand-drawn sketch

    B. A series of photographs

    C. An architect's plan

    D. A 3D model

    E. A site survey report

10. The documentation for main distribution frames (MDFs) and intermediate distribution frames (IDFs) should incorporate details on which of the following elements? (Choose all that apply.)

    A. Power

    B. Environment

    C. Distances

    D. Costs

11. Your department is experiencing frequent delays as users wait for images to be rendered by their outdated graphics software package. As a result, you are planning to submit a service request for an upgrade to a new software product at the monthly meeting of the company's change management team. Which of the following types of information are likely to be included in your service request? (Choose all that apply.)

    A. The possibility of rolling back to the previous software, if necessary

    B. The procedure for installing and configuring the new software

    C. An estimate of the productivity increase realizable with the new software

    D. A list of software and hardware upgrades or modifications needed to run the new software

12. The change request for new graphics software that you submitted to your company's change management team has been approved. Now it is time to implement the change. Which of the following administrative tasks will most likely be the change management team's responsibility during the implementation process? (Choose two.)

    A. Authorizing downtime

    B. Notifying users

    C. Designating a maintenance window

    D. Documenting all modifications made

13. A rack-mounted device that is four units tall will be approximately what height in inches?

    A. 1.75

    B. 3.5

    C. 4

    D. 7

14. Which of the following types of documentation should indicate the complete route of every internal cable run from wall plate to patch panel?

   A. Physical network diagram

   B. Asset management

   C. Logical network diagram

   D. Wiring schematic

15. Which of the following types of network diagram contains the MAC addresses used for local network communication?

   A. Layer 1

   B. Layer 2

   C. Layer 3

   D. Layer 4

16. Which of the following statements about physical network diagrams and logical network diagrams are true? (Choose two.)

   A. A physical network diagram is created automatically, and a logical network diagram is created manually.

   B. A physical network diagram depicts hardware devices and the connections between them.

   C. A logical network diagram contains all of the information you would need to rebuild your network from scratch.

   D. A logical network diagram typically contains the IP addresses of network devices.

17. What is the width of a standard equipment rack in a datacenter?

   A. 12 inches

   B. 16 inches

   C. 19 inches

   D. 24 inches

18. Many network diagrams use Cisco symbols to illustrate the locations of and relationships between network components. Cisco symbols are standardized pictographs that illustrate the basic function of a network component. In a network diagram that uses Cisco symbols, what component does the symbol in the figure represent?

   A. A switch

   B. A hub

   C. A router

   D. A gateway

19. The precise locations of devices in a datacenter are typically documented in which of the following documents?

    A. Rack diagram

    B. Network map

    C. Wiring schematic

    D. Logical diagram

    E. Business continuity plan

    F. Audit and assessment report

20. Which of the following statements about network maps is true?

    A. Network maps are typically drawn to scale.

    B. Network maps typically contain more information than network diagrams.

    C. Network maps must be read/write accessible to all personnel working on the network.

    D. Network maps diagram only the locations of cable runs and endpoints.

21. Which of the following types of documentation should contain the chemical composition of all cleaning compounds used in a datacenter?

    A. ESD

    B. MSDS

    C. NDA

    D. BYOD

    E. SOP

22. You are working for a company with numerous branch offices scattered around the country, and you are required to travel to these offices frequently. Each branch office has some means of accessing the network at the company headquarters. Some use Frame Relay, while others use virtual private networks (VPNs). During one trip, you mention to a branch office manager that you intend to connect to the headquarters network that night from your hotel room. The manager warns you that this is against company policy, but you are not so sure. Where in the company documentation should you look to confirm this?

    A. Remote access policies

    B. Service-level agreement

    C. Acceptable use policy

    D. Privileged user agreement

23. Which of the following is a document that a company's new hires might want to consult to determine whether they are permitted to install their own personal software on company computers?

    A. SLA

    B. AUP

    C. NDA

    D. BYOD

24. Many employees have been contacting the IT help desk asking how they can connect their personal smartphones and tablets to the company's wireless network. This has raised issues regarding network security and technical support. You have been asked to draft a policy for the in-house use of personal electronics that addresses these issues. Which of the following describes the document that you will be creating?

A. SLA

B. AUP

C. NDA

D. BYOD

25. You are going to work for a new company as a software developer, and the human resources (HR) department has notified you that you must sign a document guaranteeing that you will maintain confidentiality about the company's products and programming code in perpetuity. Which of the following documents contains this agreement?

A. SLA

B. AUP

C. NDA

D. MOU

E. BYOD

26. You are an IT director, and a fire has broken out on the lower floors of your company's office building. After the personnel are evacuated, the fire department asks you where they can find documentation about all chemicals and equipment used in the company's datacenter, which is threatened by the fire. You direct them to the correct filing cabinet in your office, which contains which of the following document types?

A. ESD

B. NDA

C. BYOD

D. MSDS

27. You have been asked to draft an acceptable use policy (AUP) for new hires at your company to sign that specifies what they can and cannot do when working with the company's computers and network. Which of the following is not one of the provisions typically found in this type of document?

A. Privacy

B. Ownership

C. Illegal use

D. Upgrades

28. You are starting a new job, and the company's human resources (HR) department has asked you to sign an acceptable use policy (AUP) regarding computer and network use. The document includes a privacy clause. Which of the following are specifications you can expect to find in this clause? (Choose all that apply.)

    A. Any emails you send or receive can be monitored by the company at any time.

    B. All files and data that you store on company computers must be accessible to the company for scanning and monitoring.

    C. All work that you perform for the company becomes the sole property of the company, including copyrights and patents.

    D. All hardware, software, and any proprietary data stored on the company's computers remain the property of the company.

29. Which of the following is most likely to be the last step in a change management procedure?

    A. Documentation

    B. Notification

    C. Approval

    D. Service request

    E. Scheduling

    F. Process tracking

30. Which of the following terms would apply to the procedure of adding a user's personal smartphone to the network under a bring your own device (BYOD) policy?

    A. Out-of-band

    B. On-boarding

    C. In-band

    D. Off-boarding

31. Which of the following is not likely to be a procedural element of an IT end-of-life asset disposal policy?

    A. Data deletion

    B. Recycling

    C. Data preservation

    D. Inventory

32. While negotiating a new contract with a service provider, you have reached a disagreement over the contracted reliability of the service. The provider is willing to guarantee that the service will be available 99 percent of the time, but you have been told to require 99.9 percent. When you finally reach an agreement, the negotiated language will be included in which of the following documents?

    A. SLA

    B. AUP

    C. NDA

    D. BYOD

33. Which of the following elements would you typically not expect to find in a service-level agreement (SLA) between an Internet service provider (ISP) and a subscriber?

A. A definition of the services to be provided by the ISP

B. A list of specifications for the equipment to be provided by the ISP

C. The types and schedule for the technical support to be provided by the ISP

D. The types of applications that the subscriber will use when accessing the ISP's services

34. You have just completed negotiating an annual contract with a provider to furnish your company with cloud services. As part of the contract, the provider has agreed to guarantee that the services will be available 99.9 percent of the time, around the clock, seven days per week. If the services are unavailable more than 0.1 percent of the time, your company is due a price adjustment. Which of the following terms describes this clause of the contract?

A. SLA

B. MTBF

C. AUP

D. MTTR

35. The technical support clause of a service-level agreement (SLA) typically includes which of the following elements? (Choose all that apply.)

A. Whether the provider will provide onsite, telephone, or online support

B. The time service for responses to support calls, which specifies how quickly the provider must respond to requests for support

C. The percentage of time that the service is guaranteed to be available

D. The amount of support that will be provided and the cost of additional support

36. Which of the following is the criterion most commonly used to filter files for backup jobs?

A. Filename

B. File extension

C. File attributes

D. File size

37. Which of the following backup job types does not reset the archive bits of the files it backs up?

A. Full

B. Incremental

C. Differential

D. Supplemental

38. What are the three elements in the grandfather-father-son media rotation system for network backups?

    A. Hard disk drives, optical drives, and magnetic tape drives

    B. Incremental, differential, and full backup jobs

    C. Monthly, weekly, and daily backup jobs

    D. QIC, DAT, and DLT tape drives

39. Which of the following is a tool that integrates DHCP and DNS so that each is aware of the changes made by the other?

    A. HOSTS

    B. DHCPv6

    C. IPAM

    D. APIPA

40. Which of the following storage techniques prevents version skew from occurring during a system backup?

    A. Incrementals

    B. Differentials

    C. Iterations

    D. Snapshots

41. How do tape libraries and autoloaders increase the overall storage capacity of a backup solution?

    A. By compressing data before it is stored on the medium

    B. By automatically inserting media into and removing it from a drive

    C. By running a tape drive at half its normal speed

    D. By writing two tracks at once onto a magnetic tape

42. Which of the following types of patches are most typically applied to a hardware device?

    A. Firmware updates

    B. Driver updates

    C. Feature changes

    D. Vulnerability patches

43. Which of the following software releases is a fix designed to address one specific issue?

    A. A patch

    B. An update

    C. An upgrade

    D. A driver

44. Unlike individual users, who usually have their operating system patches downloaded and installed automatically, corporate IT departments typically evaluate new patches before deploying them. Which of the following is not a common step in this evaluation process?

    A. Testing

    B. Researching

    C. Rolling back

    D. Backing up

45. Which of the following terms refers to the process of uninstalling a recently released patch to resume using the previous version?

    A. Backslide

    B. Downgrade

    C. Reset

    D. Rollback

    E. End-of-life

    F. End-of-support

46. A new shipment of bare metal workstations has just arrived, and Alice is responsible for preparing them for deployment on the company network. She first installs the Windows operating system on one computer to build a test configuration. Then, she installs some specialized drivers for the hardware in the computers and the Microsoft 365 productivity applications. After configuring the software and performing an extensive round of testing, Alice is satisfied with the performance of the workstation. She plans to install the operating system, drivers, and office software on all of the workstations, but there are other software products that she will have to install later for users in specific departments. Which of the following are appropriate terms for this basic installation? (Choose two.)

    A. Production configuration

    B. Sandbox configuration

    C. Golden configuration

    D. Baseline configuration

47. An IT department receives a shipment of 20 new computers, and Alice has been assigned the task of preparing them for deployment to end users. The first thing she does is affix a metal tag with a bar code on it to each computer. Which of the following terms best describes the function of this procedure?

    A. Asset tracking

    B. Tamper detection

    C. Device hardening

    D. Port security

48. Ralph's company has purchased new computers to replace some of the older workstations currently in use. Ralph has been assigned the task of preparing the old computers for disposal. They will be sold to a local secondhand dealer. In order for the dealer to accept the computers, they must have a functional operating system. Company policy also dictates that the computers be permanently wiped of all applications and data before disposal. Which of the following tasks will Ralph have to perform before the computers are sold? (Choose all that apply.)

A. Reinstall the operating system.

B. Uninstall all applications.

C. Delete all data files.

D. Run a disk wipe utility.

E. Perform a factory reset.

3.2 Given a scenario, use network monitoring technologies.

49. After starting work as the network administrator of Wingtip Toys, you discover that all of the switches in the company's datacenter have support for remote management, with built-in Simple Network Management Protocol (SNMP) agents in each port. Which of the following tasks must you perform to be able to gather information from the agents on those switches and display it on a central console? (Choose all that apply.)

A. Install the network management software on a network computer.

B. Install a management information base (MIB) on each of the switches.

C. Install an agent on the console computer.

D. Install an MIB on the console computer.

E. Purchase a network management product.

F. Configure SNMP with authentication credentials.

50. Which of the following technologies provides both real-time monitoring of security events and automated analysis of the event information gathered?

A. SIEM

B. SNMP

C. SEM

D. SIM

51. Which versions of the Simple Network Management Protocol (SNMP) use unencrypted community strings as their security protection? (Choose all that apply.)

A. SNMPv1

B. SNMPv2

C. SNMPv2c

D. SNMPv3

52. Which of the following statements about the Simple Network Management Protocol (SNMP) are not true? (Choose all that apply.)

A. To effectively monitor a network using SNMP, you must be sure that all of the equipment you purchase when designing and building your network supports the protocol.

B. SNMP is not only the name of a protocol; it is also the name of a network management product.

C. SNMPv1 and the original SNMPv2 rely on a community string as their only means of security.

D. Most of the network management products on the market today support SNMPv3.

E. SNMPv3 is capable of scanning network segments to monitor the availability of their IP addresses.

53. What type of network monitoring utility is shown in the accompanying figure?

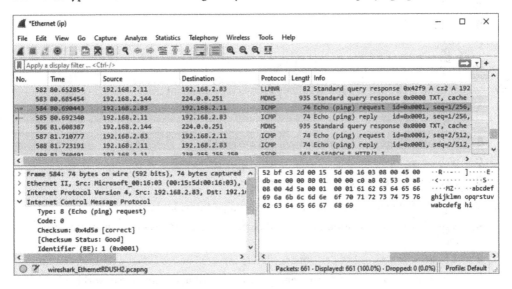

A. Protocol analyzer

B. System monitor

C. Performance monitor

D. Log viewer

54. Which of the following was created to provide logging services for the Unix sendmail program?

A. Syslog

B. Netstat

C. SNMP

D. CARP

55. You are the administrator of your company's network. Your company wants to perform a baseline analysis of network-related traffic and statistics. They want to track broadcasts, cyclical redundancy check (CRC) errors, and collisions for all traffic traversing a switched network. In addition, they want to generate alerts and cell phone notifications when anomalies occur and provide historical and daily reports for management. They also want to keep track of software distribution and metering. What type of network software product best meets these needs?

   A. SNMP management

   B. Protocol analyzer

   C. Performance monitor

   D. Network traffic monitor

56. SIEM products combine the capabilities of which of the following? (Choose all that apply.)

   A. Syslog

   B. SNMP

   C. SEM

   D. SIM

57. Which of the following statements about web server logs is not true?

   A. To analyze web server activity, you typically use an application that interprets the web server log files.

   B. Web server logs are typically maintained as text files.

   C. Web server logs record the IP addresses of all visiting users.

   D. To interpret web server logs, you use a protocol analyzer.

58. Which of the following statements best describes a performance baseline?

   A. A baseline is an estimation of expected performance levels, based on manufacturers' specifications.

   B. A baseline is a record of performance levels captured under actual workload conditions.

   C. A baseline is a record of performance levels captured under simulated workload conditions.

   D. A baseline is a record of performance levels captured before the system is actually in use.

59. When monitoring performance metrics on one of your servers, you notice that the server is utilizing 100 percent of the network bandwidth available to it. What modification could you make to the server that will most likely address the problem?

   A. Add memory to the system.

   B. Install a second network adapter.

   C. Update the network adapter's firmware.

   D. Install a second processor.

60. Which of the following indicators is typically not included in an operating system's performance monitoring tool, such as the Windows Performance Monitor or the MacOS Activity Monitor?

A. Temperature

B. CPU/processor activity

C. Memory consumption

D. Network utilization

E. Storage statistics

61. Which of the following syslog message severity levels indicates that a system is unusable?

A. 0

B. 1

C. 2

D. 3

E. 4

62. Which of the following syslog message severity levels indicates a call for immediate action?

A. 0

B. 1

C. 2

D. 3

E. 4

63. Which of the following syslog message severity levels indicates that the message is purely informational?

A. 0

B. 2

C. 4

D. 6

E. 7

64. A Simple Network Management Protocol (SNMP) console can inform administrators when a managed device requires attention. For this to occur, the agent in the device first has to send a message to the console. What is the term used for a message sent by an SNMP agent to the central console?

A. Alert

B. Notification

C. Ping

D. Trap

E. Flow

65. Which of the following metrics would you typically not find displayed by an interface monitor?

A. Error rate

B. Bandwidth utilization

C. Packet drops

D. Rollbacks

66. Which of the following are reasons contributing to the number of packet drops displayed by an interface monitor? (Choose all that apply.)

A. Resets

B. Discards

C. Errors

D. Overflows

67. Which of the following is not a statistic that you would typically find in a server performance baseline?

A. CPU utilization

B. Disk transfer rate

C. Network transmissions speed

D. OS update history

E. Memory utilization

68. Log management typically consists of which of the following tasks? (Choose all that apply.)

A. Rollback

B. Utilization

C. Security

D. Cycling

69. Which of the following security information and event management (SIEM) processes performs searches for specific criteria, during specific time frames, in logs located on different computers?

A. Data aggregation

B. Forensic analysis

C. Correlation

D. Retention

70. Which of the following terms best describes the security information and event management (SIEM) process of consolidating log information from multiple sources?

A. Data aggregation

B. Forensic analysis

C. Correlation

D. Retention

71. Which of the following Windows applications would you most likely use to create a baseline of system or network performance?

- **A.** Performance Monitor
- **B.** Event Viewer
- **C.** Syslog
- **D.** Network Monitor

72. Which of the following is the database used by the Simple Network Management Protocol (SNMP) to store information gathered from agents distributed about the network?

- **A.** Trap
- **B.** Syslog
- **C.** MIB
- **D.** SIEM

73. Which of the following are not SNMP components?

- **A.** MIBs
- **B.** Traps
- **C.** OIDs
- **D.** CRCs
- **E.** API integrations

74. Ralph's company recently switched from a standard telephone system to a Voice over Internet Protocol (VoIP) system. Since then, users have been complaining of service interruptions and problems hearing callers at certain times of the day. After analyzing a network traffic audit and assessment report, Ralph determines that traffic levels on the Internet connection are substantially higher during the first and last hours of the day, the same times when most of the users have experienced problems. Which of the following solutions can provide more reliable VoIP service during peak usage times?

- **A.** Implement traffic shaping.
- **B.** Implement load balancing.
- **C.** Upgrade the local area network (LAN) from Fast Ethernet to Gigabit Ethernet.
- **D.** Replace the router connecting the LAN to the Internet with a model that supports Simple Network Management Protocol (SNMP).

75. Which of the following abbreviations describes a product that combines real-time monitoring of security events and automated analysis of the event information gathered?

- **A.** SIEM
- **B.** SNMP
- **C.** SEIM
- **D.** SEM/SIM

76. Which of the following troubleshooting tools enables you to capture all of the packets transmitted in network traffic to a buffer, analyze the protocols used in the packets, and display the output?

A. Event Viewer

B. Performance monitor

C. Protocol analyzer

D. Management console

77. Which of the following switch features enables administrators to capture traffic generated by the computers connected to the switch?

A. Port mirroring

B. Stateful packet inspection

C. Trunking

D. Service-dependent filtering

78. Which of the following best describes the function of an administrative network monitoring tool that can perform an ad hoc network discovery?

A. The administrator starts the tool, and it scans the local subnet, displaying a list of the MAC addresses associated with it.

B. The administrator specifies an IP address, and the tool scans all of the well-known port numbers at that address for active services.

C. The administrator enters a range of IP addresses, and the tool attempts to perform a traceroute test for each one.

D. The administrator enters a range of IP addresses, and the tool scans each address to determine if a device is using it.

E. The administrator creates a network discovery schedule and identifies the network address of the subnet to be scanned.

3.3 Explain disaster recovery (DR) concepts.

79. Which of the following is the primary aim of an organization's security incident response policies?

A. To know how to respond to a particular incident

B. To prevent an incident from occurring again

C. To identify the cause of an incident

D. To document the procedures leading up to an incident

80. Which of the following tasks is not considered to be part of an IT department's incident response plan?

   A. Performing tabletop exercises to prepare for an incident

   B. Stopping an ongoing incident

   C. Containing the damage caused by an incident

   D. Remediating the damage caused by an incident

   E. Rebuilding an infrastructure destroyed by an incident

   F. Performing validation tests

81. Which of the following are occurrences that are typically addressed by an IT department's incident response policies? (Choose all that apply.)

   A. Denial-of-service (DoS) attack

   B. Hard disk failure

   C. Electrical fire

   D. Server outage

82. Which of the following Redundant Array of Independent Disks (RAID) levels provides fault tolerance by storing parity information on the disks, in addition to the data?

   A. RAID 0

   B. RAID 1

   C. RAID 5

   D. RAID 10

83. Installing an electrical generator for your datacenter is an example of which of the following fault tolerance concepts?

   A. Uninterruptible power supply (UPS)

   B. Power redundancy

   C. Dual power supplies

   D. Redundant circuits

84. Which of the following RAID levels uses disk striping with distributed parity?

   A. RAID 0

   B. RAID 1

   C. RAID 5

   D. RAID 10

85. Which of the following is not a fault tolerance mechanism?

   A. Port aggregation

   B. Clustering

   C. MTBF

   D. UPS

86. Which of the following is not a type of server load balancing mechanism?

    A. Round-robin DNS

    B. Network address translation

    C. Content switching

    D. Multilayer switching

87. Which of the following is an element of high availability systems that enables them to automatically detect problems and react to them?

    A. Backups

    B. Snapshots

    C. Failover

    D. Cold sites

88. Which of the following RAID levels does not provide fault tolerance?

    A. RAID 0

    B. RAID 1

    C. RAID 5

    D. RAID 10

89. Which of the following disaster recovery mechanisms can be made operational in the least amount of time?

    A. A cold site

    B. A warm site

    C. A hot site

    D. All of the options are the same.

90. Which of the following datacenter disaster recovery mechanisms is the least expensive to implement?

    A. A cold site

    B. A warm site

    C. A hot site

    D. A cloud site

91. Which of the following terms defines how long it will take to restore a server from backups if a complete system failure occurs?

    A. RPO

    B. RTO

    C. BCP

    D. MIB

92. In a disaster recovery scenario, which of the following terms applies to devices that are not repairable?

A. MTBF

B. MTTF

C. MTTR

D. MDT

93. If you have a server with dual power supplies, both of which are connected to a single uninterruptible power supply (UPS), with a building power circuit connected to a backup generator, which of the following failures can the server survive and keep running indefinitely? (Choose all that apply.)

A. Failure of one server power supply

B. Failure of the UPS

C. Failure of the building power circuit

D. Failure of the building backup generator

94. A network load balancing cluster is made up of multiple computers that function as a single entity. Which of the following terms is used to describe an individual computer in a load balancing cluster?

A. Node

B. Host

C. Server

D. Box

95. Which of the following networking concepts frequently use virtual Internet Protocol (IP) addresses to provide high availability? (Choose all that apply.)

A. Clustering

B. Load balancing

C. Network address translation (NAT)

D. Network interface card (NIC) teaming

96. Which of the following disaster recovery mechanisms is the least expensive to implement?

A. A cold site

B. A warm site

C. A hot site

D. All of the options cost the same.

97. Which of the following can be provided by clustering servers?

A. Fault tolerance

B. Load balancing

C. Failover

D. All of the above

98. When you configure NIC teaming on a server with two network adapters in an active-passive configuration, which of the following services is provided?

    A. Load balancing

    B. Fault tolerance

    C. Server clustering

    D. Traffic shaping

99. Which of the following is not a load balancing mechanism?

    A. NIC teaming

    B. Server clustering

    C. Round-robin DNS

    D. RAID 1

100. Which of the following best describes the difference between cold, warm, and hot backup sites?

    A. Whether the backup site is owned, borrowed, or rented

    B. The age of the most recent backup stored at the site

    C. The cost of the hardware used at the site

    D. The time needed to get the site up and running

101. Which of the following specifications would you most want to examine when comparing hard disk models for your new Redundant Array of Independent Disks (RAID) array?

    A. MTBF

    B. SLA

    C. AUP

    D. MTTR

102. Which of the following RAID levels provides fault tolerance with the smallest amount of usable disk space?

    A. RAID 0

    B. RAID 1

    C. RAID 5

    D. RAID 10

103. Disk mirroring and disk duplexing are both fault tolerance mechanisms for hard disk data storage. Which of the following statements about disk mirroring and disk duplexing is true?

    A. Disk mirroring enables a server to survive the failure of a disk drive.

    B. Disk duplexing enables a server to survive the failure of a disk controller.

    C. Disk mirroring enables a server to survive the failure of a disk drive or a disk controller.

    D. Disk duplexing enables a server to survive the failure of a disk drive or a disk controller.

104. You are installing a new Windows server with two hard disk drives in it, and you want to use RAID to create a fault-tolerant storage system. Which of the following RAID levels can you configure the server to use?

   A. RAID 0

   B. RAID 1

   C. RAID 5

   D. RAID 10

105. Which of the following RAID levels provide fault tolerance without using parity data? (Choose all that apply.)

   A. RAID 0

   B. RAID 1

   C. RAID 5

   D. RAID 10

106. If you back up your network by performing a full backup every Wednesday at 6:00 p.m. and incremental backups in the evening on the other days of the week, how many jobs would be needed to completely restore a computer with a hard drive that failed on a Monday at noon?

   A. One

   B. Two

   C. Five

   D. Six

107. For a complete restore of a computer that failed at noon on Tuesday, how many jobs would be needed if you performed full backups to tape at 6:00 a.m. every Wednesday and Saturday and incremental backups to tape at 6:00 a.m. every other day?

   A. One

   B. Two

   C. Three

   D. Four

108. If you back up your network by performing a full backup every Wednesday at 6:00 p.m. and differential backups in the evening on the other six days of the week, how many jobs would be needed to completely restore a computer with a hard drive that failed on a Tuesday at noon?

   A. One

   B. Two

   C. Six

   D. Seven

109. Why does performing incremental backups to a hard drive, rather than a tape drive, make it possible to restore a server with a single job, rather than multiple jobs?

   A. Because hard drives hold more data than tape drives.

   B. Because hard drives can transfer data faster than tape drives.

   C. Because hard drives are random access devices and tape drives are not.

   D. Because hard drives use a different block size than tape drives.

110. Which of the following is not a fault tolerance mechanism?

   A. UPS

   B. RAID 1

   C. SNMP

   D. Clustering

111. Which of the following is a term for a read-only copy of a data set made at a specific moment in time?

   A. Snapshot

   B. Incremental

   C. Hot site

   D. Differential

112. Which of the following statements about backing up a firewall's state and backing up its configuration are true? (Choose all that apply.)

   A. A backup of a firewall's state contains more data than a backup of its configuration.

   B. A backup of a firewall's configuration contains more data than a backup of its state.

   C. A backup of a firewall's state contains the exact same data as a backup of its configuration.

   D. A backup of a firewall's state includes its configuration.

   E. A backup of a firewall's configuration includes its state.

113. Redundant servers running in an active-active configuration provide which of the following advantages that the same servers in an active-passive configuration do not? (Choose all that apply.)

   A. Increased performance

   B. Fault tolerance

   C. Data encapsulation

   D. Load balancing

114. To build a network with redundant Internet connections that ensures full fault tolerance, it is necessary to use which of the following?

   A. Different ISPs

   B. Different WAN connections

   C. Different routers

   D. All of the above

115. Installing redundant firewalls in a parallel configuration, as shown in the accompanying graphic, provides which of the following benefits? (Choose all that apply.)

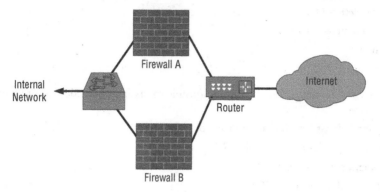

A. Load balancing

B. Fault tolerance

C. Added security

D. Enhanced performance

3.4 Given a scenario, implement IPv4 and IPv6 network services.

116. In which of the following DNS transactions does the querying system generate a recursive query? (Choose two.)

A. A DNS client sends the server name www.adatum.com from a URL to its designated DNS server for resolution.

B. A client's DNS server sends a request to a root domain server to find the authoritative server for the com top-level domain.

C. A client's DNS server sends a request to the com top-level domain server to find the authoritative server for the adatum.com domain.

D. A client's DNS server, which has been configured to function as a forwarder, sends the server name www.adatum.com from a URL to its ISP's DNS server for resolution.

E. A client's DNS server sends a request to the adatum.com domain server to find the IP address associated with the server name www.

117. Which of the following devices would you most likely configure to function as a Dynamic Host Configuration Protocol (DHCP) server?

    A. A wireless router

    B. An unmanaged switch

    C. A hub

    D. A bridge

118. Which of the following protocols are responsible for assigning IP addresses to hosts? (Choose two.)

    A. Dynamic Host Configuration Protocol (DHCP)

    B. Address Resolution Protocol (ARP)

    C. Domain Name System (DNS)

    D. File Transfer Protocol (FTP)

    E. Bootstrap Protocol (BOOTP)

119. Which of the following Domain Name System (DNS) resource records is used only for reverse name resolution?

    A. MX

    B. CNAME

    C. AAAA

    D. PTR

120. Which of the following features is supported by DHCP, but not by BOOTP and RARP?

    A. Dynamic address allocation

    B. Relay agents

    C. Manual address allocation

    D. Automatic address allocation

121. Which of the following message types are exchanged by Dynamic Host Configuration Protocol (DHCP) clients and servers during a successful IP address allocation transaction? (Choose all that apply.)

    A. DHCPDISCOVER

    B. DHCPOFFER

    C. DHCPINFORM

    D. DHCPACK

    E. DHCPREQUEST

    F. DHCPNAK

    G. DHCPRENEW

    H. DHCPRELEASE

122. Which of the following message types are exchanged by Dynamic Host Configuration Protocol (DHCP) clients and servers during a successful IP address lease renewal transaction? (Choose all that apply.)

    A. DHCPDISCOVER

    B. DHCPOFFER

    C. DHCPINFORM

    D. DHCPACK

    E. DHCPREQUEST

    F. DHCPNAK

    G. DHCPRENEW

    H. DHCPRELEASE

123. Which of the following is a protocol used to allocate IP address assignments to clients on a network?

    A. ARP

    B. ICMP

    C. DNS

    D. DHCP

124. Which of the following best describes what happens when a DNS server receives an iterative name resolution query?

    A. The DNS server responds immediately to the query with the best information it has in its resource records or in its cache, or failing that, with an error message stating that it could not resolve the requested name.

    B. The DNS server attempts to resolve the requested name by checking its own resource records and cache, or failing that, by issuing its own iterative queries to other DNS servers.

    C. The DNS server attempts to resolve the requested name by checking its own resource records and cache, or failing that, by forwarding the name resolution request to another DNS server in a recursive query.

    D. The DNS server responds immediately if it is the authoritative server for the domain in which the requested name is located. Otherwise, it returns an error message stating that it could not resolve the requested name.

125. What is the term used to refer to the DNS client mechanism that generates name resolution queries and sends them to DNS servers?

    A. Requestor

    B. Forwarder

    C. Authority

    D. Resolver

126. Which of the following TCP/IP parameters, configured on an end system, specifies the IP address of a device that performs name resolution services?

    A. IP Address

    B. Subnet Mask

    C. Default Gateway

    D. Preferred DNS Server

127. Which IP address allocation method is not supported by Dynamic Host Configuration Protocol (DHCP)?

    A. Manual

    B. Dynamic

    C. Stable

    D. Automatic

128. On a Dynamic Host Configuration Protocol (DHCP) server, what is the name of the element you create to specify which IP addresses the server should assign to clients?

    A. Range

    B. Scope

    C. Pool

    D. Subnet

129. Why is it necessary to use a relay agent to enable a Dynamic Host Configuration Protocol (DHCP) server to assign IP addresses to clients on other networks? (Choose two.)

    A. Because DHCP requires a separate license for each subnet.

    B. Because clients cannot initiate an address assignment by contacting DHCP servers on other networks directly.

    C. Because DHCP must use the Transmission Control Protocol (TCP) to communicate with clients.

    D. Because the DHCP address assignment process relies on broadcast transmissions.

130. Which of the following Domain Name System (DNS) resource records is used to resolve a hostname into an IPv6 address?

    A. MX

    B. PTR

    C. AAAA

    D. NS

131. Ralph has configured a server called NE6 to function as a web server. He does not want to change the server's existing name, but he wants it to also be accessible to clients using the name www. What Domain Name System (DNS) modification can Ralph make to accomplish this?

    A. Create an additional A resource record.

    B. Create a new CNAME resource record.

    C. Modify the existing A resource record.

    D. Create a new TXT resource record.

    E. Create a new PTR resource record.

132. Which of the following options should you configure on a Dynamic Host Configuration Protocol (DHCP) server to supply clients with a default gateway address?

    A. Router

    B. Time Server

    C. Name Server

    D. LPR Server

    E. Lease Time

133. Dynamic Host Configuration Protocol (DHCP) clients rely on which of the following types of transmissions to locate and initiate contact with DHCP servers on the local network?

    A. Unicast

    B. Broadcast

    C. Multicast

    D. Anycast

134. Which of the following Domain Name System (DNS) resource record types specifies the IP addresses of the authoritative DNS servers for a particular zone?

    A. NS

    B. PTR

    C. MX

    D. SRV

    E. SOA

    F. TXT

135. Which of the following must you create on a DHCP server if you want it to always assign the same IP address to a particular computer?

    A. Scope

    B. Exclusion

    C. Reservation

    D. Relay

136. Which of the following DHCP address allocation methods enables the server to reclaim IP addresses when they are no longer in use by clients?

    A. Automatic

    B. Dynamic

    C. Manual

    D. Static

137. Which of the following technologies enables the IP addresses assigned to clients by a Dynamic Host Configuration Protocol (DHCP) server to be automatically added to the DNS namespace?

   A. Reverse name resolution

   B. Dynamic DNS

   C. Automatic allocation

   D. HOSTS

138. Which of the following is the term used to describe the logical distance of a Network Time Protocol (NTP) server from the time source to which it is synchronized?

   A. Layer

   B. Path

   C. Iteration

   D. Stratum

139. Which of the following protocols are used to synchronize computer clocks to a time signal provided by a server? (Choose all that apply.)

   A. NTS

   B. HTTPS

   C. NTP

   D. SMTP

   E. PTP

140. Which of the words in the fully qualified domain name (FQDN) `www.paris.mydomain.org` represents the topmost layer in the DNS namespace hierarchy?

   A. `www`

   B. `paris`

   C. `mydomain`

   D. `org`

141. Which of the following Dynamic Host Configuration Protocol (DHCP) options prevents the client from transmitting IP datagrams that circulate endlessly around the network?

   A. Interface MTU

   B. Default IP TTL

   C. ARP Cache Timeout

   D. TCP Keepalive Interval

142. In designing a network for a client, Ed has decided to use both internal and external DNS servers. Which of the following resources should Ed register with the external DNS server? (Choose two.)

   A. Company database servers

   B. Internet web servers

   C. Incoming email servers

   D. Domain controllers

143. Ralph is concerned that the IP address scope of available leases on his DHCP server is nearly exhausted. What happens to DHCP clients when there are no IP addresses left in the scope for assignment?

  A. Clients are assigned a 0.0.0.0 address.

  B. Clients self-assign APIPA addresses.

  C. Client DHCP requests are forwarded to another DHCP server.

  D. Clients are forced to share IP addresses.

144. Alice is the administrator of a subnet for which she has been allotted 100 IP addresses. She has installed a DHCP server with a scope containing all 100 available addresses for lease. There are currently 99 clients configured to use the DHCP server, many of which are mobile devices, and Alice fears that systems frequently leaving and rejoining the network might cause the scope of available leases to be exhausted. Which of the following adjustments can help to prevent this from happening?

  A. Increase the lease time for the scope.

  B. Decrease the lease time for the scope.

  C. Install a second DHCP server.

  D. Create a second scope for the subnet.

145. DHCP clients use broadcast messages to contact a DHCP server on the local subnet. Which of the following are mechanisms by which DHCP broadcast messages can be forwarded to a DHCP server on another subnet when there is none on the local subnet? (Choose all that apply.)

  A. DHCP relay

  B. UDP forwarding

  C. Zone transfer

  D. IP helper

146. Which of the following mechanisms enables administrators to maintain current DNS database information on both primary and secondary name servers, for fault tolerance and load balancing purposes?

  A. Multi-master replication

  B. UDP forwarding

  C. Iterative query

  D. Zone transfer

147. If an authoritative DNS server has a forward zone for a particular domain but no reverse zone, which of the following tasks will the server be unable to perform?

  A. Resolve a DNS name into an IP address

  B. Resolve an IP address into a DNS name

  C. Respond to recursive queries from other DNS servers

  D. Send queries to the DNS root name servers

148. The Domain Name System Security Extensions (DNSSEC) are a series of specifications that add cryptographic security to DNS communications. To make this possible, the DNSSEC specifications add some new DNS resource records. Which of the following are resource records created for use with DNSSEC? (Choose all that apply.)

A. SRV

B. RRSIG

C. NS

D. DNSKEY

E. DS

F. RP

149. Which of the following are extensions to the original Domain Name System (DNS) that provide security for the data exchanged in DNS transactions? (Choose all that apply.)

A. DNS over IPsec

B. DNS over HTTPS (DoH)

C. DNS over TLS (DoT)

D. DNS over STP

E. SLAAC

F. DNSSEC

150. Systems on an IPv6 network can assign IPv6 addresses to themselves using mechanisms such as DHCPv6 and SLAAC. Which of the following statements about the primary difference between these two mechanisms are true? (Choose all that apply.)

A. DHCPv6 is stateful.

B. SLAAC is stateful.

C. DHCPv6 is stateless.

D. SLAAC is stateless.

3.5 Compare and contrast network access and management methods.

151. Which of the following technologies enables virtual private network (VPN) clients to connect directly to each other, as well as to the VPN server at the home site?

A. VPN concentrator

B. DMVPN

C. SIP trunk

D. MPLS

E. Clientless VPN

152. Which of the following virtual private networking protocols is generally considered to be obsolete?

A. IPsec

B. L2TP

C. PPTP

D. SSL/TLS

153. Which of the following virtual private networking (VPN) protocols does not provide encryption within the tunnel?

A. PPTP

B. IPsec

C. L2TP

D. SSL

154. Which of the following elements must be identical in both the client and server computers to establish a remote wide area network (WAN) connection? (Choose all that apply.)

A. The WAN type

B. The Data link layer protocol

C. The authentication method

D. The operating system

155. Which of the following is not a protocol that is typically used to secure communication between web servers and web browsers?

A. SSL

B. TLS

C. SSH

D. DTLS

156. Which of the following types of virtual private networking (VPN) connection is the best solution for allowing vendors and partners limited access to your corporate network?

A. Client-to-site

B. Site-to-site

C. Client-to-client

D. Extranet

157. Which of the following protocols is not used for remote control of computers?

A. RDP

B. TFTP

C. SSH

D. Telnet

158. Which of the following services is provided by the Remote Desktop Protocol (RDP)?

A. Thin client computing

B. Clientless virtual private networking

C. Encrypted tunneling

D. Unauthenticated file transfers

159. Which of the following types of virtual private networking (VPN) connection is the best solution for connecting a branch office to a corporate headquarters?

A. Client-to-site

B. Site-to-site

C. Client-to-client

D. Extranet

160. Ralph is a network administrator for a firm that is allowing employees to telecommute for the first time, and he is responsible for designing a remote access solution that will enable users to access network resources, such as company email and databases, securely. All of the remote users have been issued smartcards and will be connecting using virtual private network (VPN) connections on company-supplied laptop computers running Windows 11 and equipped with card readers. The users will be logging on to the company network using their standard Active Directory Domain Services (AD DS) accounts, so it is important for Ralph to design a solution that provides the maximum protection for their passwords, both inside and outside the office. Which of the following authentication protocols should Ralph configure the remote access servers and the laptop computers to use?

A. Password Authentication Protocol (PAP)

B. Challenge Handshake Authentication Protocol (CHAP)

C. Extensible Authentication Protocol (EAP)

D. Microsoft Challenge Handshake Authentication Protocol (MS-CHAP v2)

161. Which of the following remote access protocols provides users with full control over the graphical user interface (GUI) on a Windows computer? (Choose two.)

A. SSH

B. RDP

C. VNC

D. Telnet

162. Ralph has come upon the term *virtual desktop*, and he is not exactly sure what it means. After performing some Internet searches, he finds multiple definitions. Which of the following is not one of the technologies that uses the term virtual desktop?

A. A three-dimensional realization of a computer display created using a virtual reality hardware device

B. A computer display with a virtual operating system desktop that is larger than can be displayed on a monitor

    C. A cloud-based Windows 11 deployment that enables users to access their desktops using any remote device

    D. A hardware device that projects a computer desktop on a screen, rather than displaying it on a monitor

163. Which of the following types of traffic are carried by the Remote Desktop Protocol (RDP)? (Choose all that apply.)

    A. Keystrokes

    B. Mouse movements

    C. Display information

    D. Application data

164. Which of the following types of traffic are transmitted by Virtual Network Computing (VNC)? (Choose all that apply.)

    A. Keystrokes

    B. Mouse movements

    C. Display information

    D. Application data

165. Which of the following types of traffic are carried by Telnet? (Choose two.)

    A. Keystrokes

    B. Mouse movements

    C. Display information

    D. Application data

166. Which of the following describes the primary function of a remote desktop gateway?

    A. Provides multiple users with Remote Desktop client access to one workstation.

    B. Provides a single Remote Desktop client with simultaneous access to multiple workstations.

    C. Enables remote users outside the network to access network workstations.

    D. Enables remote users to access workstations without the need for a Remote Desktop client.

167. Which of the following statements about in-band management and out-of-band management are true? (Choose two.)

    A. Out-of-band management tools do not provide access to the remote system's BIOS or UEFI firmware.

    B. Out-of-band management tools enable you to reinstall the operating system on a remote computer.

    C. Secure Shell (SSH), Virtual Network Computing (VNC), and application programming interface (API) connections are in-band management tools.

    D. To perform out-of-band management on a device, it must have an IP address.

168. Which of the following statements best defines out-of-band management?

  A. Out-of-band management is a method for accessing network devices from a remote location.

  B. Out-of-band management is a method for accessing network devices using a direct cable connection.

  C. Out-of-band management is a method for accessing network devices using a connection to the system other than the production network to which the device is connected.

  D. Out-of-band management is a method for accessing network devices using any tool that operates over the production network to which the device is connected.

169. What four components are required for a computer to establish a remote Transmission Control Protocol/Internet Protocol (TCP/IP) connection? (Choose all that apply.)

  A. A Physical layer connection

  B. Remote Access Service (RAS)

  C. Common protocols

  D. TCP/IP configuration

  E. Point-to-Point Tunneling Protocol (PPTP)

  F. Host and remote software

170. Which of the following statements explains why web browsing over a client-to-site virtual private network (VPN) connection is usually so much slower than browsing locally?

  A. The browser application is running on the VPN server.

  B. The browser is using the remote network's Internet connection.

  C. The VPN tunnel restricts the amount of bandwidth available.

  D. VPN encryption is processor intensive.

171. In a site-to-site virtual private network (VPN) connection, which of the following combinations of endpoint devices would most likely be involved?

  A. Two workstations

  B. A workstation and a server

  C. A workstation and a VPN concentrator

  D. Two VPN concentrators

172. In a client-to-site virtual private network (VPN) connection, which of the following combinations of endpoint devices would most likely be involved?

  A. Two workstations

  B. A workstation and a server

  C. A workstation and a VPN concentrator

  D. Two VPN concentrators

173. Which of the following are the two most common types of Transport Layer Security/Secure Sockets Layer (TLS/SSL) virtual private network (VPN) connections? (Choose two.)

    A. TLS/SSL client

    B. TLS/SSL portal

    C. TLS/SSL tunnel

    D. TLS/SSL gateway

174. In a client-to-client virtual private network (VPN) connection, which of the following combinations of endpoint devices would most likely be involved?

    A. Two workstations

    B. A workstation and a server

    C. A workstation and a VPN concentrator

    D. Two VPN concentrators

175. Many managed switches and routers include a console port for administrative access, to which you can connect a laptop and run a terminal program to access the device's interface. Which of the following is the best term for this type of access to the device?

    A. Out-of-band

    B. In-band

    C. Client-to-site

    D. BYOD

176. Which of the following statements about running a site-to-site virtual private network (VPN) connection to join two distant local area networks (LANs) together, rather than using a wide area network (WAN) connection, are generally true? (Choose two.)

    A. The VPN is cheaper.

    B. The VPN is slower.

    C. The VPN is less secure.

    D. The VPN is harder to maintain.

177. Which of the following are examples of out-of-band device management? (Choose all that apply.)

    A. Logging on remotely from a network workstation

    B. Plugging a laptop into a console port

    C. Establishing a point-to-point modem connection

    D. Connecting dedicated ports on each device to a separate switch

    E. Accessing a device through its application programming interface (API)

178. Which of the following was the first TCP/IP terminal emulation program?

    A. Telnet

    B. SSH

    C. Windows Terminal Services

    D. Virtual Network Computing

179. Which of the following techniques do virtual private networks use to secure the data that they transmit over the Internet? (Choose all that apply.)

 A. Tunneling

 B. Socketing

 C. Message integrity

 D. Authentication

180. Virtual private networks (VPNs) use tunneling, which is the process of encapsulating a data packet within another packet for transmission over a network connection, typically using the Internet. The system encrypts the entire encapsulated data packet for protection. Split tunneling is a variation of this method that provides which of the following advantages? (Choose all that apply.)

 A. Conservation of VPN bandwidth

 B. Access to local network devices while connected to the VPN

 C. Additional data integrity protection

 D. Faster data transmission through multiplexing

181. SSH was created to be an improvement on the Telnet terminal emulation program. In which of the following ways is it an improvement?

 A. SSH is faster than Telnet.

 B. SSH provides graphical terminal emulation.

 C. SSH encrypts passwords and data.

 D. SSH is less expensive than Telnet.

182. Remote Desktop Protocol (RDP) was created for use with which of the following terminal emulation programs?

 A. Windows Terminal Services

 B. Virtual Network Computing (VNC)

 C. Citrix WinFrame

 D. Telnet

183. Alice is a new hire in the IT department of a company that, in addition to their existing Ethernet network, has recently installed a storage area network (SAN) using Fibre Channel technology and three hard drive arrays. Alice's supervisor has instructed her to set up a jump box to manage the SAN. Alice has never heard the term *jump box* before. Which of the following describes what she must do to complete the task?

 A. Connect a dumb terminal to the SAN.

 B. Install a Fibre Channel adapter in a workstation computer and connect it to the SAN.

 C. Install Ethernet and Fibre Channel adapters in a workstation computer and connect it to both the Ethernet network and the SAN.

 D. Install an Ethernet adapter in one of the drive arrays on the SAN.

Chapter

4

Network Security

THE COMPTIA NETWORK+ EXAM N10-009 TOPICS COVERED IN THIS CHAPTER INCLUDE THE FOLLOWING:

✓ **4.1 Explain the importance of basic network security concepts.**

- Logical security
  - Encryption
    - Data in transit
    - Data at rest
  - Certificates
    - Public key infrastructure (PKI)
    - Self-signed
  - Identity and access management (IAM)
    - Authentication
      - Multifactor authentication (MFA)
      - Single sign-on (SSO)
      - Remote Authentication Dial-in User Service (RADIUS)
      - LDAP
      - Security Assertion Markup Language (SAML)
      - Terminal Access Controller Access Control System Plus (TACACS+)
      - Time-based authentication
    - Authorization
      - Least privilege
      - Role-based access control
  - Geofencing
- Physical security
  - Camera
  - Locks

- Deception technologies
  - Honeypot
  - Honeynet
- Common security terminology
  - Risk
  - Vulnerability
  - Exploit
  - Threat
  - Confidentiality, Integrity, and Availability (CIA) triad
- Audits and regulatory compliance
  - Data locality
  - Payment Card Industry Data Security Standards (PCI DSS)
  - General Data Protection Regulation (GDPR)
- Network segmentation enforcement
  - Internet of Things (IoT) and Industrial Internet of Things (IIoT)
  - Supervisory control and data acquisition (SCADA), industrial control system (ICS), operational technology (OT)
  - Guest
  - Bring your own device (BYOD)

✓ **4.2 Summarize various types of attacks and their impact to the network.**

- Denial-of-service (DoS)/distributed denial-of-service (DDoS)
- VLAN hopping
- Media Access Control (MAC) flooding
- Address Resolution Protocol (ARP) poisoning
- ARP spoofing
- DNS poisoning

- DNS spoofing
- Rogue devices and services
  - DHCP
  - AP
- Evil twin
- On-path attack
- Social engineering
  - Phishing
  - Dumpster diving
  - Shoulder surfing
  - Tailgating
- Malware

✓ **4.3 Given a scenario, apply network security features, defense techniques, and solutions**

- Device hardening
  - Disable unused ports and services
  - Change default passwords
- Network access control (NAC)
  - Port security
  - 802.1X
  - MAC filtering
- Key management
- Security rules
  - Access control list (ACL)
  - Uniform Resource Locator (URL) filtering
  - Content filtering
- Zones
  - Trusted vs. untrusted
  - Screened subnet

4.1 Explain the importance of basic network security concepts.

1. Which of the following authentication protocols do Windows networks use for Active Directory Domain Services (AD DS) authentication of internal clients?

    A. RADIUS

    B. WPA2

    C. Kerberos

    D. EAP-TLS

2. Which of the following are examples of multifactor authentication? (Choose all that apply.)

    A. A system that uses an external RADIUS server for authentication

    B. A system that requires two passwords for authentication

    C. A system that requires a smartcard and a PIN for authentication

    D. A system that requires a password and a retinal scan for authentication

    E. A system that requires users to appear for authentication at specific times

3. Which of the following is not one of the mechanisms often used to implement a defense in depth strategy?

    A. Screened subnets

    B. Network segmentation enforcement

    C. Honeypots

    D. Access control vestibules

    E. Social engineering

    F. Separation of duties

4. Which of the following protocols can you use to authenticate Windows remote access users with smartcards?

    A. EAP

    B. MS-CHAPv2

    C. CHAP

    D. PAP

5. Which of the following statements best defines multifactor user authentication?

    A. Verification of a user's identity on all of a network's resources using a single sign-on

    B. Verification of a user's identity using two or more types of credentials

    C. Verification of a user's identity on two devices at once

    D. Verification of a user's membership in two or more security groups

6. Which of the following services are methods of tracking a user's activities on a network? (Choose all that apply.)
    A. Authentication
    B. Authorization
    C. Accounting
    D. Auditing

7. When a user supplies a password to log on to a server, which of the following actions is the user performing?
    A. Authentication
    B. Authorization
    C. Accounting
    D. Auditing

8. When a user swipes a finger across a fingerprint scanner to log on to a laptop computer, which of the following actions is the user performing?
    A. Authentication
    B. Authorization
    C. Accounting
    D. Auditing

9. Which of the following security protocols can authenticate users without transmitting their passwords over the network?
    A. Kerberos
    B. 802.1X
    C. TKIP
    D. LDAP

10. Which of the following statements about authentication auditing is not true?
    A. Auditing can disclose attempts to compromise passwords.
    B. Auditing can detect authentications that occur after hours.
    C. Auditing can identify the guess patterns used by password cracking software.
    D. Auditing can record unsuccessful as well as successful authentications.

11. When a user swipes a smartcard through a reader to log on to a laptop computer, which of the following actions is the user performing?
    A. Authentication
    B. Authorization
    C. Accounting
    D. Auditing

12. Combining elements like something you know, something you have, and something you are to provide access to a secured network resource is a definition of which of the following types of authentication?

A. Multifactor

B. Multisegment

C. Multimetric

D. Multifiltered

13. HVAC sensors can use the Internet of Things (IoT) to monitor which of the following? (Choose all that apply.)

A. Temperature

B. Pressure

C. Humidity

D. Printers

E. Occupancy

F. Cameras

G. Door locks

14. Which of the following describes the primary difference between single sign-on (SSO) and same sign-on?

A. Single sign-on (SSO) enables users to access different resources with one set of credentials, whereas same sign-on requires users to have multiple credential sets.

B. Single sign-on (SSO) credentials consist of one username and one password, whereas same sign-on credentials consist of one username and multiple passwords.

C. Single sign-on (SSO) requires the user to supply credentials only once, whereas with same sign-on, the user must supply the credentials repeatedly.

D. Single sign-on (SSO) requires multifactor authentication, such as a password and a smartcard, whereas same sign-on requires only a password for authentication.

15. Which of the following is the best description of biometrics?

A. Something you know

B. Something you have

C. Something you are

D. Something you do

16. Which of the following authentication factors is an example of something you have?

A. A fingerprint

B. A smartcard

C. A password

D. A finger gesture

17. Which of the following statements best describes the primary scenario for the use of TACACS+?

    A. TACACS+ was designed to provide authentication, authorization, and accounting services for wireless networks.

    B. TACACS+ was designed to provide authentication, authorization, and accounting services for the Active Directory Domain Services.

    C. TACACS+ was designed to provide authentication, authorization, and accounting services for remote dial-in users.

    D. TACACS+ was designed to provide authentication, authorization, and accounting services for network routers and switches.

18. Which of the following is not one of the functions provided by TACACS+?

    A. Authentication

    B. Authorization

    C. Administration

    D. Accounting

19. The new door lock on your company's datacenter door requires you to supply both a PIN and a thumbprint scan. Which of the following authentication factors does the lock use? (Choose all that apply.)

    A. Something you have

    B. Something you know

    C. Something you are

    D. Something you do

20. Your new smartphone enables you to configure the lock screen with a picture of your husband, on which you draw eyes, nose, and a mouth with your finger to unlock the phone. This is an example of which of the following authentication factors?

    A. Something you have

    B. Something you know

    C. Something you are

    D. Something you do

21. Which of the following authentication factors is an example of something you do?

    A. A fingerprint

    B. A smartcard

    C. A password

    D. A self-signed certificate

    E. A finger gesture

22. Which of the following authentication factors is an example of something you know?

    A. A fingerprint

    B. A smartcard

    C. A password

    D. A finger gesture

23. Which of the following authentication factors is an example of something you are?

    A. A fingerprint

    B. A smartcard

    C. A password

    D. A finger gesture

24. Which of the following data loss prevention (DLP) terms is used to describe dangers pertaining to data that is being transmitted over a network? (Choose all that apply.)

    A. Data in use

    B. Data at rest

    C. Data in motion

    D. Data in transit

25. Which of the following data loss prevention (DLP) terms is used to describe dangers pertaining to data while a user is loading it into an application?

    A. Data in use

    B. Data at rest

    C. Data in motion

    D. Data in process

26. Which of the following data loss prevention terms is used to describe potential dangers of data loss or data leakage to unauthorized parties while the data is stored without being used?

    A. Data in motion

    B. Data at rest

    C. Data in use

    D. Data on disk

27. Which of the following are not standard terms used in data loss prevention (DLP)? (Choose all that apply.)

    A. Data online

    B. Data at rest

    C. Data in motion

    D. Data in use

    E. Data locality

28. Which of the following are standards that define combined authentication, authorization, and accounting (AAA) services? (Choose two.)

  A. 802.1X

  B. RADIUS

  C. TACACS+

  D. LDAP

  E. SAML

29. Which of the following is not one of the five functional levels associated with a distributed control system such as supervisory control and data acquisition (SCADA) systems?

  A. Field level

  B. Remote access

  C. Direct control

  D. Plant supervisory

  E. Production control

  F. Production scheduling

30. Which of the following standards was originally designed to provide authentication, authorization, and accounting services for dial-up network connections?

  A. RADIUS

  B. TACACS+

  C. Kerberos

  D. LDAP

31. Which of the following statements about RADIUS and TACACS+ is correct?

  A. By default, RADIUS uses UDP, and TACACS+ uses TCP.

  B. By default, RADIUS uses TCP, and TACACS+ uses UDP.

  C. By default, both RADIUS and TACACS+ use TCP.

  D. By default, both RADIUS and TACACS+ use UDP.

32. Which of the following standards provides authentication, authorization, and accounting services for network routers and switches?

  A. RADIUS

  B. TACACS+

  C. Kerberos

  D. LDAP

33. Which of the following terms refers to the process of determining whether a user is a member of a group that provides access to a particular network resource?

  A. Authentication

  B. Accounting

  C. Authorization

  D. Access control

34. Which of the following terms refers to the process of confirming a user's identity by checking specific credentials?

A. Authentication

B. Authorization

C. Accounting

D. Access control

35. Which of the following terms refers to the process by which a system tracks a user's network activity?

A. Authentication

B. Accounting

C. Authorization

D. Access control

36. Which of the following statements about a public key infrastructure are true? (Choose two.)

A. Data encrypted with a user's public key can be decrypted with the user's public key.

B. Data encrypted with a user's public key can be decrypted with the user's private key.

C. Data encrypted with a user's private key can be decrypted with the user's private key.

D. Data encrypted with a user's private key can be decrypted with the user's public key.

37. Which of the following technologies can maintain an account database that multiple remote access servers can employ to authenticate remote users?

A. RADIUS

B. IDS

C. NGFW

D. NAS

38. Which element of the CIA triad prevents unauthorized modification of protected data?

A. Confidentiality

B. Integrity

C. Availability

D. None of the above

39. Which of the following is an example of local authentication?

A. A system that uses an external RADIUS server for authentication

B. A system that uses the Kerberos protocol for authentication

C. A system that authenticates users without network communication

D. A system that requires a password and a retinal scan for authentication

40. In some cases, network administrators create computers that function as enticing targets for attackers but do not provide access to any legitimately sensitive services or information. Which of the following is the term used to describe this technique?

A. Screened subnet

B. Honeypot

C. Root guard

D. Spoofing

41. Honeypots and honeynets belong to which of the following categories of devices?

A. Mitigation techniques

B. Network attacks

C. Switch port protection types

D. Firewall filters

42. Which of the following best describes the process of penetration testing?

A. Administrators create computers or networks that are alluring targets for intruders.

B. Administrators attempt to access the network from outside using hacker tools.

C. An organization hires an outside consultant to evaluate the security conditions on the network.

D. An organization hires an outside consultant who attempts to compromise the network's security measures.

43. Which of the following statements best describes the difference between an exploit and a vulnerability?

A. An exploit is a potential weakness in software, and a vulnerability is a potential weakness in hardware.

B. A vulnerability is a potential weakness in a system, and an exploit is a hardware or software element that is designed to take advantage of a vulnerability.

C. An exploit is a potential weakness in a system, and a vulnerability is a hardware or software element that is designed to take advantage of a vulnerability.

D. A vulnerability is a potential weakness in software, and an exploit is a potential weakness in hardware.

44. Which of the following is the best description of a software product with a zero-day vulnerability?

A. A product with a vulnerability that has just been addressed by a newly released fix

B. A product with a vulnerability that has been addressed by a fix that nearly all users have applied

C. A vulnerability in a newly released product for which no fix has yet been developed

D. A vulnerability in a product that no attackers have yet discovered or exploited

45. As part of her company's new risk management initiative, Alice has been assigned the task of performing a threat assessment for the firm's data resources. For each potential threat she discovers, which of the following elements should Alice estimate? (Choose all that apply.)

    A. Severity

    B. Mitigation

    C. Likelihood

    D. Posture

46. Alice has been assigned the task of examining her department's order entry procedure to determine whether it meets established cost, quality, and timeliness goals. Which of the following is the best term for this examination?

    A. Vendor assessment

    B. Process assessment

    C. Business assessment

    D. Risk assessment

47. Which of the following standards defines a framework for the authentication process but does not specify the actual authentication mechanism?

    A. WPA

    B. EAP

    C. TKIP

    D. TLS

    E. BYOD

48. A wireless network is configured to allow clients to authenticate only when the signal strength of their connections exceeds a specified level. Which of the following terms best describes this configuration?

    A. Local authentication

    B. Port security

    C. Geofencing

    D. Motion detection

49. Which of the following best describes a wireless network that uses geofencing as a security mechanism?

    A. A wireless network that allows clients to authenticate only when the signal strength of their connections exceeds a specified level

    B. A wireless network that requires users to log on to a wired system before they can authenticate on a wireless device

    C. A wireless network that requires users to have an Active Directory account located within the local site

    D. A wireless network that requires users to type in the local SSID before they can authenticate

50. Which of the following elements associates a public and private key pair to the identity of a specific person or computer?

A. Exploit

B. Signature

C. Certificate

D. Resource record

51. Which of the following mitigation techniques helps organizations maintain compliance with standards such as HIPAA and FISMA?

A. File integrity monitoring

B. Role separation

C. Deauthentication

D. Tamper detection

E. Router Advertisement guard

52. Which of the following functions cannot be implemented using digital signatures?

A. Integrity

B. Nonrepudiation

C. Segmentation

D. Authentication

53. When Ralph digitally signs and encrypts a document with his private key, Alice can decrypt the document only by using Ralph's public key. As long as the private key is accepted to be secure, which of the following statements are true? (Choose all that apply.)

A. Ralph cannot deny having created the document.

B. No one has altered the document since Ralph sent it.

C. No one but Ralph could have created the document.

D. No one but Alice can decrypt and read the document.

54. When Alice encrypts a document with Ralph's public key, Ralph can decrypt the document only by using his private key. As long as the private key is accepted to be secure, which of the following statements are true? (Choose all that apply.)

A. Alice cannot deny having created the document.

B. No one has opened the document since Alice sent it.

C. No one but Alice can have created the document.

D. No one but Ralph can decrypt and read the document.

55. Which of the following is the best description of geofencing?

A. Something you do

B. Something you know

C. Something you have

D. Somewhere you are

56. The Internet of Things (IoT) and the Industrial Internet of Things (IIoT) encompass a huge number of device types ranging from personal electronics to household appliances to medical equipment to industrial control systems (ICS). Many of these devices deal with sensitive information, and many perform critically important tasks. The field of IoT security is still in its infancy; there is no all-encompassing standard defining IoT protection protocols. IoT devices have vastly different security requirements and also vastly different functional capabilities, making it difficult to create a blanket protection mechanism for all of them. Which of the following are potentially viable methods for securing all IoT devices against attack? (Choose two.)

   A. Firewalls

   B. Network access control

   C. Security gateways

   D. Network segmentation

57. Which of the following technologies associated with the Internet of Things (IoT) is often used to identify pets using embedded chips?

   A. Z-wave

   B. Bluetooth

   C. NFC

   D. RFID

58. Which of the following is typically not an example of the Internet of Things (IoT)?

   A. A key fob that unlocks your car

   B. A smartphone home automation app

   C. A remotely monitored cardiac pacemaker

   D. A seismic early warning system

   E. Operational technology that controls industrial equipment

59. Which of the following are available as Internet of Things (IoT) devices?

   A. Refrigerators

   B. Doorbells

   C. Thermostats

   D. Speakers

   E. All of the above

60. The terms *on-boarding* and *off-boarding* are typically associated with which of the following policies?

   A. Data loss prevention

   B. Incident response

   C. Inventory management

    D. Identity management

    E. Disaster recovery

    F. Business continuity

61. The term *off-boarding* refers to which of the following procedures?

    A. Removing a node from a cluster

    B. Disconnecting all cables from a switch

    C. Revoking a user's network privileges

    D. Retiring old workstations

62. A server's firewall is configured using a default policy that does not allow any users remote access to the server unless an administrator creates a rule granting them access. Which of the following terms describes this default policy?

    A. Explicit allow

    B. Explicit deny

    C. Implicit allow

    D. Implicit deny

63. Alice is a consultant working in your office who has been given the SSID and the passphrase for the company's main wireless network, but she is unable to connect with her laptop. Which of the following security measures might be preventing her from connecting?

    A. MAC filtering

    B. Disabling SSID broadcast

    C. Geofencing

    D. Using WPA2

    E. Guest network isolation

64. Which of the following is a regulatory standard for the European Union?

    A. Payment Card Industry Data Security Standards (PCI DSS)

    B. Security information and event management (SIEM)

    C. General Data Protection Regulation (GDPR)

    D. Supervisory control and data acquisition (SCADA)

65. Ralph is a network administrator who wants to implement an access control scheme that allocates permissions based on an employee's job requirements. Which of the following is most suited to this type of implementation?

    A. Single sign-on (SSO)

    B. Mandatory access control (MAC)

    C. Confidentiality, integrity, and availability (CIA)

    D. Role-based access control (RBAC)

4.2 Summarize various types of attacks and their impact to the network.

66. A user calls the help desk complaining that he cannot access any of the data on his computer. A message has also appeared on his screen stating that his data has been encrypted and that it will only be decrypted after he pays $768 in digital currency to an unknown address. Which of the following types of attack has the user experienced?

   A. War driving

   B. Ransomware

   C. Denial-of-service

   D. ARP poisoning

67. Which of the following attack types typically involves modifying network packets while they are in transit? (Choose all that apply.)

   A. Spoofing

   B. On-path

   C. Denial-of-service

   D. Logic bomb

68. Which of the following types of attack involves the modification of a legitimate software product?

   A. Social engineering

   B. War driving

   C. Logic bomb

   D. Evil twin

69. Which of the following steps can help to prevent war driving attacks from compromising your wireless network? (Choose all that apply.)

   A. Configure your access point to use a longer SSID.

   B. Configure your access point not to broadcast its SSID.

   C. Configure your clients and access point to use WPA3 security.

   D. Configure your clients and access point to use WEP security.

70. Which of the following is the name for an attack in which an intruder uses a Bluetooth connection to steal information from a wireless device, such as a smartphone?

   A. Bluedogging

   B. Bluesnarfing

   C. Bluesmurfing

   D. Bluejacking

71. Which of the following types of denial-of-service (DoS) attack does not involve flooding a server with traffic?

  A. Amplified

  B. Reflective

  C. Distributed

  D. Permanent

72. Which of the following statements best describes the difference between distributed and reflective denial-of-service (DoS) attacks?

  A. A distributed DoS attack uses other computers to flood a target server with traffic, whereas a reflective DoS attack causes a server to flood itself with loopback messages.

  B. A distributed DoS attack uses malware-infected computers to flood a target, whereas a reflective DoS attack takes advantage of other servers' native functions to make them flood a target.

  C. A reflective DoS attack uses malware-infected computers to flood a target, whereas a distributed DoS attack takes advantage of other servers' native functions to make them flood a target.

  D. A distributed DoS attack floods multiple target computers with traffic, whereas a reflective DoS attack only floods a single target.

73. Which of the following terms refers to a denial-of-service (DoS) attack that places more of a burden on the target server than just the flood of incoming traffic?

  A. Amplified

  B. Reflective

  C. Distributed

  D. Permanent

74. Which of the following types of attack require no additional hardware or software components? (Choose all that apply.)

  A. Brute-force

  B. Social engineering

  C. Denial-of-service

  D. Phishing

75. Which of the following attack types are specifically targeted at wireless network clients? (Choose all that apply.)

  A. Logic bomb

  B. Deauthentication

  C. Evil twin

  D. ARP poisoning

76. Which of the following is an effective method for preventing sensitive data from being compromised through social engineering?

    A. Implement a program of user education and corporate policies.

    B. Install an antivirus software product on all user workstations.

    C. Install a firewall between the internal network and the Internet.

    D. Use IPsec to encrypt all network traffic.

77. Which of the following terms refer to denial-of-service (DoS) attacks that use other computers to flood a target server with traffic? (Choose all that apply.)

    A. Amplified

    B. Reflective

    C. Distributed

    D. Permanent

78. In which of the following ways is VLAN hopping a potential threat?

    A. VLAN hopping enables an attacker to scramble a switch's patch panel connections.

    B. VLAN hopping enables an attacker to rename the default VLAN on a switch.

    C. VLAN hopping enables an attacker to access different VLANs using 802.1q spoofing.

    D. VLAN hopping enables an attacker to change the native VLAN on a switch.

79. Which of the following types of attack can be used to enable an intruder to access a wireless network despite the protection provided by MAC filtering?

    A. Spoofing

    B. Brute-force

    C. DNS poisoning

    D. War driving

80. Which of the following terms refers to a type of denial-of-service (DoS) attack that uses multiple computers to bombard a target server with traffic?

    A. Amplified

    B. Reflective

    C. Distributed

    D. Permanent

81. Which of the following terms refers to a type of denial-of-service (DoS) attack that bombards a target server with traffic that requires a large amount of processing?

    A. Amplified

    B. Reflective

    C. Distributed

    D. Permanent

82. Which of the following types of attack are rarely seen anymore because of changes in device design that were specifically designed to prevent them? (Choose all that apply.)

    A. VLAN hopping

    B. Logic bomb

    C. Phishing

    D. Smurf

83. Which of the following terms refers to a denial-of-service (DoS) attack in which an attacker breaks into a company's datacenter and smashes its servers with a sledgehammer?

    A. Distributed

    B. Amplified

    C. Reflective

    D. Permanent

84. Which of the following terms refers to a denial-of-service (DoS) attack that involves zombies?

    A. Reflective

    B. Amplified

    C. Distributed

    D. Permanent

85. Which of the following types of attack can cause a user's attempts to connect to an Internet website to be diverted to an attacker's website instead?

    A. Evil twin

    B. ARP poisoning

    C. Spoofing

    D. DNS poisoning

86. Which of the following functions can be interfered with by a DNS poisoning attack?

    A. IP address resolution

    B. Name resolution

    C. Password protection

    D. Network switching

87. In testing the new application he has designed, Ralph has discovered that it contains a weakness that could enable an attacker to gain full administrative access. Which of the following is another term for this weakness?

    A. Exploit

    B. Mitigation

    C. Vulnerability

    D. Honeypot

88. A senior IT administrator at your company was terminated two weeks ago. Today, Friday, you arrived at the office and found that all of the hosts in the web server farm had had their data deleted. There are no unauthorized entries to the datacenter recorded, but you suspect the terminated administrator is responsible. Which of the following attack types might the administrator have directed at the web server farm?

    A. Social engineering

    B. ARP poisoning

    C. Evil twin

    D. Logic bomb

89. Which of the following attack types can be facilitated by ARP spoofing? (Choose all that apply.)

    A. Evil twin

    B. On-path

    C. Session hijacking

    D. Social engineering

90. Which of the following statements best describes a type of replay attack?

    A. An intruder reenters a resource previously compromised by another intruder.

    B. An intruder retransmits captured authentication packets to gain access to a secured resource.

    C. An intruder uses the same technique that provided access to other resources to penetrate a new resource.

    D. An intruder accesses a resource that was accidentally left unsecured by an authorized user.

91. Ed receives an email through his personal account, warning him that his checking account has been locked due to excessive activity. To confirm that the activity is fraudulent, the email instructs Ed to click the enclosed hyperlink, log on to his account, and review the list of charges. Ed clicks the link and is taken to a web page that appears to be that of his bank. He then supplies his username and password to log on. Which of the following specific types of attacks is Ed most likely to be experiencing?

    A. Evil twin

    B. Phishing

    C. Logic bomb

    D. Spoofing

92. Which of the following attack types are specifically directed at wireless networks? (Choose all that apply.)

    A. Evil twin

    B. Phishing

    C. Deauthentication

    D. War driving

93. Which of the following are not considered to be denial-of-service (DoS) attacks? (Choose all that apply.)

    A. An intruder breaks into a company's datacenter and smashes their web servers with a sledgehammer.

    B. An attacker uses the `ping` command with the `-t` parameter to send a continuous stream of large ICMP packets to a specific server.

    C. An attacker captures the packets transmitted to and from a domain controller to obtain encrypted passwords.

    D. An attacker connects a rogue access point to a company's wireless network, using their SSID in the hope of attracting their users.

    E. An attacker bombards a switch with Ethernet frames in an attempt to replace the legitimate information in its MAC table.

94. In the hacker subculture, which of the following statements best describes a zombie?

    A. A computer that is remotely controllable because it has been infected by malware

    B. A computer that is no longer functioning because it is the target of a denial-of-service (DoS) attack

    C. A user that has fallen victim to a phishing attack

    D. A program that attackers use to penetrate passwords using brute-force attacks

95. Which of the following statements best describes a ransomware attack?

    A. A website is rendered inaccessible by a denial-of-service (DoS) attack until its owner agrees to pay a fee.

    B. A user's access to a specific resource, such as a bank's website, is blocked until the user pays a fee.

    C. A message appears on a user's screen, stating that the system is locked and will only be released on payment of a fee.

    D. An application is supplied with limited usability until the user pays a license fee.

96. Which of the following types of attacks requires no computer equipment?

    A. Denial-of-service

    B. Social engineering

    C. Brute-force

    D. Dictionary

    E. Phishing

97. Which of the following best describes a brute-force attack?

    A. An attacker breaking down the door of a datacenter

    B. An attacker cracking a password by trying thousands of guesses

    C. An attacker using zombie computers to flood a server with traffic

    D. An attacker deploying an unauthorized access point on a wireless network

98. An intruder has deployed a rogue access point on your company's wireless network and is using it to access traffic generated by users who have accidentally connected to it. Which of the following is the name for this type of attack?

    A. Evil twin

    B. War driving

    C. Social engineering

    D. Spoofing

99. A person identifying herself as Trixie from the IT department telephones a user called Alice and tells her that there is a problem with her network user account that could cause all her data to be lost. Trixie says that to resolve the problem, she must log on using Alice's account and configure an important setting. All she needs to do this is Alice's account password. This call is, of course, an illicit attempt to learn Alice's password. Which of the following terms describes the type of attack that is currently occurring?

    A. On-path

    B. Spoofing

    C. Social engineering

    D. Evil twin

100. Regularly applying operating system updates and patches to network computers is an important mitigation procedure for which of the following security problems?

    A. Denial-of-service attacks

    B. Malware

    C. Social engineering

    D. Port security

101. Which of the following is not a form of social engineering?

    A. Piggybacking

    B. Tailgating

    C. Shoulder surfing

    D. Dumpster diving

    E. Evil twin

102. Which of the following types of attack can best be prevented by implementing a program of employee education and training?

    A. Social engineering

    B. War driving

    C. Logic bomb

    D. Evil twin

103. A technician in the IT department at your company was terminated today and had to be escorted from the building. Your supervisor has instructed you to disable all of the technician's accounts, change all network device passwords to which the technician had access, and have the datacenter doors rekeyed. Which of the following terms best describes your supervisor's concern in asking you to do these things?

    A. Social engineering

    B. Internal threats

    C. Logic bombs

    D. War driving

    E. External threats

104. Which of the following statements about DHCP snooping is not true?

    A. DHCP snooping detects rogue DHCP servers.

    B. DHCP snooping is implemented in network switches.

    C. DHCP snooping drops DHCP messages arriving over the incorrect port.

    D. DHCP snooping prevents DNS spoofing.

4.3 Given a scenario, apply network security features, defense techniques, and solutions.

105. Which of the following are terms for an area of an enterprise network, separated by firewalls, that contains servers that must be accessible both from the Internet and from the internal network? (Choose all that apply.)

    A. Intranet

    B. Screened subnet

    C. EGP

    D. Stateless network

    E. Perimeter network

    F. DMZ

106. Which of the following terms describes a system that prevents computers from logging on to a network unless they have the latest updates and antimalware software installed?

    A. NAC

    B. LDAP

    C. RADIUS

    D. AES

107. Which of the following are typical elements of a corporate password policy? (Choose all that apply.)

    A. Minimum password length

    B. Use of special characters

    C. Unique passwords

    D. Frequent password changes

108. Alice is implementing a new password policy that requires all users to change their passwords every seven days. What further modification can she make to the password policy to prevent users from thwarting the password change requirement?

    A. Specify a minimum password length.

    B. Require the use of special characters.

    C. Require the creation of unique passwords.

    D. Specify a maximum password change interval.

109. Which of the following are settings typically included in an account lockout policy? (Choose all that apply.)

    A. Account lockout duration

    B. Time allowed between attempts

    C. Account lockout threshold

    D. Reset account lockout threshold counter

110. How do account lockouts help to prevent intruders from cracking passwords?

    A. By forcing users to select passwords of a minimum length

    B. By preventing users from entering incorrect passwords more than a specified number of times

    C. By preventing users from reusing the same passwords

    D. By requiring an additional authentication method, such as a fingerprint

111. Password policies frequently require users to specify complex passwords. Which of the following are characteristics of a complex password?

    A. Passwords that contain mixed upper- and lowercase letters, numbers, and symbols

    B. Passwords that exceed a specific length

    C. Passwords that do not duplicate a specific number of the user's previous passwords

    D. Passwords that do not duplicate the user's account name, birth date, or other personal information

112. Password policies that contain a history requirement typically have which of the following limitations?

    A. Users cannot reuse recent passwords.

    B. Users cannot create passwords containing names of relatives.

    C. Users cannot create passwords containing names of historical figures.

    D. Users cannot create passwords that duplicate those of any other users on the network.

113. Account lockout policies are designed to protect against which of the following types of attack?

    A. Social engineering

    B. Spoofing

    C. Brute-force

    D. On-path

114. Which of the following types of password policies are designed to prevent brute-force attacks? (Choose all that apply.)

    A. Password length policies

    B. Account lockout policies

    C. Password history policies

    D. Complex password policies

115. Which of the following is an implementation of network access control (NAC)?

    A. RADIUS

    B. 802.1X

    C. LDAP

    D. TACACS+

116. Which of the following is not one of the roles involved in an 802.1X transaction?

    A. Supplicant

    B. Authenticator

    C. Authorizing agent

    D. Authentication server

117. In an 802.1X transaction, what is the function of the supplicant?

    A. The supplicant is the service that issues certificates to clients attempting to connect to the network.

    B. The supplicant is the service that verifies the credentials of the client attempting to access the network.

    C. The supplicant is the network device to which the client is attempting to connect.

    D. The supplicant is the client user or computer attempting to connect to the network.

118. In an 802.1X transaction, what is the function of the authenticator?

    A. The authenticator is the service that issues certificates to clients attempting to connect to the network.

    B. The authenticator is the service that verifies the credentials of the client attempting to access the network.

    C. The authenticator is the network device to which the client is attempting to connect.

    D. The authenticator is the client user or computer attempting to connect to the network.

119. An 802.1X transaction involves three roles: the supplicant, the authenticator, and the authentication server. Of the three, which role typically takes the form of a RADIUS implementation?

    A. The supplicant

    B. The authenticator

    C. The authentication server

    D. None of the above

120. Which of the following types of servers are typically found in a screened subnet? (Choose all that apply.)

    A. Domain controllers

    B. DHCP servers

    C. Web servers

    D. Email servers

121. EAP and 802.1X are components that help to provide which of the following areas of wireless network security?

    A. Authentication

    B. Authorization

    C. Encryption

    D. Accounting

122. Which of the following can be described as wireless network hardening techniques? (Choose all that apply.)

    A. Encryption

    B. Authentication

    C. MAC filtering

    D. Social engineering

    E. Antenna placement

123. Despite having imposed password policies on his network, compelling users to change their passwords frequently, create passwords of a specific length, and use complex passwords, Ralph has had several reports of account penetrations. The victims of the incidents had all apparently shared a "tip" suggesting that users cycle through the names of their children, nephews, nieces, and other relatives when forced to create new passwords, changing letters to numbers as needed. Which of the following actions can Ralph take to remedy the situation without creating a larger problem?

    A. Distribute a list of common passwords that are insecure, such as those based on names, birth dates, etc.

    B. Modify the password policies to force users to change passwords more frequently.

    C. Assign the users long passwords consisting of random-generated characters and change them often.

    D. Change the password history policy to a value greater than the number of children in any user's family.

124. Which of the following devices are likely to have default credentials configured into them that attackers might know? (Choose all that apply.)

    A. Wireless access points

    B. Windows servers

    C. Switches

    D. Routers

125. One of the basic principles of network device hardening is to use secure protocols. Which of the following suggestions comply with this principle? (Choose all that apply.)

    A. Use SSH instead of Telnet.

    B. Use WEP instead of WPA2.

    C. Use TKIP instead of AES.

    D. Use HTTPS instead of HTTP.

126. On which of the following types of devices should you consider disabling unused ports as a security precaution? (Choose all that apply.)

    A. Hubs

    B. Servers

    C. Switches

    D. Wireless access points

127. For which of the following reasons is disabling the SSID broadcast of a wireless network to prevent unauthorized access a relatively weak method of device hardening?

    A. Attackers have ways of connecting to the network without the SSID.

    B. Attackers can capture packets transmitted over the network and read the SSID from them.

    C. Every access point's SSID is printed on a label on the back of the device.

    D. Attackers have software that can easily guess a network's SSID.

128. Which of the following cannot be considered to be a server hardening policy?

    A. Disabling unnecessary services

    B. Leaving the default TCP and UDP ports open

    C. Upgrading firmware

    D. Creating privileged user accounts

129. Which of the following are valid reasons not to disable unused switch ports? (Choose all that apply.)

    A. The datacenter is secured from unauthorized access.

    B. The unused ports are not patched in to wall jacks.

    C. The unused ports are left open to facilitate the on-boarding of new users.

    D. The switch is configured to use a MAC-based access control list.

130. Which of the following Windows password policies includes a provision to prevent users from specifying common passwords?

    A. Maximum password age

    B. Enforce password history

    C. Minimum password length

    D. Passwords must meet complexity requirements

131. Which of the following is not a method for hardening a wireless access point?

    A. Upgrading firmware

    B. Changing default credentials

    C. Generating new pre-shared keys

    D. Deauthentication

132. Creating a policy instructing users to avoid passwords that use commonly shared information, such as birth dates and the names of children and pets, is an example of which of the following?

    A. Mitigation techniques

    B. Multifactor authentication

    C. Network hardening

    D. Access control

133. Which of the following are the default administrative user accounts found in Windows and Linux operating systems? (Select two.)

    A. Administrator

    B. root

    C. admin

    D. Control

134. Which of the following are network segmentation methods that can prevent intruders from gaining full access to a network? (Choose all that apply.)

  A. ACL

  B. VLAN

  C. NAC

  D. Screened subnet

135. Which of the following types of mitigation techniques is not applicable to servers?

  A. Role separation

  B. Applying ACLs

  C. File integrity monitoring

  D. DHCP snooping

136. Which of the following services are provided by access control lists (ACLs)?

  A. Authentication

  B. Authorization

  C. Accounting

  D. Auditing

137. Which of the following terms describes the threat mitigation technique of deploying individual applications and services on virtual servers so that no more than one is endangered at any one time, rather than deploying multiple applications on a single server?

  A. Geofencing

  B. Network segmentation

  C. Role separation

  D. VLAN hopping

138. Role separation is a threat mitigation technique that is applied to which of the following types of network components?

  A. Switches

  B. Servers

  C. Routers

  D. Wireless access points

139. Dynamic ARP inspection (DAI) is a feature in some network switches that prevents on-path (man in the middle) attacks facilitated by ARP poisoning, the deliberate insertion of fraudulent information into the ARP cache. A switch with DAI inspects incoming ARP packets and rejects those that contain incorrect pairs of IP and MAC addresses. Which of the following is the means by which the switch compiles a table of the correct ARP information for comparison with the incoming packets?

  A. DHCP snooping

  B. Secure SNMP

  C. DNS name resolution

  D. Neighbor Discovery Protocol (NDP)

140. At which layer of the OSI reference model does DHCP snooping operate?

   A.   Physical

   B.   Data link

   C.   Network

   D.   Transport

   E.   Application

141. Which of the following types of attacks on a network switch can a flood guard help to prevent?

   A.   DNS poisoning

   B.   War driving

   C.   MAC flooding

   D.   Evil twin

142. Which of the following protocols is a root guard designed to affect?

   A.   EAP

   B.   STP

   C.   LDAP

   D.   ARP

143. How does MAC address filtering increase the security of a wireless LAN?

   A.   By preventing access points from broadcasting their presence

   B.   By allowing traffic sent to or from specific MAC addresses through the Internet firewall

   C.   By substituting registered MAC addresses for unregistered ones in network packets

   D.   By permitting only devices with specified MAC addresses to connect to an access point

   E.   By isolating specific wireless clients from the rest of the network

144. MAC filtering is an access control method used by which of the following types of hardware devices?

   A.   Wireless access points

   B.   RADIUS servers

   C.   Domain controllers

   D.   Smartcards

145. Which of the following technologies utilize access control lists to limit access to network resources? (Choose all that apply.)

   A.   NTFS

   B.   LDAP

   C.   WAP

   D.   Kerberos

146. Which of the following is another term for a switching technique called port isolation?

   A. Frame Relay

   B. Private VLAN

   C. Site-to-site VPN

   D. Screened subnet

147. Which of the following statements accurately describe the difference between content filtering and URL filtering? (Choose all that apply.)

   A. URL filtering controls outbound traffic, while content filtering controls inbound traffic.

   B. Content filtering requires access to an outside database of objectionable sites, while URL filtering does not.

   C. URL filtering can provide protection against phishing attempts and other types of malware; content filtering cannot.

   D. Content filtering typically requires administrators to filter web content, email traffic, and executable files.

Chapter

5

Network Troubleshooting

✓ **5.1 Explain the troubleshooting methodology.**

- Identify the problem
    - Gather information
    - Question users
    - Identify symptoms
    - Determine if anything has changed
    - Duplicate the problem, if possible
    - Approach multiple problems individually
- Establish a theory of probable cause
    - Question the obvious
    - Consider multiple approaches
        - Top-to-bottom/bottom-to-top OSI model
        - Divide and conquer
- Test the theory to determine the cause
    - If the theory is confirmed, determine the next steps to resolve the problem
    - If the theory is not confirmed, establish a new theory or escalate
- Establish a plan of action to resolve the problem and identify potential effects
- Implement the solution or escalate as necessary
- Verify full system functionality and implement preventive measures, if applicable
- Document findings, actions, outcomes, and lessons learned throughout the process

✓ **5.2 Given a scenario, troubleshoot common cabling and physical interface issues.**

- Cable issues
  - Incorrect cable
    - Single mode vs. multimode
    - Category 5/6/7/8
    - Shielded twisted pair (STP) vs. unshielded twisted pair (UTP)
  - Signal degradation
    - Crosstalk
    - Interference
    - Attenuation
  - Improper termination
  - Transmitter (TX)/Receiver (RX) transposed
- Interface issues
  - Increasing interface counters
    - Cyclic redundancy check (CRC)
    - Runts
    - Giants
    - Drops
  - Port status
    - Error disabled
    - Administratively down
    - Suspended
- Hardware issues
  - Power over Ethernet (PoE)
    - Power budget exceeded
    - Incorrect standard
  - Transceivers
    - Mismatch
    - Signal strength

✓ **5.3 Given a scenario, troubleshoot common issues with network services.**

- Switching issues
  - STP
    - Network loops
    - Root bridge selection
    - Port roles
    - Port states
  - Incorrect VLAN assignment
  - ACLs
- Route selection
  - Routing table
  - Default routes
- Address pool exhaustion
- Incorrect default gateway
- Incorrect IP address
  - Duplicate IP address
- Incorrect subnet mask

✓ **5.4 Given a scenario, troubleshoot common performance issues.**

- Congestion/contention
- Bottlenecking
- Bandwidth
  - Throughput capacity
- Latency
- Packet loss
- Jitter
- Wireless
  - Interference
    - Channel overlap
  - Signal degradation or loss
  - Insufficient wireless coverage

- Client disassociation issues
- Roaming misconfiguration

✓ **5.5 Given a scenario, use the appropriate tool or protocol to solve networking issues.**

- Software tools
  - Protocol analyzer
  - Command line
    - ping
    - traceroute/tracert
    - nslookup
    - tcpdump
    - dig
    - netstat
    - ip/ifconfig/ipconfig
    - arp
  - Nmap
  - Link Layer Discovery Protocol (LLDP)/ Cisco Discovery Protocol (CDP)
  - Speed tester
- Hardware tools
  - Toner
  - Cable tester
  - Taps
  - Wi-Fi analyzer
  - Visual fault locator
- Basic networking device commands
  - show mac-address-table
  - show route
  - show interface
  - show config
  - show arp
  - show vlan
  - show power

5.1 Explain the troubleshooting methodology.

1. Which of the following troubleshooting steps involves prioritizing trouble tickets based on the severity of the problem?
    A. Identify symptoms of the problem.
    B. Establish a theory of probable cause.
    C. Test the theory to determine the cause.
    D. Establish a plan of action to resolve the problem and identify potential effects.
    E. Implement the solution or escalate as necessary.
    F. Verify full system functionality and implement preventive measures, if applicable.
    G. Document findings, actions, outcomes, and lessons learned throughout the process.

2. Which of the following is considered a systemwide error?
    A. A problem with an order entry or customer service call center resource
    B. A problem with a router that affects only one local area network (LAN)
    C. A fatal error that causes a single computer to fail
    D. A problem with an email server that affects all network users

3. Which of the following is a networkwide problem?
    A. A problem with an order entry or customer service call center resource
    B. A fatal error that causes a single computer to fail
    C. A problem with an application server that affects a single local area network (LAN)
    D. A problem with a router that connects an entire network to the Internet

4. A user reports that she cannot connect to a server on her network. Ed wants to identify the scope of the problem, so he tries to reproduce the problem on the user's computer. The problem still remains. No other users are reporting this problem. What is the next logical step that Ed should perform to identify the affected area?
    A. Verify that the local router is forwarding traffic.
    B. Try performing the same task on another computer attached to the same segment.
    C. Verify that the server is configured properly.
    D. Verify that the switch the client is connected to is functioning.

5. Which of the following troubleshooting steps involves asking the user preliminary questions such as, "What were you doing when the problem occurred?"
    A. Identify the problem.
    B. Establish a theory of probable cause.
    C. Test the theory to determine the cause.

    D. Establish a plan of action to resolve the problem and identify potential effects.

    E. Implement the solution or escalate as necessary.

    F. Verify full system functionality and implement preventative measures, if applicable.

    G. Document findings, actions, and outcomes.

6. When troubleshooting, you begin by taking steps to identify the problem. Which of the following steps should you perform next?

    A. Implement the solution.

    B. Establish a plan of action.

    C. Establish a theory of probable cause.

    D. Verify full system functionality.

7. In which troubleshooting step do you try to duplicate a network problem to logically and methodically eliminate elements that are not the source of the problem?

    A. Identify the problem.

    B. Establish a theory of probable cause.

    C. Test the theory to determine the cause.

    D. Establish a plan of action to resolve the problem and identify potential effects.

    E. Implement the solution or escalate as necessary.

    F. Verify full system functionality and implement preventative measures, if applicable.

    G. Document findings, actions, and outcomes.

8. Ralph is a first-tier technician working the help desk. After identifying a network problem submitted by multiple users, Ralph comes up with a theory specifying a possible source of the problem and sets about testing his theory. Unfortunately, testing indicates that Ralph's theory is wrong; the source he suspected is not the cause of the problem. Which of the following should not be the next step in Ralph's troubleshooting process?

    A. Reinterview the users to gather more information about the problem.

    B. Escalate the problem to a second-tier technician.

    C. Repeat the process of establishing a theory of probable cause.

    D. Begin replacing components that might contribute to the problem.

9. Ralph is a first-tier technician working the help desk. A user calls in, saying that when she turned her computer on that morning, nothing appeared on the screen. Which of the following should be Ralph's first question to the user?

    A. What is your computer's IP address?

    B. Have you applied the latest system updates?

    C. Are the computer and monitor plugged in to AC power?

    D. Has anyone else been using your computer?

10. You have a problem with a server or other network component that prevents many users from working. What type of problem is this?

  A. A networkwide problem

  B. A shared resource problem

  C. A systemwide problem

  D. A user application problem

11. A single Windows user suddenly cannot connect to any hosts on the network (local or remote). Alice interviews the user and finds out that he made some changes to his computer's Internet Protocol (IP) configuration properties. What should she do next?

  A. Run the `ipconfig` command to view the local configuration.

  B. Check the Domain Name System (DNS) server to see if it is resolving IP hostnames.

  C. Check the DHCP server for the local network to see if it is assigning IP addresses.

  D. Verify that the router is functioning.

12. Alice has a network with a Domain Name System (DNS) server, a proxy server, and an Internet router. A user is complaining that she suddenly cannot connect to hosts on her own local area network (LAN) and other internal LANs, and she cannot access hosts on the Internet. What is the most likely problem?

  A. The user's local configuration

  B. The proxy server

  C. The DNS server

  D. The router

13. Alice takes a call from a user who is unable to send email to a colleague in one of the company's branch offices. Alice begins by having the user try to send emails to different people at the branch office, to people in the local office, and to people on the Internet. She then checks the user's IP configuration settings, the computer's local LAN communication, and the cable connection to the network. Which of the following approaches is Alice using to troubleshoot the problem?

  A. OSI bottom-to-top

  B. Divide and conquer

  C. OSI top-to-bottom

  D. Question the obvious

14. Alice is working the help desk when a user calls and reports that she is unable to connect to the Internet. Which of the following steps is the one Alice is least likely to perform first when troubleshooting the problem?

  A. Check the configuration of the router connecting the LAN to the Internet.

  B. Ask the user if she can access resources on the local network.

  C. Check to see if anyone else is experiencing the same problem.

  D. Check the user's job title to see if she is an important person in the company.

15. In the standard troubleshooting methodology, which of the following steps appears last but must actually be practiced throughout the troubleshooting process?

   A. Test the theory to determine the cause.

   B. Document findings, actions, outcomes, and lessons learned throughout the process.

   C. Verify full system functionality and implement preventive measures, if applicable.

   D. Implement the solution or escalate as necessary.

   E. Establish a plan of action to resolve the problem and identify potential effects.

   F. Establish a theory of probable cause.

   G. Identify the problem.

16. Which step of the troubleshooting model involves identifying whether hardware or software has been recently installed or reconfigured?

   A. Identify the problem.

   B. Establish a theory of probable cause.

   C. Establish a plan of action to resolve the problem and identify potential effects.

   D. Test the theory to determine the cause.

   E. Document findings, actions, outcomes, and lessons learned throughout the process.

17. Which step of the troubleshooting model involves replacing components until a faulty hardware device is identified?

   A. Duplicate the problem, if possible.

   B. Gather information.

   C. Test the theory to determine the cause.

   D. Establish a plan of action to resolve the problem and identify potential effects.

   E. Verify full system functionality and implement preventive measures, if applicable.

   F. Document findings, actions, outcomes, and lessons learned throughout the process.

18. Which of the following are not general troubleshooting steps? (Choose all that apply.)

   A. Identify the problem.

   B. Establish a theory of probable cause.

   C. Test the theory to determine the cause.

   D. Verify that the client's Internet Protocol (IP) configuration is correct.

   E. Establish a plan of action to resolve the problem and identify potential effects.

   F. Verify that the router is forwarding.

   G. Implement the solution or escalate as necessary.

   H. Verify full system functionality and implement preventive measures, if applicable.

   I. Document findings, actions, and outcomes, and lessons learned throughout the process.

19. Which of the following are reasons for documenting a network problem or incident? (Choose all that apply.)

   A. Documentation makes it easier to escalate calls to senior technicians.

   B. Documentation makes it easier to prioritize administrative tasks.

   C. Documentation makes it easier to prioritize each help call.

   D. Documentation makes it easier to escalate calls to first-tier technicians.

20. Which of the following statements about prioritizing help calls are true? (Choose all that apply.)

   A. Individual desktop problems take precedence over problems with shared resources.

   B. Problems with shared resources take precedence over individual desktop problems.

   C. Departmental problems take precedence over networkwide problems.

   D. Networkwide problems take precedence over departmental problems.

21. Which of the following statements about multitiered technical support organizations are true? (Choose all that apply.)

   A. Help calls are typically escalated to second-tier technicians when they involve mission-critical network components such as routers.

   B. First-tier technicians generally handle desktop problems.

   C. Second-tier technicians are generally less experienced than first-tier technicians.

   D. First-tier technicians are generally less experienced than second-tier technicians.

22. Ed is a first-tier support technician. He receives the help calls listed here. His job is to assign them priorities based on their severity. Which of the following should be the problem that receives the highest priority?

   A. A problem with an order entry or customer service call center resource that affects an entire department, with multiple local area networks (LANs)

   B. A fatal error that causes a single computer to fail

   C. A problem with a mission-critical backbone router that affects an entire network

   D. A problem with an application server that affects a single LAN

23. Ed is a first-tier support technician. He receives the help calls listed here. His job is to assign them priorities based on their severity. Which of the following should be the problem that receives the lowest priority?

   A. A problem with an order entry or customer service call center resource that affects an entire department, with multiple local area networks (LANs)

   B. A fatal error that causes a single computer to fail

   C. A problem with a mission-critical backbone router that affects an entire network

   D. A problem with an application server that affects a single LAN

24. When you troubleshoot a network problem, it is possible to introduce another problem while attempting to fix the original one. In which step of the troubleshooting process should you be aware of the residual effects that changes might have on the network?

    A. Identify the problem.

    B. Establish a theory of probable cause.

    C. Test the theory to determine the cause.

    D. Establish a plan of action to resolve the problem and identify potential effects.

    E. Implement the solution or escalate as necessary.

    F. Verify full system functionality an implement preventive measures, if applicable.

    G. Document findings, actions, outcomes, and lessons learned throughout the process.

25. In which troubleshooting step do you create a record of your activities and inform the user of what happened and why?

    A. Identify the problem.

    B. Establish a theory of probable cause.

    C. Test the theory to determine the cause.

    D. Establish a plan of action to resolve the problem and identify potential effects.

    E. Implement the solution or escalate as necessary.

    F. Verify full system functionality and implement preventive measures, if applicable.

    G. Document findings, actions, outcomes, and lessons learned throughout the process.

26. On Monday morning, Alice arrives at work to find multiple messages from users who are unable to access the accounting department's file server. Which of the following are the best questions for Alice to ask during the beginning stage of the networking troubleshooting process? (Choose two.)

    A. What has changed since the users were last able to access the server?

    B. Are there any software updates that Alice should apply to the server?

    C. Has the server suffered a hard disk failure?

    D. Which users are reporting a problem and where are they located?

27. A user calls Alice at the help desk to report that her mouse has stopped working, she cannot access the Internet, and all of her email has disappeared from her inbox. Which of the following would be the best course of action for Alice to take?

    A. Create a separate trouble ticket for each problem.

    B. Escalate the call to a senior technician.

    C. Have the caller's computer replaced with a new one.

    D. Send a technician to the user's site to address all of the problems.

28. Alice receives a call in which a user reports that he is unable to send print jobs to the network-attached workgroup printer near his desk. Which of the following tasks should Alice perform first?

A. Reinstall the printer driver on the user's workstation.

B. Test network connectivity to the printer using the `ping` utility.

C. Examine the switches to which the user's workstation and the printer are connected.

D. Check to see if there are printer firmware upgrades available.

29. The entire network at Adatum Corp. is unable to access the Internet. All of the users throughout the network are complaining that their browsers are displaying DNS failure messages. The company does not have an in-house network administrator, so they call Ralph at his consulting firm. Which of the following should be the first question that Ralph asks in his attempt to pinpoint the location of the malfunction?

A. What browser are the users running?

B. Where is the DNS server located?

C. What technology is used to provide access to the Internet?

D. What sites are the users attempting to access?

30. You are the first responder to an incident of computer crime at your company. The datacenter's security has been penetrated, a server accessed, and sensitive company data stolen. The company's incident response plan lists the specific tasks that you are responsible for performing. Which of the following are likely to be among those tasks? (Choose all that apply.)

A. Turn off the server.

B. Secure the area.

C. Document the scene.

D. Collect evidence.

E. Cooperate with the authorities.

5.2 Given a scenario, troubleshoot common cabling and physical interface issues.

31. Which of the following types of unshielded twisted-pair wiring faults cannot be detected by a toner and probe?

A. Split pairs

B. Open circuits

C. Short circuits

D. Transposed wires

32. After connecting a toner or tone generator to the green wire at one end of a twisted-pair cable run, Ralph proceeds to the other end of the cable and touches the probe (or locator) to each of the eight pins in turn. The green wire and the green striped wire both produce a tone. What type of wiring fault has Ralph discovered?

    A. Split pair

    B. Far-end crosstalk

    C. Transposed wires

    D. Short circuit

    E. Delay skew

33. Which of the following types of cables is used to connect a terminal to the console port of a router or switch?

    A. Rollover

    B. Straight-through

    C. Crossover

    D. Plenum

    E. Shielded

    F. Tap

34. Which of the following types of patch cables is used to connect a computer to a wall plate?

    A. Straight-through

    B. Crossover

    C. Rollover

    D. Plenum

35. A routine test of a newly installed twisted-pair cable run indicates that there is a short circuit on one of the wires. Which of the following procedures might possibly correct the fault?

    A. Use a different pinout on both ends of the cable.

    B. Replace the connectors at both ends of the cable run.

    C. Move the cable away from any potential sources of electromagnetic interference.

    D. Use a higher grade of UTP cable.

36. Which of the following troubleshooting tools is not used to test copper cabling installations?

    A. Cable tester

    B. Multimeter

    C. Toner and probe

    D. Optical power meter

37. Which of the following devices is not one of the tools generally used by a data networking cable installer?

A. Toner and probe

B. Cable tester

C. Butt set

D. Cable certifier

38. Ralph is a new hire for a consulting firm that frequently performs cable installations. He is trying to learn more about the tools needed to install internal cable runs. To that end, which of the following statements about cable crimpers has Ralph found to be true?

A. Cable installers use a crimper to attach keystone connectors to lengths of bulk cable.

B. Cable installers use a crimper to attach RJ-45 connectors to lengths of bulk cable.

C. You need to purchase a separate crimper for each type of cable to which you want to attach connectors.

D. Making your own patch cables by applying connectors yourself is always more economical than buying prefabricated patch cables.

39. Which of the following cable faults increases a twisted-pair cable's susceptibility to crosstalk?

A. Open

B. Short

C. Split pair

D. Transposed pairs

40. Alice's company has moved to a building that was prewired for twisted-pair Ethernet. However, since installing the company's Gigabit Ethernet equipment using the existing cable runs, performance has been poor. After performing some packet captures and analyzing the traffic samples, Alice discovers that there are a great many Ethernet frames being retransmitted. Next, she examines the cable runs in the drop ceilings. They do not appear to be overly long, and they do not appear to run near any major sources of electromagnetic interference. Which of the following could be the problem?

A. Some of the cable runs are using T568A pinouts, and some are using T568B.

B. The cables only have two wire pairs connected, instead of four.

C. The existing cable is not rated for use with Gigabit Ethernet.

D. There are mismatched transceivers at the cable ends with different signal strengths.

41. Ed is experiencing poor network performance on some new twisted-pair cable runs. After ruling out all other causes, he tests the cables with a toner and probe and finds no faults. Finally, he examines the cable connectors more closely and finds that, while the pins at one end of the cable are correctly connected to their corresponding pins at the other end, in some cases there are two solid color wires twisted together in a pair. Which of the following types of faults has Ed discovered?

A. Open circuit

B. Short circuit

C. Split pairs

D. Transposed wires

42. Which of the following terms describes the progressive weakening of transmitted signals as they travel along a network medium?

- **A.** Absorption
- **B.** Latency
- **C.** Attenuation
- **D.** Crosstalk

43. After experiencing some problems with devices connected to the company's fiber-optic network, Alice brings in a contractor to test the fiber-optic cable runs. The contractor detects a significant amount of decibel (dB) loss in some of the cable runs, which could be the source of the problems. Which of the following are possible causes of the decibel loss? (Choose all that apply.)

- **A.** Electromagnetic interference
- **B.** Dirty optical cables
- **C.** Excessive cable length
- **D.** Signal crosstalk

44. Which of the following should a troubleshooter look for when a duplex mismatch is suspected on an Ethernet network? (Choose all that apply.)

- **A.** Collisions
- **B.** Runt frames
- **C.** CRC errors
- **D.** Failed ping tests

45. Ed is trying to troubleshoot a problem that has caused a wired network connection to fail completely. Which of the following wired network problems will cause a complete failure of a network connection? (Choose all that apply.)

- **A.** Bottleneck
- **B.** Speed mismatch
- **C.** Duplex mismatch
- **D.** Transmitter (TX)/receiver (RX) transposed
- **E.** Error disabled port

46. Ed has discovered that some of the twisted-pair cable runs on his newly installed Ethernet network are well over 100 meters long. Which of the following problems is his network likely to experience due to cable segments that are greater than the specified length?

- **A.** Jitter
- **B.** Attenuation
- **C.** Crosstalk
- **D.** EMI

47. Ed is trying to troubleshoot a problem with his wired network, and his research has led him to a list of possible network faults. The list is rather old, however, and Ed is wondering if some of the problems are relevant. Which of the following wired network problems no longer occur with modern Gigabit Ethernet switches and network adapters in their default configurations? (Choose all that apply.)

A. Bottleneck

B. Speed mismatch

C. Duplex mismatch

D. Transmitter (TX)/receiver (RX) transposed

48. Ed has discovered that some of the twisted-pair cables on his newly installed network are running right alongside fluorescent light fixtures in the drop ceiling. Which of the following problems is the network likely to experience due to the cables' proximity to the fixtures?

A. Jitter

B. Attenuation

C. Crosstalk

D. EMI

49. Which of the following indicators can you use to determine whether an adapter is connected to a functioning hub or switch?

A. Speed light-emitting diode (LED)

B. Collision LED

C. Link pulse LED

D. Status LED

50. Ralph wants to use Power over Ethernet (PoE) to supply power to security cameras located throughout the company's datacenter. The Ethernet network is currently running at Gigabit Ethernet speed, but Ralph is planning to downgrade the camera connections to 100Base-TX because that standard has two wire pairs free for the transmission of power. Which of the following statements about Ralph's plan is true?

A. Ralph's planning is correct; only 10Base-T and 100Base-TX support PoE.

B. Ralph's plan will not work because 100Base-TX is not compatible with PoE.

C. Ralph's plan will work, but it is not necessary to downgrade the connections to 100Base-TX.

D. Ralph's plan will not work because security cameras would exceed the PoE power budget.

51. Ed is inspecting the cable runs recently installed for some new Gigabit Ethernet systems on his company's network. Looking at the patch panel connections, he notices that they are wired using the T568B pinout standard. However, when he examines the wall plate connections, he sees that they are wired using the T568A standard. What is the best way for Ed to resolve the problem?

   A. Call the contractor and have all of the wall plate connectors rewired using the T568B standard.

   B. Purchase crossover patch cables for all of the connections between the patch panel and the switches.

   C. Configure the switches to not use a crossover circuit for all of the ports connected to the patch panel.

   D. Do nothing. The cable runs will function properly as is.

52. Ralph has two computers that he long ago networked together by plugging one end of an Ethernet cable into each machine. He recently bought an old Ethernet switch at a garage sale and wants to use it to expand his network. The switch has four numbered ports and a fifth port marked with an X. Ralph plugs one computer into port 1 using his existing cable and buys a new cable to plug the other computer into port 4. The two computers cannot communicate, however. Which of the following solutions will not enable his computers to communicate?

   A. Move the port 4 cable to port 2.

   B. Replace the old cable with a second new one.

   C. Plug the computer with the old cable into the X port.

   D. Plug the computer with the new cable into the X port.

53. Ralph is responsible for the network installation in a new building purchased by his company, and he has elected to have Category 6 unshielded twisted-pair cable installed. The company president has asked him if it is possible to run their Gigabit Ethernet network using two of the wire pairs in the cable, while using the other two pairs for telephone connections. Ralph is not sure, so he sets up a lab network using cables with only two pairs connected. When he plugs computers into the switch and turns them on, the LEDs labeled 1000 light up, indicating that a Gigabit Ethernet connection has been established. Ralph gets excited at the thought of how much money he might save the company by using the same cable for both telephone and data. However, while the LED is lit, he cannot seem to connect to another system over his test network. Which of the following describes what he must do to correct the problem?

   A. Ralph must manually configure the network adapters to use Gigabit Ethernet, rather than let them autonegotiate.

   B. Ralph is using the wrong two wire pairs for the Gigabit Ethernet connection. He must rewire the connectors.

   C. Ralph is using the wrong pinout standard on his lab network. He must use T568A.

   D. Ralph must use all four wire pairs for a Gigabit Ethernet connection.

54. Ralph recently bought an old Ethernet switch and some twisted-pair cables at a garage sale and wants to use them to build a home network. He plugs two computers into the switch using the cables but finds that the computers are unable to communicate. Then he notices that one of the ports in the switch is labeled with an X. He tries plugging one of the computers into the X port, and now they can communicate. Which of the following statements is the most likely explanation for this behavior?

A. The switch has a bad port.

B. One of the cables is a crossover cable.

C. Both of the cables are crossover cables.

D. The X port provides extra strength to the signals.

55. Alice is a consultant who has been hired to move a client's old 20-node coaxial Ethernet network to a new location. She disassembles all of the network cabling and other components and packs them for shipping. At the new site, she sets up all of the computers, plugs a T-connector into each network adapter, and connects the cables, running them from one computer to the next to form the bus. When Alice is finished, she starts the computers and tests their network connectivity. She finds that 12 consecutive computers can communicate with each other, and the other 8 can communicate with each other, but the 12 cannot communicate with the 8. She makes sure that all of the connectors are securely tightened, especially the ones on the 12th computer, but the problem persists. Which of the following is the most likely cause of the difficulty?

A. Alice has forgotten to terminate the computers at each end of the bus.

B. One of the connectors on the 12th computer has a bent pin.

C. Alice has forgotten to ground the network.

D. The transmit and receive pins are reversed on the 12th computer.

56. Ed is troubleshooting some network performance problems. After exhausting many other possibilities, he is examining the twisted-pair cable runs in the office's drop ceiling. He finds that some cables have been damaged, apparently by electricians working in that space. In some cases, the cable sheath has been split along its length, and some of the insulation on the wires inside has been scraped off as well. Which of the following types of faults might be caused by this damage? (Choose all that apply.)

A. Open circuits

B. Short circuits

C. Split pairs

D. Transposed wires

57. Which of the following types of interference on a twisted-pair network are designed to be prevented by the twists in the wire pairs inside the cable?

A. Crosstalk

B. EMI

C. Attenuation

D. Latency

58. Ralph has been asked to create some new twisted-pair patch cables that will be used to connect patch panel ports to the network switches. He has been told that the patch panel connectors are all wired using the T568A pinout standard. Which of the following instructions should Ralph use when creating the patch cables?

- **A.** Use T568A at both ends.
- **B.** Use T567B at both ends.
- **C.** Use T568A at one end and T568B at the other end.
- **D.** Use either standard, as long as both ends are the same.

59. Ed has discovered that, on some of his newly installed twisted-pair cable runs, the installer has stripped away nearly a foot of the cable sheath at each end and has untwisted the wire pairs before attaching them to the connectors. Which of the following problems is the network more likely to experience due to the untwisted wires?

- **A.** Jitter
- **B.** Attenuation
- **C.** Crosstalk
- **D.** EMI

60. Ed is the administrator of his small company's network. A user calls the help desk and reports that she cannot connect to the network. She has never had any problems connecting before now, and she says that nothing on her computer has changed. Ed goes to the user's location to investigate and notices that the link pulse light-emitting diode (LED) on the switch port for the user's computer is not lit. What should Ed do next to isolate and fix the problem? (Choose all that apply.)

- **A.** Verify that the cable is securely connected to the switch.
- **B.** Verify the patch cable is pinned and paired properly.
- **C.** Replace the existing patch cable with a straight-through cable that is known to be good.
- **D.** Replace the existing patch cable with a crossover cable that is known to be good.

61. Ed is examining some twisted-pair cable runs that were recently installed in his office by an outside contractor. Looking at the connectors, he sees a variety of pinout combinations. Which of the following pinouts must Ed have rewired because they are incorrect? (Choose all that apply.)

- **A.** White/orange, orange, white/green, blue, white/blue, green, white/brown, brown
- **B.** White/green, green, white/orange, blue, white/blue, orange, white/brown, brown
- **C.** White/orange, orange, white/green, green, white/blue, blue, white/brown, brown
- **D.** White/brown, white/green, white/orange, blue, white/blue, orange, green, brown

62. To save the company money and to provide some new hires with Gigabit Ethernet connectivity, Ralph has installed some new Category 5e cable runs, connecting his company's datacenter with a newly rented office at the far end of the building. However, the new users are complaining of intermittent connectivity problems. The company brings in a cabling contractor to investigate, and his diagnosis is attenuation. Which of the following will most likely be a sure solution to the problem?

A. Repull the runs using Category 6 cable.

B. Shorten the cable runs.

C. Configure the hardware to run at a slower speed.

D. Install high-end network adapters in the workstations.

63. Alice's network has been experiencing intermittent service slowdowns and outages ever since the company moved into their new building. She has tried every troubleshooting procedure she can think of and has not been able to determine the cause. One particular user, hoping to be the squeaky wheel that gets the grease, has taken to calling Alice every time he experiences a problem. One day, as she is working in the datacenter, Alice notices that the user calls her every time she hears an additional humming noise begin. After examining the doors in the hallway, Alice realizes that the racks containing her switches are located right next to the building's elevator machinery room. Which of the following conditions is probably causing the network communication problem?

A. EMI

B. NEXT

C. FEXT

D. Attenuation

64. Ralph is setting up a workstation for the company's new vice president. He has installed the computer in the VP's office and plugged the data cable into the wall plate. Then, back in the datacenter, he uses a patch cable to connect the corresponding port in the patch panel to a port in the network switch. However, the computer is unable to access the network. There are no complaints from other users. Which of the following could be the sources of the problem? (Choose all that apply.)

A. The DNS server is malfunctioning.

B. The switch port is administratively down.

C. The NAT server is not functioning.

D. The switch is configured to use port security.

65. Ralph is setting up a network connection for a new vice president, who is supplying his own laptop under the company's bring your own device (BYOD) policy. He plugs the computer into the wall plate, and the link pulse LED lights up. Then, back in the datacenter, he uses a patch cable to connect the corresponding port in the patch panel to a port in the network switch. Later, the VP calls Ralph to report that data transfers between his laptop and the network servers are extremely slow. Which of the following could explain the problem?

A. There is a duplex mismatch between the laptop and the network switch.

B. Ralph used a crossover cable to connect the laptop to the wall plate.

C. The switch port is disabled.

D. The network adapter drivers on the laptop are outdated.

66. Ralph recently bought an older 100Base-T Fast Ethernet switch at a garage sale and wants to use it to connect his various computers into a home network. He plugs three computers into the switch and finds that although two of his older computers can communicate with each other, his newest computer cannot connect to the network. Which of the following tasks will most likely resolve the problem?

   A. Configure the switch to run at 100 Mbps.

   B. Configure the switch to run at 1 Gbps.

   C. Configure the computer's network adapter to autonegotiate.

   D. Configure the computer's network adapter to run at 100 Mbps.

67. Ralph has installed a new Category 5e cable run himself. He has attached keystone connectors to both ends of the cable, mounted the office-side connector to a wall plate, and mounted the datacenter connector into a patch panel. Then he took a patch cord and connected the patch panel port to an open port in one of the network switches. However, the LED on the switch port does not light. What should Ralph do?

   A. Repull the cable run using Category 6 cable.

   B. Check the cable run for wiring faults.

   C. Make sure the switch port is not disabled.

   D. Plug a computer into the wall plate.

68. A user calls Ed at the help desk to report that his computer is displaying a Duplicate IP Address error message. This puzzles Ed because all of the network workstations should be configured to obtain their IP addresses from DHCP servers. Ed asks the user if he has changed the TCP/IP configuration settings on the computer recently. The user says no. Ed then asks if anybody else uses the workstation. The user says no. However, when Ed runs the `ipconfig /all` command on the user's workstation, he sees that the DHCP Enabled setting reads No. What should Ed do next?

   A. Accuse the user of changing the TCP/IP settings and then lying about it.

   B. Activate the DHCP client on the workstation and close the trouble ticket.

   C. Begin an investigation into the possibility of a rogue DHCP server on the network.

   D. Change the IP address on the workstation to one that is not already in use.

69. Alice is having trouble with a new fiber-optic cable run that has just been installed between two buildings on her company's campus. To confirm that there is a problem with the cables, Alice consults the wiring diagram provided by the cable installer and begins to calculate the optical power loss resulting from cable installation factors such as the type of cable used, the attenuation resulting from the length of the cable runs, and the number and type of splices. Which of the following terms describes the calculations that Alice is performing?

   A. Protocol analysis

   B. Routing loop

   C. Optical link budget

   D. Received signal strength indication

70. Which of the following Power over Ethernet (PoE) specifications supplies power to devices using the spare wire pair on a 10Base-T or 100Base-TX twisted-pair network?

 A. Alternative A

 B. Alternative B

 C. 4PPoE

 D. All of the above

71. Which of the following network interface occurrences are considered to be malfunctions on a full-duplex Ethernet network? (Choose all that apply.)

 A. Runts

 B. Drops

 C. Giants

 D. Collisions

 E. Late collisions

72. Which of the following is the most likely cause of runt and giant frames on an Ethernet network interface?

 A. A network adapter malfunction

 B. A router malfunction

 C. Half-duplex communication

 D. Excessive cable length

73. Which of the following is the most likely cause of cyclic redundancy check (CRC) errors on an Ethernet network interface?

 A. Half-duplex communication

 B. A network adapter malfunction

 C. Electromagnetic interference

 D. Excessive cable length

74. Which of the following is not a type of error typically found in network interface statistics?

 A. Runt

 B. Encapsulation

 C. Giant

 D. CRC

 E. Jumbo

75. At what point in the installation process should patch panel ports and wall plates be labeled?

 A. When the patch panels and wall plates are installed

 B. When a length of cable is cut from the spool

 C. When the cables are attached to the connectors

 D. When the cable runs are tested, immediately after their installation

76. Alice has been hired by a corporation to design the cabling for their network. The corporation just moved into two different floors of an older building: a retail space on the ground floor and an office space on the 43rd floor. The building has existing Category 5e (CAT 5e) unshielded twisted-pair (UTP) cable. Alice's client wants two separate local area networks (LANs), one on each of the two floors, with a backbone network connecting them. They want a 1 gigabit-per-second (Gbps) data rate for each LAN but plan on migrating to 10 Gbps in the future. The two networks are approximately 200 meters apart. Which of the following solutions best meets the client's needs?

   A. Install Category 6 (CAT 6) or Category 6a (CAT 6a) UTP cable for the LANs. These cables run at 1 Gbps and provide a migration path to 10 Gbps. Use twisted-pair cable for the backbone network.

   B. Use the existing CAT 5e cabling for the LANs, since CAT 5e runs at 1 Gbps. Use thick coaxial cable for the backbone network.

   C. Install CAT 6 or CAT 6a UTP cable for the LANs. These cables run at 1 Gbps and provide a migration path to 10 Gbps. Use multimode fiber-optic cable for the backbone network.

   D. Install CAT 6 or CAT 6a UTP cable for the LANs. These cables run at 1 Gbps and provide a migration path to 10 Gbps. Use the existing CAT 5e cable for the backbone network.

   E. Replace the UTP cables with shielded twisted-pair (STP) cables.

77. A maintenance worker, while replacing a light fixture in an office building, accidentally severs a network cable in the drop ceiling. The tenants use a variety of local area network (LAN) technologies throughout the structure, but on that particular floor, there are three separate LANs: a 10-node Thin Ethernet LAN using coaxial cable in a bus topology, a 25-node Gigabit Ethernet LAN using twisted-pair cable in a star/hub and spoke topology, and a 5-node Fiber Distributed Data Interface (FDDI) LAN using multimode fiber-optic cable in a double ring topology. Without knowing which of the LANs the severed cable belongs to, what is the maximum number of computers that could be directly affected by the cable break?

   A. 0

   B. 1

   C. 5

   D. 10

   E. 25

   F. 40

78. Which of the following twisted-pair cable types can you use to construct a 10GBase-T network with 100-meter segments? (Choose all that apply.)

   A. CAT 5

   B. CAT 5e

   C. CAT 6

D. CAT 6a

E. CAT 7

F. CAT 8

79. Which of the following twisted-pair cable types are rated for 1,000 megabit-per-second (Mbps) Gigabit Ethernet using two wire pairs? (Choose all that apply.)

A. Category 5 (CAT 5)

B. Category 5e (CAT 5e)

C. Category 6 (CAT 6)

D. Category 6a (CAT 6a)

E. None of the above

80. Which of the following twisted-pair cable types support both 10-megabit-per-second (Mbps) and 100 Mbps data rates, using only two pairs? (Choose all that apply.)

A. Category 5 (CAT 5)

B. Category 5e (CAT 5e)

C. Category 6 (CAT 6)

D. Category 6a (CAT 6a)

81. Ed has been hired to install network cabling for a small private company with 15 employees who need to share files and printers. All of the employees are physically located within the same building in two separate office spaces directly adjacent to each other, sharing a common wall and door for access. Both offices have drop ceilings. The client wants a simple Gigabit Ethernet installation that is easy to troubleshoot. In addition, Ed's client wants to keep installation costs to a minimum. Which of the following combinations of topology, cable type, and installation method would best meet the needs of Ed's client?

A. Star/hub and spoke topology, fiber-optic cabling, and internal installation

B. Bus topology, coaxial cabling, and external installation

C. Bus topology, twisted-pair cabling, and internal installation

D. Star/hub and spoke topology, coaxial cabling, and external installation

E. Star/hub and spoke topology, twisted-pair cabling, and external installation

82. Ed has been hired by a company to upgrade its network infrastructure. The current network is 10 Mbps Ethernet running on Category 5 (CAT 5) twisted-pair cable. There are 100 computers on the network, all of which have 10/100/1000 multispeed network interface adapters. The computers are all connected to hubs. Users are complaining that the network is too slow, and connections are sometimes dropped. Management wants to upgrade to the fastest Ethernet standard possible using the existing cabling, and still keep costs to a minimum. Which of the following implementations should Ed recommend to the client?

A. Upgrade to 100Base-TX and keep the existing hubs.

B. Upgrade to 1000Base-T and keep the existing hubs.

C. Upgrade to 100Base-FX and replace all of the hubs with switches.

D. Upgrade to 1000Base-T and replace all of the hubs with switches.

E. Upgrade to 100Base-SX and replace all of the hubs with switches.

83. Ralph has been asked to create some new patch cables that will be used to connect patch panel ports to the network switches. He has been told to use the T568B pinout standard for all of the cable connectors. Ralph gathers the materials and the tools needed to complete the task, but he is not sure about the T568B pinout. Which of the following pinouts must Ralph use when creating the patch cables?

A. White/orange, orange, white/green, blue, white/blue, green, white/brown, brown

B. White/green, green, white/orange, blue, white/blue, orange, white/brown, brown

C. White/orange, orange, white/green, green, white/blue, blue, white/brown, brown

D. White/brown, white/green, white/orange, blue, white/blue, orange, green, brown

84. It is Ralph's first day working for a consultancy that does network cable installations. His new boss points to a spool of Category 6 cable, hands Ralph a large plier-like device and a bag of little clear plastic components, and tells him to "get started on fives and tens." What is Ralph expected to do?

A. Pull cable runs

B. Create patch cables

C. Attach keystone connectors

D. Install a patch panel

85. Which of the following devices can you use to connect two multimode fiber-optic Ethernet networks in different buildings 2,000 meters apart using a single-mode fiber-optic cable segment running at the same speed, while maintaining a single collision domain?

A. Bridge

B. Switch

C. Router

D. Media converter

86. Alice has recently installed some new computers onto her Gigabit Ethernet network. To ensure the best possible network performance, she has configured the network adapters in the new computers to run at 1 Gbps speed and use full-duplex communication. Once the computers are in service, however, Alice begins getting reports of extremely poor network performance on those machines. She tries running some ping tests and does not see any problem. She calls in a consultant to perform a packet analysis and the consultant detects large numbers of packet collisions, late collisions, cyclic redundancy check (CRC) errors, lost packets, and runt frames. Which of the following could conceivably be the problem?

A. Duplex mismatch

B. Transmitter (TX)/receiver (RX) transposed

C. Incorrect cable type

D. Damaged cables

87. Ed is trying to troubleshoot a problem that has caused a wired network connection to slow down noticeably. Which of the following wired network problems will cause a drastic slowdown of a network connection, without causing it to fail completely? (Choose all that apply.)

   A. Bottleneck

   B. Speed mismatch

   C. Duplex mismatch

   D. Transmitter (TX)/receiver (RX) transposed

5.3 Given a scenario, troubleshoot common issues with network services.

88. A user calls Alice at the help desk to report that he cannot access the Internet. He can access systems on the local network, however. Alice examines the routing table on the user's workstation and sees the following. Which of the following statements explains why the user cannot access the Internet?

```
IPv4 Route Table
===========================================================================
Active Routes:
Network Destination    Netmask          Gateway    Interface      Metric
    127.0.0.0          255.0.0.0        On-link    127.0.0.1      331
    127.0.0.1          255.255.255.255  On-link    127.0.0.1      331
    127.255.255.255    255.255.255.255  On-link    127.0.0.1      331
    192.168.2.0        255.255.255.0    On-link    192.168.2.37   281
    192.168.2.37       255.255.255.255  On-link    192.168.2.37   281
    192.168.2.255      255.255.255.255  On-link    192.168.2.37   281
    224.0.0.0          240.0.0.0        On-link    127.0.0.1      331
    224.0.0.0          240.0.0.0        On-link    192.168.2.37   281
    255.255.255.255    255.255.255.255  On-link    127.0.0.1      331
    255.255.255.255    255.255.255.255  On-link    192.168.2.37   281
===========================================================================
Persistent Routes:
  None
```

   A. The routing table contains a loopback address.

   B. The routing table does not specify a default gateway address.

   C. The routing table does not specify a DNS server address.

   D. The routing table contains two different routes to the 224.0.0.0 network.

89. Ed is implementing a web server farm on his company's network and has created a screened subnet (or perimeter network) on which the web servers will be located. The screened subnet is using the network IP address 192.168.99.0/24. He has also installed a router connecting the screened subnet to the internal network, which uses the 192.168.3.0/24 network address. The IP addresses of the router's interfaces are 192.168.3.100 and 192.168.99.1. Ed needs to access the web servers from his Windows workstation on the internal network, but right now, he cannot do so. Because he needs to have a different router specified as his default gateway, Ed decides to add a route for the screened subnet to his computer's routing table. Which of the following commands will create a routing table entry that enables Ed to access the screened subnet?

    A. `route add 192.168.3.0 MASK 255.255.255.0 192.168.3.100`

    B. `route add 192.168.99.1 MASK 255.255.255.0 192.168.3.0`

    C. `route add 192.168.3.100 MASK 255.255.255.0 192.168.99.0`

    D. `route add 192.168.99.0 MASK 255.255.255.0 192.168.3.100`

90. Alice has recently created a new screened subnet (or perimeter network) for the company's web server cluster, along with a router to connect it to the internal network. When she is finished, she sends Ralph an email instructing him to run the following command on his Windows workstation so that he can access the servers on the screened subnet. What function does the IP address 192.168.87.226 perform in this command?

    `route add 192.168.46.0 MASK 255.255.255.0 192.168.87.226`

    A. 192.168.87.226 is the address of Ralph's workstation.

    B. 192.168.87.226 is the network address of the perimeter network.

    C. 192.168.87.226 is the address of one of the router's interfaces.

    D. 192.168.87.226 is the address of the web server cluster.

91. When you run a port scanner on a server, which of the following is the result?

    A. A list of processes running on the system

    B. A list of open ports through which the system can be accessed

    C. A list of protocols used by the system for network communication

    D. A list of IP addresses used on the network

92. A port scanner examines a system for network vulnerabilities at which layer of the Open Systems Interconnection (OSI) model?

    A. Application

    B. Transport

    C. Network

    D. Data link

93. Which of the following best describes the primary function of a port scanner?

    A. A port scanner examines a computer's hardware and compiles a list of the physical ports in the system.

    B. A port scanner examines a computer for TCP and UDP endpoints that are accessible from the network.

C. A port scanner examines a specified range of IP addresses on a network, to determine whether they are in use.

D. A port scanner accepts a computer name as input and scans the network for the IP address associated with that name.

94. Ed is working the help desk at a local computer store, and he receives a call from a customer trying to set up a home network using Windows 11 and wired Ethernet equipment. The customer reports that, from her computer, she can see the two other computers in the house, but she cannot access the Internet. Ed asks her to run the `ipconfig /all` command and read the results to him. She says that her IP address is 172.16.41.2, her subnet mask is 255.255.255.0, and her default gateway is 172.16.43.1. Which of the following is most likely the cause of the customer's problem?

A. The customer's network cable is unplugged.

B. The customer has an incorrect subnet mask.

C. The customer has an incorrect default gateway address.

D. The computer's DNS record contains the wrong information.

E. The computer is inhibited by a switching loop.

95. Ralph has a wired home network with three Windows computers, a switch, and a cable modem/router that provides access to the Internet. All three computers are able to access the Internet, but none of them can access filesystem shares on the others. Which of the following is the most likely cause of the problem on the three network computers?

A. Incorrect IP addresses

B. Incorrect subnet mask

C. Incorrect default gateway address

D. Incorrect access control list (ACL) settings

96. Which of the following IP address assignments indicates that a computer has been unable to communicate with a DHCP server?

A. 127.0.0.1

B. 255.255.255.0

C. 240.15.167.251

D. 169.254.199.22

97. A user reports to Ralph that he cannot access the Internet, although he is able to connect to computers on the local network. Ralph runs `ipconfig /all` on the user's workstation and examines the output. Which of the following is the most likely explanation for the user's problem, based on these `ipconfig` results?

```
Windows IP Configuration  Host Name . . . . . . . . . . . . : Client12
    Primary Dns Suffix . . . . . . . :
    Node Type . . . . . . . . . . . . : Hybrid
    IP Routing Enabled. . . . . . . . : No
    WINS Proxy Enabled. . . . . . . . : NoEthernet adapter Local Area Connection:
Connection-specific DNS Suffix . :
```

```
Description . . . . . . . . . . . : PCIe Family Controller
Physical Address. . . . . . . . . : 60-EB-69-93-5E-E5
DHCP Enabled. . . . . . . . . . . : No
Autoconfiguration Enabled . . . . : Yes
Link-local IPv6 Address . . . . . : fe80::c955:c944:acdd:3fcb%2
IPv4 Address. . . . . . . . . . . : 192.168.4.24
Subnet Mask . . . . . . . . . . . : 255.255.255.0
Lease Obtained. . . . . . . . . . : Monday, October 23, 2017 6:23:47 PM
Lease Expires . . . . . . . . . . : Saturday, November 18, 2017 9:49:24 PM
Default Gateway . . . . . . . . . : 192.168.6.99
DHCPv6 IAID . . . . . . . . . . . : 241232745
DHCPv6 Client DUID. . . . . . . . : 00-01-00-01-18-10-22-0D-60-EB-69-93-5E-E5
DNS Servers . . . . . . . . . . . : 202.86.10.114
NetBIOS over Tcpip. . . . . . . . : Enabled
```

A. The Subnet Mask setting is incorrect.

B. The Default Gateway setting is incorrect.

C. The DNS Servers setting is located on another network.

D. DHCP is not enabled.

98. Ralph is troubleshooting a workstation that cannot access the network. The workstation is plugged into a wall plate that should provide it with access to a DHCP-equipped network using the 192.168.4.0/24 network address. No one else on that network is reporting a problem. Ralph checks that the patch cable is properly plugged into the workstation and the wall plate, which they are, and then runs `ipconfig /all` on the user's workstation and examines the output. Which of the following could be the explanation for the user's problem, based on these `ipconfig` results?

```
Windows IP Configuration  Host Name . . . . . . . . . . . . . : Client12
  Primary Dns Suffix . . . . . . . :
  Node Type . . . . . . . . . . . . : Hybrid
  IP Routing Enabled. . . . . . . . : No
  WINS Proxy Enabled. . . . . . . . : NoEthernet adapter Local Area Connection:
Connection-specific DNS Suffix . :
  Description . . . . . . . . . . . : PCIe Family Controller
  Physical Address. . . . . . . . . : 60-EB-69-93-5E-E5
  DHCP Enabled. . . . . . . . . . . : Yes
  Autoconfiguration Enabled . . . . : Yes
  Link-local IPv6 Address . . . . . : fe80::c955:c944:acdd:3fcb%2
  IPv4 Address. . . . . . . . . . . : 169.254.203.42
  Subnet Mask . . . . . . . . . . . : 255.255.0.0
  Lease Obtained. . . . . . . . . . : Monday, October 23, 2017 6:23:47 PM
  Lease Expires . . . . . . . . . . : Saturday, November 18, 2017 9:49:24 PM
```

```
Default Gateway . . . . . . . . . :
DHCPv6 IAID . . . . . . . . . . . : 241232745
DHCPv6 Client DUID. . . . . . . . : 00-01-00-01-18-10-22-0D-60-EB-69-93-5E-E5
DNS Servers . . . . . . . . . . . : fec0:0:0:ffff::1%1
                                    fec0:0:0:ffff::2%1
                                    fec0:0:0:ffff::3%1
NetBIOS over Tcpip. . . . . . . . : Enabled
```

A. The Subnet Mask setting is incorrect.

B. The Default Gateway address is missing.

C. The DHCPv4 scope is exhausted.

D. The DNS server addresses are incorrect.

99. Ralph is troubleshooting a workstation that cannot access the network. The workstation is plugged into a wall plate that should provide it with access to a DHCP-equipped network using the 192.168.32.0/20 network address. Ralph checks that the patch cable is properly plugged into the workstation and the wall plate, which they are, and then runs `ipconfig /all` on the user's workstation and examines the output. Which of the following could be the explanation for the user's problem, based on these `ipconfig` results?

```
Windows IP Configuration  Host Name . . . . . . . . . . . . : Client12
  Primary Dns Suffix . . . . . . . :
  Node Type . . . . . . . . . . . . : Hybrid
  IP Routing Enabled. . . . . . . . : No
  WINS Proxy Enabled. . . . . . . . : NoEthernet adapter Local Area Connection:
Connection-specific DNS Suffix . . :
  Description . . . . . . . . . . . : PCIe Family Controller
  Physical Address. . . . . . . . . : 60-EB-69-93-5E-E5
  DHCP Enabled. . . . . . . . . . . : No
  Autoconfiguration Enabled . . . . : Yes
  Link-local IPv6 Address . . . . . : fe80::c955:c944:acdd:3fcb%2
  IPv4 Address. . . . . . . . . . . : 192.168.42.24
  Subnet Mask . . . . . . . . . . . : 255.255.255.0
  Lease Obtained. . . . . . . . . . : Monday, October 23, 2017 6:23:47 PM
  Lease Expires . . . . . . . . . . : Saturday, November 18, 2017 9:49:24 PM
  Default Gateway . . . . . . . . . : 192.168.42.99
  DHCPv6 IAID . . . . . . . . . . . : 241232745
  DHCPv6 Client DUID. . . . . . . . : 00-01-00-01-18-10-22-0D-60-EB-69-93-5E-E5
  DNS Servers . . . . . . . . . . . : 202.86.10.114
  NetBIOS over Tcpip. . . . . . . . : Enabled
```

A. The IPv4 Address setting is incorrect.

B. The Subnet Mask setting is incorrect.

C. The Default Gateway setting is incorrect.

D. The DNS Servers setting is located on another network.

100. Ralph is troubleshooting a workstation that cannot access the network. The workstation is plugged into a wall plate that should provide it with access to a DHCP-equipped network using the 192.168.4.0/24 network address. Ralph checks that the patch cable is properly plugged into the workstation and the wall plate, which they are, and then runs `ipconfig /all` on the user's workstation and examines the output. Which of the following could be the explanation for the user's problem, based on these `ipconfig` results?

```
Windows IP Configuration  Host Name . . . . . . . . . . . . : Client12
  Primary Dns Suffix . . . . . . . :
  Node Type . . . . . . . . . . . . : Hybrid
  IP Routing Enabled. . . . . . . . : No
  WINS Proxy Enabled. . . . . . . . : NoEthernet adapter Local Area Connection:
Connection-specific DNS Suffix . . :
  Description . . . . . . . . . . . : PCIe Family Controller
  Physical Address. . . . . . . . . : 60-EB-69-93-5E-E5
  DHCP Enabled. . . . . . . . . . . : Yes
  Autoconfiguration Enabled . . . . : Yes
  Link-local IPv6 Address . . . . . : fe80::c955:c944:acdd:3fcb%2
  IPv4 Address. . . . . . . . . . . : 10.124.16.8
  Subnet Mask . . . . . . . . . . . : 255.0.0.0
  Lease Obtained. . . . . . . . . . : Monday, October 23, 2017 6:23:47 PM
  Lease Expires . . . . . . . . . . : Saturday, November 18, 2017 9:49:24 PM
  Default Gateway . . . . . . . . . :
  DHCPv6 IAID . . . . . . . . . . . : 241232745
  DHCPv6 Client DUID. . . . . . . . : 00-01-00-01-18-10-22-0D-60-EB-69-93-5E-E5
  DNS Servers . . . . . . . . . . . : fec0:0:0:ffff::1%1
                                      fec0:0:0:ffff::2%1
                                      fec0:0:0:ffff::3%1
  NetBIOS over Tcpip. . . . . . . . : Enabled
```

A. The workstation could not connect to a DHCP server.

B. There is a rogue DHCP server on the network.

C. The workstation is not configured to use DHCP.

D. The IP address assigned by the DHCP server has expired.

101. You have three virtual LANs (VLAN2, VLAN3, and VLAN4), with each implemented on three switches. A single router provides routing among the VLANs. All of the VLAN2 users connected to one particular switch are complaining that they cannot access resources on other hosts within their own VLAN or on VLAN3 and VLAN4. Before today, they could connect to local and remote resources with no problem. What is the likeliest cause of the service interruption?

A. The router is malfunctioning and not routing among the VLANs.

B. VLAN2 is misconfigured.

C. The switch to which the VLAN2 users are connected is not functioning.

D. VLAN3 and VLAN4 are misconfigured.

102. Alice is supporting a network that consists of four internal local area networks (LANs) with 50 users each. Each internal LAN uses twisted-pair Gigabit Ethernet links that connect the users to a switch. Each of the four switches connects to a backbone router. All of the routers connect to the same backbone network, which has a single additional router to connect the company's network to the Internet, using a T-1 link. Users on one of the internal LANs are complaining that, when they came in this morning, they could not access the Internet or the other internal LANs, although they could access local resources with no problems. Which network component is the likeliest source of the problem in this scenario?

A. The router connecting the problem LAN to the backbone

B. The Internet router

C. The switch on the problem LAN

D. The cable on the backbone network

103. Ed is implementing a web server farm on his company's network and has installed a router to create a screened subnet (or perimeter network) on which the web servers will be located. However, Ed now cannot access the web servers from his workstation on the internal network. Which of the following tasks will Ed have to complete before he can access the perimeter network from the internal network? (Choose all that apply.)

A. Change IP addresses.

B. Change default gateway addresses.

C. Update the DNS records.

D. Change MAC addresses.

104. Ralph has a wired home network with three Windows computers, a switch, and a cable modem/router that provides access to the Internet. One of the computers is able to connect to the other two, but it cannot connect to the Internet. Which of the following configuration parameters on the malfunctioning computer will Ralph most likely have to change to resolve this problem?

A. IP address

B. Subnet mask

C. Default gateway

D. MAC address

105. Ralph is a network administrator attempting to use his workstation to remote into a web server called WebServ1 on a screened subnet (perimeter network). However, the remote desktop client software is unable to establish a connection to the server. Ralph can see all of the computers on his local network and on the screened subnet. He tries using the ping utility to test WebServ1's TCP/IP functionality, and the ping test is successful. Ralph then calls his colleague Ed and has him try to connect to WebServ1 using the same remote access tool. Ed connects successfully. Which of the following could be the cause of the problem Ralph is experiencing?

A. Name resolution failure

B. Unresponsive service on the web server

C. Blocked TCP/UDP ports on the web server

D. Incorrect firewall settings on Ralph's workstation

106. Alice is supporting a network that consists of four internal local area networks (LANs) with 50 users each. Each internal LAN uses twisted-pair Gigabit Ethernet links that connect the users to a switch. Each of the four switches connects to a backbone router. All of the routers connect to the same backbone network, which has a single additional router to connect the company's network to the Internet. Users on all of the internal LANs are complaining that, when they came in this morning, they could not access the Internet, although they could access resources on all of the LANs with no problems. Which network component is the likeliest source of the problem in this scenario?

    A. The router connecting the problem LAN to the backbone

    B. The Internet router

    C. The switch on the problem LAN

    D. The cable on the backbone network

107. A user calls the company's IT help desk to report that she has received an error message on her Windows workstation. The error states that her computer has an IP address that is duplicated on the network. Ralph is concerned that there might be a configuration problem with the DHCP servers on the network. He suspects that there are DHCP servers configured with scopes that overlap, resulting in two DHCP servers assigning the same IP addresses to different clients. He is worried that they are about to receive a flood of calls reporting the same problem. Alice reassures Ralph, telling him that it cannot be a DHCP problem, and that there must be two computers that are manually configured with the same IP address. How does Alice know this?

    A. Because Windows computers check the routing table before accepting an IP address from a DHCP server

    B. Because DHCP servers use DNS queries to check for duplicate IP addresses

    C. Because DHCP clients use ARP broadcasts to check for duplicate IP addresses

    D. Because it is only possible to have one DHCP server on a given subnet

108. A user calls Alice at the IT help desk and reports that she is having intermittent problems accessing both local servers and Internet websites. Which of the following potential problems can Alice rule out immediately?

    A. Duplicate MAC addresses

    B. Duplicate IP addresses

    C. Malfunctioning router

    D. Malfunctioning DNS server

109. While working in her company's datacenter, Alice notices that the LEDs on most of the network switch ports are green, but there are several that are orange. Alice asks several people why this is so and receives several different answers. Which one of the following answers is correct?

    A. The orange LEDs indicate that no device is connected to the switch port.

    B. The orange LEDs indicate that the connected device is experiencing an excessive number of collisions.

    C. The orange LEDs indicate that the device is connected to the switch at a relatively slow speed.

    D. The orange LEDs indicate that the connected devices are other switches, rather than workstations.

110. Ralph is a network administrator for a company with several branch offices, each of which has a Windows domain controller. There have been problems lately with the domain controllers synchronizing their data, and Ralph suspects that the problem is related to the Network Time Protocol (NTP) settings on the servers. Examining the server logs on the various domain controllers, he sees multiple errors saying, "Server NTP service not synchronized." All of the other server functions are running normally. Which of the following could be the cause of the problem Ralph is experiencing?

    A. Name resolution failure

    B. Unresponsive database service on the servers

    C. Incorrect TCP/IP settings on the servers

    D. Incorrect firewall settings on the servers

111. Alice's company is opening a new branch office, and Alice is responsible for building the domain controller for that office. She installs a new Windows server and configures it as a domain controller, and then ships it to the new office site. However, once it arrives and is connected to the home office network, the new domain controller fails to synchronize with the existing ones at the home office. Which of the following could be the cause of the problem?

    A. Incorrect time

    B. Server hardware failure

    C. Duplicate IP addresses

    D. Incorrect default gateway address

112. Alice is troubleshooting a problem that some users are having connecting to an application server on the local network. While testing connectivity using the `ping` tool, she discovers that she can ping the server successfully using its computer name, but pinging the computer's fully qualified domain name (FQDN) fails. Which of the following is most likely the source of the problem?

    A. DNS

    B. DHCP

    C. EMI

    D. ACL

113. Ralph has begun to receive calls from users reporting that they cannot access the local network or the Internet. Ralph checks their computers and discovers that all of the users with a problem have IP addresses in the 169.254.0.0/16 network, which is not the address used on Ralph's network. Which of the following might be the cause of the problem?

    A. The users have tried to modify their IP configuration settings.

    B. There is a rogue DHCP server somewhere on the network.

    C. The IP address leases assigned by the DHCP server have expired.

    D. The users' workstations have been infected by a form of malware.

114. Ralph is working with a multifunction router that provides Internet access and that also has a switch module with four Ethernet ports, all of which are assigned to the default VLAN1. Ralph can plug a laptop into one of the router's ports and access the Internet with no problems. Ralph now needs to connect the router to his company network, so that the wireless access points on the network can provide users with Internet access through the router's connection. However, when Ralph plugs an Ethernet port on the router into a switch port on the company network in VLAN4, the switch starts generating "Native VLAN mismatch detected" errors every minute. Which of the following steps should be part of the solution Ralph implements to stop the error messages? (Choose all that apply.)

   A. Create a VLAN1 on the company network switch.

   B. Create a VLAN4 on the Internet router's switch module.

   C. Configure the network switch port connected to the router to use VLAN1.

   D. Configure the router port connected to the network switch to use VLAN4.

115. Ralph is working with a multifunction router that provides Internet access and that also has a switch module containing four Ethernet ports, all of which are assigned to VLAN2. Ralph can plug a laptop into one of the router's ports and access the Internet with no problems. Ralph now needs to connect the router to his company network, so that the wireless access points on the network can provide users with Internet access through the router's connection. However, when Ralph plugs an Ethernet port on the router into a switch port on the company network in VLAN4, the switch starts generating "Native VLAN mismatch detected" errors every minute. To correct the problem, Ralph attempts to create a VLAN4 on the Internet access router, but he receives a "Feature not licensed" error. Which of the following actions can Ralph take to resolve the problem? (Choose all that apply.)

   A. Purchase a feature upgrade for the Internet access router.

   B. Create a VLAN2 on the switch.

   C. Configure the Internet access router to use VLAN1.

   D. Configure the switch to use VLAN1.

116. Clients of Ralph's company are calling to complain that, when they try to access the company's website, they see an error message stating that the website has an untrusted security certificate. They are afraid that they are connecting to an unprotected site or that the site has been taken over by hackers. What must Ralph do to address this problem?

   A. Obtain a security certificate from a trusted third-party company.

   B. Configure the web servers to generate a self-signed certificate.

   C. Install a certification authority on one of the network servers.

   D. Explain to the clients that it is safe to bypass the error message and proceed to the website.

117. Alice is working the IT help desk at her company, which has 500 inside salespeople who start work at 9:00 AM. The users are running Windows 11 and obtaining their IP address configuration settings from DHCP servers. Every morning, Alice receives many trouble calls from users who are experiencing extremely slow performance after they first turn on their computers. Their performance gradually improves within an hour. Which of the following is the most likely cause of the slowdown?

A. Broadcast storm

B. Network loop

C. Rogue DHCP server

D. Switching loop

E. Asymmetric routing

118. Which of the following TCP/IP parameters, configured on an end system, specifies the Internet Protocol (IP) address of a router on the local network that provides access to other networks?

A. IPv6 Address

B. Default Gateway

C. DNS Servers

D. Subnet Mask

119. Which of the following network devices do not employ access control lists (ACLs) to restrict access?

A. Routers

B. Hubs

C. Switches

D. Wireless access points (WAPs)

120. Which of the following features help to protect network switches from attacks related to the Spanning Tree Protocol (STP)? (Choose all that apply.)

A. BPDU guard

B. Root guard

C. DHCP snooping

D. Geofencing

5.4 Given a scenario, troubleshoot common performance issues.

121. Delays in the transmission of data packets over a network can result in temporary service interruptions, dropouts, or even data loss. Which of the following terms is used to describe these delays?

A. Crosstalk

B. Electromagnetic interference (EMI)

C. Jitter

D. Attenuation

122. Ralph has purchased an IEEE 802.11ac wireless access point, which he plans to use to build a home network with his two computers, both of which have 802.11ax network adapters, and a television, which has an 802.11n adapter that can only run on the 2.4 GHz band. When he connects the devices to the access point, he finds that the two computers communicate properly, but the TV does not. What can Ralph do to enable all of his devices to connect using the new access point?

 A. Nothing. The television can never connect to the new access point.

 B. Configure the access point to run on the 2.4 GHz band.

 C. Configure the computers to run on the 2.4 GHz band.

 D. Move the television closer to the access point.

123. Ralph is setting up a wireless network using the 2.4 GHz frequency band. Which of the following channels should he use to avoid channel overlap? (Choose all that apply.)

 A. 1

 B. 4

 C. 6

 D. 8

 E. 11

124. Ralph is adding new workstations to his wireless network, which uses an access point that is configured to use WPA3 encryption. However, after configuring the wireless network adapter on the first workstation, Ralph finds that it is not connecting to the network. The access point is listed on the Available Networks display, and there are no error messages or indications of a problem, just a failure to connect. Which of the following is most likely to be the problem?

 A. Incorrect passphrase

 B. Channel overlap

 C. Incorrect SSID

 D. Incorrect antenna placement

125. Ralph is adding new workstations to his wireless network, which uses a single access point that is configured to use WPA3 encryption. However, after installing the wireless network adapter on the first workstation, Ralph finds that he cannot see the wireless access point on the Available Networks display. Which of the following could be the problem? (Choose all that apply.)

 A. Incorrect passphrase

 B. Channel overlap

 C. Incorrect SSID

 D. Incorrect antenna polarization

 E. Antenna cable attenuation

 F. Roaming misconfiguration

126. Ralph is the administrator of a small company's wireless network. He has recently discovered evidence that users outside of the company's office space have been accessing its wireless network. The office is located in a narrow space against the building's outside wall. Ralph is concerned that the network's wireless access point is extending coverage outside the building. Speaking with a consultant friend of his, Ralph is advised to install a different type of antenna on his access point. Which of the following antenna types would most likely help Ralph to alleviate the problem?

A. Dipole

B. Yagi

C. Patch

D. Unidirectional

127. Trixie has recently moved to a new office in her company's building, down the hall from her old one. Since the move, she has only been able to access the wireless network with her laptop intermittently. She never had a problem in her previous location. Which of the following could possibly be the cause of her problem? (Choose all that apply.)

A. Trixie's new office is farther from the access point than her old one.

B. Her laptop is connecting to the wrong SSID.

C. The access point is using an omnidirectional antenna.

D. There are too many walls between Trixie's new office and the access point.

128. Alice is a new hire at Adatum Corp., and when she asks about wireless network access for her laptop, she is given an SSID and a WPA3 passphrase. Later, in the lunchroom when she tries to connect her laptop to the network, she cannot see the SSID she was given in the Available Networks list, although she can see other networks. What should Alice do next to try to resolve the problem?

A. Type in the WPA3 passphrase.

B. Type in the SSID manually.

C. Move closer to the wireless access point.

D. Move away from the microwave in the lunchroom.

129. Alice is a new hire at Adatum Corp., and when she asks about wireless network access for her laptop, she is given an SSID and a passphrase. She is also told that she must add the SSID manually. Later, she types in the SSID she was given, and the computer prompts her to select a security type. Not knowing which option to choose, she selects 802.1X because it sounds as though it should be the most secure. However, this option does not enable her to enter her passphrase, so she selects another option, WEP, and is able to type in the passphrase. However, her laptop says she "Can't connect to this network." Which of the following is the most likely cause of Alice's problem?

A. Overcapacity

B. Distance limitations

C. Frequency mismatch

D. Encryption protocol mismatch

130. Ralph purchases some 802.11ac wireless network adapters for desktop computers at a yard sale, which he intends to use to upgrade his outdated 802.11g home network. He installs one of the adapters in a computer and attempts to connect it to the network, but he cannot see his SSID. He tries a different adapter, thinking the first one might be broken, but that one does not work either. What can Ralph do to resolve the problem and connect the computer to his network?

   A. Move the computer closer to the access point.

   B. Configure the access point to use the 5 GHz frequency.

   C. Manually enter the SSID in the computer's client software.

   D. Nothing. 802.11ac equipment cannot connect to an 802.11g network.

131. Ralph is responsible for building a new wireless LAN for his company that consists of an 802.11n 2x2:2 access point and laptop computers with a variety of network adapters. Some of the laptops support 802.11n, most support 802.11ac, and a few older models still have 802.11g adapters. The new wireless LAN will be located in a large office building with many other wireless networks, and Ralph is having trouble finding a channel on the 2.4 GHz band that is not congested with traffic. Scanning the 5 GHz band, he finds relatively little traffic, so he reconfigures the access point to use a 5 GHz channel. The result is that some of the laptops are able to connect to the network, whereas others are not. What is the most likely reason for the connection failures, and what must Ralph do to enable all of the laptops to connect to the wireless network?

   A. The 5 GHz band does not support automatic channel selection. Ralph must configure each laptop to use the same channel as the access point in order for all the laptops to connect successfully.

   B. The 802.11ac and 802.11g standards do not support communication using the 5 GHz band. Ralph must configure the access point to support 2.4 GHz in order for all the laptops to connect successfully.

   C. The 5 GHz band does not support MIMO communications, so the 802.11n laptops are unable to connect to the network. Ralph must replace the access point with an 802.11ax unit in order for all the laptops to connect successfully.

   D. The 802.11g standard does not support communication using the 5 GHz band. Ralph must replace the network adapters in those laptops with newer models in order for them to connect successfully.

132. Alice is the administrator of a wireless network that has client computers in a number of small offices, all located on the same floor of an office building built in the mid-twentieth century. The network has an IEEE 802.11n access point located at the approximate center of the floor. Workstations in most of the rooms connect to the network using the 2.4 GHz band at 72 Mbps, but the computers in one particular room run much more slowly and rarely connect at that speed. Which of the following might be the cause of the problem?

   A. The computers in the problematic room are configured to use a different wireless encryption protocol than the access point.

   B. The computers in the problematic room are experiencing an SSID mismatch.

C. The network adapters in the problematic computers support IEEE 802.11ac, not 802.11n.

D. The RSSI of the problematic computers might be low, due to excessive distance from the access point.

133. Which of the following is not a potential solution for an IEEE 802.11n wireless computer that has intermittent problems connecting to an IEEE 802.11n access point?

A. Install a higher gain antenna on the access point.

B. Replace the access point with a model that supports 802.11ax.

C. Move the computer closer to the access point.

D. Change the channel used by the access point.

134. Ed has installed a separate 802.11n wireless network for guest users working in his company's offices. The guest network is unsecured, and Ed has recently become aware that people outside the building are able to access it. It is not possible to move the access point, and it must run at maximum power to reach the entire building. Which of the following is the most convenient way to prevent users outside the building from accessing the guest network while leaving it available to users inside the building?

A. Change the passphrase daily.

B. Switch the network frequency.

C. Disable SSID broadcasting.

D. Implement MAC filtering.

135. Alice is trying to provide users in a warehouse with wireless network connectivity for their tablets. The warehouse is a huge concrete structure with many internal cinderblock walls. Which of the following types of signal interference are inhibiting Alice's efforts?

A. Refraction

B. Reflection

C. Diffraction

D. Absorption

136. Ralph is having trouble providing satisfactory wireless network performance to some executive offices at the far end of the building. The wireless access point is based on the 802.11n standard. The offices have heavy doors and insulated walls for sound dampening, and the occupants typically leave their doors closed during work hours. Which of the following actions can Ralph take to provide the users in these offices with better wireless network performance?

A. Install an additional access point nearer to the offices.

B. Modify the access point to use higher number channels.

C. Upgrade the access point to a model based on the 802.11ax standard.

D. Configure the access point to disable SSID broadcasting.

137. Ralph is having trouble providing satisfactory wireless network performance to some executive offices at the far end of the building. The offices have heavy doors and insulated walls for sound dampening, and the occupants typically leave their doors closed during work hours. Which of the following types of radio signal interference is Ralph trying to overcome?

   A. Reflection

   B. Refraction

   C. Diffraction

   D. Absorption

138. Ralph is having trouble providing satisfactory wireless network performance to a row of glass-walled conference rooms at the far end of the building. The doors to the conference rooms are also made of glass and are always closed when meetings are in progress. Which of the following types of radio signal interference are likely to be the main issues that Ralph is trying to overcome? (Choose all that apply.)

   A. Reflection

   B. Refraction

   C. Diffraction

   D. Attenuation

139. Alice receives a call from a user who cannot connect to the company's 802.11n wireless network with a laptop that has an 802.11ac network adapter. Other users running 802.11n and 802.11g devices in the same area are able to connect to the network without difficulty. Which of the following are tasks that Alice can perform to resolve the problem? (Choose all that apply.)

   A. Replace the access point with one that supports the 802.11ac standard.

   B. Change the channel used by the wireless access point.

   C. Replace the wireless network adapter in the user's laptop.

   D. Move the user closer to the wireless access point.

140. Several accounting consultants are working in Ed's office for the first time, and they are unable to connect to the 802.11ax wireless network with their laptops. They are selecting the correct SSID from the Available Networks list, but they cannot connect, and there are no error messages of any kind. Which of the following tasks should Ed perform to try to resolve the problem?

   A. Check the network adapters in the laptops for channel overlap.

   B. Change the frequency used by the wireless access point from 2.4 GHz to 5 GHz.

   C. Examine the area where the consultants are working for possible sources of signal interference.

   D. Make sure that the consultants' laptops are configured to use the correct wireless security protocol.

141. Ed has installed a separate 802.11n wireless network for guest users working in his company's offices. The guest network uses no security protocol, and Ed has recently become aware that people outside the building are able to access it. Which of the following steps can Ed take to prevent users outside the building from accessing the guest network, while leaving it available to users inside the building? (Choose all that apply.)

A. Move the wireless access point to the center of the building.

B. Lower the power level of the wireless access point.

C. Implement MAC filtering.

D. Install a captive portal.

142. Alice receives a call from a user who cannot connect to the company's 802.11ax wireless network with a laptop that has an 802.11n network adapter. Other users working in the same area are able to connect to the network without difficulty. Which of the following steps should Alice take first to try to resolve the problem? (Choose all that apply.)

A. Change the channel used by the wireless access point.

B. Check whether the user is connecting to the correct SSID.

C. Check whether the wireless adapter in the user's laptop is enabled.

D. Provide the user with an 802.11ax wireless network adapter.

143. Users on Ed's 802.11n wireless network are dropping their connections intermittently. Which of the following might help to resolve these client dissociation issues?

A. Restart the wireless access point.

B. Change the network's SSID.

C. Change the channel the devices are using.

D. Change the wireless security protocol.

144. Several accounting consultants are working in Ed's office for the first time, and they are unable to connect to the 802.11n wireless network with their laptops. Which of the following tasks should Ed perform first to try to resolve the problem? (Choose two.)

A. Check the network adapters in the laptops for channel overlap.

B. Make sure that the consultants are attempting to connect to the correct SSID.

C. Examine the area where the consultants are working for possible sources of signal interference.

D. Make sure that the consultants' laptops are configured to use the correct wireless encryption protocol.

145. Ralph is deploying an 802.11n wireless network for a client that calls for the best possible security without deploying additional servers. When setting up the wireless access point, Ralph disables SSID broadcasts, selects Wi-Fi Protected Access Pre-shared Keys (WPA-PSK), and configures MAC address filtering. Which of the following statements about the security of this arrangement is true?

A. The configuration is as secure as Ralph can make it with the specified equipment.

B. Ralph should not disable SSID broadcasts, because this prevents users from connecting to the network.

C. Ralph should not use MAC address filtering, because it exposes MAC addresses to possible attacks.

D. Ralph should use Wi-Fi Protected Access 2 (WPA2) instead of WPA, because it is more resistant to certain types of attacks.

146. Which of the following is a power measurement of a specific transmitter and antenna combination, as used in a wireless access point?

A. RSSI

B. EIRP

C. SSID

D. MIMO

147. Alice has been asked to update an accounts receivable spreadsheet with information about the day's incoming payments, a task she has never performed before. After locating and opening the spreadsheet on the network server, she types in her new information, but when she attempts to save the changes, she receives an error message that directs her to save the file on her local drive instead of the network server. Which of the following is the probable cause of the problem?

A. Blocked TCP/UDP ports

B. Incorrect filesystem ACL settings

C. Incorrect firewall settings

D. An untrusted SSL certificate

148. Which of the following terms best describes a connectivity problem on wired networks that is caused by individual packets that are delayed due to network congestion, different routing, or queuing problems?

A. Latency

B. Attenuation

C. Jitter

D. Bottleneck

149. Which of the following network applications are most likely to be obviously affected by the wired network connectivity problem known as jitter? (Choose all that apply.)

A. Email

B. VoIP

C. Streaming video

D. Instant messaging

150. Ralph is experiencing long access point association times and generally poor performance on his home 802.11n wireless network. Ralph lives in a large apartment complex, and when he runs a Wi-Fi analyzer, he sees many other nearby networks using the often-recommended channels 1, 6, and 11 on the 2.4 GHz frequency. Using the 5 GHz frequency is not an option for Ralph's equipment. What should Ralph do to improve his network performance?

   A. Configure his equipment to use channel 2.

   B. Configure his equipment to use channel 5.

   C. Configure his equipment to use channel 9.

   D. Configure his equipment to use channel 10.

5.5 Given a scenario, use the appropriate tool or protocol to solve networking issues.

151. Ralph is a new hire working on a network that uses CAT 6 unshielded twisted-pair cable, which was installed several years ago. Over time, some of the paper labels that the original cable installers used to identify the wall plates and patch panel connectors have worn away or fallen off. As a result, Ralph has quite a few cable runs that he is unable to identify. After checking with his supervisor, Ralph discovers that the company has no cable testing equipment and is unwilling to hire a consultant just to identify cable runs. What is the most inexpensive tool Ralph can use to associate unlabeled wall plates with the correct patch panel ports?

   A. A visual fault locator

   B. A cable tester

   C. A toner and probe

   D. A protocol analyzer

152. Which of the following tools might you use when connecting internal twisted-pair cable runs to the keystone connectors that snap into wall plates? (Choose all that apply.)

   A. A crimper

   B. A punchdown tool

   C. A pigtail splicer

   D. A wire stripper

   E. A fusion splicer

153. Which of the following tools can you use to test for signal degradation in a fiber-optic cable?

   A. An optical power meter

   B. A toner and probe

   C. A protocol analyzer

   D. A visual fault locator

154. Which of the following troubleshooting tools can test cabling for length, attenuation, near-end crosstalk (NEXT), equal level far-end crosstalk (ELFEXT), propagation delay, delay skew, and return loss?

    A. Toner and probe

    B. Cable certifier

    C. Optical power meter

    D. Spectrum analyzer

155. Which of the following statements about cable certifiers are true? (Choose all that apply.)

    A. A cable certifier eliminates the need for testing tools like toners and probes.

    B. Cable certifiers are the most inexpensive cable testing solution.

    C. Cable certifiers must be reconfigured whenever a new cable specification is standardized.

    D. Cable certifiers can only test copper-based cables.

156. Which of the following tools can you use to create your own twisted-pair patch cables? (Choose all that apply.)

    A. Punchdown tool

    B. Crimper

    C. Pliers

    D. Wire stripper

157. Which of the following cable installation tools is likely to be the most expensive?

    A. A crimper

    B. A cable certifier

    C. A punchdown tool

    D. A toner and probe

158. What is the function of the tool shown in the following figure?

A. When you place the tool at one end of a wire, it generates a tone that can be detected at the other end.

B. To connect a bulk cable to a keystone connector, you use the tool to punch each wire down into the correct receptacle on the connector.

C. By touching the end of the tool to a copper cable, you can detect and measure the electrical current flowing through it.

D. By connecting the tool to the end of a fiber-optic cable, you can measure the length of the cable run.

159. What is the function of the tool shown in the following figure?

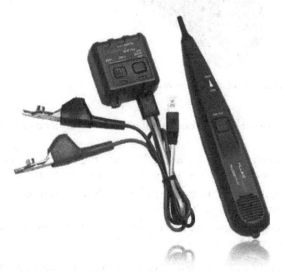

Reproduced with permission of Todd, 2015 / John Wiley & Sons.

A. When you place the tool at one end of a wire, it generates a tone that can be detected at the other end.

B. To connect a bulk cable to a keystone connector, you use the tool to punch each wire down into the correct receptacle on the connector.

C. By touching the end of the tool to a copper cable, you can detect and measure the electrical current flowing through it.

D. By connecting the tool to the end of a fiber-optic cable, you can measure the length of the cable run.

160. What is the function of the tool shown in the following figure?

Reproduced with permission of Todd, 2015 / John Wiley & Sons.

  A. When you place the tool at one end of a wire, it generates a tone that can be detected at the other end.

  B. To attach a bulk cable end to an RJ-45 connector, you use the tool to squeeze the connector closed, forcing the wire ends to contact the connector's pins.

  C. By touching the end of the tool to a copper cable, you can detect and measure the electrical current flowing through it.

  D. By connecting the clips to pins in a punchdown block, you can access telephone circuits in order to test them or place telephone calls.

161. Ralph is testing a twisted-pair cable run using a toner and probe. When he applies the toner to one particular wire at one end of the cable, he fails to detect a tone at the other end. Which of the following faults has Ralph discovered?

  A. Open

  B. Short

  C. Split pair

  D. Crosstalk

162. Ralph is testing a twisted-pair cable run using a toner and probe. When he applies the toner to a particular pin at one end of the cable, he detects a tone on two pins at the other end. Which of the following faults has Ralph discovered?

  A. Open

  B. Short

  C. Split pair

  D. Crosstalk

163. Ralph is using a toner and probe to test some newly installed twisted-pair cable runs on his network. Which of the following cable faults will he be unable to detect?

A. Open

B. Short

C. Split pair

D. Transposed pairs

164. Alice has been told by a consultant that the newly installed twisted-pair cable runs on her network might have split pairs. Which of the following cable testing tools can she use to detect split pairs?

A. Toner and probe

B. Visual fault locator

C. Multimeter

D. Cable certifier

165. Ralph is testing some newly installed twisted-pair cable runs on his network, and he has found one run that appears to have a cable break. However, the connectors at both ends are correctly installed, so the break must be somewhere inside the cable itself, which is nearly 100 meters long. Which of the following tools can Ralph use to determine the location of the cable break? (Choose all that apply.)

A. Toner and probe

B. Multimeter

C. Visual fault locator

D. Cable certifier

166. Ralph's company has engaged a firm of wiring contractors to install some new fiber-optic cable runs. Before the cables are connected to any devices, Ralph wants to confirm that they have been installed to proper specifications. He brings in a contractor from another firm to test the cable runs. To test each cable run, the contractor connects a light source to one end of the cable and a measuring device to the other end. Which of the following is the correct name for this testing device?

A. Optical power meter

B. OLTS

C. Spectrum analyzer

D. Multimeter

167. Ralph is attempting to access a Domain Name System (DNS) server located on the other side of a router, but his attempt fails with an error stating that the destination port UDP 53 is unreachable. His first step in troubleshooting the problem is to try using the nslookup utility to access that specific DNS server. This too fails. Next, he uses the ping utility with the DNS server's IP address. The ping test is successful, indicating that the server is up and running. Which of the following are possible causes of the problem? (Choose all that apply.)

A. The router connecting the networks is not running DNS and will not forward this type of datagram.

B. The DNS process on the remote server is not running.

    C. The TCP/IP host configuration on the computer is improperly configured.

    D. The TCP/IP host configuration on the DNS server computer is improperly configured.

    E. There is a firewall blocking the DNS server's UDP 53 port.

168. Which of the following Windows tools uses ICMP messages and manipulates IPv4 time-to-live (TTL) values to illustrate the route packets take through an internetwork?

    A. `ping`

    B. `netstat`

    C. `route`

    D. `tracert`

    E. `nslookup`

169. Users are having trouble connecting to Internet hosts. Alice suspects that there is a problem with the Domain Name System (DNS) server, and she wants to verify this. Which of the following steps can she take to determine whether the DNS server is resolving Internet hostnames?

    A. Issue the `ipconfig` command from a local workstation.

    B. Try to connect to a host using the IP address instead of the hostname.

    C. Ping the DNS server to see if it is functioning.

    D. Use the `tracert` command to test the functionality of the DNS server.

170. Which of the following utilities can you use to view resource record information on a particular DNS server? (Choose two.)

    A. `netstat`

    B. `nslookup`

    C. `nbtstat`

    D. `arp`

    E. `dig`

171. Which of the following Windows command-line utilities produced the output shown here?

```
Interface: 192.168.2.24 --- 0x2
Internet Address      Physical Address      Type
192.168.2.2           d4-ae-52-bf-c3-2d     dynamic
192.168.2.20          00-26-c7-7e-00-e0     dynamic
192.168.2.22          00-90-a9-a2-43-8f     dynamic
192.168.2.27          1c-c1-de-ca-1f-12     dynamic
192.168.2.28          30-f7-72-38-e9-1d     dynamic
192.168.2.255         ff-ff-ff-ff-ff-ff     static
224.0.0.22            01-00-5e-00-00-16     static
224.0.0.251           01-00-5e-00-00-fb     static
224.0.0.252           01-00-5e-00-00-fc     static
```

```
224.0.0.253        01-00-5e-00-00-fd    static
239.255.255.250    01-00-5e-7f-ff-fa    static
255.255.255.255    ff-ff-ff-ff-ff-ff    static
```

A. ping

B. tracert

C. netstat

D. arp

E. hostname

172. Which of the following Windows command-line utilities produced the output shown here?

```
 1    <1 ms    <1 ms    <1 ms RT-N86U [192.168.2.99]
 2     3 ms     5 ms     4 ms 192.168.3.1
 3    25 ms    30 ms    17 ms 10.172.1.1
 4    20 ms    19 ms    29 ms gateway-BE1-EBlocal.eh.lpod.net [207.44.123.89]
 5    26 ms    29 ms    29 ms gateway-be1-abn2abn2.ab.lpod.net [207.44.127.49]
 6      *        *        * Request timed out.
 7   111 ms   108 ms   109 ms be38.trmc0215-01.ars.mgmt.hox3.kkg [184.168.0.69]
 8   108 ms   107 ms   108 ms be38.trmc0215-01.ars.mgmt.hox3.kkg [184.168.0.69]
 9   106 ms   109 ms   108 ms ip-216-69-188-102.ip.srvr.net [216.69.188.102]
10   106 ms   108 ms    99 ms p3nlh153.shr.prod.phx3.srvr.net [97.74.144.153]
```

A. ping

B. tracert

C. netstat

D. arp

E. hostname

173. Which of the following Windows command-line utilities produced the output shown here?

```
Reply from 97.74.144.153: bytes=32 time=111ms TTL=53
Reply from 97.74.144.153: bytes=32 time=109ms TTL=53
Reply from 97.74.144.153: bytes=32 time=108ms TTL=53
Reply from 97.74.144.153: bytes=32 time=109ms TTL=53Statistics for
97.74.144.153:
    Packets: Sent = 4, Received = 4, Lost = 0 (0% loss),
Approximate round trip times in milli-seconds:
    Minimum = 108ms, Maximum = 111ms, Average = 109ms
```

A. ping

B. tracert

C. netstat

D. arp

E. hostname

174. Which of the following Windows command-line utilities produced the output shown here?

```
Active Connections Proto Local Address      Foreign Address      State
  TCP   127.0.0.1:5327       CM412:49770          ESTABLISHED
  TCP   127.0.0.1:49770      CM412:5327           ESTABLISHED
  TCP   127.0.0.1:52114      CM412:52115          ESTABLISHED
  TCP   192.168.2.24:2869    RT-M96U:42173        ESTABLISHED
  TCP   192.168.2.24:2869    RT-M96U:44356        ESTABLISHED
  TCP   192.168.2.24:51386   autodiscover:https   ESTABLISHED
  TCP   192.168.2.24:51486   autodiscover:https   ESTABLISHED
  TCP   192.168.2.24:51535   108-174-11-1:https   ESTABLISHED
  TCP   192.168.2.24:51578   aki-cache:http       TIME_WAIT
  TCP   192.168.2.24:51579   ia3s43-in-f142:http  TIME_WAIT
  TCP   192.168.2.24:51591   208:https            TIME_WAIT
  TCP   192.168.2.24:51592   208:https            TIME_WAIT
  TCP   192.168.2.24:51593   198.8.20.212:https   TIME_WAIT
```

- **A.** ping
- **B.** tracert
- **C.** netstat
- **D.** arp
- **E.** hostname

175. Which of the following command-line utilities is capable of performing the same basic function as traceroute or tracert?

- **A.** ping
- **B.** pathping
- **C.** netstat
- **D.** route

176. Which TCP/IP utility should you use to most easily identify a malfunctioning router on your network?

- **A.** ifconfig
- **B.** ping
- **C.** traceroute
- **D.** netstat

177. Which of the following protocols does the ping program never use to carry its messages?

- **A.** Ethernet
- **B.** ICMP
- **C.** IP
- **D.** UDP
- **E.** TCP

178. Which of the following commands displays the routing table on the local computer?

    A. `arp -r`

    B. `netstat -r`

    C. `ifconfig -r`

    D. `telnet -r`

    E. `show route`

179. Which of the following command lines will produce the output shown in the figure?

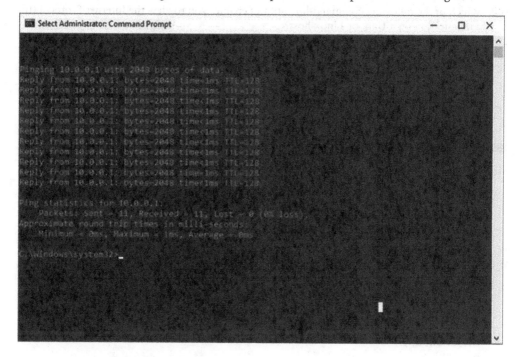

    A. `ping 10.0.0.1 -t`

    B. `ping 10.0.0.1 -n 2048`

    C. `ping 10.0.0.1 -l 2048 -n 11`

    D. `ping 10.0.0.1 -l 2048 -t`

    E. `ping 10.0.0.1 -n 2048 -t 11`

180. Which of the following commands enables you to view the ARP table stored in memory?

    A. `arp -c`

    B. `arp -d`

    C. `arp -a`

    D. `arp -s`

181. Which of the following command-line utilities enables you to generate Domain Name System (DNS) request messages?

   A. ifconfig
   B. nslookup
   C. nbtstat
   D. netstat
   E. iperf

182. Which of the following command-line utilities enables you to view the Internet Protocol (IP) configuration on a Unix or Linux host?

   A. ifconfig
   B. nslookup
   C. ipconfig
   D. netstat
   E. iperf

183. Which of the following parameters causes the ping tool to transmit messages continually until manually halted?

   A. -n
   B. -t
   C. -i
   D. -a

184. Which of the following Windows commands enables you to delete the entire ARP cache?

   A. arp -c *
   B. arp -d *
   C. arp -a
   D. show arp -d *
   E. arp -s

185. Ralph has been advised to check his Linux web servers for open ports that attackers might be able to use to penetrate the servers' security. Which of the following utilities can Ralph use to do this?

   A. tcpdump
   B. dig
   C. iptables
   D. nmap
   E. iperf

186. While performing a protocol analysis, Alice notes that there are many ICMP packets in her captured traffic samples. She attributes these to her frequent use of TCP/IP troubleshooting tools. Which of the following utilities are used to test Network layer characteristics of a host using Internet Control Message Protocol (ICMP) messages? (Choose all that apply.)

    A. ipconfig

    B. netstat

    C. ping

    D. tracert

187. Which of the following parameters enables you to specify the time-to-live (TTL) value of the messages the ping tool transmits?

    A. -n

    B. -t

    C. -i

    D. -a

188. Ralph is the network administrator of his company's network. He has had three users call the help desk to report that they are having problems connecting to the local application server. Comparing their stories, Ralph suspects that their Transmission Control Protocol (TCP) connections are being dropped. The users are not having problems connecting to any other hosts on the network. To troubleshoot this problem, Ralph decides to use a protocol analyzer. He wants to store and view only the traffic relating to the hosts and server that are having problems. How can Ralph do this?

    A. Configure a display filter.

    B. Configure a capture filter.

    C. Set a trap on the analyzer.

    D. Configure both a capture and display filter.

189. Ralph is the administrator of his company's network. All of the users on the network are reporting that they are having difficulty connecting to a particular application server that is located on a screened subnet (perimeter network) on the other side of a router. The users are not having trouble connecting to local hosts. Which of the following troubleshooting tools can Ralph use to verify the Network layer functionality of the application server and the router? (Choose all that apply.)

    A. ping

    B. route

    C. arp

    D. traceroute

190. Which of the following tools run only on Unix or Linux systems? (Choose all that apply.)

    A. tcpdump

    B. dig

    C. iptables

    D. ifconfig

    E. route

    F. show

191. Which of the following Windows command-line utilities produced the output shown here?

```
Server: trv213.pljd.net
Address: 203.186.120.114Non-authoritative answer:
Name:  microsoft.com
Addresses: 104.43.195.251
       23.100.122.175
       23.96.52.53
       191.239.213.197
       104.40.211.35
```

    A. nslookup

    B. pathping

    C. netstat

    D. route

192. Which of the following parameters enables you to specify the number of messages the ping tool transmits?

    A. -n

    B. -t

    C. -i

    D. -a

193. Which of the following command-line utilities can run on both Windows and Unix/Linux systems? (Choose all that apply.)

    A. ping

    B. traceroute

    C. ifconfig

    D. iptables

    E. nslookup

194. Which of the following command-line utilities can only run on Unix and Linux systems?

   A. `ping`

   B. `ipconfig`

   C. `tracert`

   D. `ifconfig`

   E. `netstat`

195. Which of the following command-line utilities can only run on Windows systems?

   A. `ping`

   B. `ipconfig`

   C. `traceroute`

   D. `ifconfig`

   E. `netstat`

196. Ralph is working on his company's perimeter network, which has five web servers running Linux, a Cisco router, a CSU/DSU providing a leased line connection, and a Windows-based firewall. While trying to troubleshoot a network communications failure, Ralph types the following command on one of the systems: `traceroute adatum.com`. Which of the following systems might Ralph be working on? (Choose all that apply.)

   A. The Windows-based firewall

   B. The Cisco router

   C. The CSU/DSU console

   D. One of the Linux web servers

197. Which of the following `netstat` commands can tell you how many IPv6 packets have been received on a particular Windows workstation?

   A. `netstat -a`

   B. `netstat -s`

   C. `netstat -e`

   D. `netstat -r`

198. Which of the following commands can Ralph use to display the number of bytes that a Windows workstation has transmitted?

   A. `netstat`

   B. `tcpdump`

   C. `ipconfig`

   D. `iptables`

   E. `show mac-address-table`

199. Ralph is working on his company's screened subnet (perimeter network), which has five web servers running Linux, a Cisco router, a CSU/DSU providing a leased line connection, and a Windows-based firewall. While trying to troubleshoot a network communications failure, Ralph types the following command on one of the systems: `ping 192.168.1.76`. Which of the following systems might Ralph be working on? (Choose all that apply.)

    A. The Windows-based firewall

    B. The Cisco router

    C. The CSU/DSU console

    D. One of the Linux web servers

200. While troubleshooting a Windows server, Alice runs the following command: `ping 127.0.0.1`. The command completes successfully. What has Alice proven by doing this?

    A. That the computer's network adapter is functioning properly

    B. That the computer's TCP/IP networking stack is loaded and functioning

    C. That the computer's IP address is correct for the network

    D. Nothing at all

201. Ed suspects that his workstation is experiencing TCP/IP communication problems. Which of the following commands can he use to confirm that the computer's TCP/IP stack is loaded and functioning? (Choose all that apply.)

    A. `ping loopback`

    B. `ping localhost`

    C. `ping 127.0.0.1`

    D. `ping 127.0.0.0`

202. Ralph is the administrator of his company's network. He has a Dynamic Host Configuration Protocol (DHCP) server configured to supply Internet Protocol (IP) addresses and configuration information to all of the Windows computers on the network. One of the Windows users reports that she cannot connect to the network. Which of the following commands can Ralph run on her computer to verify the status of the computer's IP settings and configuration parameters?

    A. `ifconfig`

    B. `ipconfig`

    C. `msinfo32`

    D. `tracert`

203. Which of the following are the three main categories of information that you can display by running the `netstat` command on a Windows computer?

    A. Connection state

    B. Active connections

    C. Routing table

    D. Interface statistics

204. Which of the following `route` commands displays the contents of a Windows computer's IPv6 routing table only?

A. `route print`

B. `route print -6`

C. `route list -6`

D. `route list`

205. Which of the following Windows command-line utilities produced the output shown here?

```
Interface Statistics

                        Received          Sent
Bytes                  663321544     1088192828
Unicast packets         29291610       10424979
Non-unicast packets       817568          58116
Discards                    1628              0
Errors                         0              0
Unknown protocols              0              0
```

A. `ping`

B. `tracert`

C. `netstat`

D. `arp`

206. Which of the following Linux commands generated the output shown in the figure?

A. `arp -a`

B. `arp -e`

C. `arp -d`

D. `arp -s`

207. Which of the following Windows commands enables you to create a new entry in the ARP cache?

A. `arp -N`

B. `arp -d`

C. `arp -a`

D. `arp -s`

208. Which of the following Unix/Linux tools is a packet analyzer?

A. `iptables`

B. `nmap`

C. `tcpdump`

D. `pathping`

209. Which of the following tools can administrators use to monitor network bandwidth and traffic patterns?

  A. Protocol analyzer

  B. Bandwidth speed tester

  C. NetFlow analyzer

  D. IP scanner

  E. Cable tester

210. Based on the output shown here, what is the average response time of the destination system?

```
 1   <1 ms    <1 ms    <1 ms RT-N86U [192.168.2.99]
 2    3 ms     5 ms     4 ms 192.168.3.1
 3   25 ms    30 ms    17 ms 10.172.1.1
 4   20 ms    19 ms    29 ms gateway-BE1-EBlocal.eh.lpod.net [207.44.123.89]
 5   26 ms    29 ms    29 ms gateway-be1-abn2abn2.ab.lpod.net [207.44.127.49]
 6     *        *        * Request timed out.
 7  111 ms   108 ms   109 ms be38.trmc0215-01.ars.mgmt.hox3.kkg [184.168.0.69]
 8  108 ms   107 ms   108 ms be38.trmc0215-01.ars.mgmt.hox3.kkg [184.168.0.69]
 9  106 ms   109 ms   108 ms ip-216-69-188-102.ip.srvr.net [216.69.188.102]
10  106 ms   108 ms    99 ms p3nlh153.shr.prod.phx3.srvr.net [97.74.144.153]
```

  A. 109.5 ms

  B. 104.33 ms

  C. 106 ms

  D. 99.66 ms

211. Which of the following Linux commands produced the output shown in the figure?

   A. `netstat -ns microsoft.com`

   B. `dig microsoft.com ns`

   C. `nslookup microsoft.com`

   D. `route -s microsoft.com`

212. Which of the following protocols does the `traceroute` utility on Unix and Linux systems use to test TCP/IP connectivity?

   A. ICMP

   B. HTTPS

   C. TCP

   D. UDP

   E. LLDP

213. Ed has configured his workstation to use IPsec encryption for network communications. Which of the following tools can he use to verify that his network traffic is encrypted?

   A. Multimeter

   B. Packet sniffer

   C. Port scanner

   D. Protocol analyzer

   E. IP scanner

214. Which of the following statements describes the difference between a packet sniffer and a protocol analyzer?

   A. A packet sniffer captures network traffic, and a protocol analyzer examines packet contents.

   B. A protocol analyzer captures network traffic, and a packet sniffer examines packet contents.

   C. A packet sniffer only captures the local workstation's traffic, whereas a protocol analyzer can capture all the traffic on the network.

   D. There is no difference. Packet sniffers and protocol analyzers perform the same functions.

215. Ed has recently discovered a rogue DHCP server on his network. After disabling the server, he now needs to terminate all of the rogue IP address leases currently held by Windows DHCP clients on the network and have them request new leases from the authorized DHCP server. Which of the following commands must he use on each Windows client to do this? (Choose all that apply.)

   A. `ipconfig /dump`

   B. `ipconfig /renew`

   C. `ipconfig /lease`

   D. `ipconfig /discard`

   E. `ipconfig /release`

216. Which of the following processes scans multiple computers on a network for a particular open TCP or UDP port?

A. Port scanning

B. War driving

C. Port sweeping

D. Bluejacking

217. Which of the following statements about protocol analyzers is not true?

A. To troubleshoot using a protocol analyzer, you must be familiar with the OSI model and the protocols that operate at each of its layers.

B. Protocol analyzers can be a network security risk.

C. Some network monitoring products are both analyzers and sniffers.

D. All Windows operating systems include a protocol analyzer.

218. Which of the following utilities can be classified as port scanners? (Choose all that apply.)

A. nmap

B. Nessus

C. Network Monitor

D. Performance Monitor

219. Which Unix/Linux performance monitoring tool, shown in the figure, enables you to display information about processes that are currently running on a system?

A. monitor

B. top

C. netstat

D. cpustat

220. You have finished capturing traffic with a protocol analyzer. The analyzer reports that 2,000 frames have been seen, but only 1,500 frames have been accepted. What does this mean?

  A. 2,000 frames have passed the display filter, but only 1,500 meet the criteria for display.

  B. Only 1,500 frames have passed the capture filter and are currently being held in the buffer.

  C. You lost 500 frames and need to start over—something is obviously wrong.

  D. 500 frames were damaged and never made it into the buffer.

221. Programs such as FTP and Telnet are widely criticized because they transmit all data as cleartext, including usernames and passwords. Which of the following types of tools might unscrupulous individuals use to read those passwords?

  A. Packet sniffer

  B. Terminal emulator

  C. Protocol analyzer

  D. Vulnerability scanner

  E. TFTP server

  F. Network tap

222. Which of the following best states the potential security threat inherent in running a protocol analyzer?

  A. A protocol analyzer can display the application data in packets captured from the network.

  B. A protocol analyzer can display the IP addresses of the systems on the network.

  C. A protocol analyzer can decrypt protected information in packets captured from the network.

  D. A protocol analyzer can detect open ports on network systems and launch attacks against them.

223. Which of the following tools do not provide vulnerability scanning capabilities?

  A. Nessus

  B. Spectrum analyzer

  C. nmap

  D. Visual fault locator

224. Which of the following is a function typically classified as vulnerability scanning?

  A. Network mapping

  B. Remediation

  C. Penetration testing

  D. Port scanning

225. Alice is attempting to troubleshoot a communication problem between two hosts on the same network. She decides to use a protocol analyzer to capture traffic on the network. After finishing the capture, Alice notices that there are over 15,000 frames in the protocol analyzer's capture buffer. She is having a difficult time identifying the frames that relate to the problem because there are so many in the buffer. She wants to eliminate the extraneous frames from her view, enabling her to view only the frames transmitted by these two hosts. What does Alice have to do to accomplish this?

    A. Configure a display filter.

    B. Configure a capture filter.

    C. Delete the extraneous frames from the buffer.

    D. Configure a capture and display filter.

226. Alice is examining a captured sample of network traffic to create a network performance baseline for future reference. She notices that the sample contains a flood of multicast traffic, but she does not know why. After some investigation, she learns that there is video traffic on the network being transmitted as multicasts, but it is only intended for a particular group of users, not for everyone. However, since the multicast traffic is flooding the network, all of the hosts must process the packets, possibly resulting in performance degradation or even denial of service. Which of the following can Alice use to prevent the traffic from being processed by the unintended hosts?

    A. Asymmetric routing

    B. Flow control

    C. Multipathing

    D. IGMP snooping

227. A user, Ed, is reporting what appear to be intermittent traffic interruptions on his workstation. Sometimes he receives responses to his server requests, and sometimes not. It does not seem to be an Internet issue, because the problem also occurs with local server requests. While troubleshooting the problem, Ralph performs a series of packet captures and analyzes the network traffic. He discovers that all of the request messages generated by Ed's workstation have responses on the network, but in some cases, the responses are going to a workstation other than Ed's. Which of the following conditions could be causing this to happen?

    A. Duplicate IP addresses

    B. Blocked TCP/UDP ports

    C. Duplicate MAC addresses

    D. Incorrect host firewall settings

    E. Multicast flood

228. Ralph is a network administrator who has had a Windows user report difficulties accessing certain other computers on the network. Ralph determines that the user is only experiencing problems when trying to connect to a system on the far side of a router. Therefore, Ralph decides to inspect the routing table on the user's computer. Which of the following tools can he use to do this? (Choose all that apply.)

A. nbtstat

B. route

C. nslookup

D. netstat

229. A user calls Alice at the help desk to report that he cannot access the Internet. He can access systems on the local network, however. Alice examines the routing table on the user's workstation and sees the following. Which of the following commands must Alice run to correct the user's problem?

```
IPv4 Route Table
===========================================================================
Active Routes:
Network Destination    Netmask          Gateway   Interface      Metric
    127.0.0.0          255.0.0.0        On-link   127.0.0.1      331
    127.0.0.1          255.255.255.255  On-link   127.0.0.1      331
    127.255.255.255    255.255.255.255  On-link   127.0.0.1      331
    192.168.2.0        255.255.255.0    On-link   192.168.2.37   281
    192.168.2.37       255.255.255.255  On-link   192.168.2.37   281
    192.168.2.255      255.255.255.255  On-link   192.168.2.37   281
    224.0.0.0          240.0.0.0        On-link   127.0.0.1      331
    224.0.0.0          240.0.0.0        On-link   192.168.2.37   281
    255.255.255.255    255.255.255.255  On-link   127.0.0.1      331
    255.255.255.255    255.255.255.255  On-link   192.168.2.37   281
===========================================================================
Persistent Routes:
  None
```

A. route add 0.0.0.0 MASK 0.0.0.0 192.168.2.37 METRIC 25 IF 192.168.2.99

B. route add 0.0.0.0 MASK 255.255.255.0 192.168.2.99 METRIC 25 IF 192.168.2.37

C. route add 192.168.2.0 MASK 255.255.255.0 192.168.2.99 METRIC 25 IF 192.168.2.37

D. route add 0.0.0.0 MASK 0.0.0.0 192.168.2.99 METRIC 25 IF 192.168.2.37

230. Which of the following Application layer protocols includes a program that enables a user to log on to a network device and execute commands on the remote system using a command-line interface? (Choose all that apply.)

   A. Telnet

   B. File Transfer Protocol (FTP)

   C. Simple Network Management Protocol (SNMP)

   D. Domain Name System (DNS)

   E. Nslookup

231. Which of the following utilities can display the number of packets sent and received for a specific network interface on a Unix, Linux, macOS, or Windows computer?

   A. top

   B. ifconfig

   C. netstat

   D. nbtstat

232. Which of the following is a feature included in some routers that collects and analyzes network traffic data sent or received through a network interface?

   A. netmon

   B. NetFlow

   C. netstat

   D. nbtstat

233. Which of the following tools do cable installers use to add connectors such as RJ-45 and RJ-11 to twisted-pair cabling?

   A. A crimper

   B. A splicer

   C. A pigtail

   D. A patch

234. Which of the following commands displays the routing table entries on a router?

   A. route print

   B. show route

   C. netstat -r

   D. nbtstat -t

Chapter

6

Practice Test 1

1. Which of the following are the layers in the standard three-tier datacenter architecture? (Choose all that apply.)

    A. Core

    B. Intermediate

    C. Distribution

    D. Access

2. You are a new hire at Adatum Corp., and this is your first day on the job. You are setting up your workstation, but you are unsure whether you are permitted to install your favorite software on the company's computer. The human resources server has a large library of employee documents. Which of the following documents should you consult to determine whether personal software is allowed?

    A. SLA

    B. AUP

    C. NDA

    D. BYOD

3. You are working the help desk when a user calls and reports that she is unable to connect to the Internet. Which of the following steps would you be least likely to perform first when troubleshooting the problem?

    A. Check the configuration of the router connecting the LAN to the Internet.

    B. Ask the user if she can access resources on the local network.

    C. Check to see if anyone else is experiencing the same problem.

    D. Check the user's job title to see if she is an important person in the company.

4. Which of the following is not a means of preventing unauthorized individuals from entering a sensitive location, such as a datacenter?

    A. Key fobs

    B. Motion detection

    C. Biometric scans

    D. Identification badges

5. You are an IT consultant who has been contracted to install new computers on a client's Gigabit Ethernet network. You want the performance of the new computers to be as good as it can be, so you configure their network adapters to run at the full speed of 1 Gbps and to use full-duplex communication. You test the computers after installing them, and they function well. However, once the computers are in service, you begin getting complaints from the client of extremely poor network performance on the new machines. You return to the site that evening and run some ping tests, but you do not detect any problem. You call in a colleague to perform a protocol analysis, and she detects large numbers of packet collisions,

late collisions, cyclical redundancy check (CRC) errors, and runt frames. Which of the following could be the cause of the problem?

A. Damaged cables

B. Transmitter (TX)/receiver (RX) transposed

C. Duplex mismatch

D. Incorrect cable type

6. Which of the following is a wireless topology that does not require the use of an access point?

A. Star

B. Ad hoc

C. Bus

D. Infrastructure

7. You want to create a network in which computers from different departments are assigned to separate virtual local area networks (VLANs). You also want to be able to forward traffic between the VLANs so that each computer is capable of accessing any other computer. Which of the following will enable you to perform all these functions with a single device?

A. Load balancer

B. Virtual router

C. Multilayer switch

D. Broadband router

8. Which of the following are standard terms used in data loss prevention to describe specific data states? (Choose all that apply.)

A. Data online

B. Data at rest

C. Data in transit

D. Data in use

9. Advanced Encryption Standard (AES) is an encryption algorithm that was introduced in the Wi-Fi Protected Access 2 (WPA2) security protocol to replace another algorithm that was found to be easily penetrated. Which of the following encryption algorithms did AES replace?

A. AES

B. WEP

C. WPA

D. TKIP

10. You have been asked by your supervisor in the IT department to test some newly installed cable runs. She hands you the tool shown in the following figure. What is the function of the tool and how do you use it?

Reproduced with permission of Todd, (2015) / John Wiley & Sons

   A. When you place the tool at one end of a wire, it generates a tone that can be detected at the other end.

   B. When you touch the end of the tool to a copper cable, you can detect and measure the electrical current flowing through it.

   C. When you connect the tool to the end of a fiber-optic cable, you can measure the length of the cable run.

   D. When you attach the tool to the end of a twisted-pair cable, it tests for crosstalk and other performance characteristics.

11. A multifactor authentication (MFA) system consists of at least two different identifying criteria, typically falling into two of the following categories: something you have, something you do, something you know, and something you are. Which of the following authentication factors is an example of something you have?

   A. A password

   B. A fingerprint

   C. A smartcard

   D. A finger gesture

12. Which of the following is a port number used for Structured Query Language (SQL) communications?

    A. 1433

    B. 3389

    C. 443

    D. 5060

13. At a clearance sale, you purchase some 802.11ac wireless network adapter cards for desktop computers at a very low price. Your plan is to use them to expand your 2.4 GHz 802.11n home network. After installing one of the adapters in a computer, you attempt to connect to the network, but you cannot see the SSID in the list of available networks. You try installing a different adapter, thinking the first one might be broken, but the second one does not work either. What can you do to resolve the problem and connect the computer to your network?

    A. Configure the network adapters to use the 2.4 GHz frequency.

    B. Move the computer closer to the access point.

    C. Manually enter the SSID in the computer's wireless network client software.

    D. Nothing. 802.11ac equipment cannot connect to a 2.4 GHz 802.11n network.

14. Which of the following mechanisms for the recovery from a disaster in a datacenter is the most expensive to implement?

    A. A hot site

    B. A warm site

    C. A cold site

    D. A cloud site

15. You are setting up an 802.11n wireless network using the 2.4 GHz frequency band. You plan to install three wireless access points. Which of the following channels should you use for your access points to avoid channel overlap that can result in interference? (Choose all that apply.)

    A. 1

    B. 4

    C. 6

    D. 8

    E. 11

16. Your supervisor has asked you to increase the security of the servers on your network. Which of the following procedures can be considered to be server hardening techniques? (Choose all that apply.)

    A. Installing additional memory

    B. Disabling unnecessary services

    C. Creating privileged user accounts

    D. Disabling unused TCP and UDP ports

17. You are working the IT help desk when a user calls to report that he cannot access the Internet, although he is able to connect to computers on the local network. At the user's workstation, you run the `ipconfig /all` command and examine the output. Which of the options is the most likely explanation for the user's problem, based on the following `ipconfig` results?

Windows IP Configuration

```
    Host Name . . . . . . . . . . . . . : Client12
    Primary Dns Suffix  . . . . . . . :
    Node Type . . . . . . . . . . . . : Hybrid
    IP Routing Enabled. . . . . . . . : No
    WINS Proxy Enabled. . . . . . . . : No

Ethernet adapter Local Area Connection:

    Connection-specific DNS Suffix  . :
    Description . . . . . . . . . . . : PCIe Family Controller
    Physical Address. . . . . . . . . : 60-EB-69-93-5E-E5
    DHCP Enabled. . . . . . . . . . . : No
    Autoconfiguration Enabled . . . . : Yes
    Link-local IPv6 Address . . . . . : fe80::c955:c944:acdd:3fcb%2
    IPv4 Address. . . . . . . . . . . : 192.168.23.234
    Subnet Mask . . . . . . . . . . . : 255.255.255.0
    Lease Obtained. . . . . . . . . . : Monday, October 23, 2017 6:23:47 PM
    Lease Expires . . . . . . . . . . : Saturday, November 18, 2017 9:49:24 PM
    Default Gateway . . . . . . . . . : 192.168.216.99
    DHCPv6 IAID . . . . . . . . . . . : 241232745
    DHCPv6 Client DUID  . . . . . . . : 00-01-00-01-18-10-22-0D-60-EB-69-93-5E-E5
    DNS Servers . . . . . . . . . . . : 192.168.22.114
    NetBIOS over Tcpip. . . . . . . . : Enabled
```

- **A.** DHCP is not enabled.
- **B.** The Subnet Mask setting is incorrect.
- **C.** The Default Gateway setting is incorrect.
- **D.** The DNS Servers setting is located on another network.

18. Which of the following are typical examples of the Internet of Things (IoT)? (Choose all that apply.)

- **A.** A television remote control
- **B.** A key fob that unlocks your car
- **C.** A smartphone app for your home thermostat
- **D.** A remotely monitored cardiac pacemaker
- **E.** A refrigerator with an internal camera

19. A Remote Authentication Dial-In User Service (RADIUS) server takes which of the following roles in an 802.1X transaction?

    A. The authenticator

    B. The authentication server

    C. The supplicant

    D. The accountant

20. You are installing an Internet access router for your company's new branch office. The router has a switch module containing four Ethernet ports, all of which are assigned to the default VLAN1. When you plug a laptop into one of the Ethernet ports, you can access the Internet with no difficulties. You now need to connect the router to the company network so that the wireless access points on the network can provide users with Internet access through the router. However, when you plug the router into a network switch port that is assigned to VLAN4, the switch starts generating "Native VLAN mismatch detected" errors once every minute. Which of the following steps should be part of the solution you implement to stop the error messages from appearing? (Choose all that apply.)

    A. Create a VLAN1 on the network switch.

    B. Configure the network switch port connected to the router to use VLAN1.

    C. Create a VLAN4 on the router's switch module.

    D. Configure the router port connected to the network switch to use VLAN4.

21. Which of the following cannot function as a preventative mitigation for the problem of tailgating? (Choose all that apply.)

    A. Security cameras

    B. Badge readers

    C. Access control vestibules

    D. Motion detectors

22. You have just created a new virtual machine (VM) using remote controls provided by a cloud service provider on the Internet. You then install an operating system on the virtual machine and configure it to function as a web server. Which of the following cloud architectures are you using when you do this? (Choose all that apply.)

    A. IaaS

    B. PaaS

    C. SaaS

    D. Public cloud

    E. Private cloud

    F. Hybrid cloud

23. It is your first day working for a consultant who does network cable installations. Your new boss hands you a spool of Category 6 cable, a bag of little clear plastic components, and the tool shown in the following figure. He then tells you to "get started on fives and tens." What is your new boss expecting you to do?

Reproduced with permission of Todd, (2015) / John Wiley & Sons

    A. Pull cable runs.

    B. Attach keystone connectors.

    C. Install a patch panel.

    D. Create patch cables.

24. Which of the following well-known ports do you use to configure outgoing mail on a POP3 email client?

    A. 110

    B. 25

    C. 143

    D. 80

25. You are a consultant who has been hired to extend a network by a client that is still running thin Ethernet. You have brought a spool of RG-58 coaxial cable. Which of the following types of cable connectors will you have to bring with you to add thin Ethernet network segments?

    A. ST

    B. BNC

    C. MPO

    D. RJ45

    E. RJ11

26. Which of the following types of cable is never used to connect a workstation to an Ethernet network?

   A. Rollover

   B. Straight-through

   C. Crossover

   D. Plenum

   E. Shielded

27. Which of the following protocols does IPsec use to provide data origin authentication by digitally signing packets before transmitting them over the network?

   A. AH

   B. SSL

   C. ESP

   D. RDP

28. You have constructed a network on which all of the computers are connected to a single switch. You then create virtual local area networks (VLANs) on the switch, corresponding to the company's departments, and add the switch port for each user workstation and department server to the appropriate VLAN. Later, users report that while they can access their departmental servers and the workstations of other users in the same department, they cannot communicate with any of the other departments. What is the problem, and what must you do to correct it?

   A. There is a faulty VLAN configuration on the switch. You must re-create all of the VLANs and configure each VLAN for routing.

   B. VLANs are limited to Data link layer communication only. To enable communication between the VLANs, you must install a router or a layer 3 switch on the network and configure it to route traffic between the VLANs.

   C. The VLANs are using different Data link layer protocols. You must configure the VLANs to use the same Data link layer protocol in order for them to communicate with each other.

   D. One of the VLANs is configured to filter all of the other VLAN traffic for security purposes. You must change the filter on this one VLAN.

29. The TCP/IP term *socket* consists of which of the following elements? (Choose all that apply.)

   A. Port number

   B. MAC address

   C. IP address

   D. Subnet mask

30. You are installing a cable modem to provide your home network with access to the Internet through your cable television provider. The cable modem is a multifunction device that the cable company says provides everything you need for a home network. Which of the following network functions does a home cable modem typically provide? (Choose all that apply.)

    A. DHCP server

    B. Wireless access point

    C. Broadband router

    D. Ethernet switch

    E. Proxy server

    F. RADIUS server

31. Which of the following Domain Name System (DNS) resource records is not used for forward name resolution?

    A. PTR

    B. CNAME

    C. AAAA

    D. MX

32. Which of the following are tasks that can be performed by a protocol analyzer that could provide potential intruders with information about the network? (Choose all that apply.)

    A. A protocol analyzer can decrypt protected information in packets captured from the network.

    B. A protocol analyzer can detect open ports on network systems and launch attacks against them.

    C. A protocol analyzer can display the IP addresses of the systems on the network.

    D. A protocol analyzer can display the application data in packets captured from the network.

33. Which of the following services are provided by a RADIUS server? (Choose all that apply.)

    A. Attenuation

    B. Authentication

    C. Assistance

    D. Authorization

    E. Accounting

34. Some users are having a problem connecting to an application server on their local network. You go to their department and start to troubleshoot the problem by testing connectivity using the ping tool at one of the user workstations. You discover that you can ping the server successfully using its computer name, but pinging the computer's fully qualified domain name (FQDN) fails. As a result of these tests, which of the following can you determine is the most likely source of the problem?

    A. EMI

    B. DHCP

    C. DNS

    D. ACL

35. You have been given the job of devising a plan to provide a 500-node private internetwork with access to the Internet. The primary objective of the project is to provide all of the network users with access to web and email services while keeping the client computers safe from unauthorized Internet users. There are two secondary objectives for the project: one is to provide a means of monitoring and regulating the users' Internet activities, and the other is to avoid having to manually configure IP addresses on each one of the client computers. You submit a proposal that calls for the use of private IP addresses on the client computers and a series of proxy servers with public, registered IP addresses, which are connected to the Internet. Which of the following statements about your proposed Internet access solution is true?

   A. The proposal satisfies the primary objective and both of the secondary objectives.

   B. The proposal satisfies the primary objective and one of the secondary objectives.

   C. The proposal satisfies the primary objective but neither of the secondary objectives.

   D. The proposal fails to satisfy either the primary or secondary objective.

36. Which of the following cloud service models provides the consumer with the least amount of control over the cloud resources?

   A. IaaS

   B. PaaS

   C. SaaS

   D. IaaS, PaaS, and SaaS all provide the same degree of control.

37. The jumbo frame capability is associated with which networking protocol?

   A. Ethernet

   B. Internet Protocol (IP)

   C. Point-to-Point Protocol (PPP)

   D. Transmission Control Protocol (TCP)

38. You are working your company's IT help desk, where you are required to follow a specific troubleshooting protocol when handling calls from users. In which of the following troubleshooting steps would you create a trouble ticket?

   A. Establish a theory of probable cause.

   B. Verify full system functionality and implement preventive measures, if applicable.

   C. Identify the problem.

   D. Test the theory to determine the cause.

   E. Document findings, actions, and outcomes.

   F. Implement the solution or escalate as necessary.

   G. Establish a plan of action to resolve the problem and identify potential effects.

39. You are working your company's help desk when a user calls to report that he cannot access any of the data on his computer. He says that a message has appeared on his screen stating that all of his data has been encrypted by the FBI and that it will be decrypted only after he pays $768 in Bitcoin to an unknown address. The user wants to know if he is responsible for making the payment. Which of the following types of attacks has the user experienced?

    A. Denial-of-service

    B. Social engineering

    C. Ransomware

    D. ARP poisoning

40. Which of the following are switch features that help to prevent intruders from manipulating the Spanning Tree Protocol (STP)?

    A. Geofencing

    B. Root guard

    C. DHCP snooping

    D. BPDU guard

41. Network cable runs generally connect office endpoints, such as wall plates, to a central cabling nexus, which is typically where the runs are joined to a backbone network that links them together. Which of the following are terms for such nexuses where network cabling connections are found? (Choose all that apply.)

    A. RDP

    B. IDF

    C. MDF

    D. MTBF

42. Your supervisor has asked you to call the cabling contractor your company uses and make an appointment to install some new twisted-pair cable runs. In addition to asking how many cable runs you need pulled, the contractor asks you if you need plenum or PVC. Under which of the following conditions might the local building code require that a data network use plenum cable?

    A. When cable runs exceed the maximum length specified by the Physical layer specification

    B. When cables must run through air ducts

    C. When cables run near devices that generate electromagnetic interference (EMI)

    D. When multiple cables run through the same conduit

43. Which of the following is not a term for the process of combining the bandwidth of two or more network adapters to increase the overall speed of the connection and provide fault tolerance?

    A. Port aggregation

    B. Link aggregation

    C. Bonding

    D. Clustering

    E. NIC teaming

44. You have been asked by the director of the IT department to review the security status of the network device administration procedures currently in use. You know that network device hardening has as one of its first principles the use of secure protocols over insecure ones. Which of the following suggestions are examples of this principle that you should suggest to the director? (Choose all that apply.)

   A. Use WEP instead of WPA2.

   B. Use TKIP instead of AES.

   C. Use HTTPS instead of HTTP.

   D. Use SSH instead of Telnet.

45. The Simple Network Management Protocol (SNMP) works by processing information gathered from agents installed or embedded in network devices and displaying the information on a central console. Which of the following is the term used for the database in which SNMP agents store information about their properties?

   A. MIB

   B. Trap

   C. Syslog

   D. SIEM

46. When a web browser connects to a web server using an address with the https:// prefix, the connection is secured using Transmission Control Protocol (TCP) and an encryption protocol. Which of the following protocols are typically used to secure communication between web servers and web browsers? (Choose all that apply.)

   A. TLS

   B. SSH

   C. DTLS

   D. SSL

47. A screened subnet is a segment that is exposed to the Internet and separated from the internal network by a firewall. Administrators typically use a screened subnet for servers that must be accessible to outside users, such as web and email servers. Which of the following is another term for a screened subnet?

   A. PEAP

   B. DMZ

   C. VLAN

   D. TKIP

48. Which of the following types of traffic is not exchanged by Remote Desktop clients and servers using the Remote Desktop Protocol (RDP)?

   A. Keystrokes

   B. Mouse movements

   C. Display information

   D. Application data

49. You have been engaged to design a wireless LAN for a site you have never seen. For that reason, you want the LAN to be able to support both the 2.4 GHz and 5 GHz frequencies. Which of the following IEEE 802.11 wireless LAN standards should you look for when you are shopping for equipment that supports both frequencies? (Choose all that apply.)

    A. 802.11g

    B. 802.11n

    C. 802.11ac

    D. 802.11ax

50. Which of the following statements about multitenancy in a public cloud datacenter is not true?

    A. Multitenancy presents a potential security risk because other tenants are using the same hardware.

    B. Multitenancy separates tenants by assigning each one its own virtual machine.

    C. Multitenancy reduces the cost of utilities and other overhead.

    D. Multitenancy introduces the possibility of competition for bandwidth with other tenants.

51. Which of the following specifies the name of a network using multiple APs to support a single SSID?

    A. BSS

    B. ESS

    C. SSID

    D. BSSID

    E. ESSID

52. When starting her new position as a network administrator, Alice was given two user accounts. One account is intended for standard user activities, and the other account has the additional permissions needed for Alice to perform administrative tasks. This is an example of which of the following security concepts?

    A. Zero day

    B. Least privilege

    C. Defense in depth

    D. Multifactor authentication

53. You are in the process of troubleshooting a user's computer that is malfunctioning. Which step of the troubleshooting model involves replacing computer components until you have identified a faulty hardware device?

    A. Establish a plan of action to resolve the problem.

    B. Duplicate the problem.

    C. Gather information.

    D. Verify full system functionality.

    E. Test the theory to determine the cause.

    F. Document findings, actions, and outcomes.

    G. Establish a theory of probable cause.

54. Which of the following could be an indication that there is a rogue DHCP server on your network?

    A. A user's workstation has an IP address from another subnet.

    B. A user can access local resources from his workstation but not Internet resources.

    C. The DHCP Enabled setting on a user's workstation is set to No.

    D. The user's workstation has an IP address on the 169.254.0.0/16 subnet.

55. Which of the following network interface occurrences is considered to be malfunctions on a full-duplex Ethernet network but not on a half-duplex Ethernet network?

    A. Runts

    B. Late collisions

    C. Giants

    D. Collisions

56. A protocol analyzer is a tool that captures packets from a network and examines their contents. Which of the following Unix/Linux tools is a protocol analyzer?

    A. `nmap`

    B. `tcpdump`

    C. `pathping`

    D. `iptables`

57. A storage area network (SAN) typically takes the form of a dedicated network used to provide servers with access to hard disk arrays and other storage devices. Which of the following statements about the differences between a SAN and network attached storage (NAS) are true? (Choose all that apply.)

    A. NAS devices typically provide a filesystem, while SAN devices do not.

    B. NAS provides file-level storage access, whereas a SAN provides block-level storage access.

    C. NAS devices typically contain integrated iSCSI targets.

    D. SAN devices have an operating system, whereas NAS devices do not.

58. Your supervisor has just informed you that the CIO has hired an outside consultant to perform penetration testing on the company network. Which of the following best describes what you can expect the consultant to do?

    A. Evaluate the security conditions on the network.

    B. Create computers or networks that are alluring targets for intruders.

    C. Attempt to compromise the network's security measures.

    D. Implement a new companywide security protocol.

59. Your company is a contractor for the government that regularly works with highly sensitive defense data. To prevent this data from being compromised, the company's datacenter has various special security measures installed. All of the servers have crimped metal tags holding the cases closed. All of the hardware racks are locked in clear-fronted cabinets. All of the cable runs are installed in transparent conduits. These are all examples of which of the following types of physical security measure?

    A. Asset tracking

    B. Geofencing

    C. Tamper detection

    D. Port security

60. Which of the following tools are only usable on fiber-optic networks? (Choose all that apply.)

    A. Visual fault locator

    B. Optical power meter

    C. Protocol analyzer

    D. Toner and probe

61. Which of the following mechanisms use tunneling to establish secured links between TCP/IP systems? (Choose all that apply.)

    A. VPNs

    B. IPsec

    C. GRE

    D. NAT

62. Your supervisor has given you a Class C network IP address and has asked you to create a network with 8 subnets and 30 hosts per subnet. Which of the following subnet masks will you have to use?

    A. 255.255.255.128

    B. 255.255.255.192

    C. 255.255.255.224

    D. 255.255.255.240

    E. 255.255.255.248

    F. 255.255.255.252

63. You are a consultant working at a client site. The client has supplied you with the SSID and the passphrase for the company's wireless network so that you can connect to it with your laptop. However, you are unable to establish a connection. Which of the following security measures might be preventing you from connecting your laptop to the network?

    A. Geofencing

    B. MAC filtering

    C. Using WPA3

    D. Disabling SSID broadcasts

64. You have just finished installing a new Category 6 cable run for the first time. After attaching keystone connectors to both ends of the cable, you mount the office-side connector to a wall plate and mount the datacenter connector into a patch panel. Then you take a patch cable and connect the patch panel port to an open port in one of the network switches. However, the link pulse LED on the switch port does not light as it is supposed to. What should you do next?

    A. Repull the cable run using Category 6a cable.

    B. Check the cable run for wiring faults.

    C. Make sure the switch port is not disabled.

    D. Plug a computer into the wall plate.

65. Devices on a TCP/IP network typically use the Address Resolution Protocol (ARP) to locate specific destinations on the local network by resolving IP addresses into MAC addresses (also known as hardware addresses). At which layer of the Open Systems Interconnection (OSI) model do these MAC addresses operate?

    A. Physical

    B. Data link

    C. Network

    D. Transport

66. Which of the following Network layer protocols includes a field that limits the number of times a packet can be routed on a network? (Choose all that apply.)

    A. ICMP

    B. IGMP

    C. IPv4

    D. IPv6

67. ARP poisoning is the deliberate insertion of fraudulent information into the ARP cache stored on computers and switches. Which of the following types of attack can be facilitated by ARP poisoning? (Choose all that apply.)

    A. Social engineering

    B. On-path

    C. Evil twin

    D. Session hijacking

68. Recently, your network has been the target of numerous attack attempts. To gather information about the attackers, you have created a server that is designed to function as an enticing target but that does not provide access to any legitimately sensitive services or information. Which of the following is the term used to describe this technique?

    A. Spoofing

    B. DMZ

    C. Root guard

    D. Honeypot

69. You are a consultant working on a new client's network. The network has been in place for decades, and you have been given a diagram supplied by the original installer. The diagram says that the network computers are connected to a device called a multiport bridge. Which of the following devices can also be described as a multiport bridge?

A. Repeater

B. Hub

C. Switch

D. Router

70. When you run a port scanner on a server, which of the following is the result?

A. A list of the servers currently running user processes

B. A list of the computer's hardware ports that are currently in use

C. A list specifying the numbers of packets transmitted and received by each network adapter on the system

D. A list of open ports through which the system can be accessed

E. A list of the IP addresses used by all the devices on the local network

71. Your company has a seven-node failover cluster hosting databases on SQL Server. Each server has three network interface adapters installed in it. Two are standard Gigabit Ethernet adapters that provide the nodes with access to each other and clients with access to the cluster. One is a Fibre Channel adapter that provides the cluster nodes with access to a dedicated network that also hosts a large hard disk array. Which of the following terms describe the networks to which the cluster nodes are connected? (Choose all that apply.)

A. SAN

B. WAN

C. MAN

D. LAN

72. A Windows user calls you at the help desk and reports that he cannot connect to any hosts on either the local or a remote network. This is the only report of its kind you have received today. You question the user about the problem and eventually learn that he has made some changes to his workstation's Internet Protocol (IP) settings. What should you do next?

A. Check the switches in the datacenter to see if they have logged any error messages.

B. Verify that the routers on the network are functioning.

C. Run the ipconfig command on the user's workstation to view its configuration.

D. Check the network's Domain Name System (DNS) server to see if it is resolving IP hostnames.

73. You are a network administrator attempting to use your workstation on the internal network to remotely control a web server called WebServ1 on a screened subnet. However, the remote desktop client software is unable to establish a connection to the server. You can see all the computers on your local network and on the screened subnet. You try using the ping utility to test the TCP/IP functionality of WebServ1, and the ping test is successful. You then call your colleague on the same internal network and have her try to connect to WebServ1 using the same remote access tool. She connects to WebServ1 successfully. Which of the following could be the cause of the problem you are experiencing?

A. Blocked TCP/UDP ports on the web server

B. Name resolution failure

C. Incorrect firewall settings on your workstation

D. Unresponsive service on the web server

74. The toolkit you were given when you began work for an IT consulting company contained the tool shown in the following figure. What is the function of this tool?

Reproduced with permission of Todd, (2015) / John Wiley & Sons

A. When you touch the end of the tool to a copper cable, you can detect and measure the electrical current flowing through it.

B. When you place the tool at one end of a wire, it generates a tone that can be detected at the other end.

C. To connect a bulk cable to a keystone connector, you use the tool to punch each wire down into the correct receptacle on the connector.

D. When you connect the tool to the end of a fiber-optic cable, you can measure the length of the cable run.

75. You are designing a new wireless network based on the IEEE 802.11n standard. The equipment you have selected supports both the 2.4 GHz and 5 GHz frequencies, and you are undecided about which one to use. Which of the following are possible reasons why the 5 GHz frequency tends to perform better than the 2.4 GHz frequency on a wireless LAN? (Choose all that apply.)

A. The 5 GHz frequency has more channels than the 2.4 GHz frequency.

B. The 5 GHz frequency conflicts with fewer common household devices than the 2.4 GHz frequency.

C. The 5 GHz frequency transmits at faster speeds than the 2.4 GHz frequency.

D. The 5 GHz frequency supports longer ranges than the 2.4 GHz frequency.

76. A rack-mounted device that is six units tall will be approximately what height in inches?

- **A.** 1.75
- **B.** 3.5
- **C.** 7
- **D.** 10.5

77. Which of the following server applications uses two well-known port numbers, one for control traffic and one for data traffic?

- **A.** FTP
- **B.** SNMP
- **C.** NTP
- **D.** HTTP

78. You are configuring the computers on a new network, and you have been given the network address 10.26.0.0/13. Which of the following subnet mask values must you use when configuring the computers?

- **A.** 255.248.0.0
- **B.** 255.252.0.0
- **C.** 255.254.0.0
- **D.** 255.255.248.0
- **E.** 255.255.252.0
- **F.** 255.255.254.0

79. You are testing a twisted-pair cable run using a toner and probe. When you apply the toner to each of the first seven wires at one end of the cable, you successfully detect a tone on the corresponding pin at the other end. However, when you connect the toner to the eighth wire, you fail to detect a tone at the other end. Which of the following fault types have you discovered?

- **A.** Short circuit
- **B.** Open circuit
- **C.** Split pair
- **D.** Crosstalk

80. Which of the following functions are defined as occurring at the Session layer of the Open Systems Interconnection (OSI) model? (Choose all that apply.)

- **A.** Data encryption
- **B.** Dialog control
- **C.** Datagram routing
- **D.** Dialog separation

81. You are working your company's IT help desk, and you have had several calls from users who are reporting problems with their Voice over IP (VoIP) and streaming video connections. In each case, the audio or video connection experiences frequent dropouts in sound or video, causing frustrating interruptions. Which of the following terms describes a connectivity problem on a wired network that could cause these symptoms?

A. Jitter

B. Latency

C. Bottleneck

D. Attenuation

82. You are a consultant with a client who wants to have you install a wireless network with the highest throughput currently available. What is the fastest speed achievable by a wireless LAN using the currently ratified IEEE 802.11 standards?

A. 54 Mbps

B. 600 Mbps

C. 6.9 Gbps

D. 9.6 Gbps

83. A private network uses unregistered IP addresses that are not accessible from the Internet. In order for computers on the private network to access Internet servers, there must be a device that substitutes registered IP addresses for the unregistered ones. Which of the following devices are capable of performing this kind of IP address substitution? (Choose all that apply.)

A. RADIUS server

B. NAT router

C. UTM appliance

D. Proxy server

84. A user calls you at the technical support desk in the computer store where you work. He is installing a home network and is having trouble configuring the IP addresses for his computers. He starts reading off a list of the network addresses he has tried to use. Which of the following are valid IPv4 network addresses that the user can conceivably use to configure his computers? (Choose all that apply.)

A. 1.1.1.0

B. 9.34.0.0

C. 103.256.77.0

D. 229.6.87.0

85. Which of the following terms refers to a routing protocol that relies on hop counts to measure the efficiency of routes through an internetwork?

   A.   Link state protocol

   B.   Distance vector protocol

   C.   Edge gateway protocol

   D.   Interior gateway protocol

86. You have been hired by a client to connect two local area networks that are in different buildings 500 meters apart. The cable type you use must support Gigabit Ethernet data rates of 1,000 megabits per second (Mbps) and provide a high level of resistance to electromagnetic interference (EMI). Which of the following cable types can you choose to meet the client's needs? (Choose all that apply.)

   A.   Single-mode fiber-optic cable

   B.   Thin coaxial cable

   C.   Multimode fiber-optic cable

   D.   Shielded twisted-pair (STP) cable

   E.   Unshielded twisted-pair (UTP) cable

87. You receive a call at the IT help desk from a user who has recently moved to a new office in the company building, down the hall from her old one. Since the move, she has only been able to access the company's wireless network with her laptop intermittently. The network is based on 802.11n equipment, and it is using the 2.4 GHz frequency and the WPA3 security protocol. The user never had a problem in her previous office location. Which of the following could not possibly be the cause of her problem? (Choose all that apply.)

   A.   The user's laptop is connecting to the wrong SSID.

   B.   The user's laptop is configured to use the 5 GHz frequency.

   C.   The user's new office is farther from the access point than her old one.

   D.   There are more intervening walls between the user's new office and the access point.

   E.   The user's laptop is configured with the wrong WPA3 passphrase.

88. Which of the following statements about static routing are not true? (Choose all that apply.)

   A.   Static routes are automatically added to the routing table by routing protocols when a new network path becomes available.

   B.   Static routes are manually configured routes that administrators must add, modify, or delete when a change in the network occurs.

   C.   Static routes are a recommended solution for large internetworks with redundant paths to each destination network.

   D.   Static routes are a recommended solution for small internetworks with a single path to each destination network.

   E.   Static routes adapt to changes in the network infrastructure automatically.

89. Which layer of the Open Systems Interconnection (OSI) model has its own logical addressing system and is responsible for routing packets from one network to another?

A. Physical

B. Data link

C. Network

D. Transport

E. Session

F. Presentation

G. Application

90. Several marketing consultants are working in your office for the first time, and they have approached you because they are unable to connect to the company's 802.11ac wireless network with their laptops. They are selecting the correct SSID from the Available Networks list, but they still cannot connect, and there are no error messages of any kind. Which of the following tasks should you perform first to try to resolve the problem?

A. Examine the area where the consultants are working for possible sources of signal interference.

B. Change the frequency used by the wireless access point from 5 GHz to 2.4 GHz.

C. Make sure that the consultants' laptops are configured to use the correct wireless security protocol.

D. Check the network adapters in the laptops for channel overlap.

91. You are researching the various types of storage area network (SAN) technologies currently available before making a purchasing recommendation to your IT director. Which of the following are genuine advantages of iSCSI over Fibre Channel? (Choose all that apply.)

A. iSCSI can share the same network as standard local area network (LAN) traffic, whereas Fibre Channel cannot.

B. iSCSI is routable, whereas Fibre Channel is not.

C. iSCSI is less expensive to implement than Fibre Channel.

D. iSCSI includes its own internal flow control mechanism, whereas Fibre Channel does not.

92. In which of the following DNS transactions does the querying system generate an iterative query? (Choose all that apply.)

A. A DNS client extracts the server name www.adatum.com from a URL and sends it to its designated DNS server for resolution.

B. A client's DNS server sends a name resolution request to a root domain server to discover the authoritative server for the com top-level domain.

C. A client's DNS server sends a name resolution request to the com top-level domain server to find the authoritative server for the adatum.com domain.

D. A client's DNS server, which has been configured to function as a forwarder, sends the server name www.adatum.com from a URL to its ISP's DNS server for resolution.

E. A client's DNS server sends a name resolution request to the adatum.com domain server to discover the IP address associated with the server name www.

93. A user approaches you as you are passing through his department and reports that he cannot access the Internet. After questioning him, you determine that he can access systems on the local network. You examine the routing table on the user's Windows workstation, and you see the problem. Which of the following commands must you run to correct the user's problem, based on the routing table display shown here?

```
IPv4 Route Table
===========================================================================
Active Routes:
Network Destination        Netmask          Gateway       Interface  Metric
          127.0.0.0        255.0.0.0        On-link        127.0.0.1    331
          127.0.0.1  255.255.255.255        On-link        127.0.0.1    331
    127.255.255.255  255.255.255.255        On-link        127.0.0.1    331
        192.168.2.0    255.255.255.0        On-link     192.168.2.37    281
       192.168.2.37  255.255.255.255        On-link     192.168.2.37    281
      192.168.2.255  255.255.255.255        On-link     192.168.2.37    281
          224.0.0.0        240.0.0.0        On-link        127.0.0.1    331
          224.0.0.0        240.0.0.0        On-link     192.168.2.37    281
    255.255.255.255  255.255.255.255        On-link        127.0.0.1    331
    255.255.255.255  255.255.255.255        On-link     192.168.2.37    281
===========================================================================
Persistent Routes:
  None
```

   A. route add 192.168.2.0 MASK 0.0.0.0 192.168.2.37 METRIC 25 IF 192.168.2.99

   B. route add 0.0.0.0 MASK 255.255.255.0 192.168.2.99 METRIC 25 IF 192.168.2.37

   C. route add 192.168.2.0 MASK 255.255.255.0 192.168.2.99 METRIC 25 IF 192.168.2.37

   D. route add 0.0.0.0 MASK 0.0.0.0 192.168.2.99 METRIC 25 IF 192.168.2.37

94. You are heading out to do a cabling job for a client who has coaxial and twisted-pair Ethernet networks at their facility. You want to bring connectors and cables to prepare for any eventuality. Which of the following connector types are typically associated with Ethernet networks? (Choose all that apply.)

   A. N-type
   B. BNC
   C. F-type
   D. RJ-45
   E. DB-9

95. When geofencing is used as part of a multifactor authentication system, which of the following best describes geofencing's role?

A. Somewhere you are

B. Something you do

C. Something you have

D. Something you know

96. Some organizations maintain alternative sites that they can use as datacenters should a disaster render the main datacenter unusable. Which of the following types of disaster recovery site can be made operational in the shortest amount of time?

A. A hot site

B. A warm site

C. A cold site

D. All of the site types require the same amount of preparation time.

97. Which of the following types of virtual private network (VPN) connection is the best solution for connecting a home user to a corporate network?

A. Host-to-site

B. Site-to-site

C. Host-to-host

D. Extranet

98. Which of the following are valid reasons why the leaf and spine datacenter topology is superior to the standard three-tier topology?

A. The leaf and spine topology is less expensive to implement than the three-tier topology.

B. In a leaf and spine topology, all data flows require the same number of hops.

C. The leaf and spine arrangement uses a full mesh switching topology.

D. The leaf and spine topology uses software-defined networking to direct traffic, rather than blocking ports using the Spanning Tree Protocol.

99. A baseline is a performance measurement for a device or system, taken under normal operating conditions, which you can use later to quantify any changes that might have taken place. Which of the following Windows applications would you most likely use to create a baseline of system or network performance?

A. Syslog

B. Event Viewer

C. Network Monitor

D. Performance Monitor

100. In most cases, a denial-of-service (DoS) attack refers to a deliberate attempt to overwhelm a server with incoming traffic. However, this is not always the case. Which of the following types of DoS attacks does not involve flooding a server with traffic?

A. Amplified

B. Distributed

C. Permanent

D. Reflective

Chapter

7

Practice Test 2

1. Which of the following definitions best describes the function of a firewall?

    A. A device that connects two networks forwarding traffic between them as needed

    B. A device located between two networks that enables administrators to restrict incoming and outgoing traffic

    C. A device that caches Internet data for subsequent use by internal network clients

    D. A device that enables Internet network clients with private IP addresses to access the Internet

2. Review the following figure. Each of the switches has three ports connected to computers and one port for switch-to-switch connections. All of the computer ports and links are configured for half-duplex communication. The switch-to-switch links are configured for full-duplex communication. Which of the following statements about the switched network is true?

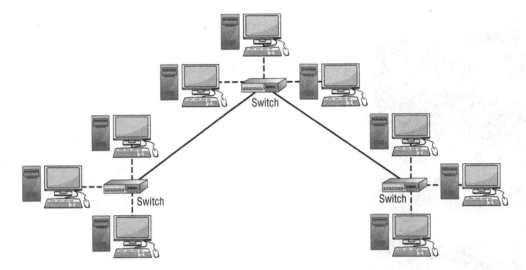

    A. There is one collision domain for this network.

    B. There are three collision domains, one for each switch-to-switch connection.

    C. There are nine collision domains, one for each half-duplex connection.

    D. There are twelve collision domains, one for each switch connection.

3. Which of the following network devices can provide authentication services for multiple remote access servers using the device's own account database?

    A. NAS

    B. IDS

    C. NGFW

    D. RADIUS

4. You are designing the network for your company's new branch office, and you need a device on which administrators can create virtual local area networks (VLANs) and that will forward traffic between them. Which of the following devices can do this?

    A. Virtual router

    B. Multilayer switch

    C. Broadband router

    D. Load balancer

5. You are setting up a new network for which you have been given the IPv4 network address 10.61.0.0/19. You want to calculate the number of hosts you can create on each subnet. How many bits are allocated to the host identifier in an IPv4 address on this network?

    A. 5

    B. 8

    C. 13

    D. 21

6. The protocols that are responsible for the delivery of data packets to their final destinations on an internetwork operate at which layer of the Open Systems Interconnection (OSI) reference model?

    A. Application

    B. Session

    C. Transport

    D. Network

    E. Data link

7. Originally, storage area networks (SANs) were dedicated solely to storage-based traffic. A local area network (LAN) was also required for other types of traffic. Today, however, it is possible for SAN and LAN traffic to coexist on a single network medium. Which of the following SAN protocols are capable of sharing a network medium with standard LAN traffic? (Choose all that apply.)

    A. Fibre Channel

    B. InfiniBand

    C. iSCSI

    D. FCoE

8. Which of the following Application layer protocols do not include a program that enables a user to log on to a remote network device and execute commands using a character-based interface? (Choose all that apply.)

    A. Telnet

    B. Simple Mail Transfer Protocol (SMTP)

    C. File Transfer Protocol (FTP)

    D. Domain Name System (DNS)

9. Which of the following statements about switches are true? (Choose all that apply.)

    A. Switches provide internal crossover circuits and use uplink ports to form a hierarchical star/hub and spoke topology.

    B. Switches are Data link layer devices that connect network devices in a star/hub and spoke topology.

    C. Switches amplify and repeat signals received through one port out all other ports regardless of the destination.

    D. Switches use IP addresses to identify the devices connected to specific ports.

10. You are planning an automated operating system deployment for 100 new Windows workstations your company has received. You intend to configure the workstations to boot using Preboot Execution Environment (PXE), during which time the system will obtain an IP address from a Dynamic Host Configuration Protocol (DHCP) server and then download a boot image file from a Trivial File Transfer Protocol (TFTP) server. Which of the following well-known ports must you open on the firewall separating the workstations from the servers? (Choose all that apply.)

    A. 64

    B. 65

    C. 66

    D. 67

    E. 68

    F. 69

11. Your department is experiencing frequent delays as users wait for images to render using their outdated graphics software package. As a result, you submitted a change request for a new software product at the monthly meeting of the company's change management team. Now that the change request has been approved, it is time to implement the change. Which of the following administrative tasks will most likely be the change management team's responsibility during the implementation process? (Choose all that apply.)

    A. Notifying users

    B. Documenting all modifications made

    C. Authorizing downtime

    D. Designating a maintenance window

12. You are installing a new server that is equipped with two power supplies. The server's firmware enables you to set the mode in which the power supplies will be used. In which of the following modes must the dual power supplies be running in order for the system to be fault tolerant?

    A. Individual mode

    B. Combined mode

    C. Redundant mode

    D. Hot backup mode

13. The Domain Name System (DNS) defines a hierarchical name space, in which locations are reflected in fully qualified domain names (FQDNs). Which of the words in the FQDN www.paris.mydomain.org represents the bottommost layer in the DNS namespace's domain hierarchy?

A. www

B. paris

C. mydomain

D. org

14. The term *datagram* is typically used by protocols offering connectionless delivery service. Which of the following protocols use the term *datagram* to describe the data transfer unit it creates? (Choose all that apply.)

A. TCP

B. IP

C. UDP

D. Ethernet

15. Which element of the CIA triad prevents unauthorized viewing of protected data?

A. Confidentiality

B. Integrity

C. Availability

D. None of the above

16. You have just received notification of a new software release for an application you are running on your servers. The release is intended to address a newly discovered security vulnerability. Which of the following is the correct term for a software release containing a fix designed to address one specific issue?

A. An upgrade

B. A patch

C. A service pack

D. An update

17. Twisted-pair cables consist of multiple pairs of wires within a sheath, with each pair of wires twisted together separately. Which of the following statements best explain the reason for the twists in twisted-pair cabling? (Choose all that apply.)

A. The twists help to prevent crosstalk in adjacent wire pairs.

B. The twists make it easier for installers to attach connectors to the cable ends.

C. The twists extend the cable's bend radius allowance, making it easier to install.

D. The twists limit the effects of electromagnetic interference (EMI) on the signals carried over the cable.

E. The twists help to prevent data collisions from occurring.

18. The figure shown here lists the processes currently running on a Linux workstation. Which of the following performance monitoring tools, provided in Linux and Unix operating systems, enables you to display information about processes that are currently running on a system?

A. netstat

B. dig

C. perfmon

D. top

19. You are contracting with a provider to obtain email services for the clients on your network, using their existing email servers in the public cloud. You do not need anything from the provider other than email. Which of the following service models will you be using?

A. PaaS

B. SaaS

C. IaaS

D. All of the above

20. Security information and event management (SIEM) is a combination tool that uses information gathered from logs and network devices to provide a real-time analysis of the network's security condition. Which of the following SIEM processes performs searches for specific criteria, during specific time frames, in logs located on different computers?

A. Data aggregation

B. Correlation

C. Retention

D. Forensic analysis

21. When you start a Dynamic Host Configuration Protocol (DHCP) client, it transmits DHCPDISCOVER messages to locate and initiate contact with DHCP servers. Which of the following types of transmissions does the client use for this purpose?

    A. Broadcast

    B. Unicast

    C. Multicast

    D. Anycast

22. Which of the following technologies enables virtual private network (VPN) users to establish a connection using only a web browser?

    A. VPN concentrator

    B. DMVPN

    C. SIP trunk

    D. MPLS

    E. Clientless VPN

23. You are installing a wireless network in a site that has many 2.4 GHz wireless telephones. Which of the following wireless networking technologies can you use that will never experience interference from the telephones? (Choose all that apply.)

    A. IEEE 802.11b

    B. IEEE 802.11g

    C. IEEE 802.11ac

    D. IEEE 802.11a

    E. IEEE 802.11n

24. Which of the following is another term for a switch?

    A. Multicast hub

    B. Multiport repeater

    C. Multiport bridge

    D. Multihomed router

25. You are working at a client site with a managed router that includes a console port for administrative access, which you can use to connect a laptop and run a terminal program to access the device's interface. Which of the following is the best term for this type of access to the device?

    A. Client-to-site

    B. In-band

    C. BYOD

    D. Out-of-band

26. Which of the following describes the primary difference between single sign-on (SSO) and same sign-on?

A. Single sign-on (SSO) credentials consist of one username and one password, whereas same sign-on credentials consist of one username and multiple passwords.

B. Single sign-on (SSO) requires the user to supply credentials only once, whereas with same sign-on, the user must supply the credentials repeatedly.

C. Single sign-on (SSO) requires multifactor authentication, such as a password and a smartcard, whereas same sign-on requires only a password for authentication.

D. Single sign-on (SSO) enables users to access different resources with one set of credentials, whereas same sign-on requires users to have multiple credential sets.

27. You have a laptop that requires you to hold your finger on a scanner pad before you can use it. A device equipped with a fingerprint scanner that is part of a multifactor authentication mechanism is using which of the following types of technology?

A. Tamper detection

B. Biometrics

C. Hand geometry

D. Pattern recognition

28. You have been asked to locate the computers on a network that the previous consultant has configured with incorrect IPv6 addresses. Which of the following are not correctly formatted IPv6 addresses? (Choose all that apply.)

A. fe00::c955:c944:acdd:3fcb

B. fe00::b491:cf79:p493:23ff

C. 2001:0:44ef68:23eb:99fe:72bec6:ea5f

D. 2001:0:49e6:39ff:8cf5:6812:ef56

29. During a physical security evaluation by an outside contractor, you are asked whether your company uses a fail open or fail closed policy for the datacenter. You do not know what the contractor means. Which of the following physical security mechanisms can either fail close or fail open?

A. Door locks

B. Motion detectors

C. Honeypots

D. Video cameras

30. A disgruntled senior associate in the IT department at your company was terminated today and had to be escorted from the building. The IT director has instructed you to disable all of the former employee's accounts, change all network device passwords to which the employee had access, and have the datacenter door locks rekeyed. Which of the following terms best describes the director's concern in asking you to do these things?

A. Logic bombs

B. Internal threats

C. Rogue devices

D. Social engineering

E. External threats

31. Ralph is troubleshooting a Windows server, and while doing so he runs the following command: `ping 127.0.0.1`. The command completes successfully. What has Ralph proven by doing this?

A. That the computer's network adapter is functioning properly

B. That the computer's IP address is correct for the network

C. That the computer's TCP/IP networking stack is loaded and functioning properly

D. Nothing at all

32. Which of the following are not examples of multifactor authentication (MFA)? (Choose all that apply.)

A. A system that requires a smartcard and a PIN for authentication

B. A system that uses an external RADIUS server for authentication

C. A system that requires two passwords for authentication

D. A system that requires a password and a retinal scan for authentication

33. A user calls Ed at the help desk to report that he cannot access the Internet. He can access systems on the local network, however. Ed examines the routing table on the user's workstation and sees the following. Which of the following statements explains why the user cannot access the Internet?

```
IPv4 Route Table
===========================================================================
Active Routes:
Network Destination   Netmask          Gateway    Interface      Metric
    127.0.0.0         255.0.0.0        On-link    127.0.0.1      331
    127.0.0.1         255.255.255.255  On-link    127.0.0.1      331
    127.255.255.255   255.255.255.255  On-link    127.0.0.1      331
    192.168.2.0       255.255.255.0    On-link    192.168.2.37   281
    192.168.2.37      255.255.255.255  On-link    192.168.2.37   281
    192.168.2.255     255.255.255.255  On-link    192.168.2.37   281
    224.0.0.0         240.0.0.0        On-link    127.0.0.1      331
    224.0.0.0         240.0.0.0        On-link    192.168.2.37   281
    255.255.255.255   255.255.255.255  On-link    127.0.0.1      331
    255.255.255.255   255.255.255.255  On-link    192.168.2.37   281
===========================================================================
Persistent Routes:
  None
```

    A. The routing table does not specify a loopback address.

    B. The routing table does not specify a DNS server address.

    C. The routing table does not specify a default gateway address.

    D. The routing table contains two different routes to the 224.0.0.0 network.

34. Which of the following statements about single-mode fiber-optic cable are true? (Choose all that apply.)

    A. Multimode cables use an LED light source, while single-mode cables use a laser.

    B. Multimode cables can span longer distances than single-mode cables.

    C. Multimode cables have a smaller core filament than single-mode cables.

    D. Multimode cables have a smaller bend radius than single-mode, making them easier to install.

    E. Multimode fiber-optic cables require a ground, whereas single-mode cables do not.

35. A user swipes a smartcard through the reader connected to a laptop and then types a password to log on to the system. Which of the following actions is the user performing?

    A. Auditing

    B. Accounting

    C. Authorization

    D. Authentication

36. Which of the following cabling topologies have never been used by standard Ethernet networks? (Choose all that apply.)

    A. Bus

    B. Ring

    C. Star/hub and spoke

    D. Mesh

37. Pulling into your company parking lot at lunchtime, you notice a person without a company parking sticker on his car working at a laptop. You have seen this more than once, and you begin to suspect that unauthorized users are connecting to the company's wireless access point and gaining access to the network. Which of the following are steps you can take to prevent this from happening in the future? (Choose all that apply.)

    A. Use RADIUS for authentication.

    B. Place the access point in a screened subnet.

    C. Disable SSID broadcasting.

    D. Implement MAC address filtering.

38. Which of the following is a fault tolerance mechanism for the default gateway on a specific TCP/IP LAN?

    A. Open Shortest Path First (OSPF)

    B. First Hop Redundancy Protocol (FHRP)

    C. Spanning Tree Protocol (STP)

    D. Network address translation (NAT)

39. Multiprotocol switches are devices that perform functions associated with two different layers of the Open Systems Interconnection (OSI) reference model. Which of the following layers are often associated with network switching? (Choose all that apply.)

    A. Application

    B. Presentation

    C. Session

    D. Transport

    E. Network

    F. Data link

    G. Physical

40. You are attempting to connect your new laptop to your company's wireless network. The wireless access point on the network has an SSID that is not broadcasted and uses WPA3 for security. Which of the following describes what you must do to connect your laptop to the network?

    A. Select the SSID from a list and allow the client to automatically detect the security protocol.

    B. Type the SSID manually and then select WPA3 from the security protocol options provided.

    C. Type the SSID manually and allow the client to automatically detect the security protocol.

    D. Select the SSID from a list and then select WPA3 from the security protocol options provided.

41. Carrier Sense Multiple Access with Collision Avoidance (CSMA/CA) is a media access control mechanism designed to prevent two systems using the same network medium from transmitting at the same time. Which of the following IEEE standards calls for the use of CSMA/CA?

    A. 802.3

    B. 802.1X

    C. 802.11ac

    D. All of the above

42. A large enterprise network will—at a minimum—have demarcation points for telephone services and a connection to an Internet service provider's network. In many cases, these services will enter the building in the same equipment room that houses the backbone switch. Which of the following is the term used to describe this wiring nexus?

    A. MTBF

    B. IDF

    C. RDP

    D. MDF

43. You have configured your company's wireless network to enable a client to authenticate only when the signal strength of their connection exceeds a specified level. Which of the following terms best describes the security mechanism provided by this configuration?

A. Geofencing

B. Local authentication

C. Motion detection

D. Port security

44. Social engineering has become an increasingly serious problem on your company network. Which of the following is an effective method for preventing sensitive data from being compromised through social engineering?

A. Install a firewall between the internal network and the Internet.

B. Install an antivirus software product on all user workstations.

C. Implement a program of user education and corporate policies.

D. Use IPsec to encrypt all network traffic.

45. You have been given a Class B network IP address with which to configure the new network you are designing. Which of the following is the default subnet mask you should use for an IPv4 Class B network?

A. 255.255.255.255

B. 255.255.255.0

C. 255.255.0.0

D. 255.0.0.0

46. Alice's company has just started working with sensitive government data. To enhance the security of the datacenter, she has implemented some additional security measures. All the servers now have crimped metal tags holding the cases closed. All the hardware racks are locked in clear-fronted cabinets. All the cable runs are installed in transparent conduits. These are all examples of which of the following physical security measures?

A. Geofencing

B. Tamper detection

C. Port security

D. Asset tracking

47. You have just installed a web server for your company that is configured to host a public Internet site using the registered domain name adatum.com. The server's hostname in the Domain Name System (DNS) is www. The web server also has an administrative site, which you want to be able to access remotely. You have configured the administrative site to be encrypted and to use the port number 12354. Which of the following URLs must you use to access the administrative website from the Internet?

A. www.adatum.com:12354

B. www.adatum.com

C. www.adatum.com:80

D. www.adatum.com:12354

48. To prevent outside users from accessing your wireless network, you configure the access point not to broadcast the network's SSID. However, you later discover that outsiders are still accessing the network. For which of the following reasons is disabling SSID broadcasts a relatively weak method of device hardening?

   A. Every access point's SSID is printed on a label on the back of the device.

   B. Attackers have software that can easily guess a network's SSID.

   C. Attackers can capture packets transmitted over the network and read the SSID from them.

   D. Attackers have ways of connecting to the network without the SSID.

49. You are installing a web server farm in your corporate headquarters that will be used to host websites for the corporation's subsidiaries, which are located all around the world. In which of the following cloud models does a single organization function as both the provider and the consumer of all cloud services?

   A. Private cloud

   B. Public cloud

   C. Ad hoc cloud

   D. Hybrid cloud

50. Your supervisor has recently begun using the terms *on-boarding* and *off-boarding*, with which you are unfamiliar. With which of the following types of policies are these terms typically associated?

   A. Incident response

   B. Identity management

   C. Inventory management

   D. Data loss prevention

51. Virtual private networks (VPNs) use a data transmission technique called tunneling, which encapsulates a data packet within another packet for transmission over a network connection, typically using the Internet. The system also encrypts the entire encapsulated data packet for protection. Split tunneling is a variation of this method that provides which of the following advantages? (Choose all that apply.)

   A. Additional data integrity protection

   B. Access to local network devices while connected to the VPN

   C. Faster data transmission through multiplexing

   D. Conservation of VPN bandwidth

52. Your supervisor wants you to disable all of the ports on the network's switches that are not in use. You tell her that this is not necessary; she wants to know why you think so. Which of the following are valid reasons not to disable unused switch ports? (Choose all that apply.)

   A. The unused ports are not patched into wall jacks.

   B. The datacenter is already secured from unauthorized access.

   C. The switch is configured to use a MAC-based access control list.

   D. Leaving some ports enabled facilitates the on-boarding of new users.

53. Which of the following are security mechanisms that fall into the category of deception technologies?

    A. Honeypots and honeynets

    B. Root guards

    C. Screened subnets

    D. Geofencing

54. Which of the following network devices can employ access control lists (ACLs) to restrict access? (Choose all that apply.)

    A. Routers

    B. Servers

    C. Switches

    D. Hubs

    E. Wireless access points

55. Which of the following terms is not associated with Data link layer communications?

    A. Administrative distance

    B. Spanning Tree Protocol

    C. Maximum transmission unit

    D. Jumbo frames

56. Which of the following statements about DHCP snooping are true? (Choose all that apply.)

    A. DHCP snooping is implemented in network switches.

    B. DHCP snooping prevents DNS cache poisoning.

    C. DHCP snooping detects rogue DHCP servers.

    D. DHCP snooping drops DHCP messages arriving over the incorrect port.

57. A user reports that she cannot connect to a server on her network. You want to identify the scope of the problem, so you try to reproduce the problem on the user's computer. The problem persists. No other users are reporting the same problem. What is the next logical step that you should perform to identify the affected area?

    A. Examine the server's configuration for the correct settings.

    B. Verify that the local router is forwarding traffic.

    C. Confirm that the switch the client is connected to is functioning.

    D. Perform the same task on another computer connected to the same segment.

58. On a wireless network, which of the following best describes an example of a captive portal?

    A. A web page stating that the data on a user's computer has been locked and will only be unlocked after payment of a fee

    B. A dedicated switch port used to connect to other switches

C. A web page with which a user must interact before being granted access to a wireless network

D. A series of two doors with an intervening airlock through which people must pass before they can enter a secured space

59. In the standard troubleshooting methodology, you begin by taking steps to identify the problem. After you have done this, which of the following steps should you perform next?

A. Verify full system functionality.

B. Establish a theory of probable cause.

C. Establish a plan of action.

D. Implement the solution.

60. The secured version of the Hypertext Transfer Protocol (HTTPS) uses a different well-known port from the unsecured version (HTTP). Which of the following ports are used by HTTP and HTTPS by default? (Choose all that apply.)

A. 25

B. 80

C. 110

D. 443

61. Which of the following are criteria typically used by load balancers to direct incoming traffic to one server out of a group of servers? (Choose all that apply.)

A. Fastest response time

B. Fastest processor

C. Lightest load

D. The next in an even rotation

62. You are responsible for a network that has a Domain Name System (DNS) server, a proxy server, and an Internet router. A user is reporting that she cannot connect to hosts on her own local area network (LAN) or other internal LANs, and she also cannot access hosts on the Internet. No one else has reported a problem. What is the most likely location of the issue preventing the user's access to the network?

A. The router

B. The DNS server

C. The proxy server

D. The user's computer configuration

63. Virtual LAN (VLAN) hopping is a type of attack directed at network switches. Which of the following best describes how VLAN hopping is a potential threat?

A. VLAN hopping enables an attacker to access different VLANs using 802.1q spoofing.

B. VLAN hopping enables an attacker to scramble a switch's patch panel connections.

C. VLAN hopping enables an attacker to change the native VLAN on a switch.

D. VLAN hopping enables an attacker to rename the default VLAN on a switch.

64. You are a first-tier support technician working the IT help desk at your company. In your first hour of duty, you receive four trouble calls. Your job is to prioritize the calls based on their severity. Which of the following should be the problem that receives the lowest priority?

    A. A fatal error that causes a single computer to fail

    B. A problem with a mission-critical backbone router that affects an entire network

    C. A problem with an application server that affects a single LAN

    D. A problem with an order entry or customer service call center resource that affects an entire department, with multiple local area networks (LANs)

65. You are attempting to access a Domain Name System (DNS) server located on the other side of a router, but your attempt fails with an error stating that the destination port UDP 53 is unreachable. Your first step in troubleshooting the problem is to try using the nslookup utility to access that specific DNS server. This attempt also fails. Next, you use the ping utility with the DNS server's IP address. The ping test is successful, indicating that the server is up and running. Which of the following are possible causes of the problem? (Choose all that apply.)

    A. The TCP/IP host settings on your computer are improperly configured.

    B. The router connecting the networks is not running DNS and will not forward this type of datagram.

    C. There is a firewall blocking the DNS server's UDP port 53.

    D. The DNS process on the remote server is not running.

    E. The TCP/IP host settings on the DNS server are improperly configured.

66. Which of the following types of switch performs a cyclical redundancy check (CRC) on an entire frame's contents prior to forwarding it out a port leading to the destination system?

    A. Packet filtering

    B. Cut-through

    C. Source route

    D. Store-and-forward

67. Which of the following attack types does not specifically target wireless network clients?

    A. Logic bomb

    B. Deauthentication

    C. Evil twin

    D. Rogue AP

68. You are having trouble installing a wireless LAN using IEEE 802.11n equipment in a new office complex. The wireless devices have trouble connecting to the access point, and when they do, they achieve only low speeds. When you use a Wi-Fi analyzer to scan the 2.4 GHz frequency band, you see literally dozens of other networks in the area, spread across all of the available channels. Which of the following tasks should you perform to enable your wireless devices to connect to the network reliably and at their best possible speeds?

    A. Configure the access point to suppress SSID broadcasts.

    B. Configure all of the wireless network devices to use the 5 GHz band.

C. Upgrade all of the network devices to the latest firmware.

D. Configure all of the network devices to use WPA3 encryption with AES.

69. Which Windows command-line utility produced the output shown here?

```
Interface: 192.168.2.24 --- 0x2
   Internet Address      Physical Address      Type
   192.168.2.2           d4-ae-52-bf-c3-2d     dynamic
   192.168.2.20          00-26-c7-7e-00-e0     dynamic
   192.168.2.22          00-90-a9-a2-43-8f     dynamic
   192.168.2.27          1c-c1-de-ca-1f-12     dynamic
   192.168.2.28          30-f7-72-38-e9-1d     dynamic
   192.168.2.255         ff-ff-ff-ff-ff-ff     static
   224.0.0.22            01-00-5e-00-00-16     static
   224.0.0.251           01-00-5e-00-00-fb     static
   224.0.0.252           01-00-5e-00-00-fc     static
   224.0.0.253           01-00-5e-00-00-fd     static
   239.255.255.250       01-00-5e-7f-ff-fa     static
   255.255.255.255       ff-ff-ff-ff-ff-ff     static
```

A. arp

B. ping

C. tracert

D. netstat

70. Your boss is working in the crawlspace under the floor of the datacenter, and he asks you to hand him the pliers. You hand him the tool shown in the following figure, and he throws it back at you. What is the real function of the tool shown in the figure?

Reproduced with permission of Todd, (2015) / John Wiley & Sons

A.   When you connect the tool to pins in a punchdown block, you can access telephone circuits in order to test them or place telephone calls.

B.   When you attach the tool to one end of a wire, it generates a tone that can be detected at the other end.

C.   To attach a bulk cable end to an RJ-45 connector, you use the tool to squeeze the connector closed, forcing the wire ends to contact the connector's pins.

D.   When you attach the tool to a copper cable, you can detect and measure the electrical current flowing through it.

71.   You are starting work for a contractor who performs telecommunications cable installations. One of the tools in the kit you have been given is unfamiliar to you. What is the name of the tool shown in the following figure?

Reproduced with permission of Todd, (2015) / John Wiley & Sons

A.   Crimper

B.   Punchdown tool

C.   Butt set

D.   Toner and probe

72.   You are seeking to upgrade your company's IEEE 802.11g access point to one that provides faster transmission speeds for your newer workstations. Which of the following wireless networking standards is capable of supporting speeds faster than the 54 Mbps of 802.11g but is still backward compatible with your existing IEEE 802.11g workstations?

A.   IEEE 802.11

B.   Bluetooth

C.   IEEE 802.11ac

D.   IEEE 802.11a

E.   IEEE 802.11n

73.   You are working on your company's screened subnet (also known as a perimeter network), which has five Linux web servers, a Cisco router, a CSU/DSU providing a leased line connection, and a Windows-based firewall on it. While trying to troubleshoot a network communications failure, you type the following command on one of the systems: traceroute adatum.com. Which of the following systems might you be working on? (Choose all that apply.)

A. The Cisco router

B. One of the Linux web servers

C. The CSU/DSU console

D. The Windows-based firewall

74. Which of the following are network topologies used by IEEE 802.11 wireless local area networks (WLANs)? (Choose all that apply.)

A. Bus

B. Spine and leaf

C. Ad hoc

D. Star/hub and spoke

E. Infrastructure

75. Which version of the Simple Network Management Protocol (SNMP) uses as its security mechanism two separate unencrypted community strings?

A. SNMPv1

B. SNMPv2

C. SNMPv2c

D. SNMPv3

76. You are working the help desk at a local computer store, and you receive a call from a customer trying to set up a home network using computers running Windows 11 and wired Ethernet equipment. The customer reports that she cannot access the other two computers in the house from her workstation, nor can she access the Internet. You ask her to run the `ipconfig /all` command and read the results to you. She says that her IP address is 192.168.0.2, her subnet mask is 255.255.255.0, and her default gateway is 192.168.0.1. Which of the following is the most likely cause of the customer's problem?

A. The customer's network address cannot include a zero.

B. The customer has an incorrect subnet mask.

C. The customer's network cable is damaged or unplugged.

D. The customer has an incorrect default gateway address.

77. Some networks are designed with a switching fabric that contains redundant paths for fault tolerance purposes. However, in this type of design it is possible for packets to circulate endlessly around the network, which is called a switching loop. Which of the following protocols prevents network switching loops from occurring by shutting down redundant links until they are needed?

A. NAT

B. RIP

C. VLAN

D. STP

78. You are responsible for an internetwork that consists of four internal local area networks (LANs) with 50 users each. Each internal LAN uses twisted-pair Gigabit Ethernet links that connect the users to a switch. Each of the four switches is connected to a separate router. All four routers connect to the same backbone network, which has a single additional router to connect the company's network to the Internet using a T-1 wide area network (WAN) link. Today, users on one of the four internal LANs are reporting that when they came in this morning, they could not access the Internet or resources on the other three internal LANs. However, they could access resources on their own LAN with no problems. Which network component is the likeliest source of the problem in this scenario?

    A. The switch on the problem LAN

    B. The Internet router

    C. The router connecting the problem LAN to the backbone

    D. The cable on the backbone network

79. You are negotiating an agreement with a provider for your company's email service. You have been told to require a 99.99 percent guaranteed rate of service reliability, but the provider is only willing to guarantee 99 percent. Eventually, you and the provider agree on a compromise of 99.9 percent. Which of the following documents will include the negotiated language on this particular point?

    A. AUP

    B. SLA

    C. BYOD

    D. NDA

80. Which of the following networking devices can split a single network into multiple collision domains while maintaining a single broadcast domain? (Choose all that apply.)

    A. Switch

    B. Bridge

    C. Router

    D. Firewall

81. You have just finished installing a web server farm on your company's network, along with a router to create a screened subnet (perimeter network) on which the web servers are located. However, you now cannot access the web servers from your workstation on the internal network. Which of the following is not one of the tasks you will have to complete before you can access the screened subnet from the internal network?

    A. Change MAC addresses.

    B. Change IP addresses.

    C. Update the DNS records.

    D. Change default gateway addresses.

82. You are testing a twisted-pair cable run using a toner and probe. When you apply the toner to a particular pin at one end of the cable, you detect a tone on two pins at the other end. Which of the following faults have you discovered?

    A. Split pair

    B. Open

    C. Short

    D. Crosstalk

83. Your network has been experiencing intermittent service slowdowns and outages ever since the company moved into their new building. You have tried every troubleshooting modality you can think of, but you have not been able to determine the cause. One particular user, per-haps hoping to be the squeaky wheel that gets the grease, has taken to calling you every time he experiences a problem. One day, as you are working in the datacenter, you notice that the user calls every time you hear an additional humming noise. After examining the doors in the hallway, you realize that the racks containing the network switches are located right next to the elevator machinery room. Which of the following conditions is probably causing this intermittent network communication problem?

    A. Bottleneck

    B. EMI

    C. Latency

    D. Crosstalk

84. Ralph is installing a pair of redundant servers and must choose whether to run them in an active-active or active-passive configuration. Running the servers in an active-active configu-ration provides which of the following advantages that the same servers in an active-passive configuration do not? (Choose all that apply.)

    A. Fault tolerance

    B. Load balancing

    C. Data encapsulation

    D. Increased performance

85. You are starting work at a new company, and on your first day you ask about wireless access for your laptop. You are given an SSID and a WPA3 passphrase. Later, in the lunchroom, when you try to connect your laptop to the network, you cannot see the SSID you were given in the list of available networks, although you can see other networks. What should you do first to try to resolve the problem?

    A. Move closer to the wireless access point.

    B. Move away from the microwave in the lunchroom.

    C. Type in the WPA3 passphrase.

    D. Type the SSID in manually.

86. You are responsible for a wireless LAN that consists of an 802.11n 2x2 access point and laptop computers with a variety of network adapters. Some of the laptops support 802.11n, and a few older models have 802.11g adapters. The wireless LAN is located in a large office building with many other wireless networks, and you are having trouble finding a channel on the 2.4 GHz band that is not congested with traffic. Scanning the 5 GHz band, you find relatively little traffic, so you reconfigure the access point to use a 5 GHz channel. The result is that some of the laptops are able to connect to the network, whereas others are not. What is the most likely reason for the connection failures, and what must you do to enable all the laptops to connect to the wireless network?

   A. The 802.11g standard does not support communication using the 5 GHz band. You must replace the network adapters in those laptops with newer models for them to connect successfully.

   B. The 5 GHz band does not support automatic channel selection. You must configure each laptop to use the same channel as the access point for all the laptops to connect successfully.

   C. The 5 GHz band does not support MIMO communications, so the 802.11n laptops are unable to connect to the network. You must replace the access point with an 802.11g unit for all the laptops to connect successfully.

   D. The 802.11g standard does not support communication using the 5 GHz band. You must configure the access point to support 2.4 GHz for all the laptops to connect successfully.

87. In the Domain Name System (DNS), a zone is a contiguous area of the DNS namespace for which authority is delegated to one or more DNS servers. Which of the following DNS resource record types specifies the IP addresses of the authoritative DNS servers for a particular zone?

   A. PTR

   B. SRV

   C. MX

   D. NS

88. You are experiencing poor performance on your home 802.11n wireless network. You live in a large apartment complex, and when you run a Wi-Fi analyzer, you see many other nearby networks using the often-recommended channels 1, 6, and 11 on the 2.4 GHz frequency. Using the 5 GHz frequency is not an option for your equipment. What should you do to improve the network's performance?

   A. Configure your equipment to use channel 10.

   B. Configure your equipment to use channel 9.

   C. Configure your equipment to use channel 5.

   D. Configure your equipment to use channel 2.

89. Your company's office building is having a fire inspection, and you are the only person on duty in the datacenter. The inspector from the fire department is reviewing the company's asset inventory and asks you where they can find documentation about all chemicals and

equipment used in the company's datacenter. You lead the inspector to the director's office, but you are not sure what the documents he needs are called. Which of the following document types contains this information?

A. MSDS

B. ESD

C. NDA

D. BYOD

90. Which of the following Power over Ethernet (PoE) specifications supplies power to devices using the spare wire pair on a 100Base-TX twisted-pair network?

A. Alternative A

B. 4PPoE

C. Alternative B

D. All of the above

91. Which of the following statements about the differences between storage area networks (SANs) and network attached storage (NAS) are not true? (Choose all that apply.)

A. NAS devices typically provide a filesystem, whereas SAN devices do not.

B. NAS devices typically contain integrated iSCSI targets.

C. NAS provides file-level storage access, whereas SAN provides block-level storage access.

D. SAN devices have an operating system, whereas NAS devices do not.

92. You are deploying an 802.11n wireless network for a client who is asking for the best possible security you can provide without deploying additional servers. When setting up the wireless access point, you disable SSID broadcasts, select Wi-Fi Protected Access Preshared Keys (WPA-PSK), and configure MAC address filtering. Which of the following statements about the security of this arrangement is true?

A. You should not disable SSID broadcasts, because this prevents users from connecting to the network.

B. The configuration is as secure as you can make it with the specified equipment.

C. You should use Wi-Fi Protected Access 3 (WPA3) instead of WPA, since it is more resistant to certain types of attacks.

D. You should not use MAC address filtering, because it exposes MAC addresses to possible attacks.

93. Which of the following connector types are used with fiber-optic cables? (Choose all that apply.)

A. DB-9

B. SC

C. BNC

D. ST

E. MPO

F. RJ-11

94. Which of the following are available as Internet of Things (IoT) devices?

   A. Refrigerators

   B. Doorbells

   C. Thermostats

   D. Speakers

   E. All of the above

95. You are designing an Ethernet network for your company's newest branch office. Your current task is to decide which Ethernet specification to use for the network, a decision that you know will determine what type of cabling you need to purchase and the topology with which the cable will be installed. Which layers of the Open Systems Interconnection (OSI) reference model apply to the cabling and topology elements of a network?

   A. The Application and Transport layers

   B. The Transport and Network layers

   C. The Network and Data link layers

   D. The Data link and Physical layers

96. You are troubleshooting a workstation that cannot access the network. The workstation is plugged into a wall plate that should provide it with access to a DHCP-equipped network using the 192.168.4.0/24 network address. No one else on that network is reporting a problem. You check that the patch cable is properly plugged into the workstation and the wall plate, which it is, and then run `ipconfig /all` on the workstation and examine the output. Which of the following could be the explanation for the workstation's problem, based on the following `ipconfig` results?

```
Windows IP Configuration

    Host Name . . . . . . . . . . . . : Client12
    Primary Dns Suffix  . . . . . . . :
    Node Type . . . . . . . . . . . . : Hybrid
    IP Routing Enabled. . . . . . . . : No
    WINS Proxy Enabled. . . . . . . . : No

Ethernet adapter Local Area Connection:

    Connection-specific DNS Suffix  . :
    Description . . . . . . . . . . . : PCIe Family Controller
    Physical Address. . . . . . . . . : 60-EB-69-93-5E-E5
    DHCP Enabled. . . . . . . . . . . : Yes
    Autoconfiguration Enabled . . . . : Yes
    Link-local IPv6 Address . . . . . : fe80::c955:c944:acdd:3fcb%2
    IPv4 Address. . . . . . . . . . . : 169.254.203.42
    Subnet Mask . . . . . . . . . . . : 255.255.0.0
    Lease Obtained. . . . . . . . . . : Monday, October 23, 2017 6:23:47 PM
```

```
Lease Expires . . . . . . . . . . : Saturday, November 18, 2017 9:49:24 PM
Default Gateway . . . . . . . . . :
DHCPv6 IAID . . . . . . . . . . . : 241232745
DHCPv6 Client DUID.  . . . . . . . : 00-01-00-01-18-10-22-0D-60-EB-69-93-5E-E5
DNS Servers . . . . . . . . . . . : fec0:0:0:ffff::1%1
                                    fec0:0:0:ffff::2%1
                                    fec0:0:0:ffff::3%1
NetBIOS over Tcpip. . . . . . . . : Enabled
```

   A. The DNS server addresses are incorrect.

   B. The Default Gateway address is missing.

   C. The Subnet Mask value is incorrect.

   D. The DHCP scope is exhausted.

97. A user calls you at the IT help desk and reports that she is having intermittent problems accessing both local servers and Internet websites. Which of the following potential problems can you rule out immediately?

   A. Malfunctioning DNS server

   B. Duplicate MAC addresses

   C. Duplicate IP addresses

   D. Malfunctioning router

98. You have recently discovered a rogue DHCP server on your network. After disabling the rogue server, you now need to terminate all of the rogue IP address leases currently held by DHCP clients on the network and then have them request new leases from the authorized DHCP server. Which of the following commands must you run on each client to do this? (Choose all that apply.)

   A. `ipconfig /dump`

   B. `ipconfig /lease`

   C. `ipconfig /release`

   D. `ipconfig /renew`

   E. `ipconfig /discard`

99. Ralph is reading an article about datacenter design, and he is puzzled by references to east-west and north-south traffic. Which of the following statements best describes the difference between east-west and north-south traffic in a datacenter?

   A. East-west is switch-to-switch traffic, while north-south is switch-to-router traffic.

   B. East-west describes traffic between devices at the same layer of the Open Systems Interconnection (OSI) reference model, while north-south describes traffic between OSI model layers.

   C. East-west traffic stays within the datacenter, while north-south traffic does not.

   D. East-west is backbone traffic among switches and routers, while north-south is traffic to end systems, such as servers.

100. Which of the following Windows command-line utilities produced the output shown here?

```
Active Connections

  Proto Local Address        Foreign Address        State
  TCP   127.0.0.1:5327       CM412:49770            ESTABLISHED
  TCP   127.0.0.1:49770      CM412:5327             ESTABLISHED
  TCP   127.0.0.1:52114      CM412:52115            ESTABLISHED
  TCP   192.168.2.24:2869    RT-M96U:42173          ESTABLISHED
  TCP   192.168.2.24:2869    RT-M96U:44356          ESTABLISHED
  TCP   192.168.2.24:51386   autodiscover:https     ESTABLISHED
  TCP   192.168.2.24:51486   autodiscover:https     ESTABLISHED
  TCP   192.168.2.24:51535   108-174-11-1:https     ESTABLISHED
  TCP   192.168.2.24:51578   aki-cache:http         TIME_WAIT
  TCP   192.168.2.24:51579   ia3s43-in-f142:http    TIME_WAIT
  TCP   192.168.2.24:51591   208:https              TIME_WAIT
  TCP   192.168.2.24:51592   208:https              TIME_WAIT
  TCP   192.168.2.24:51593   198.8.20.212:https     TIME_WAIT
```

A. arp

B. ping

C. tracert

D. netstat

E. hostname

Appendix

Answers to Review Questions

Chapter 1: Networking Concepts

1. B. The Ethernet (or IEEE 802.3) protocol at the Data link layer uses MAC addresses to identify computers on the local network. MAC addresses are coded into the firmware of physical network interface adapters by the manufacturer. The Physical layer deals with signals and is not involved in addressing. The IP protocol at the Network layer has its own addressing system. The Transport layer protocols are not involved in addressing.

2. E. ISO developed and published the OSI model to serve as a conceptual model for software and hardware developers. The ITU-T, formerly known as the CCITT, coordinates the development and advancement of international telecommunication networks and services. ANSI is a private organization that administers and coordinates a United States–based standardization and conformity assessment system. The IEEE publishes standards that define Data link and Physical layer standards. These standards are referred to collectively as the 802 series.

3. C. Network layer protocols (such as IP) contain headers that specify logical addresses for end system communication and route datagrams across a network. The Physical layer defines standards for physical and mechanical characteristics of a network. The Data link layer uses media access control (MAC) or hardware addresses, not logical addresses. The Transport layer uses port numbers, not logical addresses. Session layer protocols create and maintain a dialogue between end systems. Presentation layer protocols are responsible for the formatting, translation, and presentation of information. The Application layer provides an entry point for applications to access the protocol stack and prepare information for transmission across a network.

4. B, C, D. Before the payload data generated by an application can be transmitted over a TCP/IP network, the system must encapsulate it by applying protocol headers and footers at three layers of the OSI model. The Data link layer applies a header and footer to create an Ethernet frame. The Network layer applies a header to create an IP datagram. The Transport layer applies a TCP or UDP header to create a segment or datagram. The other model layers are involved in the payload transmission process, but they do not encapsulate the payload.

5. F. The Presentation layer implements functions that provide formatting, translation, and presentation of information. No other layers of the OSI model translate and format application data.

6. D. A router connects networks at the Network layer of the OSI model. Proxy servers operate at the Application layer. Network interface adapters operate at both the Data link and the Physical layers. Hubs are Physical layer devices.

7. G. The Application layer provides an entry point for applications to access the protocol stack and prepare information for transmission across a network. All other layers of the OSI model reside below this layer and rely on this entry point.

8. E. The Session layer is responsible for creating and maintaining a dialogue between end systems. This dialogue can be a two-way alternate dialogue that requires end systems to take turns transmitting, or it can be a two-way simultaneous dialogue in which either end system can transmit at will. No other layers of the OSI model perform dialogue control between communicating end systems.

9. B, C. The primary function of a switch is to process packets based on their media access control (MAC) addresses, which makes it a Data link layer device. However, many switches can also perform routing functions based on IP addresses, which operate at the Network layer.

10. D. There are two types of Transport layer protocols: connection-oriented and connectionless. Connection-oriented protocols guarantee the delivery of data from source to destination by creating a connection between the sender and the receiver before any data is transmitted. Connectionless protocols do not require a connection between end systems in order to pass data. The Physical layer does not use connectionless or connection-oriented protocols; it defines standards for transmitting and receiving information over a network. The Data link layer provides physical addressing and final packaging of data for transmission. The Network layer is responsible for logical addressing and routing. The Session layer is responsible for creating and maintaining a dialogue between end systems. The Presentation layer is responsible for the formatting, translation, and presentation of information. The Application layer provides an entry point for applications to access the protocol stack and prepare information for transmission across a network.

11. A, B, C. The Physical layer of the OSI model is associated with hubs, cables, and network interface adapters. The Data link layer is associated with bridges and switches. The Network layer is associated with routers. The Transport, Session, Presentation, and Application layers are typically not associated with dedicated hardware devices.

12. B. The only layer with a protocol (such as Ethernet) that adds both a header and a footer is the Data link layer. The process of adding the headers and footers is known as data encapsulation. All other protocol layers that encapsulate data add just a header.

13. C. The Ethernet protocol that handles the addressing, transmission, and reception of frames operates at the Data link layer. Each frame includes hardware addresses that identify the sending and receiving systems on the local network. Ethernet uses the CSMA/CD media access control method. Physical layer specifications include the transmission of signals in the form of electrical or light pulses to represent binary code, not frames. CSMA/CA is a Data link layer media access control method used by wireless LAN protocols, but not Ethernet.

14. B. On a TCP/IP network, the Internet Protocol (IP) at the Network layer is the protocol responsible for the delivery of data to its final destination. Data link layer protocols are only concerned with communication between devices on a local area network (LAN) or between two points connected by a wide area network (WAN) link. The Session and Application layers are not involved in the actual delivery of data.

15. D. Internet Protocol (IP), Internet Control Message Protocol (ICMP), and Internet Group Management Protocol (IGMP) are all Network layer protocols. Internet Message Access Protocol (IMAP) is a mail protocol that operates at the Application layer.

16. C. A connection-oriented Transport layer protocol, such as Transmission Control Protocol (TCP), provides guaranteed delivery of data for upper layer applications. Connectionless protocols do not guarantee delivery of information and therefore are not a good choice. Guaranteed delivery of information between end systems is generally not a function of the Data link, Network, or Application layer.

17. A. The Physical layer defines the mechanical and electrical characteristics of the cables used to build a network. The Data link layer defines specific network (LAN or WAN) topologies and their characteristics. The Physical layer standard that Alice will implement depends on the Data link layer protocol she selects. The Network, Transport, and Application layers are not concerned with cables and topologies.

18. E, F. In the TCP/IP suite, the functions of the Session layer are primarily implemented in the Transport layer protocols: Transmission Control Protocol (TCP) and User Datagram Protocol (UDP). The Presentation layer functions are often implemented in Application layer protocols, although some functions, such as encryption, can also be performed by Transport or Network layer protocols.

19. C. Transport layer protocols, such as Transmission Control Protocol (TCP) and User Datagram Protocol (UDP), have header fields that contain the port numbers of the applications that generated the data in the packet, and which will receive it. The Application, Presentation, and Network layers do not use port numbers.

20. E. The correct order of the OSI model layers, from top to bottom, is Application, Presentation, Session, Transport, Network, Data link, Physical.

21. B. Switches and bridges are involved in local area network (LAN) communications only and therefore primarily at the Data link layer. They are not primarily associated with the Physical, Network, or Transport layers, although some switches include Network layer routing capabilities.

22. C. Flow control is a process that adjusts the transmission rate of a protocol based on the capability of the receiver. If the receiving system becomes overwhelmed by incoming data, the sender dynamically reduces the transmission rate. In the TCP/IP protocol suite, Transmission Control Protocol (TCP) is responsible for implementing flow control. TCP runs at the Transport layer. None of the other layers listed have TCP/IP protocols that provide flow control.

23. A. The Physical layer of the OSI model defines the standards for the physical and mechanical characteristics of a network, such as cabling (copper and fiber), connecting hardware (hubs and switches), and signaling methods (analog and digital). None of the other layers are involved in the mechanical characteristics of the network.

24. D. The Presentation layer provides a syntax translation service that enables two computers to communicate, despite their use of different bit-encoding methods. This translation service also enables systems using compressed or encrypted data to communicate with each other.

25. A. The Physical layer of the OSI model defines the functions specific to the network medium and the transmission and reception of signals. All of the other layers are software components that do not physically send or receive signals.

26. B. IP is a connectionless protocol that operates at the Network layer of the OSI model. There are no connection-oriented protocols at this layer. The protocols at the Transport layer include Transmission Control Protocol (TCP), which is connection-oriented, and User Datagram Protocol (UDP), which is connectionless.

27. A. An Ethernet network interface adapter functions at the Data link layer by encapsulating Network layer data for transmission over the network. It provides Physical layer functions by providing the connection to the network medium and generating the appropriate signals for transmission. Network interface adapters do not operate at the Network, Transport, or Application layers.

28. A, B. Hypertext Transfer Protocol (HTTP) and Simple Network Management Protocol (SNMP) operate at the Application layer. Internet Control Message Protocol (ICMP) and Internet Group Management Protocol (IGMP) both operate at the Network layer. User Datagram Protocol (UDP) operates at the Transport layer.

29. B. The Presentation layer of the OSI model is responsible for translating different kinds of syntax, including text-encoding systems, such as EBCDIC and ASCII. The Application, Session, and Physical layers do not perform this function.

30. D. Internet Control Message Protocol (ICMP) operates at the Network layer by sending operational and error messages. It does not encapsulate upper layer protocol data. Internet Protocol (IP) operates at the Network layer, but it does encapsulate Transport layer protocol data. Transmission Control Protocol (TCP) and User Datagram Protocol (UDP) are Transport layer protocols that encapsulate upper layer protocol data. Address Resolution Protocol (ARP) does not encapsulate upper layer protocol data, but it is a Data link layer protocol.

31. B, C. A repeater is a Physical layer device that amplifies the signals entering it and transmits them again. A hub is a Physical layer device that propagates incoming signals out through all of its ports. Switches and routers have Physical layer elements but are primarily Data link and Network layer devices, respectively.

32. D. A gateway enables two devices using different protocols to communicate by performing translation and conversion services for them. Routers, hubs, and switches all require the same protocol at some of the OSI model layers.

33. A. A firewall is a filter that can prevent dangerous traffic originating on one network from passing through to another network. A device that connects two networks together and forwards traffic between them is a router, not a firewall. A device that enables Internet network clients with private IP addresses to access the Internet is a description of a network address translation (NAT) router or a proxy server, not a firewall. A device that caches Internet data is a proxy server or caching engine, not a firewall.

34. B. Service-dependent filtering blocks traffic based on the port numbers specified in the Transport layer header fields. Because port numbers represent specific applications, you can use them to prevent traffic generated by these applications from reaching a network. IP address filtering operates at the Network layer. DPI scans the contents of packets, rather than their headers. NGFW defines a device with advanced protection capabilities; port number scanning is a basic firewall function.

35. C, D. Most operating systems are capable of functioning as routers or firewalls. To route traffic, the system must have two network connections. A software firewall can be part of a computer's routing functionality, or it can be a stand-alone firewall that protects only the local system. Computers cannot function as hubs or switches because multiple ports would be required, and standard network adapters do not implement those functions.

36. D. Service-dependent filtering blocks traffic based on the port numbers specified in the Transport layer header fields. Because port numbers represent specific applications, you can use them to prevent traffic generated by these applications from reaching a network. IP address filtering enables you to limit network access to specific computers; it is not service dependent. Filtering based on hardware addresses provides the same basic functionality as IP address filtering, but it is more difficult to spoof hardware addresses than IP addresses. Filtering by protocol identifier enables you to block all traffic using TCP or UDP; it is not service dependent.

37. C. A personal firewall is an inexpensive way to protect an individual computer from Internet incursions. Installing a hardware firewall is a complex and expensive solution, not suitable for a small network. An IPS is a relatively expensive solution, suitable for larger networks. An IDS is also expensive, and connecting it to a switched port would not enable it to protect the other computers on the network. A port scanner is a device that performs scans on demand. It does not continuously monitor ports, and it does nothing to protect them.

38. B, C. Hubs operate at the Physical layer, and switches operate at the Data link layer. Hubs and switches both create a single broadcast domain for all of the connected devices. Switches create a separate collision domain for each connected device, whereas hubs create a single collision domain. There are switches (but not hubs) with Network layer (layer 3) functionality.

39. B, C. A switch is essentially a multiport bridge. Both switches and bridges process incoming packets by scanning their Data link layer hardware addresses and forwarding the packets out the port connected to the destination system. The primary difference between them is that switches have many ports, whereas bridges have only two. Hubs and routers are Physical layer and Network layer devices, respectively, and perform different functions.

40. A. Cut-through switches are fast, because they look at only the first 6 bytes (the destination media access control, or MAC, address) when forwarding a frame. They do not perform a cyclical redundancy check (CRC) on the entire frame's contents prior to forwarding it out a port leading to the destination. Source route is a bridging technique in which the source host, not the switch, determines the path a frame will take through a network to reach a destination. Store-and-forward switches take in the entire frame and verify its contents by performing a CRC calculation before forwarding it. There is no switch called a destination switch.

41. C. A firewall that supports stateful packet inspection examines other network and Transport layer header fields, looking for patterns that indicate damaging behaviors, such as IP spoofing, SYN floods, and teardrop attacks. Port number filtering is the most commonly used form of packet filtering; it is not the same as stateful packet inspection. Blocking traffic based on IP addresses prevents specific systems from accessing a network; stateful packet inspection is a much more complicated operation. Packet filtering based on protocol identifiers enables you to block TCP traffic; this is not stateful packet inspection.

42. A, C. IDSs can use anomaly-based detection to identify deviations from a known baseline of trustworthiness, or signature-based detection to locate specific malicious byte or instruction sequences. Behavior-based and statistic-based detection are not typical IDS methods.

43. B. A traditional switch is a Data link layer device that essentially performs the function of a bridge for each device connected to one of its ports. It can therefore be described as a multiport bridge. Some switches include layer 3 functionality, but they still function as bridges. Routers, hubs, and gateways are devices that operate at the Network, Physical, and Application layers, respectively, so they cannot be described as bridges.

44. A, B, D. Routers are Network layer devices that do not forward broadcast messages, so they create separate broadcast domains for each network. Switches do forward broadcasts, forming a single broadcast domain. Routers and switches can communicate using dedicated protocols. As Data link layer devices, switches read only hardware addresses from packet frames; routers forward traffic based on the IP addresses in packets' IP headers.

45. A. Security information and event management (SIEM) systems can function as a central clearinghouse for information gathered by IDSs and other security processes. Network-attached storage (NAS), Remote Authentication Dial-In User Service (RADIUS), and Voice over IP (VoIP) are not systems that collect IDS information.

46. A, B. Adding a router splits the Ethernet LAN into two LANs, creating two separate broadcast domains. Each computer, therefore, has a smaller number of broadcast messages to process. Because the network is split by the router, the amount of unicast traffic on each subnet is reduced.

47. B. Traditional bridges and switches are Data link layer devices that forward frames based on the destination MAC address contained in the frame. They operate in promiscuous mode, listening and processing all frames on each segment, and they build forwarding tables with this information. Forwarding tables are built based on source MAC addresses. Some switches include layer 3 functionality, but their primary function is still based at the Data link layer. Bridges are protocol independent; they are not involved with the upper layer protocols being carried on the LAN. Broadcast domains are defined by Network layer devices, not Data link layer devices.

48. C. A traditional switch is best described as a multiport bridge because it reads the hardware addresses of incoming packets and forwards them out through the port for the destination node. Although a traditional switch does function at layer 2 of the OSI model (the Data link layer), there are also switches with Network layer capabilities that can function as a router, which connects networks together at layer 3. Hubs and repeaters are Physical layer (layer 1) devices that are not capable of performing the functions of a switch.

49. C. The main reason why traditional layer 2 switches improve the efficiency of an Ethernet LAN is that they create a separate collision domain for each switched port, eliminating most collisions. Collisions result in packets having to be retransmitted, so fewer collisions mean fewer retransmissions, which improves performance. Layer 2 switches do not forward packets faster than hubs, but they do forward broadcast transmissions. Layer 2 switches do read hardware addresses, not IP addresses, but there are switches with layer 3 capabilities that route data packets to their destinations using IP addresses and subnetting.

50. A, D, E. Routers are Network layer devices that use IP addresses to forward frames, not MAC addresses. Routers are protocol dependent. They must support the Network layer protocol being routed. As a Network layer device, a router defines networks (or LANs) that represent a separate broadcast domain. Routers do not build their routing tables or forward frames using MAC addresses.

51. C. Routers store and maintain route information in a routing table that is stored in memory, not in a local text file. All of the other statements about routers are true.

52. D. The firewall is a conduit between the private network and the ISP's network (which provides access to the Internet), through which all traffic must pass. This ensures that the firewall has the opportunity to examine every packet that passes between the private network and the Internet and filter out those that are not authorized. If the firewall were located in the midst of the private internetwork, it would be possible for Internet computers to bypass the firewall and communicate directly with the private systems. Placing the firewall on the far side of the router would put it on the ISP's network, causing it to filter all of the ISP's traffic and not just that destined for the private network. Installing the firewall at the ISP's site would have the same effect as installing it on the far side of the router at the private network site.

53. D. A proxy server is an Application layer service because it receives Internet service requests from client computers, reads the Application layer protocol data in each request, and then generates its own request for the same service and transmits it to the Internet server the client specifies. Only an Application layer service can read and process the Application layer data in network packets. A proxy server cannot be a Data link layer device because it can provide Internet access to an entire internetwork, while the Data link layer is concerned with communications on a single subnet. Proxy servers cannot be Network layer devices because the Network layer handles all internetwork packets indiscriminately and is unaware of what application generated the data carried inside the packets. The Transport layer is not involved in processing application data, so proxy servers cannot be said to function at the Transport layer.

54. B. DPI is a firewall technique that examines the data carried in packets and not just the protocol headers. While traditional firewalls typically do not support DPI, NGFWs often do. Stateful packet inspection, NAT, and VPN support are all features that are commonly supported by traditional firewall products.

55. C. Content filters are a firewall feature that examine the data inside packets, rather than their origin, to locate objectionable material. They do not scan IP addresses, nor do they detect typical types of malware. Content filters are not implemented in switches.

56. D. In most cases, a load balancing router works by processing incoming traffic based on rules set by the administrator. The rules can distribute traffic among a group of servers using various criteria, such as each server's current load or response time, or which server is next in a given rotation. Load balancers typically do not use the hardware configuration of the servers to direct traffic since this is a factor that does not change.

57. B. In many enterprise wireless networks, the access points (APs) do not run a full operating system and are called thin or lightweight APs. The network also has a device called a wireless controller that performs some of the required tasks and manages the APs. A *wireless* *endpoint* is another term for a computer or other device that is a client on the wireless network. Hypervisors and demarcation points have nothing to do with wireless networking. A hypervisor creates and manages virtual machines (VMs) on a host server, and a demarcation point is the interface between a private network and an outside telecommunications service.

58. B. A load balancer is a type of router that forwards traffic with a single IP address to multiple servers in turn. In most cases, a load balancing router works by processing incoming traffic based on rules set by the administrator. Because a load balancer works with IP addresses, it is a Network layer device. Load balancers are not switches, gateways, or firewalls.

59. C. Next-generation firewalls (NGFWs) expand on the packet filtering capabilities of traditional firewalls by adding features such as DPI and IPSs, as well as inspection of encrypted traffic and antivirus scanning. Remote Authentication Dial-In User Service (RADIUS) servers can provide centralized authentication, authorization, accounting, and auditing (AAAA) services. A CSU/DSU is a device that provides a router on a private network with access to a leased line. A proxy server is an Application layer service that receives Internet service requests from client computers, reads the Application layer protocol data in each request, and then generates its own request for the same service and transmits it to the Internet server the client specifies.

60. A. Because the client computers use private IP addresses, they are invisible to the Internet, so users outside the private network cannot see or access them. The proxy server has a public IP address so that it can participate in service transactions with Internet servers. If the proxy server used a private IP address, it would not be able to access the Internet directly. If the clients used public IP addresses, they would be visible to the Internet and vulnerable to intrusion.

61. A. Intrusion detection systems (IDSs) are designed to monitor network traffic for anomalies and send notifications to administrators. Uninterruptible power supplies (UPSs), Remote Authentication Dial-In User Service (RADIUS) servers, denial-of-service (DoS) attacks, and Remote Access Service (RAS) servers all have nothing to do with network monitoring.

62. B. Port mirroring is a feature found in some switches that takes the form of a special port that runs in promiscuous mode. This means that the switch copies all incoming traffic to that port, as well as to the dedicated destination ports. By connecting an IDS or protocol analyzer to this port, an administrator can access all of the network's traffic. Stateful packet inspection is a firewall feature that enables the device to examine network and Transport layer header fields, looking for patterns that indicate damaging behaviors, such as IP spoofing, SYN floods, and teardrop attacks. Trunking is a switch feature that enables administrators to create VLANs that span multiple switches. Service-dependent filtering is a firewall feature that blocks traffic based on Transport layer port numbers.

63. A, C. iSCSI runs on a standard IP network, and Fibre Channel over Ethernet (FCoE) runs on a standard Ethernet network. Both of these protocols can share a network with LAN traffic, although the use of a quality of service (QoS) mechanism is usually recommended. Fibre Channel and InfiniBand both require a dedicated network medium that does not support LAN traffic.

64. C. Voice over Internet Protocol (VoIP) is a technology for the transmission of voice communications over IP networks; it is not a SAN protocol. Internet Small Computer Systems Interface (iSCSI), Fibre Channel over Ethernet (FCoE), and Fibre Channel are all SAN protocols.

65. E. The Internet Storage Name Service (iSNS) is an application that provides iSCSI initiators with automated discovery of targets located on the network. iSNS can also function as a discovery service for Fibre Channel devices. Active Directory, Internet Control Message Protocol (ICMP), and Domain Name System (DNS) are not capable of registering iSCSI targets. iWINS does not exist.

66. D. The current Fibre Channel standard calls for a maximum data transfer rate of 128 gigabits per second (Gbps), for a nominal throughput of 12,800 megabytes per second (MBps).

67. B. A NAS device is essentially a file server that connects to a network and provides users with access to shared files. A NAS is a single computer, so it cannot be associated with failover clustering. Just a bunch of disks (JBOD) is a simple storage array that provides block-level access to data, whereas NAS devices provide file-level access. Redundant Array of Independent Disks (RAID) is a fault tolerance technology that might be implemented in NAS devices, but it is not the device's primary function.

68. A, D. NAS devices are self-contained file servers that connect directly to a standard IP network. A NAS device provides file-level access to its storage devices and includes an operating system and a filesystem. NAS devices are typically not iSCSI targets.

69. A, B, D. Because it uses standard Ethernet hardware, Fibre Channel over Ethernet (FCoE) is far less expensive to implement than Fibre Channel, which requires a dedicated fiber-optic network. Because Fibre Channel requires a dedicated network, it cannot coexist with standard IP traffic, whereas FCoE can. Because it is encapsulated in Ethernet frames, FCoE is not routable on IP networks.

70. A, B, D. Common Internet File System (CIFS), Network File System (NFS), and Hypertext Transfer Protocol (HTTP) are all file sharing protocols supported by many NAS devices. Remote Direct Memory Access (RDMA) provides high-speed network data transfers, but it is not an Application layer file sharing protocol.

71. C. iSCSI does not include its own flow control mechanism. It runs over a TCP connection, which is the protocol responsible for flow control. Because it runs on any IP network, iSCSI traffic is routable, and it is less expensive to implement. Fibre Channel requires a dedicated network using fiber-optic cable. iSCSI traffic can coexist with standard LAN traffic on a single network, although some type of quality of service (QoS) mechanism is frequently recommended.

72. A. The client side of an iSCSI implementation is called an initiator. The storage device to which the initiator connects is called a target. *Controller* and *adapter* are not terms used for iSCSI clients or servers.

73. A, B, C. iSCSI runs on a standard IP network; therefore, iSCSI messages are encapsulated using Transmission Control Protocol (TCP) at the Transport layer, Internet Protocol (IP) at the Network layer, and Ethernet at the Data link layer. iSCSI does not use the User Datagram Protocol (UDP).

74. E. The Fibre Channel standard defines a unique, five-layer protocol stack that does not correspond to the OSI model layers. Therefore, Fibre Channel does not use Ethernet, nor does it use Transmission Control Protocol (TCP), Internet Protocol (IP), User Datagram Protocol (UDP), or any of the other TCP/IP protocols.

75. B. The Fibre Channel standard defines a five-layer networking stack, with layers numbered FC-0 to FC-4, that does not correspond to the layers of the OSI model. Internet Small Computer System Interface (iSCSI), Point-to-Point Protocol (PPP), and Remote Direct Memory Access (RDMA) all function within the standard OSI model layers.

76. A. Fibre Channel over Ethernet (FCoE) uses Ethernet frames in place of the bottom two layers (FC0 and FC1) of the Fibre Channel protocol stack. The remaining layers (FC2, FC3, and FC4) use the standard Fibre Channel protocols. FCoE does not use Transmission Control Protocol (TCP), Internet Protocol (IP), User Datagram Protocol (UDP), or any of the other TCP/IP protocols.

77. C. Proxy servers provide network users with access to Internet services, and the unregistered IP addresses on the client computers protect them from unauthorized access by users on the Internet, which satisfies the first objective. The proxy servers also make it possible for network administrators to regulate users' access to the Internet, which satisfies one of the two secondary objectives. However, the proxy servers cannot assign IP addresses to the client computers, and the plan makes no mention of DHCP or another automatic TCP/IP configuration mechanism. Therefore, the plan does not satisfy the other secondary objective.

78. D. A virtual private network (VPN) headend is a type of router that enables multiple client systems to access a network from remote locations. It does not distribute traffic among servers. A load balancer is a type of router that forwards traffic with a single IP address to multiple servers in turn. Round-robin DNS is a technique in which a DNS server resolves a name into several IP addresses, each in turn. A network load balancing (NLB) cluster is a group of servers, all running the same application, that distribute incoming traffic among themselves.

79. C. Network-attached storage (NAS) is a separate device that connects storage to the network; it is not a normal function of a UTM appliance. UTM appliances do typically perform VPN, firewall, and antivirus functions.

80. B, C, D. A multilayer switch typically operates at the Data link and Network layers, assuming the functions of a switch and a router by using media access control (MAC) addresses at the Data link layer (layer 2) and IP addresses at the Network layer (layer 3) to forward packets to their appropriate destinations. Some switches also function at the Transport layer (layer 4) by distinguishing between User Datagram Protocol (UDP) and Transmission Control Protocol (TCP) traffic and using port numbers to forward packets.

81. D. Control plane policing uses quality of service (QoS) policies to block, allow, or impose rate limits on the traffic processed by the router or switch. IPsec is a Network layer security mechanism that encrypts or authenticates traffic. 802.1X is a network authentication mechanism. Router Advertisement (RA) guard is a feature found on certain switches that prevents the misuse of RA messages to redirect traffic. VLAN hopping is a method for sending commands to switches to transfer a port from one VLAN to another.

82. A. A private branch exchange (PBX) switches internal calls and provides access to external lines. A VoIP PBX performs the same tasks as a traditional PBX. A VoIP gateway is the device that provides the conduit between an IP network and the public switched telephone network (PSTN). A VoIP endpoint is a device that makes use of the VoIP system, such as a computer or handset. A multilayer switch is a data networking device that includes both switching and routing capabilities.

83. C. A modem (modulator/demodulator) is any device that converts analog signals to digital signals and digital signals back to analog signals. The digital device does not have to be a computer, and the analog device does not have to be the PSTN. There are many devices that are incorrectly referred to as modems, such as devices that connect a digital LAN to a digital WAN or all-digital devices that connect computers to the Internet.

84. A, C. VoIP uses the terms *terminal* and *endpoint* to refer to the device with which users make calls, including computers and telephone handsets. A VoIP gateway is the device that provides the conduit between an IP network and the public switched telephone network (PSTN). A VoIP private branch exchange (PBX) is a device that switches calls between endpoints on the local IP network and provides access to external Internet lines.

85. C. A VoIP gateway is a device that provides a conduit between an IP network and the public switched telephone network (PSTN). The gateway enables standard telephones connected to the PSTN to place calls using VoIP services on the Internet. A proxy server is an Application layer device that provides web browsers and other client programs to access the Internet. A virtual private network (VPN) headend enables multiple client systems to access a network from remote locations. A unified threat management (UTM) appliance typically performs VPN, firewall, and antivirus functions.

86. D. TTL is a value included in the IPv4 header that specifies the maximum number of hops the packet is allowed on the network. Each router processing the packet reduces the TTL value by one and discards the packet when the value reaches zero. OSPF is a routing protocol. MTU specifies the maximum size of a frame. Administrative distance is a value that routers use to select the most efficient route to a destination.

87. A. A content delivery network (CDN) is a geographically scattered array of datacenters that provides users with access to their data from a nearby site, thereby decreasing latency delays and reducing bandwidth utilization. Quality of service (QoS) is a technique for prioritizing traffic by tagging packets based on their content. Network-attached storage (NAS) refers to a device containing shared drives that is connected to a network. A storage area network (SAN) is a separate network dedicated to shared storage devices.

88. A. The infrastructure as a service (IaaS) model provides consumers with processing, storage, and networking resources that they can use to install and run operating systems and other software of their choice. Platform as a service (PaaS) provides consumers with the ability to install applications of their choice on a server installed by the provider. Software as a service (SaaS) provides consumers with access to specific applications running on the provider's servers. Desktop as a service (DaaS) provides remote virtualization of the entire workstation desktop, instead of a single application.

89. C. The software as a service (SaaS) model provides consumers with access to a specific application running on the provider's servers. Infrastructure as a service (IaaS) provides the consumers with processing, storage, and networking resources that they can use to install and run operating systems and other software of their choice. Platform as a service (PaaS) provides consumers with the ability to install applications of their choice on a server installed by the provider. Desktop as a service (DaaS) provides remote virtualization of the entire workstation desktop, instead of a single application.

90. A. The infrastructure as a service (IaaS) model provides consumers with the most control, as the provider furnishes processing, storage, and networking resources that the consumer can use as needed. Platform as a service (PaaS) provides consumers with the ability to install applications of their choice on a server furnished by the provider, but they have only limited control over the server and no control over the underlying resources. Software as a service (SaaS) and desktop as a service (DaaS) provide consumers with access to a specific application or an entire desktop environment running on the provider's servers, but the consumers have no control over the operating system, the servers, or the underlying resources.

91. A, D. Infrastructure as a service (IaaS) provides consumers like Alice with processing, storage, and networking resources that they can use to install and run operating systems and other software of their choice. In the public cloud model, one organization or user functions as the provider, and another organization or user—in this case, Alice—consumes the services of the provider.

Platform as a service (PaaS) provides consumers with the ability to install applications of their choice on a server furnished by the provider. Software as a service (SaaS) provides consumers with access to a specific application running on the provider's servers. In a private cloud, the same organization that utilizes the cloud services is also the sole owner of the infrastructure that provides those services. A hybrid cloud is a combination of public and private infrastructure so that the consumer organization is only a partial owner of the infrastructure. A virtual private cloud (VPC) is a secured private cloud hosted within a public cloud.

92. B. In a private cloud, the same organization that utilizes the cloud services can also be the sole owner of the infrastructure that provides those services. A private cloud can also be owned by a third party, all or in part. In the public cloud model, one organization functions as the provider, and another organization consumes the services of the provider. A hybrid cloud is a combination of public and private infrastructure so that the consumer organization is only a partial owner of the infrastructure. A multicloud is an integrated environment consisting of multiple cloud services from multiple providers.

93. B. *Cloud bursting* is a common term for the offloading of excess traffic from private to public cloud resources when necessary to maintain satisfactory performance levels. Cloud busting, cloud splitting, and cloud migrating are not standard cloud computing terms.

94. C. Software as a service (SaaS) provides consumers with access to a specific application running on the provider's servers (in this case, an email service). Consumers have control over some of their email functions, but they have no control over the operating system, the servers, or the underlying resources. The infrastructure as a service (IaaS) model provides the consumers with access to processing, storage, and networking resources that the consumer can use as needed. Platform as a service (PaaS) provides consumers with the ability to install applications of their choice on a server furnished by the provider. Desktop as a service (DaaS) provides remote virtualization of the entire workstation desktop, instead of a single application.

95. C. A hybrid cloud consists of both public and private resources. One of its main advantages is that administrators can move services from private to public cloud servers and back again as needed, depending on the current workload. Public cloud resources require authentication, so while they might be less secure than a private cloud, they are not inherently insecure. The term *private cloud* refers to hardware resources that are owned and operated by either a single organization or a third party, regardless of their location. The various cloud delivery models do not impose specific hardware resource requirements.

96. B. The platform as a service (PaaS) model provides consumers with the ability to install applications of their choice on a server furnished by the provider. Infrastructure as a service (IaaS) provides the consumers with processing, storage, and networking resources that they can use to install and run operating systems and other software of their choice. Software as a service (SaaS) provides consumers with access to a specific application running on the provider's servers. Desktop as a service (DaaS) provides remote virtualization of the entire workstation desktop, instead of a single application.

97. A, B, C. Multitenancy is a software architecture in which multiple tenants share a single instance of an application running in the cloud. Because tenants share a single application, there is a chance that data could be compromised. Because a single application instance is running in the cloud, the operational overhead is reduced compared to the use of individual virtual machines. Tenants share a finite amount of bandwidth, so the possibility exists for competition to occur, such as when one tenant is the target of a denial-of-service (DoS) attack. Multitenancy does not call for tenants to have individual virtual machines.

98. C. A cloud direct connection is a private link between the client's private network and the cloud service provider. This link is independent from any ISP connection used by the client organization for other traffic, so it ensures a consistent bandwidth for the hybrid cloud network. Using a different ISP or a leased line does not replace the entire connection; there are still potential bottlenecks. A VPN can provide better performance than a standard connection and greater security, but it is not as consistent (or as expensive) as a direct cloud connection.

99. B. The NFV specification, published by the European Telecommunications Standards Institute (ETSI), calls for three main components: virtualized network functions (VNFs), which are software-based implementations of standard network services, such as firewalls and load balancers; a network functions virtualization infrastructure (NFVI), which is the hardware/software environment that hosts the VNFs; and a network functions virtualization-management and orchestration (NFV-MANO) framework, which includes the elements required to deploy and administer the NFVI and the VNFs. The Network Functions Virtualization Industry Specification Group (NFV ISG) is the group within ETSI that develops the NFV specifications; it is not one of the three components.

100. B, F. In a colocated datacenter, a client houses its own servers and other hardware in a shared third-party facility. Therefore, Ralph's company would own the hardware in a branch office or colocated datacenter. A datacenter in a public cloud is easier to expand than the other options because it is simply a matter of creating additional virtual devices. A colocated datacenter would be less expensive to implement than a branch office datacenter, but the public cloud option would require the smallest initial outlay. The administrators would set up and manage the hardware in a branch office or colocated datacenter, but not in a public cloud datacenter. In a colocated datacenter, Ralph's company would share utility costs with other tenants. A public cloud facility is not necessarily more secure.

101. C. Role-based access control (RBAC) works by assigning permissions to specific jobs or job roles. Each new user can then be associated with a role and receive the necessary permissions automatically. When a user leaves a job, removing them from their role revokes the permissions associated with it. Least privilege, zero trust, and defense in depth are all theoretical security concepts, but they are not descriptive of Alice's practice in this regard.

102. A. Security lists are virtual firewalls that contain rules that apply to all of the VNICs on a designated subnet. Network security groups are not limited to five member VNICs and can have members from any subnet in the virtual cloud network. A VNIC can be a member of no more than five network security groups, not security lists.

103. A, D. A network address translation (NAT) gateway enables elements on a virtual cloud network to connect to services on the Internet but allows no public Internet traffic onto the VNC. An Internet gateway allows traffic in both directions between the VNC and the Internet.

104. A. The default port for the Post Office Protocol (POP3) is 110. The default port for the Simple Mail Transfer Protocol (SMTP), the other protocol used by email clients, is 25. Port 143 is the default for the Internet Message Access Protocol (IMAP), a different email mailbox protocol that clients never use with POP3. Port 80 is the default for the Hypertext Transfer Protocol (HTTP), which is not used by POP3 email clients.

105. D. The File Transfer Protocol (FTP) uses two port numbers. It uses the first, port 21, for a control connection that remains open during the entire client/server session. The second port, 20, is for a data connection that opens only when the protocol is actually transferring a file between the client and the server. Network Time Protocol (NTP), Simple Network Management Protocol (SNMP), and Hypertext Transfer Protocol (HTTP) all use a single port on the server.

106. C. Ping uses the Internet Control Message Protocol (ICMP) to exchange messages with other systems. ICMP is also used to return error messages to sending systems. The User Datagram Protocol (UDP) and the Transmission Control Protocol (TCP) are both Transport layer protocols that carry Application layer data; Ping does not use either one. The Internet Group Management Protocol (IGMP) is used to create multicast groups; Ping does not use it.

107. B. The port numbers specified in a Transport layer protocol header identify the application that generated the data in the packet or the application that will receive the data. Port numbers do not identify Transport layer protocols, gateways, or proxy servers.

108. B. The IANA assigns values for well-known port numbers. The IEEE publishes Ethernet standards, among many others. The IETF develops standards for Internet technologies. The ISO developed the Open Systems Interconnection (OSI) model.

109. C. Port 80 is the default well-known port for HTTP. Port 22 is for the Secure Shell (SSH) protocol, port 20 is for File Transfer Protocol (FTP), and port 443 is for secured HTTP.

110. D. The well-known port for HTTPS is 443. Port 25 is for the Simple Mail Transfer Protocol (SMTP), port 80 is for unsecured HTTP, and port 110 is for the Post Office Protocol (POP3).

111. A. The Maximum Segment Size (MSS) field in the TCP Options subheader specifies the size (in bytes) of the largest segment a system can receive. The Window field indicates the amount of data (in bytes) that the receiver can accept. There are no MMS or WinMS fields in a TCP header.

112. A. The term for an IPv4 address and port number in combination is *socket*. An organizationally unique identifier (OUI) identifies a manufacturer of networking hardware. A well-known port is a port number assigned to a specific application. A network address is the network identifier part of an IP address. A domain is a group of computers and other resources.

113. A, B. Internet Control Message Protocol (ICMP) and Internet Group Management Protocol (IGMP) are unusual in that they generate messages that are encapsulated directly within IP datagrams. Nearly all of the other TCP/IP protocols, including Simple Mail Transfer Protocol (SMTP) and Simple Network Management Protocol (SNMP), are encapsulated within one of the Transport layer protocols—User Datagram Protocol (UDP) or Transmission Control Protocol (TCP)—which is encapsulated in turn within an IP datagram.

114. B. The Lightweight Directory Access Protocol (LDAP) is an Application layer protocol used for managing and accessing information stored in directory services. The Remote Desktop Protocol (RDP) is used to establish a graphical remote control session with another computer. The Simple Network Management Protocol (SNMP) is used to carry information gathered by management agents distributed around a network to a central management server. Server Message Block (SMB) is the primary file sharing protocol used by Windows systems.

115. A, C. SMTP Secure (SMTPS) uses port number 587. POP3 uses port number 110. Port number 25 is used for SMTP without encryption. Port number 443 is used for Hypertext Transfer Protocol Secure (HTTPS).

116. D. The port number 3389 is used by the Remote Desktop Protocol (RDP) and is not involved in SQL communication. Port 1433 is used by SQL Server; port 1521 is used by SQLnet; and port 3306 is used by MySQL.

117. B. Port number 514 is assigned to syslog, a Unix/Linux standard designed to facilitate the transmission of log entries generated by a device or process, such as the sendmail SMTP server, across an IP network to a message collector, called a syslog server. Port number

389 is assigned to the Lightweight Directory Access Protocol (LDAP). Port number 636 is assigned to LDAP over Secure Sockets Layer (SSL). Port number 993 is assigned to Internet Message Access Protocol (IMAP) over SSL.

118. A. Hypertext Transfer Protocol Secure (HTTPS) is the primary protocol used for web client/server communications. Hypertext Markup Language (HTML) is a coding language used to create web content. Simple Mail Transfer Protocol (SMTP) and File Transfer Protocol (FTP) can both be used in web communications, but neither is the primary protocol.

119. C. The Domain Name System (DNS) is a protocol that computers on a TCP/IP use to resolve host and domain names into the IP addresses they need to communicate. Dynamic Host Configuration Protocol (DHCP) and Bootstrap Protocol (BOOTP) are both IP address allocation protocols, although BOOTP has largely been superseded by DHCP, and Simple Network Management Protocol (SNMP) carries information gathered by agents to a central management console.

120. B, D. The term *datagram* is typically used by protocols offering connectionless delivery service. The two main connectionless protocols in the TCP/IP suite are the Internet Protocol (IP) and the User Datagram Protocol (UDP), both of which use the term *datagram*. Ethernet uses the term *frame*, and Transmission Control Protocol (TCP) uses *segment*.

121. D. The default file sharing protocol used on all Windows operating systems is SMB. HTTPS is the native protocol used by web clients and servers. NFS is the native file sharing protocol used on Unix/Linux networks. FTP is a protocol used for transferring files from one system to another. LDAP is a protocol for transmitting directory service information.

122. A. The receiving host uses the ACK bit to notify the sending host that it has successfully received data. The other control bits are not used to acknowledge receipt of information.

123. D. Two systems establishing a TCP connection exchange three messages before they begin transmitting data. The exchange of these synchronization messages is referred to as a *three-way handshake*. The other terms listed are not formally used to describe this exchange.

124. C, D, E. Dynamic Host Configuration Protocol (DHCP) servers use port numbers 67 and 68. The Trivial File Transfer Protocol (TFTP) uses port number 69. Neither protocol uses port 65 or 66.

125. B. TCP ports and UDP ports identify the application protocol or process that generated the information in a datagram. Client ports are chosen randomly from the range 1024 through 65,535. Server ports are well known and are chosen from the range 1 through 1023.

126. C. Ephemeral client ports are in the range of 49,152 through 65,535. Well-known TCP and UDP server ports are in the range of 0 through 1023. Registered port numbers are in the range of 1024 through 49,151.

127. A, D, E. UDP is a connectionless Transport layer protocol. It has a small, 8-byte header and does not use packet sequencing or acknowledgments.

128. A, C. FTP uses two ports: one for control messages (port 21) and one for data transfers (port 20). Port 23 is used by Telnet. Port 53 is used by the Domain Name System (DNS). Port 69 is used by the Trivial File Transfer Protocol (TFTP).

129. C. The User Datagram Protocol (UDP) provides connectionless service at the Transport layer. Transmission Control Protocol (TCP) provides connection-oriented service at the Transport layer. Hypertext Transfer Protocol (HTTP) is an Application layer protocol, and Address Resolution Protocol (ARP) is a Data link layer protocol.

130. D. Well-known TCP and UDP server ports are in the range of 1 through 1023. Registered port numbers are in the range of 1024 to 49151. Ephemeral client ports are in the range of 49152 through 65535.

131. B, D. Ralph's traffic analysis should show the addition of the Simple Mail Transfer Protocol (SMTP), which handles incoming and outgoing Internet mail, and Internet Message Access Protocol (IMAP), which provides mailboxes for users that store their mail permanently on the server. POP3 is a mailbox protocol that enables users to download their messages and therefore should not be present on the network. SNMP is a network management protocol, and RIP is a routing protocol; neither of these carries email traffic.

132. F. An ephemeral port number is a temporary port supplied by a client to a server, for use during a single session or transaction. The allowed ephemeral port number values range from 49152 to 65535. The port values below 1024 are reserved for use as well-known ports, and the values from 1024 to 49151 are reserved for ports registered by specific manufacturers for their applications. Of these answers, 50134 is the only value that the client can use as an ephemeral port.

133. A. The Transmission Control Protocol (TCP) provides connection-oriented service at the Transport layer, with guaranteed delivery. The User Datagram Protocol (UDP) provides connectionless service at the Transport layer. Hypertext Transfer Protocol (HTTP) operates at the Application layer, and Internet Protocol (IP) is a connectionless Network layer protocol.

134. A. ARP relies on broadcast transmissions, which are not routable. It is therefore limited to use on the local subnet. DHCP also relies on broadcasts, but the ability to create DHCP relay agents makes it usable on an entire internetwork. DNS and SMTP do not rely on broadcasts and therefore are not limited to the local subnet. GRE is a tunneling protocol used to establish secure point-to-point links between devices on different networks.

135. B. No matter what protocol is used to encrypt a website, you must use the HTTPS:// prefix to access it. HTTP:// is for unencrypted sites, and TLS:// and HTLS:// are nonexistent prefixes.

136. A, B. Using the prefix HTTPS:// causes a web browser to use a different port number to establish a secure connection to the web server. Security is provided by encrypting all data using Secure Sockets Layer (SSL) or Transport Layer Security (TLS). However, SSL and TLS do not replace HTTP; they just augment it. The HTTPS:// prefix does not affect the IP address used to connect to the server.

137. D. Because the administrative site is encrypted, you must use the HTTPS:// prefix to access it. Because the administrative site uses the nondefault port number 12354, you must append that number to the server name with a colon.

138. A. Encapsulating Security Protocol (ESP) is a protocol in the TCP/IP suite that is capable of providing encryption services for IPsec. Authentication Header (AH) provides digital integrity services for IPsec, in the form of a digital signature. Secure Sockets Layer (SSL) is a security protocol that provides encrypted communications between web browsers and servers. Internet Key Exchange (IKE) is a security protocol that IPsec uses to create security associations that specify agreed-upon policies between systems.

139. B, C. Authentication Header (AH) is an IPsec protocol that provides authentication and digital integrity services. Encapsulating Security Protocol (ESP) provides encryption services for IPsec. Secure Shell (SSH) is a remote administration tool, and Transport Layer Security (TLS) is a protocol that provides encrypted communications between web browsers and servers.

140. A. FTP does provide authentication capabilities, but passwords are transmitted over the network in cleartext, which is an unacceptable security condition. FTP Secure (FTPS) adds security in the form of the Transport Layer Security (TLS) protocol. SSH File Transfer Protocol (SFTP) uses Secure Shell (SSH) security. File transfer speed and size limitations are not an issue.

141. B, C. FTPS adds security to FTP in the form of the Transport Layer Security (TLS) and Secure Sockets Layer (SSL) protocols. SFTP uses Secure Shell (SSH) for security. Both of these encrypt authentication passwords before transmitting them. FTP transmits passwords over the network in cleartext, which is an unacceptable security condition. Trivial File Transfer Protocol (TFTP) does not authenticate clients, so it does not transmit passwords at all.

142. D. Trivial File Transfer Protocol (TFTP) is a simplified version of FTP that does not authenticate clients, so systems booting with PXE can download boot images invisibly after being directed to a TFTP server by the Dynamic Host Configuration Protocol (DHCP). FTP, FTPS, and SFTP all require authentication and other interaction, which would be impractical for use with PXE.

143. C. Authentication Header (AH) is a protocol in the TCP/IP suite that provides digital integrity services in the form of a digital signature, which ensures that an incoming packet actually originated from its stated source. Encapsulating Security Protocol (ESP) provides encryption services for IPsec. Secure Sockets Layer (SSL) is a security protocol that provides encrypted communications between web browsers and servers. Internet Key Exchange (IKE) is a security protocol that IPsec uses to create security associations that specify agreed-upon policies between systems.

144. A. Secure Sockets Layer (SSL) is the original security protocol for web servers and browsers and the predecessor of Transport Layer Security (TLS). Datagram Transport Layer Security (DTLS) is a protocol that provides the same encryption and other web server/browser security functions as TLS, but for User Datagram Protocol (UDP) traffic. Secure Shell (SSH) is a character-based tool that enables users to execute commands on remote computers. It does not provide web server or browser security.

145. B. Secure Sockets Layer (SSL) is the original security protocol for web servers and browsers and the predecessor of TLS. It was deprecated in 2015. Secure Shell (SSH) is a character-based tool that enables users to execute commands on remote computers. It does not provide web server or browser security like TLS and DTLS. IPsec is a set of security protocols that provide digital signing, encryption, and other services for network transmissions. It is not specifically designed for web security. Remote Desktop Protocol (RDP) is a component of Remote Desktop Services, a Windows mechanism that enables a client program to connect to a server and control it remotely. RDP is not a web security protocol.

146. A, B. The FTP protocol uses two well-known ports: 20 and 21. A firewall must have both of these ports open to admit FTP traffic. FTP does not require ports 22, 23, or 24.

147. C. The Transmission Control Protocol (TCP) uses a flow control technique in which the receiving system creates a window of a specific size and allows the transmitting system to send packets until that window is full. When the window is full, the sender stops transmitting. The receiver then sends back an acknowledgment packet that specifies the next packet it expects to receive from the sender. The User Datagram Protocol (UDP), Hypertext Transfer Protocol (HTTP), and Session Initiation Protocol (SIP) do not use the sliding window technique or any other form of flow control.

148. C. The termination phase of a TCP connection begins when either the client or the server sends a message containing the FIN control bit with a value of 1. The other control bits listed have nothing to do with the connection termination procedure, and there is no END bit.

149. D. The TCP connection establishment exchange is a three-way handshake that uses TCP flags to specify the message type for each frame. The first frame contains a SYN flag from the client; the second frame contains the SYN and ACK flags from the server; and the last frame contains an ACK flag from the client.

150. D. Anycast addresses are IPv6-only addresses designed to transmit to any one host in a multicast group. Unicast, broadcast, and multicast addresses are all traffic types used by both IPv4 and IPv6 networks.

151. A. The network medium provides the physical connection between networked computers. This connection can be made through a copper-based, fiber-optic, or wireless medium. The network medium is not a protocol, and it does not pass data packets; it only carries signals. The network medium does not process electrical or light pulses and convert them to data; it carries only the signals generated by transceivers.

152. D. Copper cables use electrical signals to transmit data. Fiber-optic is a cable type, not a signal type. Microwave signals cannot be transmitted over copper cable. Infrared signals are used only for wireless networks.

153. E. The three organizations that collectively developed the T568b document, which defines the standard for a structured cabling system for voice and data communications, are the American National Standards Institute (ANSI), the Telecommunications Industry Association (TIA), and the Electronic Industries Association (EIA). None of the other options are standards organizations or cabling standards.

154. D. The cable type and connector used to attach a television set to a CATV network is a coaxial cable with a screw-on F-type connector. Although CATV networks typically use fiber-optic cables and ST connectors for outdoor connections, they do not use fiber for internal connections to television sets. Coaxial cables with BNC connectors are most commonly used for Thin Ethernet LANs, not CATV network connections. Twisted-pair cables and RJ-45 connectors are used for Ethernet LANs and telephone networks, but not CATV networks. AUI cables and vampire tap connectors are used for Thick Ethernet networks. Twinaxial cables are used for SATA 3.0 devices and 100 Gbit Ethernet connections, but not for CATV connections.

155. A. The cable type used for Thick Ethernet segments is a coaxial cable called RG-8. RG-58 is used exclusively on Thin Ethernet segments. RJ-45 is a connector type used in twisted-pair cabling for data networks. RJ-11 is a connector type used in twisted-pair cabling for telecommunications networks.

156. B. RG-58 coaxial cable is used exclusively for Thin Ethernet segments. RG-8 cable is used for Thick Ethernet segments. RJ-45 is a connector type used in twisted-pair cabling for data networks. RJ-11 is a connector type used in twisted-pair cabling for telecommunications networks.

157. A, D. RG-6 and RG-59 are 75-ohm cables that are still used for cable television and similar connections. RG-8 and RG-58 are 50-ohm cables that were formerly used for Thick Ethernet and Thin Ethernet, respectively, but are no longer in general use.

158. A, B, C. Joining an APC to a UPC creates a mismatched connection that generates an extremely high rate of insertion loss (attenuation). APCs do generate more insertion loss than UPCs and less return loss (reflection). It is APCs, not UPCs, that use green boots or bodies on the connectors.

159. D. Bayonet-Neill-Concelman (BNC) is a type of connector used with coaxial cable. Subscriber Connector (SC), Mechanical Transfer-Registered Jack (MT-RJ), Local Connector (LC), and Straight Tip (ST) are all types of fiber-optic connectors.

160. C. The Gigabit Interface Converter (GBIC) transceiver standard was first published in 1995 and defines a maximum data transfer rate of 1.25 Gbps. It was rendered all but obsolete by the Small Form-factor Pluggable (SFP) standard, introduced in 2001, which ran at the same maximum speed but was smaller in size. Subsequent variations on the standard, such as SFP+, Quad Small Form-factor Pluggable (QSFP), and QSFP+, defined devices with faster transfer rates.

161. B. There are two main types of twisted-pair wiring used for data communications: unshielded twisted-pair (UTP) and shielded twisted-pair (STP). Both types can be used in a star/hub and spoke topology. UTP and STP cables contain eight copper conductors twisted in four pairs. UTP and STP cables use RJ-45 connectors to connect end systems to switches, patch panels, and wall plates. RG-8 and RG-58 coaxial cable can only be used in a bus topology. Fiber-optic cable can be used in a star/hub and spoke topology, but it uses either glass or plastic conductors and does not use RJ-45 connectors.

162. C. The twists in a twisted-pair cable prevent the signals on the different wires from interfering with each other (which is called crosstalk) and also provide resistance to outside electromagnetic interference. The twists have no effect on collisions. The twists cannot completely eliminate the effects of EMI. Twists have nothing to do with the bend radius allowance for the cable.

163. C. Thin Ethernet networks use a type of 50-ohm coaxial cable called RG-58, which is 0.195 inches in diameter and uses BNC connectors. A 75-ohm coaxial cable with F-type connectors is used for cable television networks, and RG-8 coaxial is the cable that Thick Ethernet networks use.

164. B, D. Thin Ethernet networks use coaxial cables with Bayonet Neill–Concelman (BNC) connectors. All unshielded twisted-pair (UTP) Ethernet networks use RJ-45 connectors. F-type connectors are used with coaxial cable, typically for cable television installations, but not for Ethernet. DB-9 connectors are commonly used for serial communications ports.

165. D. Thin Ethernet networks use a type of coaxial cable that runs from each computer to the next one, forming a bus topology. To connect the cable to the network computers, each network interface adapter has a T-connector attached to it, with two additional male Bayonet Neill–Concelman (BNC) connectors, to which you connect two lengths of network cabling.

166. B, D, E, F. Fiber-optic cable connectors all function on the same basic principles, but there are a variety of form factors from which to choose, including Straight Tip (ST), Local Connector (LC), and Mechanical Transfer–Registered Jack (MT-RJ). Multi-fiber Push On (MPO) is a fiber array connector that gathers multiple optical fibers into a single connection. RJ-11 is a twisted-pair cable connector, and F connectors are for coaxial cable.

167. E. Thick Ethernet installations used a type of coaxial cable called RG-8. To connect a node to the network, installers ran a separate cable called an Attachment Unit Interface (AUI) cable from the computer to the RG-8 and connected it using a device called a vampire tap that pierced the sheathing to make contact with the conductors within. All of the other cable types listed use different types of connectors.

168. A, C. Single-mode cables are capable of spanning longer distances than multimode because they have a narrower core diameter, reducing signal dispersion rates. Because the core consists of fewer (typically one or two) strands, single-mode cables are less flexible than multimode and cannot bend around corners as easily, making them more difficult to install. Because they use light impulses rather than electricity, all fiber-optic cables are completely immune to electromagnetic interference.

169. A, C, D. Voice telephone networks do not have performance requirements as strict as those of data networks, so they are less liable to suffer from crosstalk and other types of interference. As a result, installers often use larger UTP cables for telephone connections. UTP cables are available in configurations containing 25 wire pairs and 100 wire pairs in a single sheath, which enables installers to service multiple users with a single cable. The punchdown blocks for UTP data networks with 8P8C connectors are called 110 blocks. The older standard for punchdown blocks is the 66 block. Rarely used for data networking, 66 blocks are still found in many telephone service installations.

170. B, C. Single-mode cables have a smaller core filament and can span longer distances than multimode cables. Single-mode cables also use a laser light source, have a larger bend radius, and do not require a ground.

171. D. Installers use a punchdown block tool to connect the ends of bulk cable runs to jacks in wall plates and patch panels. A crimper or crimping tool is a jawed device that enables installers to squeeze the two halves of an RJ-45 or RJ-11 connector together, securing the connector to the cable. Installers use a splicing tool to splice two cable segments together. There is no tool called a pigtail.

172. A. Multimode fiber-optic cable best meets the client's needs. Fiber-optic cable supports the required 1,000 Mbps data rate and can connect networks that are more than 1,000 feet apart. Fiber-optic cable is immune to EMI. Although both multimode and single-mode fiber would meet the corporation's general needs, multimode is best in this scenario because it is less expensive than single-mode fiber. Twisted-pair wiring (STP or UTP) meets the data rate and cost requirements but does not support connections longer than 100 meters. Thin coaxial cable does not support the data rate or distances longer than 185 meters.

173. A, B, C. Bayonet Neill–Concelman (BNC) connectors are used for coaxial Thin Ethernet networks, and N-type connectors with Thick Ethernet. F-type connectors are used for coaxial cable television installations. Straight Tip (ST) connectors are used with fiber-optic cable, and RJ-11 connectors are used for telephone installations.

174. A. You use a punchdown block tool to connect the ends of bulk cable runs to jacks in wall plates and patch panels. The steps of the process are as follows:

1. Strip some of the sheath off the cable end to expose the wires.

2. Separate the twisted wire pairs at the ends.

3. Strip a small amount of insulation off each wire.

4. Insert the wires into the appropriate contacts in the jack.

5. Press the bare wire down between the two metal contacts that hold it in place.

6. Cut off the excess wire that protrudes past the contacts.

You must repeat the process of punching down for both ends of your internal cable runs.

175. D. ST, SC, fiber LC, and MT-RJ are all connectors used with fiber-optic cables. F-type connectors are used with coaxial cables.

176. C, D. The DB-9 and DB-25 connectors were at one time ubiquitous on personal computers, providing peripheral connections to modems, printers, and other devices. They have since been largely eliminated in favor of USB. Bayonet Neill–Concelman (BNC) connectors were used for Thin Ethernet networking, but they have been replaced by unshielded twisted-pair (UTP) cable with RJ-45 connectors. RJ-11 connectors are used for telephone connections.

177. B, D. The main cable types used in LANs today are multimode fiber-optic and unshielded twisted-pair. Single-mode fiber-optic is used primarily for long-distance wide area network (WAN) connections, and coaxial cable is no longer used for LANs.

178. B, D, F. Coaxial cable has two conductors within the same sheath that share a common axis. These conductors are surrounded by an outer insulating sheath of either PVC or Teflon. Copper cables carry electrical signals. Only fiber-optic cables carry light pulse signals.

179. A, B, D, E, F. Fiber-optic cable comes in two types: multimode and single-mode. Fiber-optic cables vary in light source (LED or laser), cable grade (glass or plastic), and size of the core conductor. Single-mode uses a higher-grade glass conductor with a laser light source. Multimode fiber uses an LED light source. Both types can use either ST or SC connectors to physically connect end devices to a fiber-optic network. Fiber-optic cable is used to extend networks over long distances. Fiber-optic cables do not use IDC connectors, which are intended for use with shielded twisted-pair (STP) cable.

180. A, D, F. The use of bulk cable with no connectors, wall plates, and rack-mounted patch panels are all characteristics of an internal wiring installation. Internal installations typically cover large geographic areas that require cabling through walls, ceilings, and around other obstacles, making the cabling difficult to move. Solid core wiring is used for longer cable runs, whereas shorter cable runs such as connections from node to wall plate use prefabricated stranded core cables with connectors attached.

181. B. 40GBase-T is a 40-gigabits-per-second (Gbps) Ethernet specification that calls for 4-pair CAT8 twisted-pair cabling for lengths up to 30 meters. 10GBase-T and 100Base-TX do not require CAT8 cable, and 1000Base-SX is a fiber-optic standard.

182. E. Ralph should use a mesh topology with redundant fiber-optic cable runs and an internal installation method. This will meet the requirements for connecting the LANs and providing redundancy and fault tolerance. Fiber-optic cable is immune to electromagnetic interference (EMI) and can span long distances. The internal installation method is most often used in larger networks, where end systems are geographically distant. The star/hub and spoke topology will not fulfill the requirements since it provides no redundancy. Twisted-pair cable cannot span distances more than 100 meters, and it is susceptible to EMI. Coaxial cable cannot span distances more than 500 meters, and it is also susceptible to EMI. The bus topology cannot use twisted-pair cabling and does not support cable runs longer than 500 meters.

183. C. The CAT 6 UTP network described in the old proposal is sufficient to connect the 20 workstations to a single LAN running at 1 Gbps, thus achieving the primary goal. The star/hub and spoke topology can tolerate a single cable break without affecting the entire network, but the UTP cable is susceptible to EMI, so one secondary goal could not be achieved.

184. D. Fiber-optic cable is not more tolerant of cable breaks than UTP. Some fiber-optic networks are fault tolerant, but the Ethernet fiber-optic specifications are not. UTP cables connecting a computer to a switch can be no longer than 100 meters, making 200 meters the maximum distance between two computers. Connecting two buildings with a copper-based cable creates an electrical connection between them, which can be hazardous. Fiber-optic cable does not create an electrical connection. Fiber-optic cable is also unaffected by the EMI generated by manufacturing equipment.

185. B. The 10GBase-CX4 specification calls for the use of a twinaxial copper cable with segments no longer than 15 meters. The10GBase-LR, 10GBase-ER, 10GBase-LX4, and 10GBase-SR specifications all call for fiber-optic cable.

186. D. The multispeed network interface adapters in the computers can run at 1 Gbps speed using the existing CAT6 cable, but the 100Base-T switch must be replaced with a 1000Base-T switch. While the network might run better with a cable upgrade, it is not immediately necessary. Replacing the network interface adapters is not necessary because the existing multispeed adapters can run at 1 Gbps if they are connected to a 1000Base-T switch.

187. C. 1000Base-T is the fastest 802.3 Ethernet specification that can run on 100-meter CAT6 UTP cables. 10GBase-T requires at least Category 6a (CAT6a) UTP cable for a 100-meter segment. 100Base-TX can use CAT6 cable, but it runs at one-tenth the speed of 1000Base-T. 1000Base-LX and 1000Base-SX are fiber-optic specifications that cannot run on CAT6 UTP or any copper cable.

188. B, C, E. The three IEEE 10 Mbps standards for Ethernet are 10Base2, 10Base5, and 10Base-T. 10Base2 is limited to 185-meter segments; 10Base5 is limited to 500-meter segments; and 10Base-T is limited to 100-meter segments. The other options are not valid.

189. A, D. The first version of DIX Ethernet (Version 1) supported RG-8 thick coaxial cable in a bus topology. Version 2 added support for thin coaxial cable (RG-58) but was still limited to a bus topology. RG-10 and RG-14 are not Ethernet cable types.

190. D. The types of wavelength division multiplexing use different spacing of the wavelengths they carry, which enables them to fit different numbers of channels on a single medium. WDM (or BWDM) carries two wavelengths for bidirectional communication. CWDM can carry up to 16 channels, and DWDM 40 or 80 (depending on the spacing used). Various amplification technologies (including EFDA and Raman) can expand the amount of usable wavelength in each type.

191. A. Media converters will enable Ralph to join the multimode fiber-optic run to the UTP at both sides of the courtyard while maintaining a single network at minimum cost. Inexpensive small-business hubs and switches cannot join different media together. Routers can join different media, but they are more expensive, and they would separate the installation into three separate networks.

192. B. Plenum cable is a type of cable intended for use within building air spaces (called plenums) that has an outer sheath that is more resistant to high temperatures and does not produce toxic fumes when it burns. The use of plenum cable has no effect on EMI or the type of traffic on the cable, nor is it required for low temperature areas.

193. C, E. IEEE 802.11n and 802.11ax support transmission speeds over 72 Mbps, and they both run on the 2.4 GHz band, so they are backward compatible with 802.11b and 802.11g equipment. IEEE 802.11 and 802.11a cannot run at 72 Mbps, and 802.11a is not compatible with 802.11b and 802.11g because it only runs on the 5 GHz band. IEEE 802.1ac can run at speeds over 72 Mbps, but it only runs on the 5 GHz band, so it is not compatible with 802.11b and 802.11g.

194. C. Time-division multiple access (TDMA) is a communication technique that splits a frequency into multiple time slots, enabling it to carry multiple data streams. Commonly used in 2G cellular systems, TDMA is no longer used by the major US carriers in their 3G systems. Code-division multiple access (CDMA), Global System for Mobile Communications (GSM), and Long-Term Evolution (LTE) are alternative communications techniques that are currently used by the major US cellular carriers.

195. E. Wireless networks using equipment based on the IEEE 802.11ax standard can span indoor distances of up to 820 feet at speeds up to 9.6 Gbps. An 802.11n network can span distances of up to 175 feet, which meets the requirement, but at much slower speeds of only 600 Mbps. An 802.11ac network can run at faster speeds—up to 1.3 Gbps—but it is limited to approximately 115-foot distances. Networks using 802.11g equipment can span 150 feet, but they run at a maximum of 54 Mbps. An 802.11a network cannot span more than 75 feet, and it runs at no more than 54 Mbps.

196. B. The word *symmetric* in symmetric digital subscriber line (SDSL) means that the service provides equal amounts of bandwidth in both directions. The asymmetric in asymmetric digital subscriber line (ADSL) means that the service provides more downstream bandwidth than upstream. Cable and satellite services are also asymmetric, providing more bandwidth downstream than upstream.

197. A, B, C, D. The 1000Base-SX standard calls for multimode cable with a maximum length of approximately 500 meters, whereas the new cable run is 4,000 meters and uses single-mode cable. The 1000Base-SX transceiver will also be incompatible with the 1000Base-BX10 transceiver at the other end. 1000Base-BX10 uses wavelengths from 1,300 to 1,600 nanometers (nm), whereas 1000Base-SX uses wavelengths of 770 to 860 nm.

198. E. Direct-attach copper (DAC) connections use twinaxial cable, which has two conductors instead of the one used in coaxial cables. DAC connections also do not use twisted-pair cables, either shielded or unshielded, or fiber-optic cables.

199. A. A cable break in a bus topology would split the network into two halves, preventing the nodes on one side of the break from communicating with those on the other. In addition, both halves of the network would be left with one unterminated end, which would prevent the computers on each side of the break from communicating effectively. A cable break in a star/hub and spoke or logical ring topology would only interrupt the connection of a single computer to the network. The mesh topology is not often used for LANs, but redundant network connections are a characteristic of mesh networks, which means that a single cable break would have no effect on the network.

200. D. A wired LAN is a group of computers within a small area, connected by a common network medium. A wired LAN can be configured using a ring, bus, or star/hub and spoke topology.

201. B. A hybrid LAN topology is a network that uses two or more of the basic topologies, connected together so that each workstation can communicate with all of the other workstations. Connecting four switches to a bus topology combines four star/hub and spoke networks in such a way that the workstations are all interconnected. Connecting a single workstation to a star/hub and spoke and a bus network enables that workstation to access both networks, but it does not enable other workstations to access both topologies. Four workstations, each with a separate connection to the other three, is a mesh network topology, not a hybrid. Four connected switches expands the star/hub and spoke topology, but it does not create a hybrid topology.

202. A. WANs (wide area networks) connect LANs that are geographically distant. A LAN (local area network), as the name implies, is a group of computers, not other LANs, and it is contained within a small area. MANs (metropolitan area networks) connect LANs in a single metropolitan area; they are not confined to a small area. A MAN is typically larger than a LAN but smaller than a WAN. A campus area network (CAN) typically includes a group of adjacent buildings, such as those of a corporation or university.

203. D. Virtually all of the new Ethernet networks installed today use the star/hub and spoke topology, with one or more switches functioning as a cabling nexus. Ethernet no longer uses the bus topology, and it does not support point-to-point or mesh topologies.

204. A. A storage area network (SAN) is a network that is dedicated to carrying traffic between servers and storage devices. A personal area network (PAN) provides communication among devices associated with a single person, such as smartphones. A wide area network (WAN) is a network that connects devices or networks at different geographic locations. A metropolitan area network (MAN) is a type of WAN that connects devices within a limited geographic area.

205. A, C. WLANs can use the ad hoc topology, in which devices communicate directly with each other, or the infrastructure topology, in which the wireless devices connect to an access point. The bus and star/hub and spoke topologies are used by wired networks only.

206. C. A switch can function as the cabling nexus at the center of an Ethernet star/hub and spoke topology. Each of the devices on the network is connected by a cable to the switch. Routers are used to connect networks to each other; they cannot function as the center of a star/hub and spoke topology. Firewalls are not cabling devices, and access points are used on wireless networks.

207. C. A mesh topology is one in which every node is directly connected to every other node, thus providing complete redundancy through the network. In a star/hub and spoke topology, each node is connected to a central nexus, providing each with a single path to the rest of the network. In a ring topology, each node is connected to two other nodes, providing two possible paths through the network. In a bus topology, nodes are chained together in a line, providing no redundancy.

208. A. 10Base2 is the Physical layer specification for Thin Ethernet, which uses coaxial cable in a bus topology. 10Base-T, 100Base-TX, and 1000Base-T all use twisted-pair cable in a star/hub and spoke topology.

209. C. A peer-to-peer network calls for each workstation to maintain accounts for authenticating users that access their shared resources. On a client-server network, authentication is centralized. Peer-to-peer networks can be more difficult to administer than client-server networks, but they are not inherently less secure. Peer networks sharing copyrighted content on the Internet are illegal, but it is not illegal to share private resources on a peer-to-peer network. Workstations on a peer-to-peer network are not required to share their resources, but they are capable of it.

210. B. For this scenario, the best of the options given is a dedicated leased line connection. This is because the bandwidth requirements are constant and the data transfer rates are high. To support the 40 Mbps data rate, Ed should recommend a T-3 dedicated leased line, running at 44.735 Mbps. Standard modem connections, CATV, and ADSL connections are all too slow.

211. D. In this scenario, the best solution is for Ralph to use his existing CATV service for the remote connection. CATV offers faster data rates than standard modem-to-modem service and supports VPN connections. A dedicated fractional T-1 line is expensive and is not typically used for remote user connections. Since Ralph's telephone lines are not run through conduit and the distance to the central office is more than 18,000 feet, he probably cannot use DSL technology, because it requires good-quality lines and close proximity to a central office.

212. A, C. A Session Initiation Protocol (SIP) trunk provides a connection between the private and public domains of a unified communications network. A Voice over Internet Protocol (VoIP) gateway provides a connection between an IP network and the public switched telephone network (PSTN). Both of these provide a conduit between a subscriber's private network and the network furnished by a service provider. A channel service unit/data service unit (CSU/DSU) is a device that provides a router on a private network with access to a leased line. A smartjack provides signal conversion, diagnostic testing, and other capabilities to leased line subscribers. A virtual private network (VPN) concentrator is a type of router that enables multiple client systems to access a network from remote locations.

213. D. Frame Relay is a packet switching service that uses a single leased line to replace multiple leased lines by multiplexing traffic through a cloud. Asynchronous Transfer Mode (ATM) uses a switched fabric, but it is not referred to as a cloud. A fractional T-1 is part of a leased line that connects two points, so there is no switching involved and no cloud. SONET is a Physical layer standard that defines fiber-optic connections; it does not call for switching or use the term *cloud*.

214. D. All coaxial-based Ethernet networks, including Thin Ethernet, use a bus topology. All UTP-based Gigabit Ethernet networks use a star/hub and spoke topology. Therefore, an upgrade from coaxial to UTP cable must include a change in topology from bus to star/hub and spoke. Ethernet networks never use a mesh topology.

215. D. In most virtualization products, when you create multiple virtual machines on one host computer, they can communicate with each other internally using a built-in virtual switching capability. A computer with multiple network adapters can function as a router, but not as a switch. Layer 3 switches can provide virtual routers that connect VLANs together, but not virtual switches. The function that enables VLANs on different switches to communicate is called trunking, not virtual switching.

216. B. You can create virtual local area networks (VLANs) on a virtual switch, just as you can create them on many physical switches. In most cases, virtual components function just like their physical counterparts. Virtual NICs are components of virtual machines and therefore do not provide functions spanning entire networks. Virtual routers function at the Network layer and virtual firewalls at the Application layer, so neither of these can host VLANs, which operate at the Data link layer.

217. A. The hypervisor is the hardware or software component responsible for managing virtual machines and providing the virtualized hardware environment on which they run. Virtual servers and virtual switches are components that are part of the virtual network infrastructure enabled by the hypervisor. A virtual private network (VPN) concentrator is a type of router that enables multiple remote clients to connect to a network; it has nothing to do with virtual networking.

218. C. A computer with a hypervisor, on which you can create virtual machines, is referred to as a host. The virtual machines themselves are called guests. Network-attached storage (NAS) refers to a device containing shared drives that is connected to a network. A storage area network (SAN) is a separate network dedicated to shared storage devices.

219. E. A virtual firewall is a service or appliance that performs the same functions as a physical network firewall: packet filtering and monitoring. In a virtual environment, firewalls can take the form of software components installed on a guest virtual machine or a hypervisor host system. A firewall can also be incorporated into a virtual switch.

220. D. Network address translation (NAT) enables workstations on private networks to access the Internet by substituting a public IP address in packets generated with private addresses. Layer 2 Tunneling Protocol (L2TP), IPsec, and Multipoint Generic Routing Encapsulation (MGRE) are all protocols that encapsulate packets in an encrypted form within another protocol to secure the contents.

221. B. The three-tier hierarchical architecture for datacenters consists of core, distribution, and access layers. The access layer in a datacenter contains servers; the distribution layer contains redundant switch connections; and the core layer provides high-speed transport between the switches. There is no intermediate layer in the architecture.

222. C. The spine and leaf topology uses a full mesh topology in its two layers of switches. This is more expensive than the three-tier topology, but it reduces latency by requiring the same number of hops in the path between any two routers. The use of software-defined networking provides adaptive path determination without the use of the Spanning Tree Protocol (STP) for layer 2 port blocking.

223. C. East-west traffic describes traffic flow within the datacenter, while north-south is traffic between devices inside the datacenter and outside devices. The terms *east-west* and *north-south* do not pertain to the OSI model layers or to specific devices used.

224. A. In a typical datacenter topology, racks contain servers that implement applications. A leaf switch at the top of the rack connects the servers in the rack together and also connects to a spine switch that links to the rest of the datacenter. The top-of-rack switches are not classified as backbone, spine, or core devices.

225. B. Switches are Data link layer devices that amplify and repeat incoming signals only through the port for which the data is destined, not through all ports. Switches are used to physically connect end systems to a star/hub and spoke topology. Switches typically provide an internal crossover circuit connection. Uplink ports are sometimes used to extend the distance of a star/hub and spoke network, forming a hierarchical star.

226. A. In a collapsed core network, the core and distribution layers are combined, creating a simpler design that is less expensive to implement. A collapsed core network does not combine the distribution and access tiers or the core and access tiers. There is no intermediate tier in the three-tier hierarchical model.

227. B. Network address translation (NAT) is a service that enables computers with unregistered IP addresses to access the Internet by substituting a registered address in packets as they pass through a router. The Dynamic Host Configuration Protocol (DHCP) is an IP address allocation service. Domain Name System (DNS) resolves domain and hostnames into IP addresses, and Network Time Protocol (NTP) enables network devices to synchronize their time settings.

228. C. You cannot extend the IPv4 address beyond its 32-bit size, and you cannot remove bits from the network identifier, or the packets will not be routed properly. You must therefore create a subnet by borrowing bits from the host identifier.

229. B, C. IPv4 addresses with first byte values from 224 to 239 are Class D addresses, which are reserved for use as multicast addresses. Therefore, you cannot assign 229.6.87.3 to a host. Option C, 103.256.77.4, is an invalid address because the value 256 cannot be represented by an 8-bit binary value. The other options, 1.1.1.1 and 9.34.0.1, are both valid IPv4 addresses.

230. B. The value after the slash in a Classless Inter-Domain Routing (CIDR) address specifies the number of bits in the network identifier. An IPv4 address has 32 bits, so if 17 bits are allocated to the network identifier, 15 bits are left for the host identifier.

231. B, E. RFC 1918 defines the private address space as the following ranges:

- 10.0.0.0–10.255.255.255
- 172.16.0.0–172.31.255.255
- 192.168.0.0–192.168.255.255

Option B, 172:33:19:7, and Option E, 172.15.2.9, both fall outside the specified private Class B range, and therefore are not valid private addresses.

232. C. To create a network with 8 subnets and 30 hosts per subnet, Alice would have to allocate 3 of the 8 bits in the last octet for subnet identifiers. This would result in a binary value of 11100000 for the last octet in the subnet mask, which converts to a decimal value of 224.

233. A. A Class A address uses only the first octet as the network identifier, which yields a binary subnet mask of 11111111 00000000 00000000 00000000. In decimal form, the subnet mask is 255.0.0.0. The 255.255.0.0 mask is for Class B addresses, and 255.255.255.0 is for Class C addresses. Option D, 255.255.255.255, is the broadcast address for the current network.

234. B. According to RFC 3927, when a DHCP client cannot access a DHCP server, APIPA assigns it an address on the 169.254/16 network, the range of addresses for which is 169.254.0.0 to 169.254.255.255.

235. D. Address 127.0.0.1 is the designated IPv4 local loopback address, and as such, it is reserved. It falls between Class A, which has first octet values from 1 to 126, and Class B, which has first octet values of 128 to 191.

236. B. All Class B addresses have first octet values between 128 and 191. The first octet range of a Class A address is 1 to 126, and the Class C first octet range is 192 to 223. Class D addresses have a first octet range of 224 to 239. Class E addresses have a first octet range of 240 to 255.

237. A. Variable-length subnet masking (VLSM) describes the process of subnetting an IPv4 network address by assigning an arbitrary number of host bits as subnet bits, providing administrators with great flexibility over the number of subnets created and the number of hosts in each subnet. Automatic Private IP Addressing (APIPA) is the process by which a DHCP client assigns itself an IP address when no DHCP servers are accessible. Virtual local area networks (VLANs) are logical structures used to create separate broadcast domains on a large, switched network. Extended Unique Identifier-64 (EUI-64) is an addressing method used to create IPv6 link local addresses out of media access control (MAC) addresses.

238. B. The 14-bit prefix indicated in the network address will result in a mask with 14 ones followed by 18 zeroes. Broken into 8-bit blocks, the binary mask value is as follows: 11111111 11111100 00000000 00000000. Converted into decimal values, this results in a subnet mask value of 255.252.0.0.

239. A. In this scenario, the company has a Class C Internet Protocol (IPv4) address, which consists of 24 network bits and 8 host bits. The company wants 10 subnets and 14 hosts per subnet, so Ed must subdivide the 8 host bits into subnet and host bits. He can allocate 4 of the 8 host bits for subnets, enabling him to create up to 16 subnets. This leaves 4 bits for host addresses, enabling Ed to create 14 hosts per subnet.

240. E. The formula for calculating the number of subnets you can create using a subnet identifier of a given length is 2^x, where x is the number of bits in the subnet identifier. Therefore, with a 14-bit subnet, you can conceivably create 2^{14}, or 16,384, subnets.

241. C. In this scenario, the last byte of the IP address assigned to the company must be subdivided into 3 subnet bits and 5 host bits. The 3 subnet bits will give Alice up to 8 subnets, with 5 host bits for up to 30 hosts per subnet. The new subnet mask is 255.255.255.224. The 224 is the decimal equivalent of the binary value 11100000, which represents the 3 subnet bits and the 5 host bits.

242. A. A standard Class B address with a mask of 255.255.0.0 has 16 bits that can be used for subnets and hosts. To get 600 subnets, you must use 10 of the available bits, which gives you up to 1024 subnets. This leaves 6 host bits, which gives you up to 62 hosts per subnet, which exceeds the requirement of 55 requested by the client. Using 9 bits would give you only 510 subnets, while 11 bits would give you 2046 subnets but leave you only 5 bits for a maximum of 30 hosts, which is not enough.

243. C. The formula for calculating the number of hosts you can create using a host identifier of a given length is 2^x-2, where x is the number of bits in the host identifier. You cannot create a host with an address of all zeroes or all ones, which is why you subtract 2. On a network that uses 20 bits for network identification, 12 bits are left for the host identifier. Using those 12 bits, you can create $2^{12}-2$ or 4,094 host addresses.

244. B. With a Class B subnet mask of 255.255.248.0, the binary form of the third and fourth bytes is 11111000 00000000. There are 5 subnet bits, providing up to 32 subnets and 11 host bits, providing up to 2,046 hosts.

245. A. The decimal value for 11111111 is 255, the value for 11100000 is 224, and the value for 00000000 is 0, so the mask is 255.255.224.0.

246. B. With a network address of 192.168.1.32 and 27 mask bits, the subnet mask value is 11111111.11111111.11111111.11100000 in binary form, or 255.255.255.224 in decimal form. This leaves 5 bits for the host identifier. The valid range of host bits is therefore 00001 (1) through 11110 (30). This gives you a range of 192.168.1.32 + 1 (33) through 192.168.1.32 + 30 (62).

247. C. To calculate the number of host addresses available, Alice must determine the number of host bits in the address, which is 10, raise 2 to that power, and subtract 2 for the network and broadcast addresses, which are unusable for hosts. The formula is therefore 2^x-2. $2^{10}-2 = 1,022$.

248. B. When a DHCP client cannot access a DHCP server, APIPA assigns it a Class B address using the network address 169.254/16, which yields the address range 169.254.0.0 to 169.254.255.255.

249. D. Class D addresses are used for multicast transmissions. Class A, Class B, and Class C addresses are used for unicast transmissions. Class E is for experimental use only.

250. C. The address 10.1.0.253 is a proper address in the private address range 10.0.0.0 to 10.255.255.255. The address 192.167.9.46 falls outside the designated private IP address range, which is 192.168.0.0 to 192.168.255.255, and is therefore not a viable address on a private network. 172.16.255.255 is a broadcast address, which you cannot assign to a host. 225.87.34.1 falls in the Class D multicast address range and cannot be assigned to a single host.

251. B. The address given uses 20 bits to identify the network, leaving 12 bits for the host identifier. In binary form, therefore, the subnet mask value would be 11111111 11111111
11110000 00000000. The decimal value for 11111111 is 255, and the decimal value for
11110000 is 240. Therefore, the subnet mask is 255.255.240.0.

252. B. A /28 address leaves 4 bits for the host identifier. To calculate the number of hosts, Ed
uses $2^4-2=14$. The first address on the subnet is therefore 192.168.2.33, and the fourteenth
is 192.168.2.46.

253. A. 1.0.0.1 is a legitimate address that falls into Class A. Option B, 127.98.127.0, falls into the
range of addresses reserved for use as loopback addresses (127.0.0.1 to 127.255.255.255).
Option C, 234.9.76.32, falls into Class D, which is reserved for use as multicast addresses.
Option D, 240.65.8.124, is a Class E address; that class is reserved for experimental use.

254. A, D, E. Teredo and 6to4 are both tunneling protocols that were intended as transitional
mechanisms, enabling the encapsulation of IPv6 datagrams within IPv4 packets. A NAT64
server functions as a gateway between IPv4and IPv6, using the basic network address translation mechanism to substitute an IPv6 address for an IPv4. IPsec uses tunneling, but it is
not used for the encapsulation of IPv6 traffic. Internet Control Message Protocol v6, like its
ICMPv4 equivalent, enables routers and hosts to transmit informational and error messages;
it does not use tunneling.

255. A. ICMPv6 hosts generate Router Solicitation messages and transmit them to the All
Routers multicast address. Routers respond using Router Advertisement messages, which
contain the prefix information that the host uses to generate a link-local address. Hosts do
not have to learn the address of the nearest router, because they can use the All Routers
multicast. Address conflict detection comes after the host has created a link-local address
and does not use Router Solicitation and Router Advertisement messages. Hosts do not use
Router Solicitation and Router Advertisement messages to encapsulate IPv4 packets.

256. B. Stateless Address Auto-Configuration (SLAAC) is the means by which IPv6 systems
self-generate link-local addresses with the prefix fe80::/64, much as IPv4 systems use APIPA
to generate addresses. IPv6 systems can use DHCPv6 to obtain stateful (not stateless)
addresses. An Extended Unique Identifier (such as EUI-64) is the format for a media access
control (MAC) address.

257. A. An IPv6 link local address is automatically assigned to each interface. Like Automatic
Private IP Addressing (APIPA), it provides communication on the local network only.
Global unicast addresses are routable; they are the functional equivalent of IPv4 registered
addresses. Site local addresses are the equivalent of private IPv4 addresses. Anycast
addresses are designed to transmit to any one host in a multicast group.

258. D. To convert a MAC address to an Extended Unique Identifier (EUI-64), you split the
6-byte MAC address into two 3-byte halves and insert the 2-byte value FFFE in between, as
follows:

001F9E FFFE FC7AD0

Then, you change the seventh bit in the first byte, the universal/local bit, from 0 to 1,
indicating that this is a locally created address. This results in a binary first byte value
of 00000010, which converts to 02 in hexadecimal.

Finally, you add the IPv6 link local prefix FE80::/10, resulting in the following complete address:

FE80::021F:9EFF:FEFC:7AD0

All of the other answers either insert the FFFE bytes in the wrong place or fail to change the universal/local bit.

259. C. The address fe00::c955:c944:acdd:3fcb is correctly formatted for IPv6, with the double colon replacing three blocks of zeroes. Uncompressed, the address would appear as follows: fe00:0000:0000:0000:c955:c944:acdd:3fcb. Option A contains a nonhexadecimal digit. Option B contains only seven 16-bit blocks (and no double colon) instead of the eight required for 128 bits. Option D contains blocks larger than 16 bits.

260. C. A dual stack is an IP implementation that includes both IPv4 and IPv6 protocol stacks, operating simultaneously. A computer with two network adapters or connections to two network segments is often called multihomed. A computer with two installed operating systems is called a dual-boot system.

261. E. The RFC 7426 document defines five planes in the SDN architecture: forwarding, operational, control, management, and application. Infrastructure is not one of the SDN planes.

262. C. In an SDN architecture, the Application layer is software, that is, the applications and services running on the network; the control layer is a centralized console through which administrators manage the applications; and the infrastructure layer consists of the switch and router hardware. Core is not one of the SDN layers.

263. B. The Common Vulnerabilities and Exposures (CVE) database is a resource that assigns identifier numbers to known security issues found in software products. By searching the database, Ralph can learn about the vulnerabilities that have already been found in the products he is evaluating. The CIA triad lists important information security concepts (confidentiality, integrity, and availability), but it does not provide information about specific products. Stock-keeping units (SKUs) are product identifiers that do not involve security issues. Security information and event management (SIEM) is a solution that gathers and analyzes information about a network's security events, but it would not help Ralph discover vulnerabilities in the products he is evaluating.

264. C. Least privilege is the practice of only providing users with the permissions they need to perform their designated tasks and no more. For her standard activities, Alice is given an account that does not have administrative permissions because she does not need those permissions to perform standard tasks. The administrative account has the additional permissions needed for Alice to perform administrative tasks. The intention is for Alice to use that account only for those administrative tasks. Zero day is a type of vulnerability; multifactor authentication calls for users to supply two identifying factors; defense in depth refers to the use of multiple security mechanisms to provide additional protection. None of these three options refers to the use of multiple user accounts.

265. D. Lateral movement is when a user gains basic access to a network by legitimate means and then uses it to gain unauthorized access to other resources inside the network. A zero trust architecture provides full protection for all sensitive resources, even from users already inside the network. A zero trust architecture does not protect against zero day vulnerabilities, which are exploits in software; external threats; or deauthentication, which is a type of denial-of-service attack.

266. D. Infrastructure as code (IaC) is a method of deploying and configuring cloud-based resources using script files. IaC deployment provides time and cost savings and improved elasticity and scalability by automating the virtual machine deployment process, providing a central repository for source control, and deploying upgrades and updates. IaC also ensures a consistent deployment, preventing configuration drift by using the same script for all newly deployed VMs. IaC does not encrypt the virtual machine configuration.

267. B. The software-defined wide area network (SD-WAN) architecture is application aware and provides routing and quality of service (QoS) adjustments based on the data source. A standard WAN architecture routes traffic through a central datacenter based on IP addresses and ACLs, but an SD-WAN does not. The SD-WAN architecture calls for the creation of a virtual network that runs on top of the physical connections and is therefore uninvolved with the underlying technology. The SD-WAN architecture does not provide end-to-end performance guarantees.

268. C. Secure access service edge (SASE) is not an element of the SSE framework. In fact, SSE is a subset of SASE. Cloud access security broker (CASB), zero trust network access (ZTNA), and secure web gateway (SWG) are all elements of the SSE framework.

269. A, B, C. The zero trust architecture (ZTA) calls for least privileges, in which users start with no access to the network at all and then receive privileges only for the resources they require to perform their jobs, continual authentication and authorization whenever users access protected resources, and the assumption that every access request is a breach by an intruder attempting to move laterally within the network. The three-tiered hierarchical model describes a physical network architecture that is not part of a zero trust architecture.

270. A, C. Zero trust provisioning is a means of automatically configuring routers, switches, or other network devices by having them download a configuration file from a Dynamic Host Configuration Protocol (DHCP) or Trivial File Transfer Protocol (TFTP) server. File Transfer Protocol (FTP) and Hypertext Transfer Protocol Secure (HTTPS) are not used in ZTP transactions.

271. A, B. VXLANs can function as an DCI overlay network connecting remote datacenters together. VLAN switches use a 12-bit identifier, which limits them to 4,096 VLANs. VXLANs use a 24-bit network identifier, which enables them to support up to 16 million networks. VXLANs use the same physical underlay network as VLANs, so they are no faster. VXLANs and VLANs both run as an overlay network, so neither is preferable for that reason. VXLANs encapsulate layer 2 Ethernet frames within UDP datagrams, not TCP segments.

Chapter 2: Network Implementation

1. B. NAT works by modifying IP addresses, which are a Network layer element. The Data link layer is concerned only with communications on the local subnet and is not involved with NAT processing. Because NAT modifies only the IP packet headers, it works with any Transport layer protocol. NAT also works with most TCP/IP applications because it operates below the Application layer of the OSI model.

2. A, C. Network address translation (NAT) is a Network layer device that converts the private IP addresses of all of a client's transmissions to a registered IP address. NAT therefore works for all applications. A proxy server is an Application layer device that performs the same type of conversion, but only for specific applications. A Remote Authentication Dial-In User Service (RADIUS) server can provide authentication, authorization, accounting, auditing (AAAA) services for remote access servers; it does not convert IP addresses. A unified threat management (UTM) appliance typically performs VPN, firewall, and antivirus functions. It too does not convert IP addresses.

3. B. The figure displays the format for a Routing Information Protocol (RIP) version 2 packet. The figure does not show the packet format for RIPv1, which lacks the Subnet Mask and Next Hop fields for the individual routes, making subnetting impossible. The figure also does not show the format of Open Shortest Path First (OSPF), Enhanced Interior Gateway Routing Protocol (EIGRP), or Border Gateway Protocol (BGP).

4. A. EIGRP can support classless IPv4 addresses. It was designed to replace the Interior Gateway Routing Protocol (IGRP), which could not support classless addresses. All of the other options contain true statements.

5. A, B. Bandwidth throttling is a traffic shaping technique that prevents specified data streams from transmitting too many packets. Rate limiting is a traffic shaping technique that controls the transmission rate of sending systems. A broadcast storm is a type of network switching loop. NAT is a method by which private networks can share registered IP addresses. Neither of these last two is a traffic shaping technique.

6. D. *Quality of service* (QoS) is a general term that refers to various mechanisms for prioritizing network traffic so that applications or data streams requiring a certain level of performance are not negatively affected by lower-priority transmissions. Port forwarding is a routing method that redirects traffic intended for one IP address and port number to another. Dynamic routing is a method by which routing tables are automatically updated with new information as the routing fabric of an internetwork changes. Virtual local area networks (VLANs) are a means for partitioning a broadcast domain into discrete units that are functionally equivalent to physical LANs.

7. A. Differentiated services (DiffServ) is a mechanism that provides quality of service (QoS) on a network by classifying traffic types using a 6-bit value in the Differentiated Services (DS) field of the IP header. Class of service (CoS) is a similar mechanism that operates at the Data link layer by adding a 3-bit Priority Code Point (PCP) value to the Ethernet frame.

Traffic shaping is a means of prioritizing network traffic that typically works by delaying packets at the Application layer. *Quality of service (QoS)* is an umbrella term that encompasses a variety of network traffic prioritization mechanisms. Administrative distance is a value that routers use to select the most efficient routing protocol.

8. B. Routing protocols typically have some mechanism for determining the best route to a destination, but those mechanisms are often incompatible with those of other routing protocols. Administrative distance is a value that enables routers to select the most reliable routing protocol to use when multiple protocols supply routes to the same destination. Metrics are values specifying the best route among those supplied by a single protocol. Class of service (CoS) is a mechanism that operates at the Data link layer by adding a 3-bit Priority Code Point (PCP) value to the Ethernet frame. The maximum transmission unit (MTU) specifies the size of the largest packet transmittable in a single Network layer transmission.

9. A, E. Administrators must manually add, modify, or delete static routes when a change in a network occurs. For this reason, static routes are not recommended for use in large internetworks where there are multiple paths to each destination network. Static routes are not automatically added by routing protocols and do not adapt to changes in a network.

10. D. Distance vector protocols rely on hop counts to evaluate the efficiency of routes. Link state protocols use a different type of calculation, usually based on Dijkstra's algorithm. The terms *interior gateway protocol* and *edge gateway protocol* do not refer to the method of calculating routing efficiency.

11. B. A single RIP broadcast packet can include up to 25 routes. If there are more than 25 routes in the computer's routing table, then RIP must generate additional packets.

12. A, C. OSPF is a link state routing protocol, which means that it does not rely solely on hop counts to measure the relative efficiency of a route. EIGRP is a hybrid protocol that can use link state routing. RIP is a distance vector routing protocol, meaning that it uses hop counts to measure route efficiency. BGP is an exterior gateway protocol that exchanges routing information among autonomous systems using path vectors or distance vectors.

13. C. OSPF does support CIDR. All of the other options contain true statements.

14. A. *Convergence* is the term for the process by which routers propagate information from their routing tables to other routers on the network using dynamic routing protocols. Distance vectoring, redistribution, and dissemination do not describe this process.

15. A. RIP is a distance vector protocol, which uses hop counts to measure the efficiency of routes. OSPF, BGP, and IS-IS are all link state protocols, which do not rely on hop counts.

16. A. Exterior Gateway Protocol (EGP) routes datagrams between autonomous systems. Interior Gateway Protocol (IGP) routes datagrams within an autonomous system. Routing Information Protocol (RIP) and Open Shortest Path First (OSPF) are examples of interior gateway protocols. OSPF shares routes within an autonomous system.

17. A, D. The route command was originally created to display a Unix or Linux system's routing table and modify its contents by adding, changing, and deleting static routes. The ip command is part of the iproute2 command-line utility package, which has replaced route in many Unix and Linux distributions. Running ip with the route parameter can manipulate the routing table. The traceroute and ifconfig tools are not commands for manipulating the routing table.

18. A. Routers that use OSPF transmit the speed of each network interface with the other OSPF routers in the network. This enables the routers to evaluate the cost of various routes through the network and transmit packets using the route with the smallest cost value. The routers do not need to share information about the Data link layer protocols or network media they use, their IP addresses, their prefix length, or their metrics.

19. B. BGP is a path vector routing protocol, not a link state routing protocol. All of the other options contain true statements.

20. A. The default route in an IPv4 routing table always has a destination address of 0.0.0.0. The other destinations are found in a routing table, but they are not the default route destination.

21. D. The Border Gateway Protocol (BGP) is a highly scalable protocol used for routing both on private autonomous systems, where it is known as the Internal Border Gateway Protocol (iBGP) and maintains full mesh communication among all of the routers, and on the Internet, where it is known as the External Border Gateway Protocol (eBGP). Routing Information Protocol (RIP), Open Shortest Path First (OSPF), and Enhanced Interior Gateway Routing Protocol (EIGRP) do not have interior and exterior designations.

22. A, B. The Internet Protocol (IP) in both of its versions (IPv4 and IPv6) includes a TTL field in its message header that limits the number of times a packet can be routed on a network. Each router processing the packet reduces the TTL value by one until it reaches zero, after which it is discarded. The Internet Control Message Protocol (ICMP) and the Internet Group Management Protocol (IGMP) do not have a TTL field.

23. B. WAN optimization is not a form of traffic shaping, because it compresses data streams and transmits incremental file updates. Traffic shaping uses techniques like rate limiting, bandwidth throttling, and self-limiting to delay the transmission of specific types of data packets to optimize network performance.

24. B, C. To provide clients with Internet access, a NAT or proxy server must have direct access to the Internet, which requires using a registered, or public, IP address. Both NAT and proxy servers function as the middleman in transactions between the client computers on a private network and Internet servers. The NAT or proxy server transmits the client's service request to the Internet server as though it was its own and, after receiving the reply, relays the response back to the client. Because NAT servers function at the Network layer, clients can use any application to access the Internet through the server. Proxy servers, however, operate at the Application layer and can provide Internet access only to certain types of client applications. Proxy servers are capable of caching web data for later use, because they are Application layer devices that read the Application layer protocol data in the message packets they receive. NAT servers are Network layer processes that forward packets with no knowledge of the Application layer information in their contents.

25. C, E. Broadband routers generally do not function as proxy servers, which are Application layer devices used to regulate access to the Internet. They are also typically not virtual private network (VPN) headends, which enable multiple remote VPN clients to connect to the network. Many broadband routers are also WAPs, enabling users to construct a LAN without a complicated and expensive cable installation. Many broadband routers have switched ports for connections to wired devices, such as printers and computers. Most broadband routers use DHCP to assign IP addresses to devices on the private network.

26. E. SOHO multifunction devices typically function as routers connecting the local network to an Internet service provider (ISP), switches providing wired connections to host devices, Dynamic Host Configuration Protocol (DHCP) servers assigning IP addresses, Domain Name System (DNS) servers resolving names into IP addresses, network address translation (NAT) routers providing hosts with private IP addresses access to the Internet, and APs providing wireless devices with access to the network. They do not function as hubs.

27. A. Each port on a router defines a separate collision domain. Hubs forward all traffic to all of the connected nodes, so each network segment is a single-collision domain. Routers do not forward broadcasts, so each network segment is also a separate broadcast domain.

28. D. A collision domain is a LAN with a shared network medium, so that two devices transmitting at the same time generate a signal quality error, also known as a collision. Ethernet LANs connected by hubs create a shared medium, whereas switched networks create a separate collision domain for each connected node. Routers create separate collision domains. A group of computers able to receive broadcasts is the definition of a broadcast domain, not a collision domain. Overlong cables can precipitate collisions but do not define a collision domain.

29. B. A virtual private network (VPN) headend is a type of router that enables multiple client systems to access a network from remote locations. Because the device provides an interface between networks, it is considered to be a type of router, not a switch, a gateway, or a bridge.

30. A. Link states and Dijkstra's algorithm are used by link state routing protocols, such as Open Shortest Path First (OSPF). Routing Information Protocol (RIP) and Enhanced Interior Gateway Routing Protocol (EIGRP) are distance vector protocols, which do not use link states. Border Gateway Protocol (BGP) is a distance vector protocol and an exterior (not interior) gateway protocol.

31. A, B, D. CMR is a technique in which routers transmit data packets using multiple routes to the destination. This provides load balancing and improved performance by spreading the transmission among multiple paths and a measure of fault tolerance because a failure of one route only endangers part of the data. Data encapsulation is not involved in the CMR process.

32. C. FHRPs provide a fault tolerant default gateway for network hosts by automatically failing over to an alternative router address in the event of a router failure. Protocols such as Virtual Router Redundancy Protocol (VRRP) and Hot Standby Router Protocol (HSRP) create a virtual router that hosts use for their default gateway. The virtual router contains the addresses of multiple physical routers, to which it sends packets transmitted by the hosts. This provides fault tolerance in the event that a router fails, and in some cases provides load balancing as well. FHRPs do not affect the hosts' IP addresses, subnet masks, or DNS server addresses.

33. D. FHRPs provide a fault tolerant default gateway for network hosts by automatically failing over to an alternative router address in the event of a router failure. The Reverse Address Resolution Protocol (RARP) is a deprecated Internet Protocol (IP) address assignment protocol; it is not an FHRP. Common Address Redundancy Protocol (CARP), Virtual Router Redundancy Protocol (VRRP), and Hot Standby Router Protocol (HSRP) are all FHRPs.

34. A, B. Unlike network address translation (NAT), port address translation (PAT) uses a single public IPv4 address for all of the client workstations. Instead of assigning each workstation a unique address, PAT assigns each workstation a unique port number.

35. B, D. A virtual IP address is an address that does not correspond to a physical network interface. Network address translation (NAT) uses virtual public IP addresses as substitutes for the private IP addresses associated with the client hosts. A network interface in a virtual machine is virtual as well, so the IP address associated with that interface must also be virtual. Dynamic Host Configuration Protocol (DHCP) and Automatic Private IP Addressing (APIPA) both can assign IP addresses to physical network interfaces; these addresses are therefore not virtual.

36. A. A subinterface is a logical (or virtual) network interface associated with a specific physical network interface. Devices (such as routers) can use multiple subinterfaces to connect to different subnets using a single physical network interface adapter. A subinterface is a logical device, so it is not one port on a physical network interface adapter or a physical adapter connected to a subnet. A subinterface is a complete logical interface, not just an IP address.

37. B. The route with the longest matching prefix is the most specific route, which the router always uses first when evaluating routing table entries. Routers use administrative distance to evaluate routes with the same prefix length. The next hop value is not used to evaluate preferred routes. Metrics are valid only in comparison to other routes generated by the same protocol.

38. D. Ethernet uses jumbo frames at the Data link layer to transfer large amounts of data more efficiently. Ethernet typically restricts frame size to 1,500 bytes, but jumbo frames enable Ethernet systems to create frames up to 9,000 bytes. Frames are protocol data units (PDUs) associated only with the Data link layer, so they do not apply to the Network, Transport, or Application layers.

39. C. When implemented in an Ethernet switch, port security uses port-by-port MAC address filtering to allow only one MAC address to access each switch port. Deny listing blocks the MAC addresses on the list from using all of the ports on the switch. Allow listing allows the listed MAC addresses to use any port on the switch. MAC address spoofing is a method for defeating port security, deny lists, or allow lists.

40. A, B. Bridge protocol data units (BPDUs) are messages that switches running the Spanning Tree Protocol exchange to learn about the available paths through a switched network and the states of other switches. Switches should only receive BPDUs through ports that are connected to other switches. BPDU guard is a feature that prevents BPDU messages from arriving through ports connected to end systems, such as computers, thus preventing an attacker from manipulating the STP topology. A root guard affects the behavior of the STP by enforcing the selection of root bridge ports on a switched network. Without root guards, there is no way for administrators to enforce the topology of a network with a redundant switching fabric. DHCP snooping is a security feature implemented on layer 2 network switches that prevents unauthorized DHCP servers from accessing the network. Geofencing is a wireless technology that uses radio frequency identification (RFID) or GPS coordinates to define a geographic perimeter.

41. A. Distributed switching describes a hierarchical switching architecture in which remote switches (departmental switches in this case) handle most of the network traffic, with a host switch used only for traffic between the remote locations. Port forwarding is a routing method that redirects traffic intended for one IP address and port number to another. Traffic shaping is a series of techniques that optimizes the allocation of network bandwidth. Neighbor discovery is an IPv6 technique used to find addresses of devices and services on the local network. Flow control is a technique for regulating a system's transmission speed.

42. A. All half-duplex port connections on a store-and-forward switch represent a different collision domain. Full-duplex connections are not subject to collisions, so they do not define separate collision domains.

43. C. A media access control (MAC) address is a 6-byte hexadecimal value, with the bytes separated by colons, as in 00:1A:6B:31:9A:4E. Option A, 10.124.25.43, is all decimals and uses periods; this is an IPv4 address. Option B, FF:FF:FF:FF:FF:FF, is a valid MAC address, but this value is reserved for use as a broadcast address. Option D, 03:AE:16:3H:5B:11, is not a valid hexadecimal address, which should contain only numerals and the letters A to F. Option E, fe80::89a5:9e4d:a9d0:9ed7, is too long for a MAC address; this is a valid IPv6 address.

44. B. The Spanning Tree Protocol (STP) prevents packets from endlessly looping from switch to switch due to redundant links. Creating redundant links is a good preventive against switch failure, but packets transmitted over multiple links can circulate from switch to switch infinitely. STP creates a database of switching links and shuts down the redundant ones until they are needed. The Routing Information Protocol (RIP) propagates routing table information. A virtual local area network (VLAN) is an organizational tool that operates within switches by creating multiple broadcast domains. Network address translation (NAT) is a routing method that enables private networks to share registered IP addresses. Address Resolution Protocol (ARP) is a protocol that discovers a system's MAC address by broadcasting its IPv4 address.

45. A, B. When connecting an MDI port to an Auto-MDI-X port, it is possible to use either a straight-through or a crossover cable because the Auto-MDI-X port can self-adjust to implement the necessary crossover circuit if it is needed. MDI and Auto-MDI-X ports are used only with twisted-pair cables, so there is no need for coaxial or fiber-optic cables.

46. B. IEEE 802.1Q is a standard defining a mechanism (called Ethernet trunking by some manufacturers) that identifies the virtual local area network (VLAN) to which a packet belongs by inserting an extra 32-bit field into its Ethernet frame. IEEE 802.1P is a standard that defines a mechanism for implementing quality of service (QoS) at the Data link layer by adding a 3-bit field into Ethernet frames. IEEE 802.1X is a standard defining an authentication mechanism called port-based network access control (PNAC). IEEE 802.1AB is a standard defining the Link Layer Discovery Protocol (LLDP). IEEE 802.1AX is a specification for the Link Aggregation Control Protocol (LACP), which is a mechanism for combining physical ports into a single logical channel.

47. C. Stations on a CSMA/CD network first check the medium to see if it is idle. If they detect an idle medium, they begin transmitting. If two or more devices transmit at the same time, a collision occurs. Immediately after a collision occurs, the two stations involved stop transmitting. After that, they send out a jam signal. Then, the two stations back off for a random interval, and the transmission process begins again.

48. A. For CSMA/CD to function properly, a system must detect a packet collision while it is transmitting the packet. If cable segments are too long, the packet might leave the transmitting system before the collision is detected, resulting in a late collision, which cannot be retransmitted. Incorrect pinouts, too many systems, and excessive collisions typically will not prevent the collision detection system from occurring.

49. B. After transmitting their jam signals, the two systems wait for a randomized interval. This is to prevent them from retransmitting their packets at the same time, resulting in another collision. It is not necessary for the systems to reassemble, rebuffer, or recalculate checksums for their packets.

50. C. Replacing routers with switches turns an internetwork into a single large subnet, and virtual local area networks (VLANs) exist as logical elements on top of the switching fabric. Although VLANs are the functional equivalent of Network layer subnets, the systems in a single VLAN are still physically connected by switches, not routers. Bridges connect network segments at the Data link layer and selectively forward traffic between the segments. However, bridges do not provide a dedicated connection between two systems like a switch does, and they do not make it possible to convert a large, routed internetwork into a single switched network. Therefore, they have no role in implementing VLANs. Hubs are physical layer devices that propagate all incoming traffic out through all of their ports. Replacing the routers on an internetwork with hubs would create a single shared broadcast domain with huge amounts of traffic and many collisions. Hubs, therefore, do not connect the computers in a VLAN.

51. A. Collisions are a normal occurrence on an Ethernet network; they occur when two nodes transmit at exactly the same time. There need not be a network fault for collisions to occur. When collisions occur, the nodes involved retransmit their packets so that no data is lost. Collisions are a phenomenon of Data link layer protocols; they have nothing to do with IP addresses, which are Network layer constructs.

52. D. Collisions are a normal occurrence on an Ethernet network, but late collisions are not normal. Late collisions occur when two packets collide after one or more finishes transmitting. Packet retransmissions, collision detection, and jam signals are all normal occurrences on an Ethernet network.

53. B. Connecting subnets with routers at the Network layer maintains the Data link layer administrative boundaries that prevent broadcast transmissions from being propagated throughout the entire internetwork. Switching eliminates those Data link layer boundaries, and administrators can use virtual local area networks (VLANs) to simulate them. Because hubs propagate all of the traffic they receive out through all of their ports indiscriminately, they create no administrative boundaries. Domains are logical groups of network devices defined by the Domain Name System (DNS). Their functions are not related to VLANs in any way. Switches are essentially multiport bridges that forward incoming traffic only to the device for which it is destined. Therefore, bridges are more closely related to eliminating administrative boundaries than to establishing them.

54. B, D. The computers in a single virtual local area network (VLAN) can be located anywhere on a switched network, irrespective of the switches' physical configuration. A broadcast message generated by a computer in a VLAN is transmitted to all of the other computers in that VLAN only, just as if the systems were physically located on a separate LAN or subnet. Unicast transmissions between computers on a switched network do not require VLANs, because the switches create what amounts to a direct connection between the two systems. VLANs are needed only for communication processes that require the use of broadcasts, which if transmitted without VLANs, would flood the network. Even though they are a purely logical construction, VLANs function just like physical subnets and require routers for communication between them. Routing capabilities are often integrated into switches to enable communication between VLANs.

55. A, D. Every network device has a unique hardware address coded into its network interface adapter, and administrators can use these addresses to select the devices that will be part of a specific virtual local area network (VLAN). When VLANs are implemented in the switch's VLAN database, selecting the ports to which specific computers are attached is a simple way to identify the computers in a particular VLAN. IP addresses are layer 3 (Network layer) constructs, so they do not apply to layer 2 (Data link layer) devices like switches. Although DNS names do uniquely identify computers on a network, DNS is an Application layer process and has nothing to do with the switching and routing processes, which occur at the Data link and Network layers. Therefore, you cannot use DNS names to identify the computers in a VLAN.

56. C. VLANs are Data link layer local area networks (LANs) defined within switches. Only devices (and users) connected to ports belonging to the same VLAN can communicate with each other until a layer 3 device, such as a router or a layer 3 switch, is added to the network. Re-creating and reconfiguring the VLANs will not correct this problem. Traffic filters are usually implemented on routers. VLANs do not have to use the same Data link protocol.

57. C, D. SOHO networks typically consist of a single subnet and require only a basic switch without the advanced virtual local area network (VLAN) capabilities that enable administrators to create separate subnets. Most SOHO networks have a Dynamic Host Configuration Protocol (DHCP) server that assigns IP addresses and other TCP/IP configuration settings to clients. The DHCP server can be integrated into a broadband router or another Internet access sharing solution. Most SOHO networks support network address translation (NAT), enabling them to use private IP addresses and still access the Internet. 10GBase-T is the designation for UTP-based 10 Gigabit Ethernet, which is an advanced standard for network interface adapters often found in servers.

58. A. To join ports on different switches into one VLAN, you designate a trunk port on each switch for the traffic between switches. Initially, the native VLAN uses the default VLAN1 for trunk traffic, and that traffic is left untagged. Untagged traffic is susceptible to attacks using double-tagged packets. When you configure the native VLAN to use tagging, this makes it impervious to double-tagging. Changing the native VLAN does not create root guards or bridge protocol data unit (BPDU) guards, and all traffic continues to be switched, not routed.

59. C. The IEEE 802.1Q protocol is responsible for VLAN tagging, a procedure that enables network switches to support VLANs. Through the insertion of VLAN identifier tags into frames, switches can determine which VLAN each packet is destined for and forward it to the correct ports. IEEE 802.3x is one of the standards for wired Ethernet networks. IEEE 802.1X is a standard that defines a port-based network access control (PNAC) mechanism used for authentication on wireless and other networks. IEEE 802.11ac is a standard defining the physical and Data link layer protocols for wireless networks.

60. B. When in-band switch management traffic, such as that generated by a Secure Shell (SSH) connection to a switch, uses the native VLAN, it is untagged by default. This is because the native VLAN is at first the default VLAN1, which is not tagged by the 802.1Q protocol, leaving it open to certain types of double-tagging attacks. When you tag the native VLAN traffic, it is rendered immune to double-tagging. The default VLAN cannot be renamed in the VLAN database, and SSH traffic is already encrypted by the sending workstation. Changing the native VLAN does not move the management traffic off that VLAN, although many authorities advocate the creation of a separate VLAN dedicated to in-band management traffic.

61. D. Ethernet implementations, such as 100Base-TX, which use separate wire pairs for transmitting and receiving data, require a crossover circuit to ensure that the transmit pins on each end of a connection are wired to the receive pins at the other end. This crossover circuit can be implemented in a patch cable—called a crossover cable—or by a switch port. Switches with auto-medium-dependent interface crossover (MDI-X) ports can detect the need for a crossover circuit and implement it automatically in the port. This eliminates the need for crossover cables. Auto-medium-dependent interface crossover (MDI-X) ports do not eliminate the need for 8P8C connectors, connections between switches, or straight-through cables.

62. B. When connecting an MDI port to an MDI-X port, the necessary crossover circuit is implemented in the MDI-X port. Therefore, the connection needs a straight-through cable and there is no need for a crossover cable. MDI and MDI-X ports are used only with twisted-pair cables, so there is no need for coaxial or fiber-optic cables.

63. A, C. STP disables redundant links between switches that can allow packets to circulate endlessly around the network. This is called a bridging loop. As a result of a bridging loop, the network can be flooded with broadcast traffic, which is called a broadcast storm. STP does nothing to prevent late collisions, which is an Ethernet timing problem, or crosstalk, which is a cabling fault.

64. B. Switches use media access control (MAC) addresses to identify the ports associated with specific hosts. The switch reads the destination MAC address from each incoming packet and forwards it out through the port associated with that address. Switches are Data link layer devices, so they do not use IP addresses or DNS names to forward packets. The maximum transmission unit (MTU) value specifies the maximum size of Data link layer frames; the switch does not use it to forward packets.

65. D. STP operates at the Data link layer of the OSI model, so it works with hardware addresses, not IP addresses. Switches use STP to prevent redundant links from causing traffic loops on the network.

66. C. The best choice is to replace the hubs with switches, since the network is relatively small and cost is an issue. On the existing network, all users share the same 100 Mbps communication channel, and each computer must take turns transmitting. By replacing the hubs with switches, you provide each computer with a dedicated 100 Mbps connection to the switch, while reducing unnecessary traffic and collisions on the network. There is no such thing as a dedicated hub. Splitting the network into two routed LANs is not the best solution, because all users must share information on a constant basis. Also, cost is a factor, and routers are more expensive than switches. Replacing the hubs with a layer 3 switch and defining two VLANs with 20 users each is not a reasonable solution because layer 3 switches are very expensive.

67. B. The process by which STP populates its database with information about each port in a switch and designates the ports as forwarding or blocking is called convergence. *Assimilation*, *tree-building*, and *listening* are not terms for STP path evaluation.

68. A, B. All switches operate at the Data link layer of the OSI model, but multilayer switches usually also function as routers, which are Network layer devices, through the use of a switch virtual interface (SVI). They are not usually transport or Application layer devices.

69. A. If the fifth computer was in a different VLAN from the other four, it would be unable to communicate with them. A switching loop would affect communication between all of the computers, not just the fifth one. An MTU black hole is a condition in which a system is unable to complete the Path MTU Discovery process, due to an intervening firewall. Because these five computers are all on the same LAN, they all have the same MTU, and Path MTU Discovery is not necessary. A virtual router would enable switched computers on different subnets to communicate with each other; it would not prevent them from communicating.

70. B. Standard switchports have a crossover circuit, which ensures that the transmit signals at one end of the connection arrive at the receive pins at the other end. The uplink port in a switch bypasses the crossover circuit, so that two connected switches do not have crossover circuits that cancel each other out. A connection between a standard port and an uplink port, using a standard cable, results in a single crossover, which is correct wiring. Each of the other solutions results in either two crossovers or no crossovers, both of which are incorrect.

71. D, E. By default, a switched LAN consists of a single broadcast domain. To create multiple broadcast domains, you can install routers to split the installation into two or more networks, because routers do not forward broadcasts. The other possibility is to create VLANs in the switches. Each VLAN is a separate broadcast domain. All of the other options would have no effect on the number of broadcast domains on the network.

72. D. A multilayer switch is a network connectivity device that functions at both layer 2 and layer 3 of the OSI model. At layer 2, the device functions like a normal switch, providing individual collision domains to each connected node and enabling administrators to create multiple VLANs. At layer 3, with the implementation of a switch virtual interface (SVI), the device also provides routing capabilities by forwarding packets between the VLANs. Virtual routers, load balancers, and broadband routers are strictly layer 3 devices that can route traffic but cannot create VLANs.

73. D. When transmitting voice traffic on a network along with data traffic, the voice traffic should have priority, to ensure the quality of the stream. Separating data and voice traffic on separate VLANs enables switches to assign voice traffic a higher priority by applying appropriate tags to the voice packets. Separate VLANs are not needed to prevent packet conflicts or to encrypt either voice or data packets.

74. A, B. There are two methods for identifying packets carrying voice traffic: by recognizing the MAC address of the sending system as a voice device, and by recognizing packets that have already been tagged as voice VLAN traffic. It is not possible to identify voice traffic using IP addresses or DNS names.

75. A, B, D, E. *Bonding, link aggregation, port aggregation,* and *network interface card* (NIC) teaming are all terms for the same basic technology, in which the bandwidth of multiple network adapter connections is joined to speed up transmissions. The technology also enables the network communication to continue if one of the adapters is disconnected. Clustering refers to combining servers into a single unit, not network adapters.

76. D. Load balancing refers to the distribution of traffic between two or more channels. Port aggregation combines ports into a single logical channel with a single media access control (MAC) address and provides greater throughput. Port aggregation also provides fault tolerance in the event of a port failure.

77. C. This redundant switch arrangement can result in broadcast storms, which are caused by packets being read by multiple switches as originating on different networks. The result is endless circulation of packets from switch to switch.

78. A. A content switch is an Application layer device, which is what renders it capable of reading the incoming Hypertext Transfer Protocol (HTTP) and Hypertext Transfer Protocol Secure (HTTPS) messages. HTTP is an Application layer protocol. Multilayer switches do not operate above the Transport layer. Failover clustering and (DNS) round-robin are both techniques for distributing incoming traffic without actually processing it.

79. B, D. The default VLAN in the VLAN database on most switches has the ID VLAN 1, not VLAN 0, and it cannot be deleted or renamed. The default VLAN does not have to be created by the administrator; it is the one to which all ports are assigned in the default configuration.

80. C. Source route bridging was a technique used on token ring (and not Ethernet) networks, in which a routing information field (RIF) in the packet header identified the network segments the packet should follow to reach its destination. Store and forward, transparent, and multiport bridges have all been used on Ethernet networks.

81. C. The MTU is the largest amount of data (in bytes) that a protocol operating at a given layer of the OSI model can transmit in one packet. The MTU does not include any header and footer fields supplied by that protocol. For Ethernet, the maximum frame size is 1,518 bytes, which includes 18 bytes of header and footer fields. Therefore, the MTU for Ethernet is 1,500 bytes. Protocols operating at other OSI model layers can have different MTUs. For example, the typical MTU for an Internet Protocol (IPv4) implementation is smaller than that of Ethernet.

82. C. Replacing routers with switches turns an internetwork into a single large subnet, and VLANs exist as logical elements on top of the switching fabric. Although VLANs are the functional equivalent of Network layer subnets, the systems in a single VLAN are still connected by switches, not routers. Bridges connect network segments at the Data link layer and selectively forward traffic between the segments. However, bridges do not provide a dedicated connection between two systems like a switch does, and they do not make it possible to convert a large, routed internetwork into a single switched network. Therefore, they have no role in implementing VLANs. Hubs are physical layer devices that propagate all incoming traffic out through all of their ports. Replacing the routers on an internetwork with hubs would create a single shared network with huge amounts of traffic and collisions. Hubs, therefore, do not connect the computers in a VLAN.

83. A. Ethernet uses jumbo frames to transfer large amounts of data more efficiently. On a packet-switched network, each packet requires header data, which adds to the network's transmission overhead. Splitting large files into a great many small packets can lead to so much overhead that network efficiency is impaired. Ethernet typically restricts frame size to 1,500 bytes, but jumbo frames enable Ethernet systems to create frames up to 9,000 bytes. Frames are Data link layer protocol data units, so Internet Protocol (IP), operating at the Network layer, is not involved in creating them. Fibre Channel and iSCSI are specialized storage area networking protocols that do not use jumbo frames.

84. A. The IEEE 802.11ac standard, like all of the wireless LAN standards in the 802.11 working group, uses CSMA/CA for MAC. The 802.1X standard defines an authentication mechanism and does not require a MAC mechanism. The IEEE 802.3 (Ethernet) standard uses Carrier-Sense Multiple Access with Collision Detection (CSMA/CD).

85. C. An infrastructure topology uses a wireless access point (WAP) to connect wireless devices to a wired network. An ad hoc topology connects wireless devices to each other, without connecting to a wired network. A mesh topology calls for complete interconnection of wireless nodes, which need not provide access to wired resources. The star/hub and spoke and bus topologies do not support wireless devices.

86. D. An ad hoc topology describes wireless computers that communicate directly with each other, without the need for any hardware other than their wireless network adapters. Therefore, the ad hoc topology does not require a router, an Internet connection, an access point (AP), or a special antenna.

87. A, E. IEEE 802.11b, 802.11g, 802.11n, and 802.11ax networks can use the 2.4 GHz frequency band for their transmissions, which can experience interference from a wireless phone using the same frequency. IEEE 802.11a and IEEE 802.11ac, however, use the 5 GHz band, which will not experience interference from a 2.4 GHz phone.

88. C, D, E. The IEEE 802.11n, 802.11ac, and 802.11ax standards include MIMO, which enables them to effectively multiplex signals using multiple antennas. This capability was first introduced in the 802.11n standard, so the 802.11a and 802.11b/g standards do not support it.

89. B. The IEEE 802.11b standard calls for DSSS signal modulation. All of the other standards listed call for orthogonal frequency-division multiplexing (OFDM) encoding.

90. D. By placing a unidirectional antenna against an outside wall, you can limit network access to users inside the structure. Unidirectional antennas provide greater signal strength than omnidirectional antennas, enabling their signals to penetrate more interior walls. It is possible to focus a unidirectional antenna to a wider or narrower signal pattern.

91. B. The IEEE 802.11n and 802.11ac standards support a transmission technique called multiple input, multiple output (MIMO), which combines the bandwidth of multiple data streams to achieve greater throughput. IEEE 802.11n and 802.11ac do use the 5 GHz band, but this in itself does not yield greater transmission speeds. The specified standards do not call for the use of DSSS modulation, nor do they sacrifice range for speed. In fact, 802.11n and 802.11ac networks can achieve greater ranges than the previous technologies.

92. A, C, D. The 5 GHz frequency has 23 channels available in the United States, while the 2.4 GHz frequency has only 11. Many household devices, such as cordless telephones, use the 2.4 GHz frequency band, but relatively few devices use the 5 GHz band. Higher frequencies typically support faster transmission speeds, because with all other conditions equal, they can carry more data in the same amount of time. The 5 GHz frequency typically has a shorter range than 2.4 GHz, because it is less able to penetrate barriers.

93. A, C. Upgrading the devices to 802.11n will enable them to use the 5 GHz band and evade the traffic generated by the surrounding networks. Configuring the devices to use the 5 GHz band will provide many more channels to choose from and will avoid the interference from the surrounding 2.4 GHz networks. The type of encryption that a wireless network uses has no bearing on the ability of the devices to avoid the interference generated by surrounding networks. Suppressing SSID broadcasts will not help the devices to connect to the network. Upgrading the firmware on the devices is not likely to have any effect on the connection problems when they are the result of interference from other networks.

94. D. The multiple input, multiple output (MIMO) technology introduced in the IEEE 802.11n standard enables wireless devices to transmit and receive signals using multiple antennas simultaneously. The multiuser MIMO (MU-MIMO) variant defined in the 802.11ac standard advances this technique by enabling wireless devices to transmit multiple frames to different users simultaneously, using multiple antennas. Carrier-Sense Multiple Access with Collision Avoidance (CSMA/CA) is a Media Access Control (MAC) mechanism used by all 802.11 networks. Channel bonding is a wireless networking technique that combines channels to increase bandwidth.

95. A. Wireless LAN regulations call for 22 MHz channels in the 2.4 GHz band that are spaced 5 MHz apart, which means that they overlap. Channels 1, 6, and 11 are the only three channels that are distant enough from each other not to overlap. Therefore, they do not interfere with each other. Channels 1, 6, and 11 do not differ from the other channels in their bandwidth or their transmission range. Each wireless device can be set to use only one channel. Therefore, channels 1, 6, and 11 cannot all be the default setting.

96. A. Multiple input, multiple output (MIMO) calls for the use of two or more antennas, enabling wireless devices to effectively multiplex signals, thereby increasing their transmission speeds. Time-division multiple access (TDMA) is a communication technique that splits a frequency into multiple time slots, enabling it to carry multiple data streams. A personal area network (PAN) provides communication among devices associated with a single person, such as smartphones. Ant+ is a wireless protocol that is typically used to monitor data gathered by sensors, such as those in cardiac pacemakers.

97. D. Using a technique called channel bonding, the 802.11ax and 802.11ac standards define the combination of up to eight 20 MHz channels, for a total possible channel width of 160 MHz, in a single 160 MHz channel or a non-contiguous 80+80 configuration. The 802.11n standard can bond up to two channels, for a 40 MHz width. Earlier standards are limited to a single 20 MHz channel.

98. A, E. The IEEE 802.11a and IEEE 802.11ac standards can use the 5 GHz band only. IEEE 802.11b and IEEE 802.11g can use the 2.4 GHz band only. IEEE 802.11n and IEEE 802.11ax can use either the 2.4 or the 5 GHz band.

99. F. Only the 802.11ax standard defines wireless LAN devices that can support the 6 GHz frequency band. The 802.11a and 802.11ac standards use only 5 GHz, and the 802.11b and 802.11g standards use only 2.4 GHz. The 802.11n standard supports both the 2.4 and 5 GHz bands.

100. C. The IEEE 802.11ax standard provides the greatest possible throughput, up to a theoretical maximum of 9.6 Gbps. This is a 37% improvement over 802.11ac, at 7 Gbps. The 802.11n standard runs at speeds up to 600 Mbps. The 802.11a and 802.11g standards run at up to 54 Mbps. The 802.11b standard runs at up to 11 Mbps.

101. D, F. The 802.11n and 802.11ax standards define wireless LAN devices that can support both the 2.4 GHz and 5 GHz frequency bands. The 802.11a and 802.11ac standards use only 5 GHz, and the 802.11b and 802.11g standards use only 2.4 GHz.

102. C. The 802.11ax and 802.11ac standards support multiple input, multiple output (MIMO) through the use of up to eight antennas on a single device. 802.11n is the only earlier 802.11 standard that supports MIMO, but it can only use a maximum of four antennas.

103. C. The service set identifier (SSID) is the name that you use when connecting to a wireless network. A basic service set (BSS) refers to the wireless network itself, consisting of a single AP and a number of clients. An extended service set (ESS) consists of two or more BSSs, using multiple APs. The basic service set identifier (BSSID) is the MAC address of the access point associated with a BSS. The extended service set identifier (ESSID) specifies the name of a network using multiple APs to support a single SSID.

104. A, B. Devices conforming to the IEEE 802.11a and 802.11g standards can only use a single 20 MHz channel. IEEE 802.11n devices can use channel bonding to join two channels together and achieve an aggregate channel width of 40 MHz. IEEE 802.11ax and 802.11ac devices can bond up to eight channels, for an aggregate width of 160 MHz, in a single channel or a non-contiguous 80+80 configuration.

105. A. Wireless range extenders are Physical layer devices that receive signals from wireless access points (WAPs) and network adapters and retransmit them, enabling devices to connect that are farther apart than the network would normally support. Because the extenders do not process the packets in any way, but just retransmit the signals, they do not operate at any layer above the Physical.

106. D. Wi-Fi Protected Access 3 (WPA3) is the most secure of the wireless protocols, providing the greatest degree of network device hardening. Wi-Fi Protected Access (WPA) was created to replace the insecure Wired Equivalent Privacy (WEP) protocol, and Wi-Fi Protected Access 2 (WPA2) was created to replace the Temporal Key Integrity Protocol (TKIP) used in the first version of WPA with Advanced Encryption Standard (AES). Extensible Authentication Protocol (EAP) is a framework for the encapsulation of authentication messages.

107. B. WPA was created to replace the insecure Wired Equivalent Privacy (WEP) protocol and used Temporal Key Integrity Protocol (TKIP) with the RC4 cipher for encryption. Counter Mode with Cipher Block Chaining Message Authentication Code Protocol (CCMP) with Advanced Encryption Standard (AES) is an encryption protocol that is used with the Wi-Fi Protected Access 2 (WPA2) security protocol. Extensible Authentication Protocol (EAP) is a framework for the encapsulation of authentication messages. EAP is used on wireless networks and point-to-point connections and supports dozens of different authentication methods, including Transport Layer Security (TLS). It is not the encryption protocol used with WPA. Terminal Access Controller Access Control System Plus (TACACS+) is a protocol designed to provide AAA services for networks with many routers and switches.

108. B. Wi-Fi Protected Access (WPA) was created to replace the insecure Wired Equivalent Privacy (WEP) protocol and used the Temporal Key Integrity Protocol (TKIP) with the RC4 cipher. WPA was replaced by WPA2 and later WPA3, both of which use Counter Mode with Cipher Block Chaining Message Authentication Code Protocol (CCMP) with Advanced Encryption Standard (AES) for encryption. Extensible Authentication Protocol (EAP) is a framework for the encapsulation of authentication messages.

109. A. Wi-Fi Protected Access (WPA) is a wireless security protocol that was designed to replace the increasingly vulnerable Wired Equivalent Privacy (WEP). WPA added an encryption protocol called Temporal Key Integrity Protocol (TKIP). This too became vulnerable, and WPA2 was introduced, which replaced TKIP with the stronger CCMP-Advanced Encryption Standard (CCMP-AES). Extensible Authentication Protocol and 802.1X do not provide encryption.

110. B. The WPA3 protocol replaces the pre-shared key of WPA2 with a Simultaneous Authentication of Equals (SAE) exchange that provides better security. SAE still requires the client and the access point (AP) to be configured with the same passphrase. The base key, the serial number, and the MAC address are all components that WPA3 uses to generate the encryption key for each packet.

111. C, D. A replay attack is one in which an attacker utilizes the encryption key found in a previously captured packet to gain access to the network. Simultaneous Authentication of Equals (SAE) prevents replay attacks by including a mutual authentication process, as well as correlation of a shared passphrase. Perfect Forward Secrecy (PFS) prevents replay attacks by issuing a unique key for every session, so that data illicitly retained from previous sessions is rendered unusable.

Pre-shared key (PSK) is the passphrase mechanism from WPA2 that has been replaced by SAE in WPA3. Near field communication (NFC) is a contact-based short-range authentication method used by some wireless implementations. Neither prevents replay attacks.

112. C, D. Wi-Fi Protected Access (WPA) is a wireless security protocol that was designed to replace the increasingly vulnerable Wired Equivalent Privacy (WEP). WPA added an encryption protocol called Temporal Key Integrity Protocol (TKIP). This too became vulnerable, and WPA2 and later WPA3 were introduced, both of which replace TKIP with CCMP-Advanced Encryption Standard (CCMP-AES) encryption.

113. D. WPA3-Personal addresses WPA2's KRACK vulnerability with a more secure cryptographic handshake, replacing the PSK four-way handshake with Simultaneous Authentication of Equals (SAE), a version of the Internet Engineering Task Force's dragonfly handshake in which either client or AP can initiate contact. Each device then transmits its authentication credentials in a discrete, one-off message, instead of in a give-and-take, multipart conversation. Importantly, SAE also eliminates the reuse of encryption keys, requiring a new code with every interaction. Without open-ended communication between AP and client or encryption key reuse, cybercriminals can't as easily eavesdrop or insert themselves into an exchange. Wired Equivalent Privacy (WEP), Wi-Fi Protected Access (WPA), and Wi-Fi Protected Access 2 (WPA2) all support the use of a pre-shared key.

114. A. WPA2 adds Counter Mode with Cipher Block Chaining Message Authentication Code Protocol - Advanced Encryption Standard (CCMP-AES), a new symmetric key encryption algorithm that strengthens the protocol's security. Multiple-input and multiple-output (MIMO) is a multiplexing technology added to the IEEE 802.11n standard, not to WPA2. Wired Equivalent Protocol (WEP) is the predecessor to WPA; it is not part of WPA2. Temporal Key Integrity Protocol (TKIP) is the encryption algorithm used in the first version of WPA; it was not added in the second version.

115. A. Of the options listed, Wi-Fi Protected Access 3 (WPA3) will provide the maximum security for the wireless network, in part because it uses long encryption keys that change frequently. IPsec is a Network layer security standard that does not provide the security needed for IEEE 802.11 wireless networks. Transport Layer Security (TLS) is a protocol that encrypts data exchanged by web servers and clients at the Application layer; it does not provide adequate security for wireless LANs. Layer 2 Tunneling Protocol (L2TP) is a virtual private networking protocol; it does not provide adequate security for wireless networks.

116. C, D. Counter Mode with Cipher Block Chaining Message Authentication Code Protocol (CCMP) with Advanced Encryption Standard (AES) is an encryption protocol that is used with the Wi-Fi Protected Access 2 (WPA2) and Wi-Fi Protected Access 3 (WPA3) security protocols. WPA was created to replace the insecure Wired Equivalent Privacy (WEP) protocol, and WPA2 was created to replace the Temporal Key Integrity Protocol (TKIP) used in the first version of WPA. Extensible Authentication Protocol (EAP) is a framework for the encapsulation of authentication messages.

117. C. Wi-Fi Protected Access 3 (WPA3) and Wi-Fi Protected Access 2 (WPA2) are both wireless security protocols that control access to the network and provide encryption, using protocols like Counter Mode with Cipher Block Chaining Message Authentication Code Protocol (CCMP) with Advanced Encryption Standard (AES). These protocols do not provide authentication services, however. Extensible Authentication Protocol (EAP) is a framework for the encapsulation of authentication messages. Its many variants provide support for the use of smart cards and other authentication factors, such as biometrics, in addition to traditional passwords.

118. C, D. WPA-Enterprise, also known as WPA-802.1X, can use the Extensible Authentication Protocol (EAP) to support various types of authentication factors and requires a Remote Authentication Dial-In User Service (RADIUS) server. WPA-Personal, also known as WPA-PSK (Pre-Shared Key), is intended for small networks and does not require RADIUS.

119. A. WPA-Personal, also known as WPA-PSK, is intended for small networks and requires a PSK. WPA-Enterprise, also known as WPA-802.1X, uses the Extensible Authentication Protocol (EAP) to support various types of authentication factors and requires a Remote Authentication Dial-In User Service (RADIUS) server.

120. A. TKIP uses the RC4 stream cipher for its encryption. Advanced Encryption Standard (AES) is used with CCMP on versions 2 and 3 of the Wi-Fi Protected Access (WPA2 and WPA3) security protocol, not version 1 (WPA), which uses TKIP. Secure Hash Algorithm (SHA) is a file hashing algorithm, not used for wireless network encryption.

121. B, C. CCMP (Counter Mode with Cipher Block Chaining Message Authentication Code Protocol) is based on the Advanced Encryption Standard (AES) and is the encryption protocol used with the Wi-Fi Protected Access 2 (WPA2) and Wi-Fi Protected Access 3 (WPA3) security protocols on wireless networks. CCMP is not used with version 1 of the WPA protocol. 802.1X is an authentication protocol and is not used for encryption.

122. C. CCMP (Counter Mode with Cipher Block Chaining Message Authentication Code Protocol) is based on the Advanced Encryption Standard (AES) and is the encryption protocol used with the Wi-Fi Protected Access 2 and 3 (WPA2 and 3) security protocols on wireless networks. CCMP is not based on the Temporal Key Integrity Protocol (TKIP), which uses RC4 as its stream cipher. 802.1X is an authentication protocol and is not used for encryption.

123. D. An SSID that is not broadcast is not detectable by clients, so Ralph must type it in manually. Security protocols are also not detectable, so Ralph must configure the clients to use the same protocol he selected on the WAP.

124. A. Counter Mode with Cipher Block Chaining Message Authentication Code Protocol (CCMP) with Advanced Encryption Standard (AES) is an encryption protocol that is used with the Wi-Fi Protected Access 2 (WPA2) security protocol, as well as the Wi-Fi Protected Access 3 (WPA3) protocol that followed it. WPA was created to replace the insecure Wired Equivalent Privacy (WEP) protocol, and WPA2 was created to replace the Temporal Key Integrity Protocol (TKIP) used in the first version of WPA. Extensible Authentication Protocol (EAP) is a framework for the encapsulation of authentication messages. EAP is used on wireless networks and point-to-point connections and supports dozens of different authentication methods, including Transport Layer Security (TLS). It is not the encryption protocol used with WPA2. Terminal Access Controller Access Control System Plus (TACACS+) is a protocol designed to provide AAA services for networks with many routers and switches.

125. A, B. Wired Equivalent Privacy (WEP) was one of the first commercially available security protocols for wireless LANs, but it was soon found to be easily penetrated and was replaced by Wi-Fi Protected Access (WPA). WPA was also deprecated in 2015 due to multiple security weaknesses, leading to the introduction of Wi-Fi Protected Access 2 (WPA2) and then WPA3. Extensible Authentication Protocol (EAP) is a framework for the encapsulation of authentication messages.

126. C. WPA2 was introduced when the earlier version of Wi-Fi Protected Access (WPA) was determined to be increasingly vulnerable to attack. WPA used an encryption protocol called Temporal Key Integrity Protocol (TKIP). WPA2 replaced TKIP with an Advanced Encryption Standard (CCMP-AES) protocol.

127. B, C, D. Roaming from one AP to another without interruption requires that the APs all use the same SSID, the same security protocol, and the same passphrase. The APs will not function properly if they have the same IP address.

128. D. The 5G cellular network specification calls for maximum theoretical download speeds of 10 Gbps, although the actual speed realized will be less.

129. A, B. 5G networks can operate on three frequency bands—low, medium, and high—with the high frequencies having the fastest speeds and reduced range. 4G devices cannot function on 5G networks.

130. D. IEEE 802.1X is a standard that defines a port-based network access control (PNAC) mechanism used for authentication on wireless and other networks. IEEE 802.11ac and 802.11n are standards defining the physical and Data link layer protocols for wireless networks. IEEE 802.11h is a standard that addresses the coexistence of wireless LANs with other services using the same frequencies. IEEE 802.3x is one of the standards for wired Ethernet networks.

131. A, D. Disabling SSID broadcasting prevents a wireless network from appearing to clients. The clients must specify the SSID to which they want to connect. MAC address filtering is a form of access control list (ACL) that is maintained in the AP and contains the addresses of devices that are to be permitted to access the network. Both of these mechanisms make it more difficult for unauthorized devices to connect to the access point (AP). Kerberos is an authentication protocol used by Active Directory, and relocating the AP to a screened subnet will not resolve the problem.

132. D. WAPs use the layer 2 MAC addresses coded into devices in their ACLs. Usernames, IP addresses, and device names can more easily be impersonated.

133. C. Allow listing is the process of using MAC filtering to specify the hardware addresses of devices that are permitted to access a wireless network. Deny listing, by contrast, is making a list of addresses that are denied access to the network.

134. A, B. The Control and Provisioning of Wireless Access Points (CAPWAP) protocol and the Lightweight Access Point Protocol (LWAPP) both enable wireless controllers to manage and control access points (APs). Lightweight Directory Access Protocol (LDAP) is used by directory services, and Point-to-Point Tunneling Protocol (PPTP) is used for virtual private networking.

135. B. A captive portal is a web page displayed to a user attempting to access a public wireless network. The user typically must supply credentials, provide payment, or accept a user agreement before access is granted. A captive portal does not refer to a switch port, a secured entryway to a room, or a type of extortionate computer attack.

136. A. A web page that prompts users for payment, authentication, or acceptance of a EULA is a captive portal. Ransomware is a type of attack that extorts payment. Port security and root guards are methods for protecting access to switch ports.

137. D. A WAP is a device with a wireless transceiver that also connects to a standard cabled network. Wireless computers communicate with the WAP, which forwards their transmissions over the network cable. This is called an infrastructure topology. A star/hub and spoke or bus network requires the computers to be physically connected to the network cable, and an ad hoc topology is one in which wireless computers communicate directly with one another.

138. B. Band steering is a wireless network adapter mechanism that evaluates the available wireless signals and automatically chooses the best frequency for the current conditions. Channel bonding is a wireless networking technique that combines channels to increase bandwidth. *Link aggregation* is a term for technology in which the bandwidth of multiple network adapter connections is joined to speed up transmissions. Traffic shaping is a means of prioritizing network traffic by delaying packets at the Application layer.

139. A. Lightweight wireless access points are designed to facilitate the expansion of the network by using a single wireless LAN controller (WLC) to store and deploy the configuration parameters for multiple lightweight access points configured to use the same SSID. *Stand-alone* and *autonomous* are terms for the same type of combined switch and access point commonly used today. There is no such thing as a traffic access point.

140. B. Humidity prevents the buildup of static electricity that can cause discharges that damage equipment. Humidity levels of 50 percent or lower can cause equipment to be susceptible to electrostatic shock.

141. C. Unless there is a specific known threat at the datacenter location, radon is not one of the environmental factors that typically can affect equipment uptime and that needs to be monitored. Temperature, humidity, flooding, and static electricity, however, are factors that should be monitored in a datacenter, as variations of these elements can result in equipment damage and downtime.

142. A, C. A large enterprise network will—at minimum—have demarcation points for telephone services and a connection to an Internet service provider's (ISP's) network. In many cases, these services will enter the building in the same equipment room that houses the backbone switch. This room is then called the main distribution frame (MDF). An intermediate distribution frame (IDF) is the location of localized telecommunications equipment such as the interface between the horizontal cabling and the backbone. Mean time between failure (MTBF) and Remote Desktop Protocol (RDP) are not locations of network wiring.

143. C. An intermediate distribution frame (IDF) is the location of localized telecommunications equipment such as the interface between a horizontal network, which connects to workstations and other user devices, and the network backbone. A large enterprise network will typically have demarcation points for telephone services and a connection to an Internet service provider's (ISP's) network. In many cases, these services will enter the building in the same equipment room that houses the backbone switch. This room is then called the main distribution frame (MDF). Mean time between failure (MTBF), service-level agreements (SLAs), and memoranda of understanding (MOUs) are not locations of network wiring.

144. C. A fail closed policy for the datacenter specifies that any open doors should lock themselves in the event of an emergency. To support this policy, the datacenter will have to have a self-contained fire suppression system, which uses devices such as fire detectors and oxygen-displacing gas systems.

145. C. If a server is connected to two building circuits, it can continue to function if the breaker for one circuit trips and remains uncorrected. All of the other options will bring the server down unless additional redundancies are in place.

146. B. A server with dual power supplies can run in one of two modes: redundant or combined. In redundant mode, both power supplies are capable of providing 100 percent of the power needed by the server. Therefore, the server can continue to run if one power supply fails, making it fault tolerant. In combined mode, both power supplies are needed to provide the server's needs, so a failure of one power supply will bring the server down. *Individual mode* and *hot backup* mode are not terms used for this purpose.

147. B, D. It is an online UPS that runs devices using battery power all the time so that there is no gap in the power supplied to devices during a failure. It is a standby UPS that switches devices to battery power during a main power failure. Both online and standby UPSs provide only enough power for an orderly shutdown of the devices.

148. B. Online UPSs run devices from their battery all the time, while simultaneously keeping the battery charged. There is therefore no switchover gap when a power failure occurs. Online UPSs do not necessarily run longer than standby UPSs, nor do they provide more protection against power spikes and sags. Both online and standby UPSs can be managed devices.

149. B. UPSs can provide servers with battery backup power, but usually only for a few minutes, so that the servers can be powered down safely, without the potential for data corruption or loss. UPSs typically cannot keep servers running for two hours. UPSs can protect against power spikes, but that is not their primary function. A computer power supply failure will bring a server down, regardless of the presence of a UPS.

150. A, B, D. If one of the server's power supplies fails, the other will continue to function. If the UPS fails, the server will continue to use the power supply plugged into the wall socket. If the building's backup generator fails, the server will continue to run as long as the building still has outside power. If the breaker for the building power circuit trips, the server will run only as long as the UPS battery holds out.

151. A, B, C, D. If one of the server's power supplies fails, the other will continue to function. If one of the UPSs fails, the server will continue to run using the other. If one of the building power circuit breakers trips, the server will continue to run using the other one. If the building's backup generator fails, the server will continue to run as long as the building still has outside power.

152. D. Clean agents are non-conductive inert gases that extinguish flame by rapid cooling and oxygen displacement without leaving any residue behind to damage equipment. Both pre-action sprinklers and water mist systems spray water, which can damage electronic equipment. Carbon dioxide is a fire suppressant, but it is also too toxic to be used on a large scale.

153. B. A PDU for a datacenter performs the same basic function as an office power strip, but it typically has a larger power input. It does not necessarily have more outlets or a larger voltage output.

154. C. An insider threat by definition originates with an authorized user. Smart cards, motion detection, and biometrics will only detect the presence of someone who is authorized to enter sensitive areas. Video surveillance, however, can track the activities of anyone, authorized or not.

155. A. A large enterprise network will—at minimum—have demarcation points for telephone services and a connection to an Internet service provider's (ISP's) network. In many cases, these services will enter the building in the same equipment room that houses the backbone switch. This room is then called the main distribution frame (MDF). An intermediate distribution frame (IDF) is the location of localized telecommunications equipment such as the interface between the horizontal cabling and the backbone. Mean time between failure (MTBF), Remote Desktop Protocol (RDP), and memorandum of understanding (MOU) are not locations of network wiring.

156. D. The terms *fail close* and *fail open* refer to the default position of an electric or electronic door lock when there is a power failure. Security is often a trade-off with safety, and in the event that an emergency occurs that results in the power being cut off, whether secured doors are permanently locked or left permanently open is a critical factor. The terms *fail close* and *fail open* do not apply to motion detectors or video cameras. A honeypot is a computer configured to lure potential attackers; it is not a physical security mechanism.

157. F. Smart lockers are available with a wide variety of authentication mechanisms, ranging from the relatively unsecure PIN to near field communication (NFC) and Bluetooth devices to high security biometric scans and radio-frequency identification (RFID) tags.

158. A, C. Closed circuit television (CCTV) cameras are part of a self-contained system in which the cameras feed their signals to dedicated monitors, usually located in a security center. IP cameras are standalone devices that transmit signals to a wireless access point. While CCTV cameras can only be monitored by users in the security center, or another designated location, IP cameras can be monitored by any authorized user with a web browser. LDAP is a directory services protocol and Network Access Control is a service; neither one is a type of video surveillance device.

159. C. A door that is configured to fail open reverts to its unsecured state—open—when an emergency occurs. This must be a carefully considered decision, as it can be a potential security hazard. However, configuring the door to fail closed is a potential safety hazard in the event of a fire or other disaster.

160. C. The technology that uses human physical characteristics to authenticate users is called biometrics. Biometric devices can identify users based on fingerprints, retinal pattern, voice prints, and other characteristics.

161. A, B, C. Biometric scans, identification badges, and key fobs are all mean of distinguishing authorized from unauthorized personnel. Motion detection cannot make this distinction.

162. A. Video surveillance can monitor all activities of users in a sensitive area. With properly placed equipment, event specific actions, such as commands entered in a computer, can be monitored. Identification badges, key fobs, motion detection, and locking cabinets can indicate the presence of individuals in a sensitive area, but they cannot monitor specific activities.

163. A, C, E. A radio-frequency identification (RFID) device is a small chip that can be electronically detected by a nearby reader. The chip can contain small amounts of data, such as the authentication credentials needed to grant an individual access to a secured area. Key fobs, proximity cards (prox cards), and smart lockers can use RFIDs to enable users to unlock a door by waving the device near a reader. Keycard locks typically require the card to be inserted into a reader and typically use magnetic strips to store data. Cypher locks rely on data supplied by the user—that is, the combination numbers.

164. B, D. Possession of the key fob is something you have, but the key fob could be lost or stolen, so its security is confirmed by the entrance of a PIN, something you know. Unless the user both loses the key fob and shares the PIN, the device remains secure.

165. A, C. Key fobs and proximity cards (prox cards) often use RFIDs to enable users to unlock a door by waving the device near a reader. Keycard locks typically use magnetic strips to store data and require the card to be physically inserted into a reader. Cypher locks rely on data manually supplied by the user—that is, the combination numbers.

166. B, D. Video surveillance can conceivably prevent an evil twin attack, which takes the form of a rogue access point deliberately connected to the network for malicious purposes. Video surveillance can also help to prevent insider threats by monitoring the activities of authorized users. Video surveillance cannot prevent social engineering, which involves nothing more than communicating with people, or brute-force attacks, which are usually performed remotely.

167. D. When a false positive occurs during a biometric authentication, a user who should not be granted access to the secured device or location is granted access. A false negative is when a user who should be granted access is denied access.

168. A. All of the mechanisms listed are designed to make any attempts to tamper with or physically compromise the hardware devices immediately evident. This is therefore a form of tamper detection. Asset tracking is for locating and identifying hardware. Geofencing is a wireless networking technique for limiting access to a network. Port security refers to network switch ports.

169. C. The technology that uses human physical characteristics to authenticate users is called biometrics. Biometric devices can identify users based on fingerprints, retinal pattern, voice prints, and other characteristics.

170. D. A tailgater is a type of intruder who enters a secure area by closely following an authorized user. Most people are polite enough to hold the door open for the next person without knowing if they are authorized to enter. A tailgater is therefore not an intrusion prevention mechanism. Identification badges, locks, and key fobs are methods of preventing intrusions.

171. A. Identification badges, key fobs, and access control vestibules (mantraps) are all physical security mechanisms, in that they prevent unauthorized personnel from entering sensitive areas, such as datacenters. These mechanisms are not used for data file security, asset tracking, or switch port security.

172. C, D. Biometrics and smart cards are both means of preventing intrusions, whereas motion detection and video surveillance are mechanisms for detecting them.

173. B. A door that is configured to fail closed reverts to its secured state—locked—when an emergency occurs. This must be a carefully considered decision since it can be a potential safety hazard in the event of a fire or other disaster. However, configuring the door to fail open is a potential security hazard.

174. B. An entrance arrangement in which people must close one door before they can open the next one is called an access control vestibule. Security personnel can evaluate potential entrants while they are in the vestibule and detain attempted intruders there.

175. D. The cabling nexus in a telecommunications room is called a patch panel. A telepole is a tool used for installing cables. A demarcation point, or demarc, is the location at which a telecommunication provider's service meets the customer's private network. A backbone is a network that connects other local area networks (LANs) together. A fiber distribution panel is used for fiber-optic cable, not unshielded twisted-pair (UTP), connections.

176. B. A single rack unit is 1.75 inches, or 44.5 mm. Option A, 1.721 inches, is the height used for many components that are one rack unit tall, leaving a small space between components for easy insertion and removal.

177. C. The port-side intake/exhaust option controls the flow of air through the switch. An administrator can specify whether the vents on the front of the switch take air in and exhaust it out the back or exhaust air taken in through the back. This enables administrators to designate specific aisles in the datacenter as warm or cold. The port-side intake/exhaust option has nothing to do with the signal propagation through the switch or which ports the switch should use.

178. A, B, C, E, F. In addition to the actual networking equipment, such as servers, switches, and routers, the power load calculations for a datacenter must include HVAC (and particularly cooling and fire suppression), room lighting, and any other powered security equipment. The intermediate distribution frame (IDF) is not located in the datacenter and therefore does not factor in Alice's power load calculations.

Chapter 3: Network Operations

1. A. A network map is a depiction of network devices, not drawn to scale, with additional information added, such as IP addresses and link speeds. In most cases, network maps are automatically created by a software product that scans the network and creates a display from the information it discovers. The term *network diagram* is most often used to refer to a manually created document containing pictograms of network devices, with lines representing the connections between them, usually not drawn to scale. A cable diagram is a precise depiction of the cable runs installed at a site. Often drawn on an architect's floor plan or blueprint, cable diagrams enable network administrators to locate specific cables and troubleshoot connectivity problems. A management information base (MIB) is a component of a network management system that is based on the Simple Network Management Protocol (SNMP) and contains information about only one device; it does not depict all of the devices on the network.

2. C. A cable diagram is a precise depiction of the cable runs installed at a site. Often drawn on an architect's floor plan or blueprint, cable diagrams enable network administrators to locate specific cables and troubleshoot connectivity problems. A wireless survey/heat map is a depiction of the wireless signal strengths found at various locations in a site, also overlaid on a floor plan or blueprint. A network map is a depiction of network devices, not drawn to scale, with additional information added, such as IP addresses and link speeds. In most cases, network maps are automatically created by a software product that scans the network and creates a display from the information it discovers. The term *network diagram* is most often used to refer to a manually created document containing pictograms of network devices, with lines representing the connections between them; the diagram is usually not drawn to scale. A management information base (MIB) is a component of a network management system that is based on the Simple Network Management Protocol (SNMP) and contains information about only one device; it does not depict all of the devices on the network.

3. C. Devices designed to fit into IT equipment racks typically have heights measured in units. One unit equals 1.75 inches. Most rack-mounted devices are one (1U), two (2U), or four units (4U) tall.

4. A. A reputable cable installer should supply a cable diagram that indicates the locations of all the cable runs on a plan or blueprint of the site. Alice should be able to use this to determine which ports go with which wall plates. A busy cable installer is unlikely to remember specific details about an installation performed years ago. Using a tone generator and locator is an effective way to associate ports and wall plates, but it can be incredibly time consuming and is certainly not the easiest method. A cable certifier can test the cable run for faults, measure its length, and perform other tests, but it cannot specify which wall plate goes with which port, unless the user entered that information earlier.

5. B. ISO 19770 is a family of IT asset management (ITAM) standards that defines procedures and technology for the inventory and management of software and related assets in a corporate infrastructure. ISO 19770-2 defines the creation and use of SWID tags, which are XML files containing management and identification information about a specific software product. The other standards define other ITAM elements, such as compliance with corporate governance (ISO 19770-1) and resource utilization measurement (ISO 19770-4).

6. C. Rack diagrams use vertical measurement called *units*, each of which is 1.75 inches. Most rack-mounted devices are one (1U), two (2U), or four units (4U) tall.

7. A. The Cisco symbol shown in the figure is used in network diagrams to represent a router, as symbolized by the arrows pointing both in and out. This symbol is not used to represent a hub, a switch, or a gateway.

8. A, C. A physical diagram, in this case, represents the actual physical locations of the cable drops connected to the patch panels. A logical diagram uses artificial divisions that correspond to the organization of the company.

9. C. IDF diagrams should be based on an architect's plan whenever possible so that actual lengths and locations of cable runs can be documented. In situations where an architect's plan is not available, a detailed sketch, drawn to scale, can be acceptable. Photographs, models, and reports are impractical for this purpose.

10. A, B, C. MDF and IDF documentation should take into account the power sources available at the locations, the HVAC equipment needed to keep the temperature and humidity levels under control, and the distances the cable runs must span. This type of documentation is typically used for installation and troubleshooting purposes, so the costs of components and services are unnecessary and can be covered elsewhere.

11. A, B, C, D. A change management team typically requires thorough documentation for all requested service changes, specifying exactly what is needed; how the change will affect the current workflow, both to the direct recipients of the change and the rest of the organization; and what ramifications might come from the change.

12. A, C. The change management team is usually not responsible for tasks directly involved in the implementation of the changes they approve. Therefore, they would not be the ones to notify users exactly when the change will take place or document the procedure afterward. They would, however, be responsible for providing a maintenance window during which the change must occur and authorizing any downtime that would be needed.

13. D. The standard unit height for IT equipment racks is 1.75 inches, which is the equivalent of one unit. Therefore, four units would be 7 inches.

14. D. The main purpose of a wiring schematic—also called a *layer 1 network diagram*—is to indicate where cables are located in walls and ceilings. A physical network diagram identifies all of the physical devices and how they connect together. Asset management is the identification, documentation, and tracking of all network assets, including computers, routers, switches, software, licenses, warranties, and so on. A logical network diagram contains addresses, firewall configurations, access control lists (ACLs), and other logical elements of the network configuration.

15. B. A layer 2 network diagram depicts the mechanisms by which devices communicate on a local area network. Each device is uniquely identified on the LAN by a media access control (MAC) address associated with its network interface. Layer 2 is associate with LAN communications only. A layer 3 diagram would identify the routers used by LANs to communicate with other networks. A layer 1 diagram specifies the physical characteristics of the

network, such as where cables are installed in the facility. Layer 4 of the OSI models defines the Transport layer protocols in use on the network; it generally does not require a diagram.

16. B, D. A physical network diagram identifies all of the physical devices and how they connect together. A logical network diagram contains IP addresses, firewall configurations, access control lists (ACLs), and other logical elements of the network configuration. Both physical and logical network diagrams can be created automatically or manually. It is the physical network diagram that contains the information needed to rebuild the network from scratch.

17. C. The standard width of an equipment rack in a data center is 19 inches. Network hardware manufacturers use this width when designing rack-mountable components.

18. A. The Cisco symbol shown in the figure is used in network diagrams to represent a switch, as symbolized by the multiple arrows pointing outward. This symbol is not used to represent a hub, a router, or a gateway.

19. A. Datacenters typically mount components in racks, 19-inch-wide and approximately 6-foot-tall frameworks in which many networking components are specifically designed to fit. A rack diagram is a depiction of one or more racks, ruled out in standardized 1.752-inch rack units, and showing the exact location of each piece of equipment mounted in the rack. Network maps, wiring schematics, and logical diagrams are documents that define the relationships between components, not their precise locations. A business continuity plan describes the organization's disaster prevention and recovery policies. An audit and assessment report is a document—often prepared by a third party—that summarizes the organization's security posture.

20. B. Network diagrams typically specify device types and connections for layers 1, 2, and 3 of the OSI reference model, but network maps can also include IP addresses, link speeds, and other information. Network maps diagram the relationships between devices and provide information about the links that connect them, but they are not drawn to scale and usually do not indicate the exact location of each device. Although universal accessibility would be desirable, there are individuals who should not have access to network maps and other documentation, including temporary employees and computer users not involved in IT work. A network map includes all networking devices, not just cable runs and endpoints.

21. B. A material safety data sheet (MSDS) is a document created by manufacturers of chemical, electrical, and mechanical products, specifying the potential dangers and risks associated with them, particularly in regard to exposure or fire. A properly documented network should have MSDS documents on file for all of the chemical and hardware products used to build and maintain it. MSDSs can be obtained from the manufacturer or the Environmental Protection Agency (EPA). Electrostatic discharges (ESDs), non-disclosure agreements (NDAs), bring your own device (BYOD) policies, and standard operating procedures (SOPs) are not concerned with the chemical composition of cleaning compounds.

22. A. Remote access policies specify when and how users are permitted to access the company network from remote locations. A service-level agreement (SLA) is a contract between a provider and a subscriber that specifies the guaranteed availability of the service. Acceptable use policies (AUPs) specify whether and how employees can utilize company-owned hardware and software resources. A privileged user agreement specifies the abilities and limitations of users with respect to the administrative accounts and other privileges they have been granted.

23. B. Acceptable use policies (AUPs) specify whether and how employees can utilize company-owned hardware and software resources. AUPs typically specify what personal work employees can perform, what hardware and software they can install, and what levels of privacy they are permitted when using company equipment. A service-level agreement (SLA) is a contract between a provider and a subscriber. A non-disclosure agreement (NDA) specifies what company information employees are permitted to discuss outside the company. A bring your own device (BYOD) policy specifies how employees can connect their personal devices to the company network.

24. D. A bring your own device (BYOD) policy specifies the personal electronics that employees are permitted to use on the company network and documents the procedures for connecting and securing them. A service-level agreement (SLA) is a contract between a provider and a subscriber that specifies the percentage of time that the contracted services are available. Acceptable use policies (AUPs) specify whether and how employees can use company-owned hardware and software resources. A non-disclosure agreement (NDA) specifies what company information employees are permitted to discuss outside the company.

25. C. A non-disclosure agreement (NDA) specifies what company information employees are permitted to discuss outside the company. A service-level agreement (SLA) is a contract between a provider and a subscriber that specifies the percentage of time that the contracted services are available. Acceptable use policies (AUPs) specify whether and how employees can utilize company-owned hardware and software resources. A memorandum of understanding (MOU) is a document outlining an agreement between two parties that precedes the signing of a contract. A bring your own device (BYOD) policy specifies the personal electronics that employees are permitted to use on the company network and documents the procedures for connecting and securing them.

26. D. Material safety data sheets (MSDSs) are documents, created by manufacturers of chemical, electrical, and mechanical products, that specify the potential risks and dangers associated with them, particularly in regard to flammability and the possibility of toxic outgassing. A properly documented network should have MSDS documents on file for all of the chemical and hardware products used to build and maintain it. MSDSs can be obtained from the manufacturers or the Environmental Protection Agency (EPA). Electrostatic discharges (ESDs), non-disclosure agreements (NDAs), and bring your own device (BYOD) policies are not concerned with the dangers inherent in building contents.

27. D. Software and hardware upgrades are typically not part of an AUP, because they are handled by the company's IT personnel. An AUP for a company typically includes a clause indicating that users have no right to privacy for anything they do using the company's computers, including email and data storage. An AUP usually specifies that the company is the sole owner of the computer equipment and any proprietary company information stored on it or available through it. The AUP also prohibits the use of its computers or network for any illegal practices, typically including spamming, hacking, or malware introduction or development.

28. A, B. Clauses regarding company property, including the copyrights and patents for the work performed for the company, typically do appear in an AUP but not in the privacy clause. This information would be more likely to appear in an ownership clause. The privacy clause commonly explains that the company has the right to access and monitor anything stored on its computers.

29. A. After a change is requested, approved, scheduled, performed, and tracked, everyone involved should be notified, and the entire process should be documented for future reference.

30. B. The process of adding a user's personal device and allowing it to access the company network is called on-boarding. Removing the personal device from the network would be called off-boarding. *In-band* and *out-of-band* are terms defining methods for gaining administrative access to a managed network device.

31. C. An IT end-of-life (EOL) asset disposal policy typically includes procedures to be performed on assets that have reached the end of their system life cycle and that are ready for final processing. This includes the wiping of all data, the completion of inventory records, and the possible recycling of the assets. The policy assumes that all data requiring preservation has already been preserved before the asset is submitted for disposal. Therefore, data preservation procedures are not needed at this phase.

32. A. A service-level agreement (SLA) is a contract between a provider and a subscriber that specifies the percentage of time that the contracted services are available. Acceptable use policies (AUPs) specify whether and how employees can utilize company-owned hardware and software resources. A non-disclosure agreement (NDA) specifies what company information employees are permitted to discuss outside the company. A bring your own device (BYOD) policy specifies the personal electronics that employees are permitted to use on the company network and documents the procedures for connecting and securing them.

33. D. An ISP provides subscribers with access to the Internet. The applications that the subscriber uses on the Internet are typically not part of the SLA. An SLA does typically specify exactly what services the ISP will supply, what equipment the ISP will provide, and the technical support services the ISP will furnish as part of the agreement.

34. A. A service-level agreement (SLA) is a contract between a provider and a subscriber that specifies the percentage of time that the contracted services are available. Mean time between failure (MTBF) is a hardware specification that estimates how long a particular component can be expected to function. Acceptable use policies (AUPs) specify whether and how employees can utilize company-owned hardware and software resources. Mean time to repair (MTTR) specifies the average time it will take to repair a specific hardware company when it malfunctions.

35. A, B, D. The technical support clause of an SLA typically defines the type of support that the provider will furnish, the time service for support, and the amount of support that is included in the contract, as well as the cost for additional support. An SLA will typically guarantee service ability in the form of a percentage, but this refers to problems at the provider's end and is not a customer technical support matter.

36. C. The archive bit that backup software uses to perform incremental and differential jobs is a file attribute, so this is the most commonly used filter type. It is possible to filter files based on their names, their extensions, and their size, but these are not used as often as the archive file attribute.

37. C. Differential backups use the archive bit to determine which target files to back up. However, a differential backup does not reset the archive bit. Full backups do not pay attention to the archive bit, because they back up all of the files. A full backup, however, does clear the archive bit after the job is completed. Incremental backups also use the archive bit to determine which files have changed since the previous backup job. The primary difference between an incremental and a differential job, however, is that incremental backups clear the archive bit so that unchanged files are not backed up. There is no such thing as a supplemental backup job.

38. C. The generational media rotation system uses the terms *grandfather*, *father*, and *son* to refer to backup jobs that are run monthly, weekly, and daily. The jobs can be full, incremental, or differential, and the terms have nothing to do with whether the backup medium is a hard disk, optical, or any type of tape drive.

39. C. IP address management (IPAM) is a system for planning, managing, and monitoring the IP address space for an entire enterprise network. IPAM provides links between the Dynamic Host Configuration Protocol (DHCP) and the Domain Name System (DNS) so that each is aware of the naming and addressing changes made by the other. DHCPv6 is an IPv6 version of the DHCP service, which enables it to allocate IPv6 addresses to network clients. HOSTS is a text-based name resolution method for individual systems that predates DNS. Automatic Private IP Addressing (APIPA) is the mechanism that enables a DHCP client to assign itself an address when no DHCP servers are accessible.

40. D. Version skew can occur when a data set changes while a system backup is running. A file written to a directory that has already been backed up will not appear on the backup media, even though the job might still be running. This can result in unprotected files or, worse, data corruption. A snapshot is a read-only copy of a data set taken at a specific moment in time. By creating a snapshot and then backing it up, you can be sure that no data corruption has occurred due to version skew. Incrementals and differentials are types of backup jobs, and iteration is not a specific storage technology.

41. B. Tape libraries and autoloaders are robotic devices containing one or more removable media drives, such as magnetic tape or optical disk drives. The robotic mechanism inserts and removes media cartridges automatically so that a single backup job can span multiple cartridges without human intervention, increasing the overall capacity of the backup solution.

42. A. Firmware is a type of software permanently written to the memory built into a hardware device. A firmware update overrides the read-only nature of this memory to update the software. Driver updates, feature updates, and vulnerability patches are typically applied to software products, such as applications and operating systems.

43. A. A patch is a relatively small update that is designed to address a specific issue, often a security exploit or vulnerability. Patches do not add features or new capabilities; they are fixes that target a specific area of the software. Updates and upgrades are larger packages that might include new features and/or many different fixes. Drivers are the software products that enable an operating system to communicate with hardware devices.

44. C. Rolling back, the process of uninstalling a patch to revert to the previous version of the software, is not part of the patch evaluation process. The evaluation process for new patches in a corporate environment usually consists of a research stage, in which you examine the need and purpose for the patch; a testing stage, in which you install the patch on a lab machine; and a backup of the production systems to which you will apply the patch.

45. D. *Rollback* is a term used in change management to describe the process of reversing a change that has been made, to restore the original configuration. In the case of patch management, a rollback is the process of uninstalling a recently installed software update. The terms *backslide, downgrade,* and *reset* are not used for this procedure. End-of-life is a phase marking the end of a device's marketing, sales, and upgrades. However, the manufacturer might still offer security patches for the product. End-of support (EOS) marks the point at which the manufacturer discontinues all support for the product.

46. C, D. The golden or baseline configuration is one that administrators will apply to all workstations. In Alice's case, this is not a production configuration because there are other software products to be added later. A sandbox configuration is used for testing purposes only.

47. A. Bar coding the new computers enables the IT department to record their locations, status, and conditions throughout their life cycle, a process known as asset tracking. Bar codes are not used for tamper detection and device hardening. Port security refers to switches, not computers.

48. A, D. Deleting files on a hard disk drive leaves them available for retrieval, even though they appear to be gone. A disk wipe utility deletes all of the files on the hard drive and then overwrites the entire disk with zeroes, rendering all files unretrievable. Ralph can then reinstall the operating system to prepare the computer for sale. Performing these two steps eliminates the need to uninstall applications, delete data files manually, or perform a factory reset.

49. A, E. An SNMP-based network management system consists of three components: a management console software product installed on a network computer, agents installed on the devices you want to manage, and MIBs for each of the agents. Because the switches support SNMP management and already have agents, they have MIBs also. Therefore, all you have to do is purchase the network management software and install the console on a network computer.

50. A. Security information and event management (SIEM) is a product that combines two technologies: security event management (SEM) and security information management (SIM). Together, the two provide a combined solution for gathering and analyzing information about a network's security events. Simple Network Management Protocol (SNMP) is a technology that gathers information about managed devices.

51. A, B, C. SNMP version 1 (SNMPv1), SNMP version 2 (SNMPv2), and SNMP version 2c (SNMPv2c) all rely on unencrypted community strings that are sent with GET requests as a security mechanism. SNMP version 3 (SNMPv3), the one most often seen today, uses fully encrypted transmissions for more advanced security and does not use a community string.

52. B, C. SNMP is not the name of a network management product; it is just the name of the protocol that provides a framework for the interaction of the various components in a network management product. SNMPv1 uses a community string, but the original SNMPv2 did not, as it had a newer security system that was not widely adopted. The interim version SNMPv2c retains the community string from version 1 in place of the new version 2 security system. When you see a network interface adapter, switch, router, access point, or other device that purports to be managed or that claims to have network management capabilities, this usually means that the device includes an SNMP agent. Most of today's network management products do support SNMPv3. In addition, many network management products that implement SNMPv3 also include support for the earlier, unprotected versions, such as SNMPv1 and SNMPv2c. SNMPv3 does not perform IP address availability monitoring.

53. A. The utility shown in the figure is Wireshark, a packet capture and protocol analyzer application. The top pane contains a list of captured packets, and the bottom two panes display the parsed contents of the selected packet. System monitors, performance monitors, and log viewers do not display the parsed contents of individual packets.

54. A. Syslog is a standard that was designed to facilitate the transmission of log entries generated by a device or process, such as the sendmail Simple Mail Transfer Protocol (SMTP) server, across an Internet Protocol (IP) network to a message collector, called a syslog server. Since its inception, syslog has come to support message logging on other platforms, including operating systems, printers, and routers. Netstat is a program that displays status information about a system's network connections; it does not provide logging services. SNMP is a protocol that carries network management information from agents to a central console; it was not created specifically for sendmail. The Cache Array Routing Protocol (CARP) enables proxy servers to exchange information; it does not provide logging services.

55. A. The best solution is to implement Simple Network Management Protocol (SNMP). This includes a management console, agents, and management information bases (MIBs). SNMP allows you to generate alerts, track statistical network information (historical and current), and produce reports for baseline analysis and troubleshooting. Some SNMP products also allow you to track software distribution and metering. Protocol analyzers are best used for troubleshooting problems in real time and are not used for software distribution and metering. A performance monitor is a tool that allows you to track performance statistics for one system at a time and does not include software distribution and metering. There is no such product as a network traffic monitor.

56. C, D. Security information and event management (SIEM) is a product type that combines two technologies: security event management (SEM) and security information management (SIM). Together, the two provide a combined solution for gathering and analyzing information about a network's security events. Simple Network Management Protocol (SNMP) is a technology that gathers information about managed devices. Syslog is a standard designed to facilitate the transmission of log entries generated by a device or process, such as the sendmail Simple Mail Transfer Protocol (SMTP) server, across an Internet Protocol (IP) network to a message collector, called a syslog server. Neither SNMP nor syslog capabilities is typically included in SIEM products.

57. D. A protocol analyzer provides information about network traffic; it does not interpret web server logs. Most web servers maintain logs that track the Internet Protocol (IP) addresses and other information about all hits and visits. The logs are stored as text files and contain a great deal of information, but in their raw form, they are difficult to interpret. Therefore, it is common practice to use a traffic analysis application that reads the log files and displays their contents in a more user-friendly form, such as tables and graphs.

58. B. A baseline is a record of a system's performance under real-world operating conditions, captured for later comparison as conditions change. The workload during a baseline capture should be genuine, not simulated or estimated.

59. B. If a server is using all of its network bandwidth, then the most logical solution is to add more. You can do this by installing a second network adapter and connecting it to a different subnet. The other solutions could conceivably address the problem, but their success is less likely.

60. A. Performance monitoring utilities typically provide statistics on the central processing unit (CPU), memory, network, and disk usage, but not computer temperature monitoring.

61. A. Every syslog message includes a single-digit severity code. Code 0 is the most severe, indicating an emergency that has rendered the system unusable. Severity code 1 is an alert message, indicating that immediate action is needed. Severity code 2 is a critical condition message, and code 3 is an error condition. Code 4 is a warning message.

62. B. Every syslog message includes a single-digit severity code. Severity code 1 is an alert message, indicating that immediate action is needed. Code 0 is the most severe, indicating an emergency that has rendered the system unusable. Severity code 2 is a critical condition message, and code 3 is an error condition. Code 4 is a warning message.

63. D. Every syslog message includes a single-digit severity code. Code 6 indicates that the message is purely informational. Code 0 is the most severe, indicating an emergency that has rendered the system unusable. Severity code 2 is a critical condition message, and code 4 is a warning message. Code 7 is used strictly for debugging.

64. D. Messages that SNMP agents send to consoles when an event needing attention occurs are called traps. *Alerts* and *notifications* are terms for the messages that the console sends to administrators. A ping is an Internet Control Message Protocol (ICMP) echo request message sent from one TCP/IP computer to another. A flow describes the transaction between network devices, but it is not an SNMP feature.

65. D. The term *rollback* refers to the process of uninstalling or downgrading an update patch; it has nothing to do with monitoring a network interface. An interface monitor does typically display the number of transmission errors that occur on an interface, the amount of the available bandwidth that the interface is using, and the number of packets that have been dropped due to errors or discards.

66. B, C. The packet drops displayed by an interface monitor are caused by errors, such as malformed or unreadable packets, or discards, which are packets that are dropped because they are destined for another interface. Resets and overflows are not reasons for packet drops.

67. D. Performance baselines characterize hardware performance, so the OS update history would be of little or no use for future comparisons. A baseline typically consists of CPU, memory, disk, and network performance statistics.

68. C, D. Logs frequently contain sensitive information, so securing them with the appropriate permissions is an essential part of log management. Logs also can grow to overwhelm the storage medium on which they are stored, so cycling is a technique for managing log size by configuring it to delete the oldest record each time a new one is added. Rollback and utilization are not log management tasks.

69. B. In SIEM, forensic analysis is a process of searching logs on multiple computers for specific information based on set criteria and time periods. Data aggregation is a process of consolidating log information from multiple sources. Correlation is the process of linking logged events with common attributes together. Retention is the long-term storage of log data.

70. A. In SIEM, data aggregation is a process of consolidating log information from multiple sources. Forensic analysis is a process of searching logs on multiple computers for specific information based on set criteria and time periods. Correlation is the process of linking logged events with common attributes together. Retention is the long-term storage of log data.

71. A. Performance Monitor is a Windows application that can create logs of specific system and network performance statistics over extended periods. Such a log created on a new computer can function as a baseline for future troubleshooting. Event Viewer is a Windows application for displaying system log files; it cannot create a performance baseline. Syslog is a log compilation program originally created for Unix systems; it does not create performance baselines. Network Monitor is a protocol analyzer. Although it can capture a traffic sample that can function as a reference for future troubleshooting efforts, this capability cannot be called a performance baseline.

72. C. A management information base (MIB) is the database on an SNMP console where all of the information gathered from the network is stored. A trap is an alert message that SNMP agents send to the network management console. Syslog is a standard for message logging components. Security information and event management (SIEM) is a combination tool that uses information gathered from logs and network devices to provide a real-time analysis of the network's security condition.

73. D. Cyclical redundancy checks (CRCs) are faults that occur when data does not arrive at its destination in the same state as when it was sent; they are not Simple Network Management Protocol (SNMP) components. Management information bases (MIBs), traps, and object identifiers (OIDs) are all components of a Simple Network Management Protocol (SNMP) implementation. API integration, such as that using the Representational State Transfer (REST) architecture, can enable clients on the network to access SNMP information through simple web-based requests, rather than giving them direct access to the SNMP back end.

74. A. Ralph's traffic analysis led him to the conclusion that traffic shaping, a technique for prioritizing packets by buffering those that are not time sensitive for later transmission, will improve the VoIP performance. Ralph can use this technique to give VoIP packets priority over other types of traffic. Load balancing can conceivably improve the performance of a server, but it cannot help to relieve traffic congestion on the Internet link. The traffic congestion is on the Internet connection, not the LAN, so upgrading to Gigabit Ethernet will not help. SNMP is a protocol used by network management products; it will not relieve the traffic congestion problem.

75. A. Security information and event management (SIEM) is a product that combines two technologies: security event management (SEM) and security information management (SIM). Together, the two provide a combined solution for gathering and analyzing information about a network's security events. Simple Network Management Protocol (SNMP) is a technology that gathers information about managed devices. SEIM and SEM/SIM are not correct abbreviations for security information and event management.

76. C. A protocol analyzer captures all network traffic, interprets the protocol headers and fields, and displays the output. The Event Viewer displays system, application, and security event logs on a single computer. Performance monitor tracks the values of specific metrics, but it does not capture packets. A management console is a remote monitoring and management device that queries Simple Network Management Protocol (SNMP) agents.

77. A. Port mirroring is a feature found in some switches that takes the form of a special port that runs in promiscuous mode. This means that the switch copies all incoming traffic to that port, as well as to the dedicated destination ports. By connecting a protocol analyzer to this port, an administrator can access all of the network's traffic. Stateful packet inspection is a firewall feature that enables the device to examine Network and Transport layer header fields, looking for patterns that indicate damaging behaviors, such as IP spoofing, SYN floods, and teardrop attacks. Trunking is a switch feature that enables administrators to create VLANs that span multiple switches. Service-dependent filtering is a firewall feature that blocks traffic based on Transport layer port numbers.

78. D. An ad hoc network discovery is a one-time scan of a range of IP addresses to determine whether they are in use. The tool does not scan the port numbers for each address, list the MAC addresses, or perform traceroute tests. While scheduled network discoveries are possible, the term *ad hoc* refers to a one-time, on-demand procedure.

79. B. While incident response policies might include the process of responding to an incident and identifying and documenting its cause, the primary function of incident response policies is to ensure that the same incident does not happen again.

80. A, E. Tabletop exercises and validation tests can be a useful part of an incident preparedness plan, but they are not part of the incident response. Once a network infrastructure has been partially or completely destroyed, rebuilding it is no longer a matter of incident response; the responsibility passes over to the disaster recovery plan, which requires a different set of policies. Stopping, containing, and remediating an incident are all considered incident response policies.

81. A, B, D. Attacks, hardware failures, and crashes are all events that can be addressed by incident response policies that define what is to be done to analyze and remediate the problem. An electrical fire typically would not be addressed by an IT department's incident response team; it is a job for trained firefighters. Once the fire is out, the company's response falls under the heading of disaster recovery.

82. C. RAID is a technology for storing data on multiple hard disk drives, providing fault tolerance, increased performance, or both. The various RAID levels provide different levels of functionality and have different hardware requirements. RAID 5 combines disk striping with distributed storage of parity information, which provides fault tolerance. The parity information enables the array to rebuild a disk whose data has been lost. RAID 0 uses data striping only (blocks written to each disk in turn), which does not provide any form of fault tolerance. RAID 1 provides fault tolerance through disk mirroring. RAID 10 creates fault-tolerant mirrored stripe sets.

83. B. *Power redundancy* is a general term describing any fault tolerance mechanism that enables equipment to continue functioning when one source of power fails. A UPS is a device that uses battery power, not a generator. The term *dual power supplies* refers to the power supply units inside a computer, not a separate generator. The term *redundant circuits* refers to multiple connections to the building's main power, not to a generator.

84. C. Redundant Array of Independent Disks (RAID) is a technology for storing data on multiple hard disk drives, providing fault tolerance, increased performance, or both. The various RAID levels provide different levels of functionality and have different hardware requirements. RAID 5 combines disk striping (blocks written to each disk in turn) with distributed storage of parity information, for fault tolerance. RAID 0 provides data striping only. RAID 1 provides disk mirroring. RAID 10 creates mirrored stripe sets.

85. C. Mean time between failure (MTBF) is a hardware specification used to predict the approximate lifetime of a component; it does not refer to any type of fault tolerance mechanism. Port aggregation, clustering, and uninterruptible power supplies (UPSs) are all mechanisms that provide fault tolerance in the event of network adapter, server, and power failures, respectively.

86. B. Load balancing is a method of distributing incoming traffic among multiple servers. Network address translation (NAT) is a routing mechanism that enables computers on a private network to share one or more public Internet Protocol (IP) addresses; it is not a load balancing method. Domain Name System (DNS) round-robin, multilayer switching, and content switching are all mechanisms that enable a server cluster to share client traffic.

87. C. Highly available systems often have redundant failover components that enable them to continue operating even after a failure of a router, switch, hard disk, server, or other component. Backups, snapshots, and cold sites can all contribute to a system's high availability, but they do not function automatically.

88. A. Redundant Array of Independent Disks (RAID) is a technology for storing data on multiple hard disk drives, providing fault tolerance, increased performance, or both. The various RAID levels provide different levels of functionality and have different hardware requirements. RAID 0 uses data striping only (blocks written to each disk in turn), which does not provide any form of fault tolerance. RAID 1 provides disk mirroring; RAID 5 combines disk striping with distributed storage of parity information; and RAID 10 creates mirrored stripe sets—these three levels all provide fault tolerance.

89. C. Cold, warm, and hot backup sites differ in the hardware and software they have installed. A cold site is just a space at a remote location. The hardware and software must be procured and installed before the network can be restored; therefore, it is the least expensive and takes the most time. A warm site has hardware in place that must be installed and configured. A hot site has all of the necessary hardware already installed, configured, and ready to go in the event of a disaster. A warm site is more expensive than a cold site, and a hot site is the most expensive and takes the least amount of time to be made operational.

90. D. A cloud site is the least expensive to implement. Cold, warm, and hot backup sites differ in the hardware and software they have installed, but they all require the maintenance of a facility for a new datacenter. A cold site is just a space at a remote location. The hardware and software must be procured and installed before the network can be restored. It is the least expensive of the cold, warm, and hot options and takes the most time. A warm site has hardware in place that must be installed and configured. A hot site has all of the necessary hardware already installed, configured, and ready to go in the event of a disaster. A warm site is more expensive than a cold site, and a hot site is the most expensive and takes the least amount of time to be made operational. A cloud site is a virtual facility maintained with a cloud service provider. The cloud site does not require physical space or physical hardware, so it is the least expensive.

91. B. The recovery time objective (RTO) specifies the amount of time needed to restore a server from the most recent backup if it should fail. This time interval depends on the amount of data involved and the speed of the backup medium. A recovery point objective (RPO) specifies how much data is likely to be lost if a restore from backups should be necessary. This figure is based on the frequency of the backups and the amount of new data generated by the system. *Business contingency planning* (BCP) is an umbrella term for procedures enacted to keep the organization functioning in the event of a disaster. A management information base (MIB) is a database used by Simple Network Management Protocol (SNMP) systems.

92. B. Mean time to failure (MTTF) refers to devices that will eventually fail once and then be discarded, rather than repaired. Mean time between failure (MTBF), mean time to repair (MTTR), and mean down time (MDT) all refer to devices that will eventually fail and then be repaired and reused.

93. A, D. If one of the server's power supplies fails, the other will continue to function. If the building's backup generator fails, the server will continue to run as long as the building still has outside power. If the UPS fails, the server will go down. If the breaker for the building power circuit trips, the server will run only as long as the UPS battery holds out.

94. B. In a network load balancing cluster, each computer is referred to as a *host*. Other types of clusters use other terms. For example, in a failover cluster, each computer is called a *node*. The terms *server* and *box* are not used in clustering.

95. A, B. A high availability virtual IP address implementation is when multiple servers are identified by a single address, enabling all of the servers to receive incoming client traffic. In the case of server clustering and network load balancing arrangements, the cluster itself has a unique name and IP address, separate from those of the individual servers. Clients address themselves to the cluster, not to one of the servers in the cluster. NAT is not a high availability technology, and NIC teaming does not use virtual IP addresses.

96. A. Cold, warm, and hot backup sites differ in the hardware and software they have installed. A cold site is just a space at a remote location. The hardware and software must be procured and installed before the network can be restored. It is the least expensive. A warm site has hardware in place that must be installed and configured. A hot site has all of the necessary hardware installed and configured. A warm site is more expensive than a cold site, and a hot site is the most expensive.

97. D. A cluster is a group of computers configured with the same application that function as a single unit. The cluster can function as a fault tolerance mechanism by failing over from one server to the next, when necessary, or provide load balancing by distributing traffic among the servers.

98. B. NIC teaming enables you to combine the functionality of two network interface cards (NICs) in one connection. However, when you configure a NIC team to use an active-passive configuration, one of the network adapters remains idle and functions as a fault tolerance mechanism. If the other NIC should fail, the passive NIC becomes active. In this configuration, NIC teaming does not provide load balancing, server clustering, or traffic shaping.

99. D. Redundant Array of Independent Disks (RAID) level 1 is a fault tolerance mechanism that is also known as disk mirroring. A storage subsystem writes data to two or more disks at the same time so that if a disk fails, the data remains available. Because data is written to the disks at the same time, this RAID level does not provide load balancing. NIC teaming balances a network traffic load among two or more network interface cards (NICs), whereas server clustering and Domain Name System (DNS) round-robin balance a traffic load among multiple servers.

100. D. Cold, warm, and hot backup sites are disaster recovery mechanisms that enable a network to be activated at a remote location when a catastrophe occurs. The temperature refers to a site's readiness to assume the role of the network. A cold site is just a space at a remote location. The hardware and software must be procured and installed before the network can be restored. A warm site has hardware in place that must be installed and configured. It takes less time to restore the network than at a cold site, but more than at a hot site. A hot site has all of the necessary hardware installed and configured. The network can go live as soon as the most recent data is restored.

101. A. Mean time between failure (MTBF) specifies how long you can expect a device to run before it malfunctions. For a hard disk, this specification indicates the life expectancy of the device. Service-level agreements (SLAs) and acceptable use policies (AUPs) are not specifications associated with hard disk drives. Mean time to repair (MTTR) can conceivably be specified for a hard disk, but hard disk drives in a RAID array are typically replaced, not repaired.

102. B, D. Redundant Array of Independent Disks (RAID) is a technology for storing data on multiple hard disk drives, providing fault tolerance, increased performance, or both. The various RAID levels provide different levels of functionality and have different hardware requirements. RAID 1 provides disk mirroring, and RAID 10 creates mirrored stripe sets. Both provide fault tolerance by maintaining two copies of every stored file, for a usable disk space percentage of 50 percent. Some mirroring configurations store more than two copies of each file, for even less usable space. RAID 0 provides data striping only, with no fault tolerance. RAID 5 combines disk striping (blocks written to each disk in turn) with distributed storage of parity information, for fault tolerance with a usable disk space percentage of at least 66 percent.

103. D. Disk mirroring and disk duplexing both use multiple hard disk drives to store duplicate copies of all data. However, disk duplexing calls for each disk to be connected to a separate controller so that the data remains available if there is a disk failure or a disk controller failure.

104. B. Redundant Array of Independent Disks (RAID) is a technology for storing data on multiple hard disk drives, providing fault tolerance, increased performance, or both. The various RAID levels provide different levels of functionality and have different hardware requirements. RAID 1 provides disk mirroring for fault tolerance and requires two or more disk drives. RAID 0 provides data striping only, with no fault tolerance. RAID 5 combines disk striping (blocks written to each disk in turn) with distributed storage of parity information for fault tolerance, but it requires a minimum of three disk drives. RAID 10 creates mirrored stripe sets and requires at least four disk drives.

105. B, D. Redundant Array of Independent Disks (RAID) is a technology for storing data on multiple hard disk drives, providing fault tolerance, increased performance, or both. The various RAID levels provide different levels of functionality and have different hardware requirements. RAID 1 and RAID 10 both use disk mirroring to provide fault tolerance, which does not require parity data. RAID 0 uses data striping only (blocks written to each disk in turn), which does not provide any form of fault tolerance. RAID 5 combines disk striping with distributed storage of parity information.

106. C. An incremental backup is a job that backs up all of the files that have changed since the last backup of any kind. Therefore, to restore a system that failed on Monday at noon, you would have to restore the most recent full backup from the previous Wednesday and the incrementals from Thursday, Friday, Saturday, and Sunday.

107. D. An incremental backup is a job that backs up all of the files that have changed since the last backup of any kind. Therefore, to restore a system that failed on Tuesday at noon, you would have to restore the most recent full backup from the previous Saturday and the incrementals from Sunday, Monday, and Tuesday morning.

108. B. A differential backup is a job that backs up all the files that have changed since the last full backup. Therefore, to restore a system that failed on Tuesday at noon, you would have to restore the most recent full backup from the previous Wednesday and the most recent differential from Monday.

109. C. Data is stored on tape drives in a linear fashion. Once you write backup data to a tape, you cannot selectively replace individual files. When you perform a restore job, you might have to restore the most recent full backup, followed by incremental backups, which overwrites some of the full backup files with newer ones. Hard disk drives are random access devices, meaning that individual files can be written to and read from any location on the disk. When you perform incremental backup jobs to a hard disk, the software can restore data using any version of each file that is available. Data capacity, transfer speed, and block size are not relevant.

110. C. Simple Network Monitoring Protocol (SNMP) is a means of tracking the performance and functionality of network components. Software or firmware components called agents are embedded in network devices and communicate with a central monitoring console. SNMP does not provide fault tolerance. An uninterruptible power supply (UPS) is a battery backup device that enables a computer to continue functioning in the event of a power failure. Redundant Array of Independent Disks (RAID) level 1 is a disk mirroring mechanism that provides fault tolerance by maintaining duplicate copies of all stored data. Clustering is a mechanism by which multiple servers function as a single unit, running the same application, so that if a server should fail, the others continue to function.

111. A. A snapshot is a read-only copy of a data set taken at a specific moment in time. By creating a snapshot and then backing it up, you can be sure that no data corruption has occurred due to version skew. A hot site is an alternative network location in which all hardware and software is installed and ready. Incrementals and differentials are types of backup jobs.

112. A, D. A backup of a firewall's state includes its configuration as well as other elements, such as templates and policies. The state therefore contains more data than the configuration.

113. A, D. In an active-active configuration, servers can balance the incoming client load between them. Because the active servers are all servicing clients, the overall performance of the cluster is increased. Both active-active and active-passive configurations provide fault tolerance. Data encapsulation is not a factor in either configuration.

114. D. Access to the Internet can be interrupted by a failure on the Internet service provider's (ISP's) network, by a failure on the wide area network (WAN) provider's network, or by a router failure on the local network. Building redundancy into all of these elements is the best way to ensure continuous access to the Internet.

115. A, B, D. Configuring the router to split incoming packets between the two firewalls provides load balancing and a resulting performance increase. If one firewall should fail, the parallel arrangement enables the other one to take over the processing of all incoming packets, providing fault tolerance. Two firewalls in parallel do not provide additional security.

116. B, D. When a client sends a name resolution query to its DNS server, it uses a recursive request so that the server will take on the responsibility for resolving the name. The only other use of recursive requests is in the case of a forwarder, which is configured to pass that responsibility on to another server. All of the other queries issued by the client's server to the various domain authorities are iterative queries.

117. A. Most wireless routers are designed to provide connecting workstations with IP addresses and other TCP/IP configuration parameters. Switches and bridges are Data link layer devices, and hubs are Physical layer devices, none of which are capable of providing clients with Network layer IP addresses.

118. A, E. DHCP and BOOTP are both designed to allocate IP addresses to hosts. The primary difference between the two is that DHCP is capable of dynamic allocation and BOOTP is not.

DNS resolves hostnames into IP addresses, and ARP resolves IP addresses into Data link layer hardware (or MAC) addresses. FTP is designed to transfer files between systems and has no role in IP address allocation.

119. D. Like A and AAAA records, pointer records (PTRs) contain hostnames and IP addresses, but they are used for reverse name resolution—that is, resolving IP addresses into hostnames. A mail exchange (MX) record specifies the mail server that the domain should use. Canonical name (CNAME) records specify aliases for a given hostname. An AAAA resource record maps a hostname to an IPv6 address for name resolution purposes.

120. A. Dynamic Host Configuration Protocol (DHCP) can dynamically allocate IP addresses to clients and reclaim them when their leases expire. Bootstrap Protocol (BOOTP) and Reverse Address Resolution Protocol (RARP) can allocate addresses automatically or manually, but they cannot reclaim them. DHCP and BOOTP both support relay agents.

121. A, B, D, E. In a successful DHCP address allocation, the client issues DHCPDISCOVER broadcasts to locate servers, and the servers reply with DHCPOFFER messages containing addresses. Then, the client sends a DHCPREQUEST message to one server accepting an offered address, to which the server replies with a DHCPACK. DHCPNAK messages are only used in unsuccessful transactions, and DHCPRENEW, DHCPRELEASE, and DHCPINFORM messages are not used during the address allocation process.

122. D, E. In a successful DHCP address renewal transaction, the client issues a DHCPDREQUEST message, and the server replies with a DHCPACK. DHCPNAK messages are only used in unsuccessful transactions, and the other message types are not used during the address renewal process.

123. D. Dynamic Host Configuration Protocol (DHCP) is a protocol designed to allocate IP addresses to clients. Address Resolution Protocol (ARP), on the other hand, resolves existing IP addresses into Data link layer MAC (or hardware) addresses. Internet Control Message Protocol (ICMP) is a protocol used to perform Network layer tests and exchange error messages. The Domain Name System (DNS) protocol is used to exchange name resolution traffic.

124. A. When a DNS server receives an iterative query, it responds immediately with the best information that it has available, or with an error message. It does not send queries to other servers.

125. D. The client component of the Domain Name System (DNS) is called the resolver. *Requestor* is a generic term for any system issuing requests, and only DNS servers can be authorities or forwarders.

126. D. The Preferred DNS Server parameter contains the address of a server that resolves domain names into IP addresses. The IP address parameter specifies the address of the current computer, not the address of a server. The Subnet Mask parameter differentiates the network bits of the IP address from the host bits. The Default Gateway parameter defines the local router to be used to access other networks.

127. C. Stable is not a DHCP allocation method. DHCP supports three allocation methods: manual, dynamic, and automatic.

128. B. On a DHCP server, you create a scope that consists of a beginning and an ending IP address. *Range*, *pool*, and *subnet* are not technical terms for DHCP.

129. B, D. DHCP clients cannot contact servers on different networks to initiate an address assignment. Clients locate DHCP servers by transmitting broadcast messages, and broadcasts are limited to the local network. Relay agents forward the broadcast messages to other networks, enabling the server to assign IP addresses to clients on other subnets. DHCP does not require special licenses. DHCP uses User Datagram Protocol (UDP) transmissions, not TCP.

130. C. An AAAA resource record maps a hostname to an IPv6 address for name resolution purposes. A mail exchange (MX) record specifies the mail server that the domain should use. Pointer records (PTRs) also contain hostnames and IP addresses, but they are used for reverse name resolution—that is, resolving IP addresses into hostnames. Name server (NS) records identify the authoritative name servers used for the current zone.

131. B. A canonical name (CNAME) resource record specifies an alternative host name (or alias) for a system already registered in the DNS. By creating a CNAME record specifying the www name, the server can be addressed using either NE6 or www. Creating an additional A resource record will cause the server to be recognized using one name or the other, but not both. Modifying the existing A record will change the hostname. Text (TXT) records associate administrator-supplied text with a zone but perform no other functions. PTR resource records are used only for reverse name resolution.

132. A. The Router option specifies the addresses of routers on the local network, including the default gateway router. The Time Server option specifies the addresses of servers that provide time signals to the network. The Name Server option specifies the addresses of up to 10 name resolution servers (other than DNS servers) on the network. The LPR Server option specifies the addresses of line printer servers on the network. The Lease Time option specifies the length of the default address lease.

133. B. DHCP clients use broadcasts to transmit DHCPDISCOVER messages on the local network. DHCP servers are then required to respond to the broadcasts. DHCP clients cannot use unicast, multicast, or anycast messages to initiate contact with DHCP servers, because they have no way of learning their addresses.

134. A. The name server (NS) resource record identifies the authoritative name servers for a particular DNS zone. Pointer records (PTRs) are used to resolve IP addresses into hostnames. Mail exchange (MX) records identify the mail servers for a particular domain. Service records (SRVs) identify the designated servers for a particular application. The start of authority (SOA) record indicates the delegation of a domain's administrative control from its parent domain. A text (TXT) record associates administrator-supplied text with a zone but performs no other function.

135. C. On a DHCP server, a reservation is a permanent IP address assignment to a specific MAC address. A scope is a range of IP addresses to be allocated to clients. An exclusion is a range of IP addresses that is to be excluded from a scope. A relay is a component that routes DHCP traffic between networks.

136. B. Dynamic allocation enables a Dynamic Host Configuration Protocol (DHCP) server to lease IP addresses to clients for a specific time interval. When the lease period expires, the client can renew it, if it is still using the address. If the address is no longer in use when the lease expires, it is returned to the scope of available leases for reallocation. Automatic allocation permanently assigns an IP address from the scope to a client. *Manual* and *static allocation* are two terms that describe the allocation of a specific IP address to a specific client.

137. B. Dynamic DNS (DDNS) is an addition to the DNS standards that eliminates the need for administrators to manually create certain DNS resource records. For example, when a DHCP server allocates an address to a client, DDNS creates a host (A) record containing the hostname of the client and the newly allocated IP address. Reverse name resolution is the process of looking up hostnames based on IP addresses. Automatic allocation is a DHCP process by which IP addresses are permanently assigned to clients. HOSTS is a text-based name resolution method that predates DNS.

138. D. The term *stratum*, plus an integer, describes the distance in time of an NTP server from its time source in terms of the NTP server hierarchy. Stratum 0 represents an atomic clock or other precision timekeeping device. Stratum 1 represents an NTP server synchronized to within a few milliseconds of its Stratum 0 time source. Stratum 2 is a server synchronized to a Stratum 1 server, and so on. *Layer*, *path*, and *iteration* are not technical terms used by the NTP.

139. C, E. The Network Time Protocol (NTP) is used to synchronize computer clocks. Time signals can be provided by internal servers or time servers on the Internet. The Precision Time Protocol (PTP) performs a similar function, except that it can achieve greater accuracy than NTP on a local network. Network Time Security (NTS) is a protocol that provides cryptographic security for NTP transactions. The Hypertext Transfer Protocol Secure (HTTPS) is used to exchange web traffic between clients and servers. The Simple Mail Transfer Protocol (SMTP) is used to transmit email traffic between clients and servers.

140. D. The topmost layer in the DNS hierarchy is represented by `org`, which is a top-level domain. `mydomain` is a second-level domain registered by a particular organization; `paris` is a subdomain within `mydomain`; and `www` is the name of a particular host in the `paris .mydomain.org` domain.

141. B. The Default IP Time-to-Live (TTL) option specifies the maximum number of seconds or hops allowed to an IP datagram before a router removes it from the network. This prevents datagrams from circulating endlessly. The Interface Maximum Transmission Unit (MTU) option specifies the maximum size of an IP datagram. The Address Resolution Protocol (ARP) Cache Timeout specifies how long entries containing the IP address assigned by the server can remain in the cache maintained by a client's ARP implementation. The Transmission Control Protocol (TCP) Keepalive Interval option specifies the number of seconds that the client should wait before transmitting a keepalive message over a TCP connection.

142. B, C. The external DNS server should contain records only for the resources that must be accessible from the Internet, such as web servers and public email servers. For security reasons, servers containing sensitive data, such as database servers and domain controllers, should be registered on the internal DNS server.

143. B. When there are no IP addresses available for lease in a DHCP scope, Automatic Private IP Addressing (APIPA) takes over, and the system self-assigns an address on the 169.254.0.0/16 network. Clients are not assigned a 0.0.0.0 address, nor are their requests forwarded to another DHCP server. Sharing IP addresses is not possible on a TCP/IP network.

144. B. Decreasing the lease time for the scope will cause abandoned IP addresses to be returned to the scope for reallocation more quickly, which would lessen the chances of exhausting the scope. Increasing the lease time will make scope exhaustion more likely. Installing another DHCP server or creating another scope will have no effect, because the limitation is the number of addresses allocated for the subnet.

145. A, B, D. DHCP relay, UDP forwarding, and IP helper are all router mechanisms that perform the same task, forwarding broadcast messages on one subnet to a specific IP address on another subnet as a unicast message. This enables DHCP clients to contact DHCP servers on another subnet to obtain IP addresses. Zone transfer is a DNS zone replication mechanism not used by DHCP clients or servers.

146. D. A zone transfer is a client/server transaction between two DNS servers in which one server requests a copy of the other server's entire zone database, to update its own. None of the other options are used for DNS database replication. Multi-master replication is a technique that enables two systems to exchange database information as needed to update each other. UDP forwarding is a router mechanism used by DHCP to forward broadcast messages on one subnet to a specific IP address on another subnet. An iterative query is a type of DNS message that transfers responsibility for a name lookup to another server.

147. B. A forward zone uses a hierarchy based on domain names to allow resolution of DNS names into IP addresses. A reverse zone is based on the in.addr-arpa domain and uses a hierarchy based on the individual decimal values in IP addresses. Without the reverse zone, the server will be unable to resolve IP addresses into DNS names. DNS servers can send and respond to queries without a reverse zone.

148. B, D, E. Resource record signature (RRSIG), DNSKEY, and delegation signer (DS) are all resource records created specifically for use with DNSSEC. The SRV, NS, and RP resource records are defined in the original DNS specifications.

149. B, C, F. To provide security for DNS data, the DNS over HTTPS (DoH) and DNS over TLS (DoT) specifications enable DNS transactions to use secured protocols to exchange messages. DNSSEC provides cryptographic security directly within the DNS messages. Stateless address autoconfiguration (SLAAC) does not provide security to DNS. DNS over IPsec and DNS over STP do not exist.

150. A, D. DHCPv6 is stateful, meaning that the IPv6 address assignment are stored on the DHCPv6 server. Stateless address autoconfiguration (SLAAC), as the name implies, is stateless, meaning that the mechanism does not keep track of the addresses it assigns.

151. B. VPN typically enables remote clients to connect to a VPN router at a central site, much like the star/hub and spoke topology of a local area network, in which computers are all connected to a central switch. Dynamic multipoint virtual private network (DMVPN) is a technology that creates a mesh topology between the remote VPN sites, enabling the remote sites to connect directly to each other, rather than to the central VPN server. A virtual private network (VPN) concentrator is a type of router that enables multiple client systems to access a network from remote locations. A Session Initiation Protocol (SIP) trunk provides a connection between the private and public domains of a unified communications network. Multiprotocol Label Switching (MPLS) is a data transfer mechanism that assigns labels to individual packets, and then routes the packets based on those labels. Clientless VPN creates an encrypted tunnel to a server using a browser, without the need to install additional client software.

152. C. Point-to-Point Tunneling Protocol (PPTP) is considered to be obsolete for VPN use because of several serious security vulnerabilities that have been found in it. IPsec, Layer 2 Tunneling Protocol (L2TP), and Secure Sockets Layer/Transport Layer Security (SSL/TLS) are all still in use.

153. C. Layer 2 Tunneling Protocol (L2TP) is used to create the tunnel forming a VPN connection, but it does not encrypt the traffic passing through the tunnel. To do this, it requires a separate protocol that provides encryption, such as IPsec. Although both are now obsolete, Point-to-Point Tunneling Protocol (PPTP) and Secure Sockets Layer (SSL) are both capable of encrypting tunneled traffic.

154. A, B, C. Although the computers do not have to use hardware made by the same manufacturer, both must use the same basic type of WAN connection, such as a leased line or an Internet connection. Both of the computers must also use the same Data link layer protocol, such as PPP, to establish a remote network connection. Most remote network connections use some form of authentication mechanism, even if it is nothing more than the exchange of a username and cleartext password. To establish the remote network connection, both computers must be configured to use the same type of authentication, even if it is no authentication at all. As long as all of the other elements are in place, such as the Physical layer connection and the protocols, there is no need for both of the computers involved in a remote network connection to be running the same operating system.

155. C. Secure Shell (SSH) is a character-based tool that enables users to execute commands on remote computers. It does not provide web server/browser security. Secure Sockets Layer (SSL) is a security protocol that provides encrypted communications between web browsers and servers. Transport Layer Security (TLS) is an updated security protocol that is designed to replace SSL. Datagram Transport Layer Security (DTLS) is a security protocol that provides the same basic functions as TLS, but for User Datagram Protocol (UDP) traffic.

156. D. An extranet VPN is designed to provide clients, vendors, and other outside partners with the ability to connect to your corporate network with limited access. A client-to-site VPN is a remote access solution, enabling users to access the corporate network from home or while traveling. A site-to-site VPN enables a branch office to connect to the home office using the Internet rather than a more expensive wide area network (WAN) connection. A client-to-client VPN enables two individual users to establish a protected connection to each other.

157. B. Trivial File Transfer Protocol (TFTP) is typically used to download boot image files to computers performing a Preboot Execution Environment (PXE) startup. It is not used for remote control. Remote Desktop Protocol (RDP) is used by Remote Desktop Services in Windows to provide clients with graphical control over servers at remote locations. Secure Shell (SSH) and Telnet are both character-based tools that enable users to execute commands on remote computers.

158. A. RDP is a component of Remote Desktop Services, a Windows mechanism that enables a client program to connect to a server and control it remotely. RDP does not carry actual application data; it just transfers keystrokes, mouse movements, and graphical user interface (GUI) display information. Because the client program does not participate in the application computing on the server, it is known as a thin client. RDP does not provide clientless virtual private networking, encrypted tunneling, or unauthenticated file transfers.

159. B. A site-to-site VPN enables one network to connect to another, enabling users on both networks to access resources on the other one. This is usually a more economical solution for branch office connections than a wide area network (WAN) link. A client-to-site VPN is a remote access solution, enabling users to access the corporate network from home or while traveling. A client-to-client VPN enables two individual users to establish a protected connection to each other. An extranet VPN is designed to provide clients, vendors, and other outside partners with the ability to connect to a corporate network with limited access.

160. C. EAP is the only authentication protocol included with Windows 11 that supports hardware-based authentication, so this is the only viable option. PAP transmits passwords in cleartext and is therefore not a viable option. Neither is CHAP, because it must store passwords using reversible encryption. MSCHAPv2 provides sufficient password protection but does not support the hardware-based authentication needed for smartcard use.

161. B, C. RDP is a component of Remote Desktop Services, a Windows mechanism that enables a client program to connect to a server and control it remotely. RDP does not carry actual application data; it just transfers keystrokes, mouse movements, and graphic display information. Virtual Network Computing (VNC) is a similar desktop sharing system that is platform independent and open source. Secure Shell (SSH) and Telnet are console-based remote control solutions.

162. D. The term *virtual desktop* does not refer to a projection device that can display a computer desktop on a screen. A virtual desktop can be a realization of a computer monitor in a virtual reality environment; a virtualized desktop larger than the monitor, which users can scroll to view all parts of the display; or a cloud-based service provided by Microsoft Azure that provides users with access to their desktops using remote devices.

163. A, B, C. RDP is a component of Remote Desktop Services, a Windows mechanism that enables a client program to connect to a server and control it remotely. RDP does not carry actual application data; it just transfers keystrokes, mouse movements, and graphic display information.

164. A, B, C. VNC is a graphical desktop sharing system that uses a protocol called Remote Frame Buffer (RFB) to connect a client to a server and control it remotely. VNC does not transmit actual application data; it just transfers keystrokes, mouse movements, and graphic display information.

165. A, C. Telnet is a console-based remote control protocol and application that is available on virtually all computing platforms. Because it is strictly character based, Telnet clients transmit only keystrokes and receive only character-based display information from the server. They do not carry mouse movements or application data.

166. C. Remote Desktop Gateway is a Windows Server role that enables remote users outside the network to establish a Remote Desktop Protocol (RDP) connection without the need for a virtual private network (VPN) connection. The gateway does not provide multiple Remote Desktop client access to one workstation, Remote Desktop client access to multiple workstations, or access to workstations without a Remote Desktop client.

167. B, C. Out-of-band management uses a dedicated channel to devices on the network. This means that the device to be managed does not require an IP address. The dedicated channel provides access to the BIOS or UEFI firmware and makes it possible to reinstall the operating system on a remote computer. SSH, VNC, and API connections are not out-of-band management tools.

168. C. Out-of-band management refers to the use of an alternative communications channel to a network device. The channel can be a modem connection, a direct cable connection, a wireless or cellular connection, or a dedicated Ethernet connection.

169. A, C, D, F. A computer requires four components to establish a remote connection. First, a Physical layer wide area network (WAN) connection is needed. Second, the two systems must share common protocols from the Data link layer and above. Third, if TCP/IP is being used to establish a remote session, then TCP/IP parameters must be configured on the systems. Fourth, host and remote software are needed. The remote client must have software that enables it to establish a remote session, and the server must have software that enables it to receive and grant remote sessions. Microsoft RAS supports both client and server remote access software; however, this is not a required component since other types of software can be used. PPTP is an obsolete tunneling protocol and is not a required component for establishing a remote session.

170. B. When users connect to a remote network using VPN, they become a participant on that network, which includes using the remote network's Internet connection. Therefore, when a user opens a browser, the application passes the user's requests through the VPN tunnel to the remote server, which uses the default gateway and Internet connection at the remote site to connect to the desired address. This is inherently slower than connecting the browser directly to the Internet from the client computer.

171. D. A site-to-site VPN connection connects two remote local area networks (LANs) together, enabling users on either network to access the other one. The typical configuration would consist of two VPN concentrators, one at each site, functioning as the endpoints of the connection.

172. C. A client-to-site VPN connection connects a single workstation to a remote local area network (LAN), enabling the workstation user to access the remote network's resources. The typical configuration would consist of a standalone workstation and a VPN concentrator at the network site functioning as the endpoints of the connection.

173. B, C. The two most common types of TLS/SSL VPN connection are TLS/SSL portals, which provide users with access to selected remote network resources through a standard website, and TLS/SSL tunnels, which require the client web browser to run an active control, typically using a language such as Java. TLS/SSL client and TLS/SSL gateway are not common TLS/SSL VPN connections.

174. A. A client-to-client VPN connection connects two individual workstations at different locations, enabling the users on each workstation to access the other one through a secure tunnel. The typical configuration would consist of two workstations, one at each site, functioning as the endpoints of the connection.

175. A. The term *out-of-band* is used to describe any type of management access to a device that does not go through the production network. Plugging a laptop into the console port avoids the network, so it is considered to be an example of out-of-band management. In-band management describes an access method that goes through the production network. Client-to-site is a type of VPN connection, and bring your own device (BYOD) is a policy defining whether and how users are permitted to connect their personal devices to the network.

176. A, B. Because the two endpoints of a VPN are connecting to local Internet service providers (ISPs), the ongoing connection costs are typically much less than a long distance WAN connection. However, in most cases, a VPN is slower because it is affected by Internet bandwidth use and other factors. VPN connections are not inherently less secure than WANs, and they are not necessarily more difficult to maintain.

177. B, C, D. Any method of connecting to a router, switch, or other managed device that does not use the production network is considered to be out-of-band management. This includes connecting a computer or terminal directly to the device, using a point-to-point modem connection, or consolidating dedicated ports on all of the devices by connecting them to an isolated switch. Logging on remotely using a workstation on the production network would be considered in-band management, as would API access.

178. A. Telnet (TELetype NETwork) was the first TCP/IP terminal emulation program, but it is rarely used today because of its limitations. It is character-based only, and it transmits all data as cleartext, which is insecure. Secure Shell (SSH) addresses the security problem, but it too is character-based. Windows Terminal Services and Virtual Network Computing (VNC) were both created to provide graphical terminal emulation.

179. A, C, D. Tunneling is the process of encapsulating a data packet within another packet. The system then encrypts the entire data packet. Message integrity enables the recipient to detect any data tampering. Authentication ensures that only the intended recipient can access the data. There is no applicable technique called socketing.

180. B, C. A basic VPN typically uses full tunneling, in which all of the system's network traffic is encapsulated and encrypted for transmission. Split tunneling is a variation of this method in which only part of the system's traffic uses the VPN connection; the rest is transmitted over the network in the normal manner. Administrators can select which applications and devices use the VPN. Split tunneling can conserve internet bandwidth used by the VPN and provide access to local services without the need for encapsulation. Split tunneling does not provide additional data integrity protection or improved performance through multiplexing.

181. C. Telnet transmits keystrokes in cleartext, including usernames and passwords. It is therefore insecure. Secure Shell (SSH) improves on the performance of Telnet by encrypting the passwords and other data it transmits over the network. Like Telnet, SSH is free and does not support graphical terminal emulation. SSH is also no faster than Telnet.

182. A. RDP is the client/server protocol created for use with Windows Terminal Services, now known as Remote Desktop Services. It is not used with VNC, Citrix products, or Telnet.

183. C. A jump box is a workstation that is connected both to the standard LAN and to the new SAN, enabling administrators to use SAN management tools in a secure environment. To do this, Alice must install two network adapters in the jump box: an Ethernet adapter to connect to the LAN and a Fibre Channel adapter to connect to the SAN. None of the other options would create a jump box.

Chapter 4: Network Security

1. C. Windows networks that use AD DS authenticate clients using the Kerberos protocol, in part because it never transmits passwords over the network, even in encrypted form. RADIUS is an authentication, authorization, and accounting (AAA) service for remote users connecting to a network. Windows does not use it for internal clients. WPA2 is a security protocol used by wireless LAN networks; it is not used for AD DS authentication. EAP-TLS is a remote authentication protocol that AD DS networks do not use for internal clients.

2. C, D. *Multifactor authentication* (MFA) combines two or more authentication methods and reduces the likelihood that an intruder would be able to successfully impersonate a user during the authentication process. A password and a retinal scan is an example of a multifactor authentication system. A smartcard and a PIN, which is the equivalent of a password, is an example of multifactor authentication because it requires users to supply something they know and something they have. Multifactor authentication refers to the proofs of identity a system requires, not the number of servers used to implement the system. Therefore, the use of a RADIUS server does not make for an example of multifactor authentication. A system that requires two passwords is not an example of multifactor authentication, because an attacker can compromise two passwords as easily as one. A multifactor authentication system requires two different forms of authentication. Time-based authentication is possible, but the time itself is not an authentication factor.

3. E. Social engineering is a means for gaining unauthorized access to a network by convincing users to disclose passwords or other sensitive information; it is not part of a defense in depth strategy. Defense in depth can include physical protection, such as access control vestibules; division of resources using network segmentation, separation of duties, or screened subnets; and deceptive lures, such as honeypots.

4. A. The Extensible Authentication Protocol (EAP) is the only Windows remote authentication protocol that supports the use of authentication methods other than passwords, such as smartcards. MS-CHAPv2 is a strong remote access authentication protocol, but it supports password authentication only; users cannot use smartcards. The Challenge Handshake Authentication Protocol (CHAP) is a relatively weak authentication protocol that does not support the use of smartcards. The Password Authentication Protocol (PAP) supports only cleartext passwords, not smartcards.

5. B. Multifactor authentication (MFA) combines two or more authentication methods, requiring a user to supply multiple credentials. This reduces the likelihood that an intruder would be able to successfully impersonate a user during the authentication process. The term *multifactor* does not refer to the number of resources, devices, or groups with which the user is associated.

6. C, D. Accounting and auditing are both methods of tracking and recording a user's activities on a network, such as when a user logged on and how long they remained connected. Authentication is the confirmation of a user's identity, and authorization defines the type of access granted to authenticated users.

7. A. Authentication is the process of confirming a user's identity. Passwords are one of the authentication factors commonly used by network devices. Authorization defines the type of access granted to authenticated users. Accounting and auditing are both methods of tracking and recording a user's activities on a network, such as when a user logged on and how long they remained connected.

8. A. Authentication is the process of confirming a user's identity. Fingerprints and other biometric readers are some of the authentication factors commonly used by network devices. Authorization defines the type of access granted to authenticated users. Accounting and auditing are both methods of tracking and recording a user's activities on a network, such as when a user logged on and how long they remained connected.

9. A. Kerberos is a security protocol used by Active Directory that employs a system of tickets to authenticate users and other network entities without the need to transmit credentials over the network. IEEE 802.1X does authenticate by transmitting credentials. Temporal Key Integrity Protocol (TKIP) and Lightweight Directory Access Protocol (LDAP) are not authentication protocols.

10. C. Auditing of authentication activities can record both successful and unsuccessful logon attempts. Large numbers of logon failures can indicate attempts to crack passwords. Auditing tracks the time of authentication attempts, sometimes enabling you to detect off-hours logons that indicate an intrusion. Auditing does not record the passwords specified during authentications, so it cannot identify patterns of unsuccessful guesses.

11. A. Authentication is the process of confirming a user's identity. Smartcards are one of the authentication factors commonly used by network devices. Authorization defines the type of access granted to authenticated users. Accounting and auditing are both methods of tracking and recording a user's activities on a network, such as when a user logged on and how long they remained connected.

12. A. Multifactor authentication combines two or more authentication methods and reduces the likelihood that an intruder would be able to successfully impersonate a user during the authentication process. A password (something you know) and a retinal scan (something you are) is an example of a multifactor authentication system. A smartcard and a PIN, which is the equivalent of a password, is another example of multifactor authentication because it requires users to supply something they know and something they have. *Multisegment,* *multimetric,* and *multifiltered* are not applicable terms in this context.

13. A, B, C, E. HVAC sensors can measure temperatures and humidity in climate-controlled areas, such as datacenters; atmospheric pressure in devices like boilers and compressors; and occupancy, to control conditions based on the presence of people. Printers, cameras, door locks, and other physical access control devices are not part of an HVAC system.

14. C. Single sign-on (SSO) uses one set of credentials and requires the user to supply them only once to gain access to multiple resources. Same sign-on also uses a single set of credentials, with one password, but the user must perform individual logons for each resource. Neither single sign-on nor same sign-on calls for multifactor authentication.

15. C. Biometrics is a type of authentication factor that uses a physical characteristic that uniquely identifies an individual, such as a fingerprint or a retinal pattern. Therefore, biometrics is best described as something you are, as opposed to something you know, something you have, or something you do.

16. B. Something you have refers to a physical possession that serves to identify a user, such as a smartcard. This type of authentication is typically used as part of a multifactor authentication procedure because a smartcard or other physical possession can be lost or stolen. A fingerprint would be considered something you are, a password something you know, and a finger gesture something you do.

17. D. Terminal Access Controller Access Control System Plus (TACACS+) is a protocol designed to provide AAA services for networks with many routers and switches, enabling administrators to access them with a single set of credentials. It was not designed to provide AAA services for wireless networks, Active Directory, or remote dial-in users.

18. C. Terminal Access Controller Access Control System Plus (TACACS+) is a protocol that was designed to provide AAA services for networks with many routers and switches. AAA stands for authentication, authorization, and accounting, but not administration.

19. B, C. A PIN, like a password, is something you know, and a thumbprint, or any other biometric factor, is something you are. An example of something you have would be a smartcard, and an example of something you do would be a finger gesture.

20. D. The act of drawing on the screen with your finger is a gesture, which is an example of something you do. A PIN or a password is something you know; a thumbprint, or any other biometric factor, is something you are; and a smartcard is an example of something you have.

21. E. Something you do refers to a physical action performed by a user, such as a finger gesture, which helps to confirm their identity. This type of authentication is often used as part of a multifactor authentication procedure because a gesture or other action can be imitated.

A fingerprint would be considered something you are, a password something you know, and a smartcard something you have. A self-signed certificate is not an authentication factor because it provides no outside verification of identity.

22. C. Something you know refers to information you supply during the authentication process, such as a password or PIN. This is the most common type of authentication factor because it cannot be lost or stolen unless the user violates security policies. A fingerprint would be considered something you are, a finger gesture something you do, and a smartcard something you have.

23. A. Something you are refers to a physical characteristic that uniquely identifies an individual, such as a fingerprint or other form of biometric. This type of authentication is often used as part of a multifactor authentication procedure because a biometric element can conceivably be compromised. A finger gesture would be considered something you do, a password something you know, and a smartcard something you have.

24. C, D. *Data in motion* and *data in transit* are the terms used to describe network traffic. Data in use describes endpoint actions, and data at rest describes data storage.

25. A. *Data in use* is the DLP term used to describe endpoint access, such as a user loading data into an application. Data at rest describes data storage. *Data in motion* is the term used to describe network traffic. *Data in process* is not one of the standard DLP terms.

26. B. Data at rest describes data that is currently in storage while not in use. *Data in motion* is the term used to describe network traffic. Data in use describes endpoint actions working with the data, and *data on disk* is not one of the standard data loss prevention terms.

27. A, E. *Data online* and *data locality* are not standard data loss prevention (DLP) terms. *Data at rest* is a DLP term that describes data that is currently in storage while not in use. *Data in motion* is the term used to describe network traffic. Data in use describes endpoint actions.

28. B, C. Remote Authentication Dial-In User Service (RADIUS) and Terminal Access Controller Access Control System Plus (TACACS+) are both services that provide networks with authentication, authorization, and accounting. 802.1X provides only authentication, and Lightweight Directory Access Protocol (LDAP) provides communication between directory service entities. Security Assertion Markup Language (SAML) is a standard for the exchange of authentication and authorization data, but it does not define a full-featured authentication, authorization, and accounting (AAA) solution.

29. B. The five functional levels in a distributed control system such as SCADA are field level, direct control, plant supervisory, production control, and production scheduling. Remote access is not one of the levels.

30. A. Remote Authentication Dial-In User Service (RADIUS) was originally conceived to provide AAA services for Internet service providers (ISPs), which at one time ran networks with hundreds of modems providing dial-up access to subscribers. Terminal Access Controller Access Control System Plus (TACACS+) is a protocol that was designed to provide AAA services for networks with many routers and switches, but not for dial-up connections. Kerberos and Lightweight Directory Access Protocol (LDAP) are not AAA services.

31. A. RADIUS uses User Datagram Protocol (UDP) ports 1812 and 1813 or 1645 and 1646 for authentication, whereas TACACS+ uses TCP port 49.

32. B. Terminal Access Controller Access Control System Plus (TACACS+) is a protocol designed to provide AAA services for networks with many routers and switches, enabling administrators to access them with a single set of credentials. Remote Authentication Dial-In User Service (RADIUS) provides AAA services, but not for routers and switches. Kerberos and Lightweight Directory Access Protocol (LDAP) are not AAA services.

33. C. Authorization is the process of determining what resources a user can access on a network. Typically, this is done by assessing the user's group memberships. Authentication is the process of confirming a user's identity. Accounting is the process of tracking a user's network activity. Access control is the creation of permissions that provide users and groups with specific types of access to a resource.

34. A. Authentication is the process of confirming a user's identity by checking credentials, such as passwords, ID cards, or fingerprints. Authorization is the process of determining what resources a user can access on a network. Accounting is the process of tracking a user's network activity. Access control is the creation of permissions that provide users and groups with specific types of access to a resource.

35. B. Accounting is the process of tracking a user's network activity, such as when the user logged on and logged off and what resources the user accessed. Authentication is the process of confirming a user's identity by checking credentials. Authorization is the process of determining what resources a user can access on a network. Access control is the creation of permissions that provide users and groups with specific types of access to a resource.

36. B, D. In a public key infrastructure (PKI), data encrypted with a user's public key can only be decrypted with the user's private key and data encrypted with a user's private key can only be decrypted with the user's public key. This enables the system to provide both message encryption and nonrepudiation. If data encrypted with a user's public key could be decrypted with that same public key, the system would provide no security at all. If data encrypted with a user's private key could be decrypted with that same private key, the user could only send secure messages to him- or herself.

37. A. A Remote Authentication Dial-In User Service (RADIUS) server can provide authentication, authorization, and accounting services for remote access servers. Intrusion detection systems (IDSs), next-generation firewalls (NGFWs), and network attached storage (NAS) devices do not provide authentication services.

38. B. The integrity element of the CIA triad prevents data from being modified by unauthorized users. Confidentiality is protection against unauthorized viewing of data. Availability provides users with access to the data they need.

39. C. Systems that use local authentication have user accounts stored on the computer, enabling users to log on without the need for any network communication. Systems that use RADIUS or Kerberos for authentication require network communication. A password and a retinal scan is an example of a multifactor authentication system, which might or might not be local.

40. B. A honeypot is a computer configured to function as bait for attackers, causing them to waste their time penetrating a resource that provides no significant access. A screened subnet (also called a perimeter network, a demilitarized zone, or a DMZ) is the part of a network where administrators locate servers that must be accessible from the Internet. A root guard provides protection to switch ports. Spoofing is an attack technique in which an intruder modifies packets to assume the appearance of another user or computer.

41. A. A honeypot or honeynet is a type of deception technology that takes the form of a computer or network configured to function as bait for attackers, causing them to waste their time penetrating a resource that provides no significant access.

42. D. Penetration testing is a process in which an outside consultant is engaged to attempt an unauthorized access to protected network resources. Testing by an internal administrator familiar with the security barriers would not be a valid test. While having a consultant examine the network's security from within can be useful, this is not a penetration test. Computers or networks that are alluring targets for intruders are called honeypots or honeynets.

43. B. A vulnerability is a weakness, whether in software or hardware, of which an exploit is designed to take advantage. Neither term is specific to hardware or software.

44. C. A zero-day vulnerability is a serious software problem with a potential for exploitation in a newly released software product. The vulnerability has not yet been discovered, addressed, or patched by the software's developer, but it has been discovered by potential attackers. A zero-day vulnerability is one that has not yet been patched or fixed.

45. A, C. A threat assessment should estimate the potential severity of a threat, such as the damage that the loss of a specific resource can cause to the organization. The assessment should also estimate the likelihood of a particular threat occurring, as the organization will have to devote more attention to the more likely threats. An assessment of the organization's current posture (or status) with regard to a specific threat and the mitigation techniques used to counter it are both elements that come later in the risk management process, after the threat assessment has been completed.

46. B. A process assessment is an examination of an existing procedure to determine its compliance with a specific set of goals that can include cost, quality, and timeliness. A vendor assessment is an examination of the organization's relationship with a specific business partner. *Business assessment* and *risk assessment* are more general terms that can include process assessments.

47. B. Extensible Authentication Protocol (EAP) is a framework for the encapsulation of authentication messages. EAP is used on wireless networks and point-to-point connections and supports dozens of different authentication methods. Wi-Fi Protected Access (WPA) is a wireless encryption standard. Temporal Key Integrity Protocol (TKIP) is an encryption algorithm. Transport Layer Security (TLS) is an encryption protocol used for Internet communications. Bring your own device (BYOD) is a policy allowing users to connect their personal smartphones or other devices to the company network.

48. C. *Geofencing* is the generic term for a technology that limits access to a network or other resource based on the client's location. In wireless networking, geofencing is intended to prevent unauthorized clients outside the facility from connecting to the network. Local authentication is an application or service that triggers an authentication request to which the user must respond before access is granted. Port security is a method for protecting access to switch ports. Motion detection is a system designed to trigger a notification or alarm when an individual trespasses in a protected area.

49. A. Geofencing is a mechanism that is intended to prevent unauthorized clients outside the facility from connecting to the network. The mechanism can take the form of a signal strength or power level requirement, a GPS location requirement, or strategic placement of the antennae for wireless access points. The other options listed are not descriptions of typical geofencing technologies.

50. C. As part of the key management element of a public key infrastructure (PKI), digital certificates are associated with a key pair, consisting of a public key and a private key. The certificate is issued to a person or computer as proof of identity. An exploit is a hardware or software element that is designed to take advantage of a vulnerability. A signature does not associate a person or computer with a key pair. Resource records are associated with the Domain Name System (DNS).

51. A. File integrity monitoring (FIM) is a process that typically consists of a comparison of files in their current state to a known baseline copy stored elsewhere. The comparison can be direct, or it could involve the calculation of checksums or other types of file hashes. The object of the comparison is to detect changes in documents, both in content and in sensitive areas, such as credentials, privileges, and security settings, which might indicate the presence of a potential or actual security breach. Role separation applies to the deployment of applications on servers. Deauthentication is a type of wireless network attack. *Tamper detection* is a term used to describe a physical security measure for hardware. Router Advertisement (RA) guard is a feature found on certain switches that prevents the misuse of RA messages to redirect traffic.

52. C. Digital signatures can be used for the following functions: authentication, to confirm that data originated from a specific individual; nonrepudiation, to prevent the sender from denying the data's origin; and integrity, to confirm that the data has not been modified in transit. Segmentation is not a function of digital signatures.

53. A, B, C. Because only Ralph possesses the private key, only he could have signed and encrypted it. Although it is possible for someone other than Alice to have decrypted the document while it was in transit, using Ralph's public key, that individual could not have modified it and encrypted it again.

54. B, D. Because anyone can obtain Ralph's public key, the document can have been created and encrypted by anyone. However, because only Ralph possesses the private key that can decrypt the document, he can be sure that no one else has opened it while it was in transit.

55. D. *Geofencing* is the generic term for a technology that limits access to a network or other resource based on the client's location. Therefore, it is best described as somewhere you are. A finger gesture would be considered something you do, a password something you know, and a smartcard something you have.

56. B, C. Because many IoT devices are mobile or located in unprotected areas, a firewall is not a viable protection mechanism for all of them, nor is the practice of placing them on separate network segments. Network security mechanisms such as access control policies and centralized gateways providing authentication and authorization could conceivably be incorporated into a general IoT security standard.

57. D. Radio-frequency identification (RFID) uses tags containing data, frequently embedded in pets, which can be read using electromagnetic fields. Z-wave is a short-range wireless technology, frequently used for home automation. Bluetooth is a short-range wireless protocol, frequently used for computer peripherals and personal area networks (PANs). Near-field communication (NFC) provides wireless communication over ranges of 4 cm or less, and it is often used for contactless payment systems.

58. A. A key fob that unlocks your car is typically a short-range radio or infrared device that does not use the Internet for its communications. Each of the other examples describes a device with an IP address that uses the Internet to communicate with a controller, monitoring station, or other equipment.

59. E. The IoT consists of devices that are ordinarily passive but which have been made intelligent by configuring them to participate on an IP network. All of the devices listed are available as "smart" devices that enable remote users to interact with them over the Internet.

60. D. On-boarding and off-boarding are identity management processes in which users are added or removed from an organization's identity and access management (IAM) system. This grants new users the privileges they need to use the network, modifies their privileges if they change positions, and revokes privileges when they leave the company. On-boarding and off-boarding are not data loss prevention, incident response, inventory management, disaster recovery, or business continuity processes.

61. C. On-boarding and off-boarding are identity management processes in which users are added or removed from an organization's identity and access management (IAM) system. Off-boarding revokes a user's privileges when they leave the company. The term *off-boarding* does not refer to cluster management, disconnecting a switch, or retiring workstations.

62. D. An implicit deny is a policy that denies access to a resource by default, without a user-specific rule defining that denial. This type of policy is part of a least privilege authorization philosophy. Creating a new rule denying access is an explicit deny. If anyone were able to access the server remotely by default, that would be an implicit allow. An explicit allow is a rule granting specific users remote access.

63. A. MAC filtering takes the form of an access control list (ACL) on the wireless network's access points, listing the MAC addresses of all the devices that are to be permitted to access the network. If the MAC address of Alice's laptop is not included in the ACL, she will be unable to connect to the network. Alice has been given the service set identifier (SSID) of the network, so she should be able to connect, even if the access points are not broadcasting the SSID. Geofencing is intended to prevent users outside the office from accessing the network, so this should not be the problem. Alice has been given the passphrase for the network, so she should be able to configure WPA2 on her laptop. Alice is not using a separate guest network, so this is not preventing her from connecting.

64. C. General Data Protection Regulation (GDPR) is a European Union (EU) standard defining the protection of information privacy. PCI DSS is a US standard governing the handling of credit cards. SIEM is a combined solution for gathering and analyzing information about a network's security events, and SCADA is an industrial control system architecture; neither is an EU standard.

65. D. Role-based access control (RBAC) sets permissions based on each individual's job role or title, enabling administrators to create role configurations and apply them to multiple users. Single sign-on (SSO) allows a user to log on once with a single identity and then access multiple systems without the need to reauthenticate. Mandatory access control (MAC) is commonly used in government systems, which grant access to resources based on categorical assignments such as classified, secret, or top secret. Confidentiality, integrity, and availability are the elements that form the CIA triad, which is a common model used for the development of information security policies within an organization.

66. B. Ransomware is a type of attack in which a user's access to their data is blocked unless a certain amount of money is paid to the attacker. The blockages can vary from simple screen locks to data encryption. War driving is an attack method that consists of driving around a neighborhood with a computer, scanning for unprotected wireless networks. Denial-of-service is a type of attack that overwhelms a computer with traffic, preventing it from functioning properly. Address Resolution Protocol (ARP) poisoning is the deliberate insertion of fraudulent information into the ARP cache stored on computers and switches.

67. A, C. Spoofing is the process of modifying network packets to make them appear as though they are transmitted by or addressed to someone else. One way of doing this is to modify the MAC address in the packets to one that is approved by the MAC filter. An on-path (or man-in-the-middle) attack is one in which an attacker intercepts network traffic, reads the traffic, and can even modify it before sending it on to the destination. Denial-of-service is a type of attack that overwhelms a computer with traffic, preventing it from functioning properly, whereas a logic bomb is a code insert placed into a legitimate software product that triggers a malicious event when specific conditions are met. Neither of these last two involves modifying network packets.

68. C. A logic bomb is a code insert placed into a legitimate software product that triggers a malicious event when specific conditions are met. Social engineering is the practice of obtaining sensitive data by manipulating legitimate users, such as by pretending to be someone with a genuine need for that data. War driving is an attack method that consists of driving around a neighborhood with a computer, scanning for unprotected wireless networks. An evil twin is a fraudulent access point on a wireless network that mimics the SSID of a legitimate access point, in the hope of luring in users.

69. B, C. Configuring the access point not to broadcast its SSID will prevent an unsophisticated war driving attacker from seeing the network. Configuring your equipment to use Wi-Fi Protected Access 3 (WPA3) security will make it difficult for a war driver who detects your network to connect to it. The SSID is just an identifier; its length has no effect on security. Wired Equivalent Privacy (WEP) is a security protocol that has been found to have serious weaknesses.

70. B. Bluesnarfing is an attack in which an intruder connects to a wireless device using Bluetooth, for the purpose of stealing information. Bluejacking is the process of sending unsolicited messages to a device using Bluetooth. The other options do not exist.

71. D. Although a denial-of-service (DoS) attack typically involves traffic flooding, any attack that prevents a server from functioning can be called a DoS attack. A permanent DoS attack is one in which the attacker actually damages the target system and prevents it from functioning. This can be a physical attack that actually damages the hardware, or the attacker can disable the server by altering its software or configuration settings. Flood-based attacks include the distributed denial-of-service (DDoS) attack, one in which the attacker uses hundreds or thousands of computers, controlled by malware and called bots or zombies, to send traffic to a single server or website, in an attempt to overwhelm it and prevent it from functioning. An amplified DoS attack is one in which the messages sent by the attacker require an extended amount of processing by the target servers, increasing the burden on them more than simpler messages would. A reflective DoS attack is one in which the attacker sends requests containing the target server's IP address to legitimate servers on the Internet, such as DNS servers, causing them to send a flood of responses to the target.

72. B. Distributed DoS attacks use hundreds or thousands of computers that have been infected with malware, called bots or zombies, to flood a target server with traffic, in an attempt to overwhelm it and prevent it from functioning. A reflective DoS attack is one in which the attacker sends requests containing the target server's IP address to legitimate servers on the Internet, such as DNS servers, causing them to send a flood of responses to the target. Neither attack type causes a computer to flood itself.

73. A. An amplified DoS attack is one in which the messages sent by the attacker require an extended amount of processing by the target servers, increasing the burden on them more than simpler messages would. Reflective and distributed DoS attacks use other computers to flood a target with traffic. A reflective DoS attack is one in which the attacker sends requests containing the target server's IP address to legitimate servers on the Internet, such as DNS servers, causing them to send a flood of responses to the target. A distributed denial-of-service (DDoS) attack is one in which the attacker uses a botnet consisting of hundreds or thousands of computers, controlled by malware and called bots or zombies, to send traffic to a single server or website, in an attempt to overwhelm it and prevent it from functioning. A permanent DoS attack is one in which the attacker actually damages the target system and prevents it from functioning.

74. A, B, C. A brute-force attack is one in which an attacker uses repeated guesses to find a password, an open port, or some other type of sensitive data. A denial-of-service (DoS) attack floods a target server with traffic so that it is unable to function normally. While both of these attack types can be mounted using specialized software, they can also be the work of a lone attacker using nothing more than the tools provided on a standard workstation. Social engineering is the practice of obtaining sensitive data by contacting users and pretending to be someone with a legitimate need for that data. It requires nothing more than a telephone or an email client. *Phishing* is the term for an attack that uses bogus emails or websites designed to infect users with some type of malware.

75. B, C. Deauthentication is a type of denial-of-service (DoS) attack in which the attacker targets a wireless client by sending a deauthentication frame that causes the client to be disconnected from the network. The object of the attack is often to compel the client to connect to a rogue access point called an evil twin. An evil twin is a fraudulent access point on a wireless network that mimics the SSID of a legitimate access point, in the hope of luring in users. A logic bomb is a code insert placed into a legitimate software product that triggers a malicious event when specific conditions are met. ARP poisoning is the deliberate insertion of fraudulent information into the ARP cache stored on computers and switches. Neither of these last two is specifically targeted at wireless clients.

76. A. Social engineering is the practice of obtaining sensitive data by contacting users and pretending to be someone with a legitimate need for that data. No software or hardware solution can prevent it; the only way is to educate users of the potential dangers and establish policies that inform users what to do when they experience a social engineering attempt. Social engineering is not a virus or other form of malware, so an antivirus product has no effect against it. Social engineering is not implemented in network traffic, so a firewall cannot filter it. Social engineering is not implemented in network traffic, so IPsec cannot protect it.

77. B, C. Reflective and distributed DoS attacks use other computers to flood a target with traffic. A reflective DoS attack is one in which the attacker sends requests containing the target server's IP address to legitimate servers on the Internet, such as DNS servers, causing them to send a flood of responses to the target. A distributed denial-of-service (DDoS) attack is one in which the attacker uses hundreds or thousands of computers, controlled by malware and called bots or zombies, to send traffic to a single server or website, in an attempt to overwhelm it and prevent it from functioning. An amplified DoS attack is one in which the messages sent by the attacker require an extended amount of processing by the target servers, increasing the burden on them more than simpler messages would. A permanent DoS attack is one in which the attacker actually damages the target system and prevents it from functioning.

78. C. VLAN hopping is a method for sending commands to switches to transfer a port from one VLAN to another. This can enable the attacker to connect their device to a potentially sensitive VLAN. VLAN hopping does not modify the switch's patch panel connections, only its VLAN assignments. It is not possible to rename a switch's default VLAN. VLAN hopping does not enable an attacker to change a switch's native VLAN.

79. A. Spoofing is the process of modifying network packets to make them appear as though they are transmitted by or addressed to someone else. One way of doing this is to modify the MAC address in the packets to one that is approved by the MAC filter. Brute-force is the method of repeated guessing, which is impractical with MAC addresses. DNS works with IP addresses, not MAC addresses. War driving is the process of looking for unprotected wireless access points.

80. C. A distributed denial-of-service (DDoS) attack is one in which the attacker uses hundreds or thousands of computers, controlled by malware and called bots or zombies, to send traffic to a single server or website, in an attempt to overwhelm it and prevent it from functioning. An amplified DoS attack is one in which the messages sent by the attacker require an extended amount of processing by the target servers, increasing the burden on them more than simpler messages would. A reflective DoS attack is one in which the attacker sends requests containing the target server's IP address to legitimate servers on the Internet, such as DNS servers, causing them to send a flood of responses to the target. A permanent DoS attack is one in which the attacker actually damages the target system and prevents it from functioning.

81. **A.** An amplified DoS attack is one in which the messages sent by the attacker require an extended amount of processing by the target servers, increasing the burden on them more than simpler messages would. A reflective DoS attack is one in which the attacker sends requests containing the target server's IP address to legitimate servers on the Internet, such as DNS servers, causing them to send a flood of responses to the target. A distributed denial-of-service (DDoS) attack is one in which the attacker uses hundreds or thousands of computers, controlled by malware and called bots or zombies, to send traffic to a single server or website, in an attempt to overwhelm it and prevent it from functioning. A permanent DoS attack is one in which the attacker actually damages the target system and prevents it from functioning.

82. **A, D.** Smurf attacks rely on routers to forward broadcast traffic. Routers no longer forward broadcast messages, so smurf attacks have been rendered ineffective. In the same way, VLAN hopping, which is a method for sending commands to switches to transfer a port from one VLAN to another, is rarely seen because switches are now designed to prevent them. A logic bomb is a code insert placed into a legitimate software product that triggers a malicious event when specific conditions are met. *Phishing* is the term for a bogus email or website designed to infect users with some type of malware. Both of these are still commonly used attack types.

83. **D.** Although denial-of-service (DoS) attacks typically involve traffic flooding, any attack that prevents a server from functioning can be called a DoS attack. A permanent DoS attack is one in which the attacker actually damages the target system and prevents it from functioning. This can be a physical attack that damages the hardware, or the attacker can disable the server by altering its software or configuration settings. A distributed denial-of-service (DDoS) attack is one in which the attacker uses hundreds or thousands of computers, controlled by malware and called bots or zombies, to send traffic to a single server or website, in an attempt to overwhelm it and prevent it from functioning. An amplified DoS attack is one in which the messages sent by the attacker require an extended amount of processing by the target servers, increasing the burden on them more than simpler messages would. A reflective DoS attack is one in which the attacker sends requests containing the target server's IP address to legitimate servers on the Internet, such as DNS servers, causing them to send a flood of responses to the target.

84. **C.** Distributed DoS attacks use hundreds or thousands of computers that have been infected with malware, called bots or zombies, to flood a target server with traffic, in an attempt to overwhelm it and prevent it from functioning. A reflective DoS attack is one in which the attacker sends requests containing the target server's IP address to legitimate servers on the Internet, such as DNS servers, causing them to send a flood of responses to the target. A reflective attack does not require infected computers; it takes advantage of the servers' native functions. An amplified DoS attack is one in which the messages sent by the attacker

require an extended amount of processing by the target servers, increasing the burden on them more than simpler messages would. A permanent DoS attack is one in which the attacker actually damages the target system and prevents it from functioning.

85. D. DNS poisoning is a type of attack in which an attacker adds fraudulent information into the cache of a DNS server. Then, when a client attempts to resolve the name of a website or other server, the DNS server supplies the incorrect IP address, causing the client to access the attacker's server instead. An evil twin is a rogue wireless access point on a network. ARP poisoning is the deliberate insertion of fraudulent information into the ARP cache stored on computers and switches, which can interfere with the resolution of IP addresses into MAC addresses on a local level. Spoofing is the process of modifying network packets to make them appear as though they are transmitted by or addressed to someone else.

86. B. DNS poisoning is a type of attack in which an attacker adds fraudulent information into the cache of a DNS server. This can interfere with the name resolution process by causing a DNS server to supply the incorrect IP address for a specified name. The process of resolving an IP address into a MAC address can be interfered with by ARP poisoning. DNS has nothing to do with passwords or switching.

87. C. A vulnerability is a potential weakness in a system that an attacker can use to their advantage. An exploit is a hardware or software element that is designed to take advantage of a vulnerability. A mitigation is a form of defense against attacks on system security. A honeypot is a computer configured to function as bait for attackers, causing them to waste their time penetrating a resource that provides no significant access.

88. D. A logic bomb is a code insert placed into a legitimate software product that triggers a malicious event when specific conditions are met. The terminated administrator might have created code designed to trigger the deletions after the administrator's departure from the company. Social engineering is a form of attack in which an innocent user is persuaded by an attacker to provide sensitive information via email or telephone. The Address Resolution Protocol (ARP) is responsible for resolving IP addresses into media access control (MAC) addresses. ARP poisoning is the deliberate insertion of fraudulent information into the ARP cache stored on computers and switches. An evil twin is a fraudulent access point on a wireless network.

89. B,C. ARP spoofing is the deliberate insertion of fraudulent information into the ARP cache stored on computers and switches. This can enable an attacker to intercept traffic intended for another system. In an on-path (man-in-the-middle) attack, the attacker can read the intercepted traffic and even modify it before sending it on to the destination. In a session hijacking attack, the attacker can use the intercepted traffic to obtain authentication information, including passwords. An evil twin is a fraudulent access point on a wireless network. Social engineering is a form of attack in which an innocent user is persuaded by an attacker to provide sensitive information via email or telephone.

90. B. A replay attack is one in which an attacker utilizes the information found in previously captured packets to gain access to a secured resource. In many cases, the captured packets contain authentication data. In this way, the attacker can make use of captured passwords, even when they are encrypted and cannot be displayed. The other options all describe valid attack methodologies, but they are not called replay attacks.

91. B. This is a classic example of a phishing scam. In all likelihood, the link in the email Ed received has taken him not to the real website of his bank, but rather a duplicate created by an attacker. By supplying his logon credentials, he is in effect giving them to the attacker, who can now gain access to his real bank account. An evil twin is a fraudulent access point on a wireless network that mimics the SSID of a legitimate access point, in the hope of luring in users. A logic bomb is a code insert placed into a legitimate software product that triggers a malicious event when specific conditions are met. Spoofing is the process of modifying network packets to make them appear as though they are transmitted by or addressed to someone else.

92. A, C, D. An evil twin is a fraudulent access point on a wireless network that mimics the SSID of a legitimate access point, in the hope of luring in users. War driving is an attack method that consists of driving around a neighborhood with a computer scanning for unprotected wireless networks. Deauthentication is a type of denial-of-service (DoS) attack in which the attacker targets a wireless client by sending a deauthentication frame that causes the client to be disconnected from the network. Phishing is an attack type that is targeted at all users, not just wireless ones.

93. C, D. Capturing packets and installing rogue access points are not typically characterized as DoS attacks. A denial-of-service (DoS) attack is one designed to prevent a target from fulfilling its function. While ping floods are a common form of server DoS attacks, physically damaging the server hardware also prevents it from performing its function. Therefore, this too is a type of DoS attack. MAC flooding is another type of DoS attack that can overwhelm network switches, leading to a loss of confidentiality, integrity, and availability of network resources.

94. A. A zombie (or bot) is a computer that has been infected by malware—usually some form of Trojan—which an attacker can control remotely, causing the computer to flood a target system with traffic. An attack using multiple zombies is known as a distributed denial-of-service (DDoS) attack. The other options are not examples of zombies.

95. C. Ransomware is a type of attack in which a user's access to their computer or data is blocked unless a certain amount of money is paid to the attacker. The blockages can vary from simple screen locks to complete data encryption.

96. B. Social engineering is the practice of obtaining sensitive data by contacting users and pretending to be someone with a legitimate need for that data. No computer equipment is required, and no software or hardware solution can prevent it; the only way is to warn users of the potential dangers and establish policies that inform users what to do when they experience a social engineering attempt. All of the other answer options require the use of some form of computer equipment to send traffic to or manipulate target systems. Denial-of-service is a type of attack that overwhelms a computer with traffic, preventing it from functioning properly. A brute-force or dictionary attack is one in which an attacker uses repeated guesses to find a password, an open port, or some other type of sensitive data. *Phishing* is the term for a bogus email or website designed to infect users with some type of malware.

97. B. A brute-force attack (also called a dictionary attack) is one in which an attacker uses repeated guesses to find a password, an open port, or some other type of sensitive data. Brute-force does not refer to a physical attack. Flooding a server with traffic created by zombies is a distributed denial-of-service (DDoS) attack. Deploying an unauthorized access point is an evil twin attack.

98. A. An evil twin is a fraudulent access point on a wireless network, which an intruder can use to obtain passwords and other sensitive information transmitted by users. *War driving* is the term for seeking out open wireless networks. Social engineering is a form of attack in which an innocent user is persuaded by an attacker to provide sensitive information via email or telephone. Spoofing is the process of modifying network packets to make them appear as though they are transmitted by or addressed to someone else.

99. C. *Social engineering* is the term for a type of attack in which a smooth-talking intruder contacts a user and convinces them to disclose sensitive information, such as account passwords. An on-path (man-in-the-middle) attack is one in which an attacker intercepts network traffic, reads the traffic, and can even modify it before sending it on to the destination. Spoofing is the process of modifying network packets to make them appear as though they are transmitted by or addressed to someone else. An evil twin is a fraudulent access point on a wireless network.

100. B. Operating system updates and patches are frequently released to address newly discovered exploits that make computers vulnerable to malware infestation. Applying updates on a regular basis can help to mitigate the impact of malware. Updates and patches typically cannot mitigate DoS attacks, and they have no effect on nontechnical dangers such as social engineering or dangers that apply to switches, such as port security hazards.

101. E. The term *social engineering* refers to various methods attackers can use to gain access to secured resources by manipulating authorized users, either physically or digitally. An evil twin is a rogue access point deliberately connected to the network for malicious purposes, so it is not a form of social engineering. Piggybacking and tailgating typically refer to the practice of closely following an authorized individual through a physical security barrier, such as a locked door or a guarded entrance. Shoulder surfing is a method of gathering sensitive information by passing behind a user and looking at their monitor. Dumpster diving is the process of looking for valuable network or user information in the trash.

102. A. Social engineering is the practice of obtaining sensitive data by manipulating legitimate users, such as by pretending to be someone with a genuine need for that data. Because it is not a technological vulnerability, the only means of preventing this type of attack is to educate and train users to recognize potential threats. War driving is an attack method that consists of driving around a neighborhood with a computer, scanning for unprotected wireless networks. A logic bomb is a code insert placed into a legitimate software product that triggers a malicious event when specific conditions are met. An evil twin is a fraudulent access point on a wireless network that mimics the SSID of a legitimate access point, in the hope of luring in users.

103. B. Your supervisor's concern is that the disgruntled technician might take advantage of his access to devices and facilities to sabotage the network. When an individual takes advantage of information gathered during their employment, it is called an internal (or insider) threat. An external threat is one originating from a non-employee. Social engineering is a form of attack in which an innocent user is persuaded by an attacker to provide sensitive information via email or telephone. A logic bomb is a code insert placed into a legitimate software product that triggers a malicious event when specific conditions are met. War driving is an attack method that consists of driving around a neighborhood with a computer scanning for unprotected wireless networks.

104. D. DHCP snooping is a feature found in some network switches that prevents rogue DHCP servers from assigning IP addresses to clients. It can also detect when DHCP release or decline messages arrive over a port other than the one on which the DHCP transaction originated. Although DHCP snooping can prevent DHCP clients from being assigned an incorrect IP address, it does not directly prevent DNS spoofing, the poisoning of DNS server caches with erroneous information.

105. B, E, F. Servers that must be accessible both from the trusted internal network and from the untrusted Internet are typically located in an area of the enterprise called a screened subnet, a perimeter network, or a demilitarized zone (DMZ). This area is separated from both the Internet and the internal network by firewalls, which prevents unauthorized Internet users from accessing the internal network. *Intranet* is another term for the internal network. Exterior Gateway Protocol (EGP) is a type of routing protocol, and stateless is a type of firewall; neither apply to this definition.

106. A. Network access control (NAC) is a mechanism that defines standards of equipment and configuration that systems must meet before they can connect to the network. Lightweight Directory Access Protocol (LDAP) provides communication between directory service entities. RADIUS is an authentication, authorization, and accounting service for remote users connecting to a network. Advanced Encryption Standard (AES) is an encryption protocol used on wireless networks running the Wi-Fi Protected Access 2 or 3 (WPA2 or WPA3) security protocol.

107. A, B, C, D. The longer the password, the more difficult it is to guess. Corporate policies typically require passwords of a minimum length. A larger character set also makes a password more difficult to guess, so requiring upper- and lowercase, numeric, and special characters is common. Changing passwords forces the attack process to start over, so policies typically require frequent password changes and prevent users from reusing passwords.

108. C. Requiring unique passwords can prevent users from thwarting a password change policy by reusing the same passwords over and over. Password length, password character sets, and password change interval maximums can do nothing to thwart a frequent password change policy.

109. A, C, D. Account lockout threshold specifies the number of incorrect logon attempts that are allowed before the account is locked out. Account lockout duration is the amount of time that an account remains locked out. Reset account lockout threshold counter specifies the amount of time before the number of incorrect attempts is reset to zero. Account lockout policies typically do not include a setting that regulates the amount of time allowed between logon attempts.

110. B. Account lockouts limit the number of incorrect passwords that a user can enter. This prevents intruders from using a brute-force attack to crack the account by trying password after password. After a specified number of incorrect tries, the account is locked for a specified length of time or until an administrator unlocks it.

111. A. Although all of the options are characteristics of a strong password, the definition of a complex password is one that expands the available character set by using a mixture of upper- and lowercase letters, numerals, and symbols. The larger the character set used to create passwords, the more difficult they are to guess.

112. A. A history requirement in a password policy prevents users from specifying any one of their most recently used passwords. Although creating passwords using the names of relatives and historical figures is not recommended, it is not something that is easy to prevent. Each user maintains their own password history; there is no conflict with the passwords of other users.

113. C. A brute-force password attack is one in which the perpetrator tries as many passwords as possible in an effort to guess or deduce the right one. Account lockout policies are intended to prevent this type of attack by limiting the number of incorrect password attempts. Social engineering is the practice of obtaining sensitive data by manipulating legitimate users, such as by pretending to be someone with a genuine need for that data. Spoofing is the process of modifying network packets to make them appear as though they are transmitted by or addressed to someone else. An on-path (or man-in-the-middle) attack is one in which an attacker intercepts network traffic, reads the traffic, and can even modify it before sending it on to the destination. Account lockout policies are not designed to protect against social engineering, spoofing, or on-path attacks.

114. A, B, D. A brute-force password attack is one in which the perpetrator tries as many passwords as possible in an effort to guess or deduce the right one. Password length and complexity policies produce passwords that are harder to guess, making the attack statistically less likely to succeed. Account lockout policies are intended to prevent brute-force attacks by limiting the number of incorrect password attempts. Password history policies do not help to prevent brute-force attacks.

115. B. Network access control (NAC) is a set of policies that define security requirements that clients must meet before they are permitted to connect to a network. 802.1X is a basic implementation of NAC. RADIUS and TACACS+ are authentication, authorization, and accounting (AAA) services. They are not NAC implementations themselves, although they can play a part in their deployment. Lightweight Directory Access Protocol (LDAP) provides directory service communications.

116. C. An 802.1X transaction involves three parties: the supplicant, which is the client attempting to connect to the network; the authenticator, which is a switch or access point to which the supplicant is requesting access; and the authentication server, which is typically a RADIUS implementation that verifies the supplicant's identity. There is no party to the transaction called an authorizing agent.

117. D. An 802.1X transaction involves three parties: the supplicant, which is the client attempting to connect to the network; the authenticator, which is a switch or access point to which the supplicant is requesting access; and the authentication server, which is typically a RADIUS implementation that verifies the supplicant's identity. The supplicant is not involved in issuing certificates.

118. C. An 802.1X transaction involves three parties: the supplicant, which is the client attempting to connect to the network; the authenticator, which is a switch or access point to which the supplicant is requesting access; and the authentication server, which is typically a RADIUS implementation that verifies the supplicant's identity. The authenticator is not involved in issuing certificates.

119. C. The authentication server role is typically performed by a Remote Authentication Dial-In User Service (RADIUS) server. In an 802.1X transaction, the supplicant is the client attempting to connect to the network, the authenticator is a switch or access point to which the supplicant is requesting access, and the authentication server verifies the client's identity.

120. C, D. A network segment that is separated from the trusted zone (the internal network) by a firewall and exposed to the untrusted zone (the Internet) is called a screened subnet, a demilitarized zone (DMZ), or a perimeter network. Administrators typically use a screened subnet for servers that must be accessible by outside users, such as web and email servers. For security reasons, domain controllers and DHCP servers should be located on internal network segments, which are part of the trusted zone.

121. A. Extensible Authentication Protocol (EAP) and 802.1X are both components of an authentication mechanism used on many wireless networks. EAP and 802.1X do not themselves provide authorization, encryption, or accounting services.

122. A, B, C, E. Encryption, authentication, MAC filtering, and antenna placement are all techniques for hardening a wireless network against attack. Social engineering is a type of attack in which an intruder contacts a user and convinces them to disclose sensitive information, such as account passwords; it is not specifically associated with wireless networks.

123. A. There are no policies that can prevent users from creating easily guessed passwords. The only action that can help is to educate users of the fact that attackers are frequently able to guess passwords by using information such as familiar names and dates. Forcing more frequent password changes would not compel users to alter their method for choosing passwords, nor would increasing the password history value. Assigning random passwords would address the issue, but user complaints and forgotten passwords would likely create greater problems than it would solve.

124. A, C, D. Access points, switches, and routers all require authentication to access their administrative interfaces, and many have a standard username and password configured at the factory. The purchaser can modify the default credentials, but many people fail to do so. Windows servers do not have default credentials assigned; the installer is prompted to specify an Administrator password during the setup process.

125. A, D. Secure Shell (SSH) and Telnet are both remote terminal programs, but Telnet passes instructions (including passwords) in cleartext, whereas SSH is encrypted. Hypertext Transfer Protocol Secure (HTTPS) is the encrypted version of HTTP. In both of these cases, the suggested substitute is more secure. However, Temporal Key Integrity Protocol (TKIP) provides less secure encryption than Advanced Encryption Standard (AES), and Wired Equivalent Protocol (WEP) is less secure than Wi-Fi Protected Access 2 (WPA2).

126. B, C. Servers and switches are both devices on which unused ports can be a security hazard, but they use the term *port* differently. Servers have Application layer ports that permit specific types of service traffic to enter the server. Switches have ports to which administrators can connect computers and other devices. Both can provide attackers with unauthorized access to the device, so port security is an important administrative function. It is not possible to disable hub ports, and the access points used on enterprise networks typically have only a single port.

127. B. Disabling SSID broadcasts is a way of hiding the presence of a wireless network, but if an intruder knows that a network is there, it is a simple matter to capture packets transmitted by the wireless devices and read the SSID from them. It is not possible to connect to a wireless network without the SSID. SSIDs are set by the administrator of the access point; they are not printed on the device's label. SSIDs can be found relatively easily, but guessing them is no easier than guessing a password.

128. B. Open TCP and UDP ports are a security hazard, so disabling unused ports is a standard server hardening technique. Disabling services that are not in use reduces the attack surface of a server. Updating firmware for hardware devices can help to protect them from deliberate attacks. Creating privileged user accounts reduces the chance that privileged accounts will be compromised. Therefore, these are all forms of server hardening.

129. A, D. If there is no way for unauthorized people to access the datacenter, then there is no danger of someone plugging a device into a port that is left enabled. If the switch uses an access control list (ACL) that specifies the MAC addresses of systems permitted to connect to it, then there is no need to disable unused ports. However, disabling the ports is probably far easier than creating and maintaining the ACL. Ports that are not patched in can still be compromised at the switch location. Enabling ports is not difficult, so accommodating new users is not a valid reason for leaving them enabled.

130. D. The "Passwords must meet complexity requirements" policy includes a provision that new passwords cannot include the user's account name or full name. If the full name is delimited by spaces or punctuation, the individual words cannot appear in the password either. The other options do not prevent the use of common passwords.

131. D. Deauthentication is a type of denial-of-service attack in which the attacker targets a wireless client by sending a deauthentication frame that causes the client to be disconnected from the network. Therefore, it is not a method for hardening an access point. Upgrading the device's firmware to apply security fixes, changing the default administrative credentials applied at the factory, and frequent pre-shared key (PSK) changes are all means of hardening the security of an access point.

132. C. *Network hardening* is term used to describe any method of making the network more difficult for intruders to penetrate. In many cases, network hardening techniques are based on education rather than technology. Compelling users to create passwords that are difficult to guess is one example of this. Mitigation techniques are methods for reducing the severity of an attack. Multifactor authentication calls for the use of two different identity confirmation mechanisms, such as a password and a fingerprint. Access control is a technique for creating a list of approved users or systems.

133. A, B. Administrator is the default administrative user account in Windows, and root is the administrative account in Linux. Control and admin are not privileged user accounts provided with the operating systems.

134. B, D. Virtual LANs can be used to isolate systems on a separate network segment. A screened subnet, also called a demilitarized zone (DMZ) or a perimeter network, is a network segment accessible from the Internet and separated from the internal network by a firewall. Therefore, the screened subnet lies between the trusted (or private) zone and the untrusted (or public internet) zone. Both of these are methods for isolating systems to prevent security breaches from spreading beyond their bounds. Access control lists (ACLs) and network access control (NAC) are both methods for enhancing network security, but they are not segmentation methods.

135. D. DHCP snooping is a feature found in some network switches that prevents rogue DHCP servers from assigning IP addresses to clients. It can also detect when DHCP release or decline messages arrive over a port other than the one on which the DHCP transaction originated. The other options are all techniques that are applicable to servers.

136. B. Access control lists (ACLs) define the type of access granted to authenticated users. This process is known as authorization. Authentication is the confirmation of a user's identity. Accounting and auditing are both methods of tracking and recording a user's activities on a network.

137. C. Role separation is the practice of creating a different virtual server for each server role or application. In addition to providing other benefits as well, this forces intruders to mount attacks on multiple servers to disable an entire network. Geofencing is a technique for limiting access to a wireless network. Network segmentation describes the process of creating multiple VLANs or deploying firewalls to isolate part of a network. VLAN hopping is a type of attack in which an intruder sends command messages to a switch to transfer a port from one VLAN to another.

138. B. Role separation is the practice of creating a different virtual server for each server role or application. In addition to providing other benefits as well, this forces intruders to mount attacks on multiple servers to disable an entire network. Switches, routers, and access points do not use this technique.

139. A. Dynamic Host Configuration Protocol (DHCP) snooping is a process in which the switch examines DHCP traffic to determine the IP addresses that DHCP servers have assigned to specific MAC addresses. DAI detects ARP poisoning attempts by comparing the IP and MAC address pairs in ARP packets with those in the DHCP snooping table it has compiled. The switch then discards packets with address pairs that do not match. Secure SNMP, DNS name resolution, and Neighbor Discovery Protocol (NDP) are not used to implement DAI.

140. B. Although DHCP is an Application layer service that uses the UDP Transport layer protocol to assign Network layer IP addresses, DHCP snooping is a Data link layer process in which a network switch examines incoming DHCP traffic to determine whether it originates from an authorized server and is arriving over the correct port.

141. C. By flooding a switch with packets containing many different false MAC addresses, an attacker can cause the legitimate entries in the switch's MAC table to be aged out of the device and replaced with bogus entries. When the destinations of incoming packets are not found in the table, the switch broadcasts them throughout the network, where they can be more readily captured and compromised. A flood guard is a mechanism that prevents confirmed MAC addresses in the table from being replaced. A flood guard in a switch cannot protect against DNS poisoning, war driving, or evil twin attacks.

142. B. A root guard affects the behavior of the Spanning Tree Protocol (STP) by enforcing the selection of root bridge ports on a switched network. Without root guards, there is no way for administrators to enforce the topology of a network with a redundant switching fabric. Root guards do not affect the Extensible Authentication Protocol (EAP), the Lightweight Directory Access Protocol (LDAP), or the Address Resolution Protocol (ARP).

143. D. MAC address filtering enables administrators to configure an access point to allow only devices with specific addresses to connect; all other traffic is rejected. Access points broadcast their presence using an SSID, not a MAC address. MAC address filtering protects wireless LANs when implemented in an access point, not a firewall. MAC address filtering does not call for the modification of addresses in network packets. MAC filtering does not isolate clients from the network.

144. A. Wireless access points (WAPs) typically include the ability to maintain an access control list, which specifies the MAC addresses of devices that are permitted to connect to the wireless network. The technique is known as MAC address filtering. RADIUS servers, domain controllers, and smartcards typically do not include MAC filtering capabilities.

145. A, C. NTFS files and folder all have access control lists (ACLs), which contain access control entries (ACEs) that specify the users and groups that can access them and the specific permissions they have been granted. Wireless access points (WAPs) have access control lists that contain the MAC addresses of the devices that are permitted to connect to the wireless network. Lightweight Directory Access Protocol and Kerberos are protocols that provide directory service communication and authentication, respectively. Neither one uses access control lists to limit network access.

146. B. Port isolation, also known as private VLAN, is a feature in some switches that enables administrators to restrict selected ports to a given uplink, essentially creating a separate, secondary VLAN that is isolated from the switch's default, primary VLAN. Screened subnets (also called perimeter networks or DMZs), Frame Relay, and VPNs are not switching techniques.

147. A, D. URL filters examine the web addresses requested by users and prevent any outgoing traffic from being transmitted to them. Content filtering examines inbound traffic, looking for objectionable material, malware, and other potential dangers. Because network users have several avenues for potentially dangerous incoming traffic, a proper content filtering implementation typically screens all of them. It is URL filtering that requires access to an outside database. It is content filtering that provides protection against phishing attempts and other types of malware.

Chapter 5: Network Troubleshooting

1. **A.** The first step in troubleshooting is to identify the problem by establishing the symptoms related to the network issue being reported. In this step, problems are typically reported as trouble tickets, which are prioritized based on the severity of the problem. You complete the other steps after the trouble ticket has been prioritized and is being investigated.

2. **C.** A systemwide error is a problem that renders an individual user's system (computer) completely unusable. All the other problems listed would affect more than one system or user.

3. **D.** Any problem that affects all the users on the network is a networkwide problem and should be given the highest priority. An example of this would be a problem with an Internet router. All other problems listed do not affect the entire network.

4. **B.** In this scenario, only one user is reporting a problem. Therefore, the likeliest next step is to perform the same task on another computer attached to the same segment. If Ed can perform the task successfully, the problem most likely lies within the user's computer or the connection to the switch. Since no other users are reporting the same problem, the server and switches on the network are probably up and functioning. Checking the router is not necessary since the user and server are on the same network.

5. **A.** The first step in troubleshooting is to identify the problem by establishing symptoms related to the network problem being reported. In this step, you ask the user many questions to identify and define the symptoms of the problem and prioritize the trouble ticket. Although you might continue to ask the user questions throughout the troubleshooting process, this is typically associated with the first step of the troubleshooting process.

6. **C.** After identifying the problem, the next step is to establish a theory for the probable cause of the problem. After that, you can test your theory, establish a plan of action, implement a solution, verify the functionality of the system, and document the entire process.

7. **B.** The second step in troubleshooting is to attempt to duplicate a problem and develop a theory of its probable cause. As you troubleshoot a problem, you then test your theory to confirm your findings. You complete the other troubleshooting steps after the specific cause has been identified.

8. **D.** Replacing components by guesswork could resolve the problem through chance, but it would more likely be a waste of time and hardware. When Ralph's first theory is disproven, the next logical step would be to devise another theory. This could conceivably involve reinterviewing the users or escalating the issue to a senior technician. If the theory had been confirmed, the next step would be to devise a plan of action to resolve the problem.

9. **C.** In troubleshooting, one of the first steps in the process of identifying the problem is to question the obvious, such as whether the computer is plugged in or switched on. It would be unlikely that the user would know her computer's IP address or what updates had been installed when the screen is blank. Questioning whether other people have used the computer might come up later, but it will be little help at this stage of the troubleshooting process.

10. B. If a problem lies within a specific server or other network component that prevents many users from working, it is a shared resource problem. A problem that lies within resources that provide services to the entire network is a networkwide problem. Systemwide problems put a specific computer out of commission, preventing a user from getting any work done. An application problem is a problem that affects only a single user's access to a device or application.

11. A. Since only one user is reporting the problem, and he had admitted to making changes to his IP configuration, Alice should probably start by checking the configuration using the `ipconfig` command. If the router, DNS server, or DHCP server were causing the problem, more than one user would be experiencing difficulties.

12. A. Since only one user is reporting the problem, the user's computer and its configuration are the likeliest suspect components. A DNS, proxy, or router problem would affect more than one user.

13. C. Alice is using a top-to-bottom approach, based on the OSI reference model. She begins at the top of the model (the Application layer) by checking the system's email capabilities, then proceeds downwards to check the computer's IP configuration (the Network layer), the local network connectivity (the Data link layer), and the computer's cables (the Physical layer). A bottom-to-top approach would begin with the cables. The divide and conquer approach and questioning the obvious would not involve the steps Alice took in the order that she took them.

14. A. There are many possible causes for the problem that are more likely than a router configuration error, so this is not something Alice would check first. Asking if the user can access the local network attempts to isolate the problem. If she cannot, the problem could be in her computer; if she can, then the problem lies somewhere in the Internet access infrastructure. If other users are experiencing the problem, then the issue should receive a higher priority, and Alice knows that the problem does not lie in the user's computer. While it might not be the first thing she checks, it is a political reality that higher ranking users often get preferential treatment.

15. B. Documenting the findings, actions, outcomes, and lessons learned throughout the process is a crucial part of the troubleshooting method that must begin before any other action whatsoever. However, it appears as the last step in the troubleshooting methodology.

16. A. During the troubleshooting process, the identify the problem step includes determining what has changed recently on the system. This typically involves asking the user whether any new or existing hardware or software has been installed or reconfigured.

17. C. After you have established a theory of probable cause, you can try to test the theory by replacing hardware components one by one until you find the faulty device.

18. D, F. Verifying that a router is functioning and forwarding traffic and verifying that a client's IP configuration is correct are not considered general troubleshooting steps. You might perform these two steps as a subset of general troubleshooting steps.

19. **A, C.** When a network problem or incident is reported, documentation begins. Proper documentation makes it easier for a first-tier support technician to prioritize and to escalate the call to senior technicians, if necessary.

20. **B, D.** When establishing priorities, networkwide problems take precedence over departmental problems, and problems with shared resources take precedence over individual desktop problems.

21. **A, B, D.** First-tier technicians are generally less experienced than second-tier technicians. First-tier technicians are the first point of contact for users. They receive and prioritize help desk calls and escalate problems to second-tier technicians, if necessary. First-tier technicians generally handle individual desktop problems, whereas second-tier technicians troubleshoot mission-critical network components such as routers and switches.

22. **C.** A problem that affects the entire network should be given highest priority. This includes a mission-critical backbone router. Problems that affect multiple LANs or an entire department are generally given the next highest priority. An application problem that affects a shared application server on a LAN should be given the next highest priority. A problem with a single user's computer should be given the lowest priority if the other problems have been reported.

23. **B.** A problem that affects the entire network should be given highest priority. This includes a mission-critical backbone router. Problems that affect multiple LANs or an entire department are generally given the next highest priority. An application problem that affects a shared application server on a LAN should be given the next highest priority. A problem with a single user's computer should be given the lowest priority if the other problems have been reported.

24. **D.** After you identify a problem and establish and test a theory of its probable cause, you must create a plan of action to resolve the problem and identify any potential effects (positive or negative) your solution might have. Then, you implement your solution, test the results, and finish documenting the incident.

25. **G.** The last step of the troubleshooting process is to document the solution and explain to the user what happened and why. In reality, documentation should begin when the problem is reported, and the documentation should be updated throughout the troubleshooting process.

26. **A, D.** The first stage of the troubleshooting process calls for Alice to identify the problem by gathering information. Learning about who is reporting the problem and what has changed since the server was last accessible can provide Alice with information that could help her determine whether the problem is located in the users' workstations, somewhere in the network, or in the file server itself. The other options are intended to test a theory about a probable cause, a troubleshooting stage that comes later.

27. **A.** Because the multiple problems seem to be unrelated, Alice should handle them individually by creating a separate trouble ticket for each one and prioritizing each one. None of the problems seem to be severe enough to warrant escalation, nor should it be necessary to replace the computer. While it would be possible to send a technician to address all of the problems at once, it would be more efficient to assign each its own priority and handle it like any other trouble call.

28. B. The first phase of the troubleshooting process is gathering information. Learning whether the printer is accessible over the network can help Alice to isolate the location of the problem and develop a theory of probable cause. Installing drivers, checking switches, and upgrading firmware are all part of a later phase in the troubleshooting process: testing a theory to determine the cause of the problem.

29. B. The users' browsers are failing to resolve the host names of the requested web sites into IP addresses, which they must do before they can connect to the web servers. By asking where the company's DNS server is located, Ralph can determine if the problem is the DNS server itself or the router that provides access to the Internet. If the DNS server is located on Adatum's company network, then the DNS server could be failing to resolve the website names. However, the DNS server could be located on the Internet service provider's network, in which case the problem might be in the router that provides access to the ISP's network.

30. B, C, D, E. While securing the area to prevent contamination of evidence, documenting the scene with photographs or video, collecting any evidence that might be visible, and cooperating with the authorities are tasks that are likely to be in the company's incident response policy. Turning off the server most certainly would not, because this could disturb or delete evidence of the crime.

31. A. A toner and probe is a tester that consists of a main unit that connects to one end of a wire in a UTP cable and a locator that you touch to the other end, enabling you to test each wire. A toner and probe can detect opens and shorts, as well as transposed wires. However, it cannot detect split pairs, because in that fault the pins are properly connected.

32. D. The first and most essential test that installers must perform on every cable run is a continuity test, which ensures that each wire on both ends of the cable is connected to the correct pin and only the correct pin. If a pin on one end of a cable run is connected to two or more pins on the other end, the cable has a short circuit.

33. A. A rollover cable is a type of null modem cable, usually flat and light blue in color, with the pinouts reversed on either end, to enable a terminal to communicate with a router or switch through the device's dedicated console port. None of the other options are suitable for this purpose. A straight-through cable is the standard network cable used to connect a computer to a switch. A crossover cable is designed to connect two network adapters (in computers or similar devices) to each other directly. A plenum cable is a type of cable intended for use within air spaces that has an outer sheath that does not produce toxic fumes when it burns. A shielded cable is intended to protect signals from electromagnetic interference. A tap is a device used to branch a coaxial cable to two devices.

34. A. A straight-through cable is the standard network patch cable used to connect a computer to a wall plate. A crossover cable is designed to connect two network adapters (in computers or similar devices) to each other directly. A rollover cable is used to enable a terminal to communicate with a router or switch through the device's console port. A plenum cable is a type of cable intended for use within air spaces that has an outer sheath that does not produce toxic fumes when it burns.

35. B. A short circuit is a wiring fault indicating that a pin at one end of a cable run is connected to two pins at the other end. To correct the problem, you must replace the connector with the faulty wiring. None of the other suggestions are solutions for a wiring fault.

36. D. An optical power meter measures the signal strength on fiber-optic cables to locate breaks; it cannot be used on copper cables. Multimeters, toners, and cable testers are all devices that work with copper networks.

37. C. A butt set is a one-piece telephone handset with alligator clips that enables its operator to connect to a telephone line anywhere that the cables are accessible. They are used by telephone cable technicians but generally not by installers of network data cables. The other options are all standard tools used by data networking cable installers.

38. B. A crimper is a plier-like device that cable installers use to create patch cables by attaching RJ-45 connectors to lengths of bulk cable. Installers use a punchdown tool, not a crimper, to attach a cable end to a keystone connector. It is not always necessary to purchase a crimper for each cable type. Some crimpers are designed for a single cable/connector combination, but many crimpers have replaceable bits, supporting a variety of cables and connectors. Making patch cables yourself can represent a false economy. Buying bulk cable and connectors and making patch cables yourself can conceivably be cheaper than purchasing prefabricated cables. However, when you factor in the time needed to attach the connectors, the learning curve required to attach the connectors correctly, and the failure rate requiring the re-application of connectors, it might be more economical to purchase prefabricated patch cables in quantity instead.

39. C. A split pair is a connection in which two wires are incorrectly mapped in exactly the same way on both ends of the cable. Each pin on one end of the cable is correctly wired to the corresponding pin at the other end, but the wires inside the cable used to make the connections are incorrect. In a properly wired connection, each twisted pair should contain a signal wire and a ground wire. In a split pair, it is possible to have two signal wires twisted together as a pair. This can generate excessive amounts of crosstalk, corrupting both of the signals involved. Open circuits, shorts, and transposed pairs interfere with cable performance but do not make it more susceptible to crosstalk.

40. C. Of the options provided, the only possible source of the problem is that the cable runs are using a cable type not rated for Gigabit Ethernet. Some older buildings might still have the original Category 5 cable installed, rather than the Category 5e and higher cables now currently in use. Cat 5 can be unsuitable for use with Gigabit Ethernet and can result in the poor performance that Alice is experiencing. A cable installation with runs wired using different pinout standards will not affect performance as long as each run uses the same pinouts at both ends. Gigabit Ethernet will not function at all if only two wire pairs are connected. The transceivers are located in the equipment that Alice company brought from the old location, so they are not mismatched.

41. C. A split pair is a connection in which two wires are incorrectly mapped in exactly the same way on both ends of the cable. In a properly wired connection, each twisted pair should contain a colored signal wire and a striped ground wire. In a split pair, it is possible to have two signal wires twisted together as a pair. This can generate excessive amounts of crosstalk, corrupting both of the signals involved. Because all of the pins are connected properly, a toner and probe cannot detect this fault. An open circuit would manifest as a failure to detect a tone on a wire, indicating that there is either a break in the wire or a bad connection in one or both connectors. A short is when a wire is connected to two or more pins or when the conductors of two or more wires are touching. Transposed pairs is a fault in which both of the wires in a pair are connected to the wrong pins at one end of the cable. All three of these faults are detectable with a toner and probe.

42. C. Attenuation is the weakening of a signal as it travels long distances, whether on a wired or wireless medium. The longer the transmission distance, the more the signal weakens. Absorption is the tendency of a wireless signal to change as it passes through different materials. Latency is a measurement of the time it takes for a signal to travel from its source to its destination. Crosstalk is a type of interference that occurs on wired networks when a signal bleeds over to an adjacent wire.

43. B, C. Dirt on fiber-optic cable connectors can reduce the strength of the signal resulting in decibel loss. Excessive cable length can result in greater attenuation and weaker signals due to the decibel loss. Electromagnetic interference and signal crosstalk are both factors that can affect copper cable transmissions, but not fiber-optic.

44. A, B, C. There should be no collisions at all on a full-duplex network, so collisions indicate that at least one side of the connection is trying to operate in half-duplex mode. Ethernet running over twisted-pair cable, in its original half-duplex mode, detects collisions by looking for data on the transmit and receive pins at the same time. In full-duplex mode, data is supposed to be transmitted and received at the same time. In a duplex mismatch, in which one side of a connection is configured to use full duplex and the other end is configured to use half duplex, the full-duplex communications originating from one side look like collisions to the half-duplex side. The half-duplex adapter transmits a jam signal as a result of each collision, which causes the full duplex side to receive an incomplete or damaged frame, which is perceived as a runt, or a cyclic redundancy check (CRC) error. A runt is a frame that is too small—under 64 bytes. Both sides then start to retransmit frames in a continuing cycle, causing network performance to diminish. Ping tests do not detect a duplex mismatch, because ping only transmits a small amount of data in one direction at a time. The mismatch only becomes apparent when the systems transmit large amounts of data.

45. B, D, E. A speed mismatch on a wired network only occurs when two devices are configured to use a specific transmission speed and those speeds are different. In that case, network communication stops. For network communication to occur on a twisted-pair network, transmit (TX) pins must be connected to receive (RX) pins. If the connections are transposed (reversed), no communication occurs. If the switch port to which a computer is connected is disabled due to an error state, there will be no network communication. Bottlenecks and duplex mismatches will slow down network communications, but they will not stop them completely.

46. B. Attenuation is the weakening of a signal as it travels long distances, whether on a wired or wireless medium. The longer the transmission distance, the more the signal weakens. Cable length specifications are designed in part to prevent signals from attenuating to the point at which they are unviable. Jitter, crosstalk, and electromagnetic interference (EMI) are all conditions that can affect the performance of a wired network, but they are not directly related to the length of the cable.

47. B, C. The Gigabit Ethernet standards call for switches and network adapters to support autonegotiation by default, which enables devices to communicate and select the best network speed and duplex mode available to them both. Therefore, speed mismatches and duplex mismatches no longer occur unless someone modifies the speed or duplex settings to incompatible values on one or both devices.

48. D. Fluorescent light fixtures and other devices in an office environment can generate magnetic fields, resulting in electromagnetic interference (EMI). When a copper-based cable runs too near to such a device, the magnetic fields can generate an electric current on the cable that interferes with the signals exchanged by network devices. Jitter, attenuation, and crosstalk are all conditions that can affect the performance of a wired network, but they are not directly related to the cables' proximity to light fixtures.

49. C. The link pulse LED indicates the adapter is connected to a functioning hub or switch. The speed LED specifies the data rate of the link. The collision LED lights up when collisions occur. There is no status LED on a network interface adapter.

50. C. The Alternative B PoE variant can use the spare wire pairs in a CAT 5 or better 10Base-T or 100Base-TX cable to supply power to connected devices. The Alternative A and 4PPoE variants cannot use the spare wire pair in this manner; they supply power using the wire pairs that carry data at the same time. For Gigabit Ethernet or faster installations, Alternative B is capable of using the data wire pairs. Security cameras are ideal candidates for PoE without exceeding the power budget.

51. D. Cable runs are traditionally wired "straight through," that is, with the transmit pins at one end wired to the transmit pins at the other end. It is the switch that is supposed to implement the crossover circuit that connects the transmit pins to the receive pins. Cable runs wired using T568A at one end and T568B at the other end create a crossover circuit in the cable run. At one time, this would have been a serious problem, but today's switches automatically configure crossover circuits as needed, so they will adjust themselves to adapt to the cable runs. All of the other options would correct the problem, but doing nothing is certainly the easiest and best option.

52. A. The problem is unlikely to be a bad switch port or a bad cable, so moving the cable from port 4 to port 2 will not help. The problem is the crossover circuit between the two computers. The two systems were once connected directly together, which means that Ralph was using a crossover cable. The switch also provides a crossover circuit (except in the X port), and old switches often do not autonegotiate crossovers. Therefore, the connection has two crossovers, which is the equivalent of wiring transmit pins to transmit pins, instead of transmit pins to receive pins. All of the other options eliminate one of the crossover circuits, enabling the computers to be wired correctly.

53. D. The autonegotiation mechanism is not the problem, nor is the pinout standard or Ralph's wire pair selection. The speed autonegotiation mechanism in Gigabit Ethernet uses only two wire pairs, so although the LEDs do light up successfully, a functional Gigabit Ethernet data connection requires all four wire pairs.

54. B. Older Ethernet switches do not autonegotiate crossovers. Instead, they have an X (or uplink) port that provides a connection without a crossover circuit, so you can connect one switch to another. If both of the cables had been standard straight-through Ethernet cables or if both had been crossover cables, then plugging them into two regular ports should have worked. Because plugging one cable into the X port worked, this means that only one of the cables must be a crossover cable. The problem, therefore, was the cable, not the port. The X port does not provide extra strength to the signals.

55. B. A bent pin on one of the twelfth computer's connections would cause a break in the bus, essentially forming two networks that operate independently. The failure to terminate or ground the network would not produce this type of fault. Reversing the transmit and receive pins is not possible on a coaxial connection, due to the architecture of the cable.

56. A, B. An open circuit is caused either by a break in the wire somewhere inside the cable or a bad connection with the pin in one or both connectors. A short is when a wire is connected to two or more pins at one end of the cable or when the conductors of two or more wires are touching inside the cable. In this instance, the damage to the cables could have resulted in either condition. A split pair is a connection in which two wires are incorrectly mapped in exactly the same way on both ends of the cable. Having transposed pairs is a fault in which both of the wires in a pair are connected to the wrong pins at one end of the cable. Both of these faults are the result of incorrect wiring during installation; they are not caused by damaged cables.

57. A. Crosstalk is a type of interference that occurs on copper-based networks when a signal transmitted on one conductor bleeds over onto another nearby conductor. Twisted-pair cables, which have eight or more conductors compressed together inside one sheath, are particularly susceptible to crosstalk. Twisting each of the separate wire pairs tends to reduce the amount of crosstalk to manageable levels. Twisting the wire pairs does not prevent signals from being affected by electromagnetic interference (EMI) or attenuation. Latency is a measurement of the time it takes for a signal to travel from its source to its destination.

58. D. Either the T568A or the T568B pinout standard is acceptable. The patch cables will function properly as long as both ends are wired using the same pinout standard.

59. C. Crosstalk is a type of interference that occurs on copper-based networks when a signal transmitted on one conductor bleeds over onto another nearby conductor. Twisted-pair cables, which have eight or more conductors compressed together inside one sheath, are particularly susceptible to crosstalk. Twisting each of the separate wire pairs tends to reduce the amount of crosstalk to manageable levels. Untwisting the pairs leaves them more susceptible to crosstalk. Jitter, attenuation, and electromagnetic interference (EMI) are all conditions that can affect the performance of a wired network, but they are not directly related to untwisted wire pairs.

60. A, C. In this scenario, the user was previously able to connect to the network. There have been no hardware or software changes to the computer. These factors indicate that there is possibly a Physical layer problem, such as a loose or faulty cable, a suspended or error disabled switch port, or a bad network interface adapter in the computer. Since the user's cable previously worked, there is no need to verify that it is pinned and paired properly, and crossover cables are not used to connect workstations to switches. The first thing Ed should do is verify that all cable connections are secure. If he finds a loose cable and the link pulse LED lights up when he reseats it, then the cable was the problem. If the link pulse LED does not light, Ed should replace the existing cable with a straight-through cable that is known to be good. If the LED lights up, the existing cable was probably faulty. If the LED does not light up, Ed should suspect a faulty network interface adapter or switch port and try moving the cable to a port on the switch that is known to function. If the connection works, the problem is probably a failed switch port. If the connection still does not work, then the fault is probably the network interface adapter in the user's computer.

61. C, D. Option A is the T568B pinout, and option B is the T568A pinout. Both of these are correct and can be used. Options C and D are both incorrect and can result in excessive amounts of crosstalk.

62. B. Attenuation is the weakening of the signals as they traverse the network medium. In this case, the problem is most likely the result of cable runs that exceed the 100-meter maximum defined in the Ethernet twisted-pair specification. Therefore, shortening the cable runs will be likely to solve the problem. All of the Ethernet twisted-pair specifications have a 100-meter maximum length, so running the network at a slower speed, installing a higher-grade cable, and installing higher end network adapters might have no effect if the runs are overly long.

63. A. Elevator machinery, fluorescent light fixtures, and other electrical devices in an office environment can generate magnetic fields, resulting in electromagnetic interference (EMI). When copper-based data cables are located too near to such a device, the magnetic fields can generate an electric current on the cable that interferes with the signals exchanged by network devices. If the network users experience a problem every time the elevator machinery switches on, EMI is a likely cause of the problem. Near-end crosstalk (NEXT), far-end crosstalk (FEXT), and attenuation can all cause intermittent network communication problems, but they cannot be caused by elevator machinery.

64. B, D. It is common practice on many networks to disable switch ports that are not in use—leaving them in an administratively down state—so that unauthorized individuals cannot plug devices into them. Some networks also use port security, in which switches are configured with access control lists (ACLs) that specify the MAC addresses of devices that are permitted to use them. Either of these could be the source of Ralph's problem. Because there are no other network users reporting problems, malfunctioning services such as NAT and DNS are not likely to be the cause.

65. A. A duplex mismatch is the most likely of the options. Ethernet running over twisted-pair cable, in its original half-duplex mode, detects collisions by looking for data on the transmit and receive pins at the same time. In full-duplex mode, data is supposed to be transmitted and received at the same time. When one side of a connection is configured to use full duplex and the other end is configured to use half duplex, the full-duplex communications on the one side look like collisions to the half-duplex side. The half-duplex adapter transmits a jam signal as a result of each collision, which causes the full-duplex side to receive an incomplete frame. Both sides then start to retransmit frames in a continuing cycle, causing network performance to diminish drastically. If the problem were a crossover cable or a disabled switch port, the link pulse LED would not light. Outdated drivers would not be likely to slow network performance, and if they did, the slowdown would be minor.

66. C. Ralph's new computer is probably equipped with a network adapter that supports Gigabit Ethernet (1000Base-T). Fast Ethernet and newer network adapters support autonegotiation of the connection speed and duplex state, but most adapters have settings that can control the autonegotiation process. If the computer tries to set a specific speed or state that the switch does not support, the connection will fail, as it has in Ralph's case. Configuring the switch or the network adapter to run at any specific speed will prevent the autonegotiation process from occurring.

67. D. For the link pulse LED on the switch port to light up, there must be a completed connection between the switch and a computer at the other end. None of the other options will cause the LED to light.

68. B. Because Ed knows that the network workstations should be using DHCP to obtain their IP addresses, the best thing to do is to enable the DHCP client and close the ticket rather than configure the system with another static address. There is no indication that there is a rogue DHCP server on the network since the workstation's DHCP client is disabled. This is not the first time that Ed has had a user lie to him, nor will it be the last. He should just let it go and work on addressing the problem.

69. C. Alice's calculations are called an optical link budget. By adding up the various loss factors in decibels (dB), she can determine whether the budget is low, resulting in communication problems over the link. Protocol analysis is an examination of network packet contents. A routing loop is a condition in which packets are circulating endlessly around a network. Received signal strength indication (RSSI) is a wireless networking statistic that does not apply to fiber-optic connections.

70. B. The Alternative B PoE variant can use the spare wire pair in a CAT 5 or better 10Base-T or 100Base-TX cable to supply power to connected devices. The Alternative A and 4PPoE variants cannot use the spare wire pair in this manner; they supply power using the wire pairs that carry data at the same time. For Gigabit Ethernet or faster installations, Alternative B is also capable of using the data wire pairs.

71. A, C, D, E. Runts, giants, collisions, and late collisions are all malfunctions on a full-duplex Ethernet network. Runt frames occur when a network interface generates packets that are smaller than the 64-byte minimum allowable length. Giants occur when frames are larger than the 1,518-byte maximum allowable length. Collisions are normal on a half-duplex network, but on a full-duplex network, collisions are considered to be malfunctions. Late collisions occur when network cables are too long. Drops occur when there are more packets to be transmitted than the network interface can handle.

72. A. Runts and giants are typically the result of a network interface adapter malfunction. Runt frames occur on an Ethernet network when a network interface generates packets that are smaller than the 64-byte minimum allowable length. Giants occur when frames are larger than the 1,518-byte maximum allowable length. Ethernet is a local area networking protocol, so routers are not involved in frame communications. Collisions are normal on a half-duplex network, but runts and giants are not. Late collisions occur when network cables are too long.

73. C. Electromagnetic interference is the likely cause of CRC errors. A network interface adapter malfunction can cause runts and giant frames. Collisions are normal on a half-duplex network, but CRC errors are not. Late collisions occur when network cables are too long, but they do not cause CRC errors.

74. E. Jumbo frames is a feature supported by some Ethernet implementations that enable frames to exceed the 1,500-byte maximum data payload defined in the IEEE 802.3 standard. Runt frames, giant frames, cyclic redundancy check (CRC) errors, and encapsulation errors are all types of errors typically reported in network interface diagnostics.

75. C. Patch panel ports and wall plates should be labeled when the cable runs are attached to them. Labeling them at any earlier time can result in cable runs being connected incorrectly.

76. C. Either CAT 6 or CAT 6a UTP cable will provide the currently required 1 Gbps data rate, with a migration path to 10 Gbps in the future. The backbone cabling connecting the two LANs needs to be fiber-optic, since it exceeds the distance limitations of twisted-pair and coaxial cable. CAT 5e cable conceivably runs at 1 Gbps; however, it does not run at 10 Gbps. Shielded cable alone would not guarantee a 1 Gbps data rate and an upgrade path to 10 Gbps.

77. D. The Thin Ethernet LAN is the network most endangered by the cable break. If a bus network is severed, all of the workstations on it are affected because the cable segments are no longer terminated at one end. The Gigabit Ethernet network uses a star/hub and spoke topology, which means that only the one computer using the severed cable could be disconnected from the network. An FDDI double ring network can survive a single cable break without any workstations being affected.

78. D, E, F. Category 6a (CAT 6a) twisted-pair cable is a variant on CAT 6 that enables you to create 10GBase-T networks with segments up to 100 meters long. Category 7 (CAT 7) cable adds shielding both to the individual wire pairs and to the entire cable, for even greater resistance to crosstalk and noise. CAT 7 supports 100-meter 10GBase-T segments as well. CAT 8 cable supports bandwidth up to 2 GHz, making it even more suitable for 10GBase-T networks than CAT 6a (500 MHz) or CAT7 (600 MHz). CAT 5 and CAT 5e are not suitable for use with 10GBase-T. You can use CAT 6 for 10Gbase-T, but it is limited to 55-meter segments.

79. E. All twisted-pair Gigabit Ethernet implementations require all four wire pairs to achieve 1,000 Mbps transfer rates.

80. A, B, C, D. CAT 5 cable was the original cable standard intended for transfer rates up to 100 Mbps. CAT 5e, CAT 6, and CAT 6a all support 100 Mbps and are also rated for data rates up to 1,000 Mbps. CAT 6 and CAT 6a can also support 10 Gbps. All of these standards also support the 10 Mbps transfer rate.

81. E. Because the company has few employees, a single location, and cost restrictions, the best solution is a star/hub and spoke topology with prefabricated twisted-pair cabling and an external installation method. The star/hub and spoke topology uses a central switch. Prefabricated twisted-pair cabling, with the connectors already attached, will keep the cost to a minimum. Since the employees are all located in the same building, with a common wall and a drop ceiling, the external installation method is the best choice. It is not possible to use a bus topology or coaxial cable for Gigabit Ethernet. Ed could use fiber-optic cable in a star/hub and spoke topology for Gigabit Ethernet, but it is more difficult and expensive to install. An internal installation, which uses a combination of bulk cable and prefabricated cables, is more expensive than an external installation and is typically used for larger networks.

82. D. The best solution in this scenario is to upgrade to 1000Base-T and replace the existing hubs with switches. 1000Base-T provides the fastest transfer speeds supported by the existing cable. Since users are complaining that the network is slow with the existing hubs, it makes sense to replace the shared hub environment with switches that offer dedicated bandwidth on each port. Any solution that does not replace the hubs would not address the users' complaints. 100Base-TX would provide a speed increase, but it runs at ~1/10 the speed of 1000Base-TX. Upgrading to 100Base-FX or 100Base-SX would require the cabling to be replaced with fiber-optic, which would be very expensive.

83. A. Option A is the T568B pinout that Ralph should use when attaching connectors to the cables. Option B is the T568A pinout, which would also work but Ralph has been instructed not to use it. Options C and D are both incorrect and can result in excessive amounts of crosstalk.

84. B. The plier-like device is a crimper, which cable installers use to attach RJ-45 connectors, like those in the bag, to lengths of bulk cable. This is the process of creating patch cables, which are used to connect computers to wall plates and patch panels to switches. The boss is telling Ralph to start making patch cables in 5-foot and 10-foot lengths. You do not use a crimper to attach keystone connectors, and the boss has not given Ralph the tools and components needed to pull cable runs or install a patch panel.

85. D. A media converter is a Physical layer device that can connect different types of network media together, as long as they have the same speed and duplex settings. Because the converter simply retransmits the signals, the single-collision domain is maintained. Bridges and switches are Data link layer devices that create multiple-collision domains. Routers are Network layer devices that create separate collision and broadcast domains.

86. A. There should be no collisions at all on a full-duplex network, so the problem is clearly related to the duplexing of the communications. Ethernet running over twisted-pair cable, in its original half-duplex mode, detects collisions by looking for data on the transmit and receive pins at the same time. In full-duplex mode, data is supposed to be transmitted and received at the same time. When one side of a connection is configured to use full duplex, as Alice's new computers are, and the other end is configured to use half duplex (as the switches must be), the full-duplex communications on the one side look like collisions to the half-duplex side. The half-duplex adapter transmits a jam signal as a result of each collision, which causes the full-duplex side to receive an incomplete frame. Both sides then start to retransmit frames in a continuing cycle, causing network performance to diminish drastically. The ping tests do not detect a problem because ping only transmits a small amount of data in one direction at a time. The other options would likely cause the ping tests to fail as well. The solution to the problem is to configure all of the devices to autonegotiate their speed and duplex modes.

87. A, C. A bottleneck is a component involved in a network connection that is not functioning correctly, causing a traffic slowdown that affects the entire network. A duplex mismatch occurs when one side of a connection is configured to use full duplex and the other end is configured to use half duplex. When this occurs, the full-duplex communications on the one side look like collisions to the half-duplex side. The half-duplex adapter transmits a jam signal as a result of each collision, which causes the full-duplex side to receive an incomplete frame. Both sides then start to retransmit frames in a continuing cycle, causing network performance to diminish drastically. A speed mismatch or a transmitter (TX)/receiver (RX) transposition will stop network communication completely.

88. B. To access the Internet, the workstation's routing table must include a default gateway entry, which would have a Network Destination value of 0.0.0.0. A workstation's routing table does not specify the address of a DNS server. The loopback and 224.0.0.0 multicast addresses are normal routing table entries.

89. D. The correct syntax for the Windows `route add` command is to specify the destination network address, followed by the subnet mask for the destination network, followed by the address of the router interface on the local network that provides access to the destination network. The other options do not specify the correct addresses in the syntax.

90. C. The correct syntax for the Windows `route add` command is to specify the destination network address, followed by the subnet mask for the destination network, followed by the address of the router interface on the local network that provides access to the destination network. Therefore, 192.168.87.226 is the address of the router interface on the internal network, where Ralph's workstation is located.

91. B. A port scanner examines a system for open endpoints, accessible using the TCP or UDP protocols, which intruders can conceivably use to gain access to the system from the network.

92. B. A port is a numbered service endpoint identifying an application running on a TCP/IP system. A port scanner examines a system for open endpoints, accessible using the TCP or UDP protocols at the Transport layer, which intruders can conceivably use to gain access to the system from the network.

93. B. The ports that a port scanner examines are the system endpoints identified by port numbers in TCP and UDP protocol headers. An open port provides network access to an application running on the computer, which can conceivably be exploited by an intruder.

94. C. Because the customer can access the other two computers in the house, Ed knows that her IP address and subnet mask are properly configured, that the network cable is plugged in and functional, and that a switching loop is not preventing access to the Internet. Ed also knows that the computer's DNS record does not play a role in outgoing connections. The problem is most likely in the default gateway because the gateway address the customer specified is on another network, 172.16.43.0, rather than on her own network, 172.16.41.0.

95. D. The problem is most likely incorrect ACL settings. Because the computers are all able to access the Internet, their TCP/IP settings, including their IP addresses, subnet mask, and default gateway address, must be correct. However, if the users do not have the correct permissions in the access control lists (ACLs) of the filesystem shares, they will not be able to access the shares over the network.

96. D. The address 169.254.199.22 is from the 169.254.0.0/16 network address assigned to Automatic Private IP Addressing (APIPA), a standard for the assignment of IP addresses to Dynamic Host Configuration Protocol (DHCP) clients when they cannot obtain an address from a DHCP server. 127.0.0.1 is the standard IPv4 loopback address. 240.15.167.251 is from the 240.0.0.0 network address, which is reserved for experimental use. Neither of these are ever assigned by DHCP. 255.255.255.0 is not an IP address at all; it is a subnet mask.

97. B. The Default Gateway setting should contain the address of a router on the local network that provides access to other networks, such as the Internet. In this case, therefore, the Default Gateway address should be on the 192.168.4.0 network, but it contains an address on the 192.168.6.0 network, which is not local. Therefore, the user can only access systems on the 192.168.4.0 network. The Subnet Mask setting must be correct, or the user would not be able to access any other systems. Unlike the default gateway, the DNS server does not have to be on the local network, so the address shown can be correct. DHCP is not necessary to access the Internet.

98. C. The 169.254.203.42 address assigned to the workstation is from the 169.254.0.0/16 network address assigned to Automatic Private IP Addressing (APIPA), a standard for the assignment of IP addresses to DHCP clients when they cannot obtain an address from a DHCP server. Since no one else is experiencing a problem, the DHCP server is presumably functioning. The Subnet Mask value is correct for an APIPA address, and APIPA does not provide Default Gateway or DNS server addresses. Therefore, an exhausted DHCP scope is the only one of the explanations provided that could be the cause of the problem.

99. B. For a computer connected to the 192.168.32.0/20 network, the Subnet Mask value should be 255.255.240.0, not 255.255.255.0, as shown in the `ipconfig /all` output. The IPv4 Address, Default Gateway, and DNS Servers settings are appropriate for the network. The workstation apparently has DHCP disabled, so it has not retrieved appropriate IP address settings from the DHCP server.

100. B. The DHCP client on the workstation is enabled, but the IP address assigned to the workstation is not from the 192.168.4.0/24 network. The assigned address is not an APIPA address, nor is it expired, so the only conclusion is that there is a rogue DHCP server on the network assigning addresses from a wholly different subnet.

101. C. In this scenario, some, but not all, users on VLAN2 cannot connect to local and remote resources. Since users connected to other switches within the same VLAN and on other VLANs are not reporting any problems, the router is not the issue. This also excludes a VLAN2 configuration problem because this would affect the VLAN2 users on all of the switches. VLAN3 and VLAN4 users can communicate through the router, so they are also not the problem. The likeliest problem is the common component, which is the switch to which the VLAN2 users experiencing the outage are connected.

102. A. In this scenario, only users on one LAN are experiencing problems connecting to the Internet and other internal LANs. This isolates the problem to a component within that LAN only. Since users can connect successfully to local resources, the problem does not lie within the individual computers, the switch that connects the users to the network, or the backbone network cable. The likeliest problem is in the router connecting the problem LAN to the backbone network. Since users on the other internal LANs are not reporting problems connecting to the Internet, the problem most likely does not involve the Internet router.

103. A, B, C. Ed will first have to change IP addresses. This is because the computers on the other side of the router, on the screened subnet, must use an IP network address that is different from the internal network's address. Next, Ed will have to change the default gateway address setting on the internal network computers to the address of the router so that traffic can be directed to the screened subnet. Finally, Ed will have to update the resource records on the DNS server to reflect the IP address changes. MAC addresses are hard-coded into network interface adapters and are not easily changed.

104. C. The problem is most likely the default gateway address, which directs all traffic intended for the Internet to the cable modem/router. If that address is incorrect, the traffic will never reach the router or the Internet. Because the computer can access the other two systems on the local network, the IP address and subnet mask are not the problem. It is not necessary (and not always possible) to change the MAC address on a Windows workstation.

105. D. Because Ed can connect to WebServ1 successfully, the problem is not an unresponsive service or blocked ports on the server. The problem is not a name resolution failure because Ralph can successfully ping WebServ1 by name. Therefore, of the options listed, the only possible problem must be that the firewall on Ralph's workstation is not configured to allow the remote desktop client's traffic out.

106. B. In this scenario, all of the internal users are experiencing problems connecting to the Internet, so the router that provides access to the Internet is the suspected component. Since users can connect to resources on the internal LANs, the problem probably is not in any of the routers connecting the LANs to the backbone or the backbone cable itself. This also eliminates the probability that the switches on the LANs are the problem.

107. C. When a Dynamic Host Configuration Protocol (DHCP) client is offered an IP address by a DHCP server, the client broadcasts Address Resolution Protocol (ARP) requests using that address before accepting it. If another computer on the local network is using the offered address, the computer responds to the ARP request and the DHCP client declines the address. The DHCP server then offers another address. DNS queries and routing table checks are not reliable means of checking for duplicate IP addresses. It is possible to have two DHCP servers on the same local network, but they must be configured with scopes that do not overlap.

108. B. Operating systems detect duplicate IP addresses immediately and display error messages or notifications on the computers involved. Therefore, the user with the problem would have been informed immediately if another system were using her IP address. All of the other options are possible causes of the problem that are more difficult to troubleshoot.

109. C. Green LEDs indicate the device is running at the full speed supported by the switch, whereas orange LEDs indicate that the device is running at a reduced speed. If no device is connected, the LED does not illuminate at all. The LED does not indicate the occurrence of collisions or the type of device connected to the port.

110. D. On all of the servers, NTP uses the well-known User Datagram Protocol (UDP) port 123 for its communications with a Coordinated Universal Time (UTC) server. If a server's firewall is blocking that port, it cannot synchronize its clock time. If the domain controllers have clocks that are not synchronized, their data synchronization processes can be affected. The problem is not a name resolution failure, an unresponsive database service, or incorrect TCP/IP settings because other server functions are not affected.

111. A. If the time on the domain controller at the new office is more than 5 minutes off the time held by domain controller at the home office, then the new domain controller will not synchronize. Duplicate IP addresses or an incorrect default gateway address would prevent the new domain controller from connecting to the home office network. A server hardware failure would manifest as an outage far more serious than a domain controller synchronization issue.

112. A. Only DNS servers perform FQDN resolutions, so that is likely to be the source of the problem. It is possible to ping a device on the local network using its computer name without the use of DNS. Electromagnetic interference (EMI) would inhibit all network communication, and access control lists have no effect on ping tests.

113. C. The 169.254.0.0/16 network is used by Automatic Private IP Addressing (APIPA), a standard that provides DHCP clients with an IP address when they cannot contact a DHCP server. Unknown to Ralph, the DHCP server on his network has been down for over a week, and the users' IP address leases have begun to expire. This causes them to revert to APIPA addresses. Multiple users changing their IP addresses would not result in them all using the same network address. A rogue DHCP would not be likely to deploy APIPA addresses to clients. Malware infections that modify IP addresses are rare.

114. B, D. The solution should call for Ralph to create a VLAN on the Internet router that matches the VLAN the network switch port is using. Therefore, he should create a VLAN4 on the router and assign a port to it, which will be the port Ralph uses to connect the router to the network switch. There is no need to create a VLAN1 on the network switch because all switches have a default VLAN called VLAN1. Modifying the VLAN assignments on the network switch is not a good idea, because it might interfere with the existing VLAN strategy in place.

115. A, B. Ralph could purchase a license upgrade for the Internet access router enabling him to create a VLAN4. However, the simpler and less expensive solution would be to create a VLAN2 on the network switch. As long as both ends of the cable are plugged into ports using the same VLAN, the router should be able to service the network. Configuring the devices to use the default VLAN1 might interfere with the existing VLAN strategy.

116. A. For the website's security certificate to be trusted, it must be signed by a source that both parties in the transaction trust. Many security firms are in the business of providing certificates to companies that have confirmed their identities. This is what Ralph must do to prevent the error message from appearing to the company's clients. Creating a self-signed certificate or installing a certification authority in-house is not sufficient and is probably already the cause of the problem. Users are not likely to be convinced that everything is all right just because Ralph says so.

117. A. The most likely cause for the slowdown is a broadcast storm. DHCP relies on broadcast messages to assign IP addresses to users, so 500 users all turning on their computers at the same time in the morning can generate an abnormally high number of broadcast packets. This can degrade network performance until all of the users have completed their DHCP address assignments. Network loops, switching loops, and asymmetric routing can degrade network performance, but the degradation would not be limited to the early morning hours. A rogue DHCP server can cause problems but not the one described here.

118. B. The Default Gateway parameter specifies the address of the local router that the end system should use to access other networks. The IPv6 Address parameter is the 128-bit address the end system uses on IP version 6 networks. The DNS Servers parameter contains the addresses of servers used to resolve names into IP addresses. The Subnet Mask parameter specifies the sizes of the network and host identifiers in an IPv4 address.

119. B. ACLs restrict access to network devices by filtering usernames, MAC addresses, IP addresses, or other criteria. Routers, switches, and WAPs all use ACLs to control access to them. Hubs are purely Physical layer devices that relay electrical or optical signals; they have no way of controlling access to them.

120. A, B. Bridge protocol data units (BPDUs) are messages that switches running the STP exchange to learn about the available paths through a switched network and the states of other switches. Switches should receive BPDUs only through ports that are connected to other switches. BPDU guard is a feature that prevents BPDU messages from arriving through ports with other roles, such as those connected to computers, thus preventing an attacker from manipulating the STP topology. A root guard affects the behavior of the STP by enforcing the selection of root bridge ports on a switched network. Without root guards, there is no way for administrators to enforce the topology of a network with a redundant switching fabric. DHCP snooping is a feature found in some switches that prevents rogue DHCP servers from assigning IP addresses to clients. Geofencing is a wireless networking technique for limiting access to a network. Neither is related to the STP.

121. C. Jitter is defined as delays in the transmission of individual network packets. For audio or video transmissions, jitter can result in dropped words or frames. For data file transmissions, jitter can require the retransmission of packets.

122. A. The 802.11ac standard calls for the use of the 5 GHz frequency band only, which means that it will never be able to connect to 2.4 GHz devices like the television. It is not possible to configure the access point to run on the 2.4 GHZ band, and configuring the computers to use that band will prevent them from connecting to the access point. The distance between the devices has no bearing on the connections in this instance.

123. A, C, E. The 2.4 GHz band used by wireless LANs (WLANs) consists of channels that are 20 (or 22) MHz wide. However, the channels are only 5 MHz apart, so there is channel overlap that can result in interference. Channels 1, 6, and 11 are the only channels that are far enough apart from each other to avoid any overlap with the adjacent channels. Channels 4 and 8 are susceptible to overlap.

124. A. Specifying the wrong passphrase for the encryption protocol is the most common cause of a failure to connect to the network with no indication of an error. Incorrect antenna placement and channel overlap could result in a weak signal or no signal, either of which would be indicated in the Available Networks list. An incorrect SSID is not likely to be the error, as long as Ralph selected the access point from the list.

125. B, D, E. Interference resulting from channel overlap, signal degradation due to incorrect antenna polarization, and signal loss due to antenna cable attenuation could render the workstation unable to make contact with the access point. An incorrect WPA3 passphrase would not be the problem, unless Ralph had already seen the access point and attempted to connect to it. An incorrect SSID would be the problem only if Ralph had already attempted to manually enter an SSID. The network has only a single access point, so there is no chance of roaming misconfiguration causing the problem.

126. C. A patch antenna is a flat device that transmits signals in a half-spherical pattern. By placing the antenna against the building's outer wall, Ralph can provide coverage inside the building and minimize coverage extending to the outside. A dipole antenna is another name for the omnidirectional antenna usually provided with an access point. A unidirectional antenna directs signals in a straight line, which would not provide the coverage Ralph needs. A Yagi antenna is a type of unidirectional antenna.

127. A, D. Greater distance from the access point or interference from intervening walls can both cause a weakening of wireless signals, resulting in the insufficient wireless coverage and intermittent connectivity that Trixie is experiencing. An incorrect SSID would prevent Trixie's laptop from ever connecting to the network. An omnidirectional antenna generates signals in every direction, which would not account for Trixie's problem.

128. B. It is possible that the wireless access point has been configured not to broadcast the network's SSID as a security measure, so Alice should first attempt to access it by typing in the SSID manually. She would not be able to type in the WPA3 passphrase until she is connecting to the SSID. Moving the laptop closer to the access point or away from possible sources of electromagnetic interference might be solutions to the problem, but they should not be the first thing Alice tries.

129. D. The most likely cause of Alice's problem is that she has selected an incorrect encryption protocol. Wired Equivalent Privacy (WEP) is still provided as an option on many wireless devices, but it has long since been found to be insecure and is almost never used. Alice should try selecting the other security types that enable her to enter her passphrase, such as Wi-Fi Protected Access 3 (WPA3). Although the other options are possible causes of the problem, encryption protocol mismatch is the most likely cause.

130. D. Wireless LAN equipment built to the 802.11ac standard can only use the 5 GHz frequency. However, an 802.11g access point can only use the 2.4 GHz frequency. Therefore, the network adapters cannot connect to Ralph's access point. Moving the devices closer together or manually entering the SSID will have no effect on the connections.

131. B. The 802.11g standard does not support 5 GHz communications. Replacing the 802.11g adapters with those of a newer standard, such as 802.11n, 802.11ac, or 802.11ax, is the only way to connect these devices to the 5 GHz network. The 5 GHz band does support automatic channel selection, so there is no need to configure the channel on each laptop manually. The 802.11ac standard supports only the 5 GHz band, so configuring the access point to use 2.4 GHz will prevent these devices from connecting. The 5 GHz band does support MIMO, and the 802.11n laptops should be able to connect.

132. D. As wireless computers move farther away from the access point, their signals attenuate (weaken), their received signal strength indicators (RSSI) go down, and the maximum speed of their connections drops. If the computers were using a different encryption protocol than the access point, there would be no connection at all, not a diminished connection speed. An SSID mismatch would cause the computers to connect to a different network, not necessarily connect at a slower speed. If the computers had 802.11ac adapters, they would fail to connect to the access point at all because 802.11ac requires the use of the 5 GHz frequency band, and the 802.11n network uses 2.4 GHz.

133. B. Replacing the access point with an 802.11ax model is not likely to have any effect at all unless you upgrade the computer's network adapter as well. Installing a higher gain antenna on the access point can improve its range, enabling the computer to connect more readily. Moving the computer closer to the access point can strengthen the signal and raise its received signal strength indicator (RSSI), enabling it to connect more reliably. Changing the channel on the access point to a lesser used one can enable the computer to connect more easily.

134. C. Disabling SSID broadcasts will not defeat dedicated attackers, but it can prevent casual intruders from accessing the network. MAC filtering would require Ed to configure the access point with the MAC addresses of all devices that will access the network, which would be impractical in this case. The network is unsecured, so there is no passphrase to change, and a frequency change will have no effect on the problem.

135. D. Absorption is a type of interference that occurs when radio signals have to pass through barriers made of dense materials, such as concrete or cinderblock walls. The density of the material's molecular structure causes the radio signals to be partially converted to heat, which weakens them. Reflection is when signals bounce off of certain surfaces, such as metal. Refraction is when signals bend as they pass through certain barriers, such as glass or water. Diffraction is when signals have to pass around barriers to reach a particular destination. All of these phenomena can weaken the radio signals used in wireless networking, but absorption is the primary problem for Alice in this case.

136. A. The closer the users are to the access point, the stronger the signals will be. Installing an additional access point nearer to the executive offices will likely enable the signals to pass through the barriers more efficiently. The channel used by the access point, the standard on which the access point is based, and the broadcasting of SSID signals have no effect on the strength of the signals reaching the executive offices and will not resolve Ralph's problem.

137. D. Absorption is a type of interference that occurs when radio signals have to pass through barriers made of dense materials, such as walls and doors. In this case, the construction of the barriers has made them more formidable. Reflection is when signals bounce off of

certain surfaces, such as metal. Refraction is when signals bend as they pass through certain barriers, such as glass or water. Diffraction is when signals have to pass around barriers to reach a particular destination. All of these phenomena can weaken the radio signals used in wireless networking, but absorption is the primary problem for Ralph in this case.

138. B, D. Attenuation is the tendency of signals to weaken as they travel through a network medium. In the case of a wireless network, the medium is the air, and the farther away a wireless device is from the access point, the weaker the signal will be. Refraction is when signals bend as they pass through certain types of barriers, such as the glass walls of conference rooms. The bending changes the direction of the signals, possibly causing them to weaken in the process. Reflection is when signals bounce off of certain surfaces, such as metal. Diffraction is when signals have to pass around barriers to reach a particular destination. All of these phenomena can weaken the radio signals used in wireless networking, but attenuation and refraction are likely to be the primary problems for Ralph in this case.

139. C. The network is supporting 802.11n and 802.11g devices, so it must be running on the 2.4 GHz band. The 802.11ac standard is fundamentally incompatible with the network because it only runs on the 5 GHz band. Therefore, the only viable solution is to install a network adapter in the laptop that supports 2.4 GHz. Installing an 802.11ac access point would prevent the 2.4 GHz devices from connecting. Changing channels on the access point and moving the user will have no effect on the problem.

140. D. The use of an incorrect wireless security protocol is a well-known source of errorless connection failures, so checking this will most likely enable Ed to locate the source of the problem. Channel overlap is a problem that Ed would check and resolve at the access point, not the users' workstations. While it is possible to change the frequency on an 802.11ax access point, this would likely interfere with the connectivity of the other network devices. Although signal interference could conceivably be the cause for a connection failure, the users can see the network, so this is probably not the problem.

141. A, B. Moving the access point to the center of the building will keep as much of its operational range inside the structure as possible. If the signals still reach outside the building, Ed can reduce the power level of the access point until the network is only accessible inside. MAC filtering would require Ed to configure the access point with the MAC addresses of all devices that will access the network, which would be impractical in this case. Installing a captive portal would not block outside users unless Ed configures the portal to require user authentication, which defeats the purpose of the guest network.

142. B, C. The first steps Alice should take are the simplest ones: make sure that the wireless interface in the user's laptop is turned on and that she is attempting to connect to the correct SSID for the company network. Changing the channel would not be necessary unless other users in the area are also having problems due to interference. The 802.11n wireless networking standard is compatible with 802.11ax, so it should not be necessary to provide the user with a new network adapter.

143. C. If the users are losing their connections due to interference from other types of devices, changing the channel alters the frequency the network uses and can enable it to avoid the interference. The other options are not likely to affect any condition that would cause clients to dissociate.

144. B, D. Of the options provided, the ones most likely to be causing the problem are the use of an incorrect SSID or encryption protocol. Although signal interference could possibly be a cause, it is more likely that the new users have devices that are incorrectly configured for Ed's network. Channel overlap is a problem that Ed would check and resolve at the access point, not the users' workstations.

145. D. WPA has been found to be vulnerable, and WPA2 increases security by replacing the Temporal Key Integrity Protocol (TKIP) with the Advanced Encryption System (AES), so Ralph should use WPA2 instead of WPA. Suppressing SSID broadcasts does not prevent users from connecting to the network, and MAC filtering strengthens security without exposing MAC addresses to undue risk.

146. B. Effective isotropic radiated power (EIRP) is a measurement of the signal strength generated by an access point (or other radio transceiver) with a particular antenna. Received signal strength indicator (RSSI) is a measurement of the strength of the signal received by a device from an access point. Service set identifier (SSID) is a designation assigned to a specific wireless network, which appears in the Available Networks list of a Wi-Fi client. Multiple input, multiple output (MIMO) is a technology used by some IEEE wireless networking standards to increase throughput capacity by using multiple antennas.

147. B. Because Alice is able to access the server and open the spreadsheet file, the problem is not related to blocked ports, firewall settings, or an untrusted certificate. The problem is most likely that though she has the necessary filesystem access control list (ACL) permissions to open and read the file, she does not have the permissions needed to modify it.

148. C. When individual packets in a data stream are delayed, the resulting connectivity problem is called jitter. Although this condition might not cause problems for asynchronous applications, real-time communications, such as Voice over Internet Protocol (VoIP) or streaming video, can suffer interruptions, from which the phenomenon gets its name. Latency describes a generalized delay in network transmissions, not individual packet delays. Attenuation is the weakening of a signal as it travels through a network medium. A bottleneck is a condition in which all traffic is delayed, due to a faulty or inadequate component.

149. B, C. Jitter is a connectivity problem on wired networks that is caused by individual packets that are delayed due to network congestion, different routing, or queuing problems. When individual packets in a data stream are delayed, the resulting connectivity problem is called jitter. While this condition might not cause problems for asynchronous applications, such as email and instant messaging, real-time communications, such as Voice over Internet Protocol (VoIP) or streaming video, can suffer intermittent interruptions, from which the phenomenon gets its name.

150. C. The 2.4 GHz band used by wireless LANs (WLANs) consists of channels that are 20 (or 22) MHz wide. However, the channels are only 5 MHz apart, so there is channel overlap that can result in interference, possibly causing long AP association times and degraded performance. Channels 1, 6, and 11 are the only channels that are far enough apart from each other to avoid any overlap with the adjacent channels. This is why they are often

recommended. However, in Ralph's case, these channels are too crowded with other networks. Therefore, Ralph should use a channel that is as far as possible from the crowded ones. Channels 2, 5, and 10 are all immediately adjacent to a crowded channel, but channel 9 is at least two channels away from the nearest crowded channel. Therefore, Ralph should configure his equipment to use channel 9.

151. C. A toner and probe is by far the most inexpensive solution for testing both ends of cable runs. A cable tester could do the job, but it is much more expensive. A visual fault locator is a tool for testing fiber-optic cables, and a protocol analyzer looks at packet contents.

152. B, D. The punchdown tool is critical to this operation. In one motion, the tool strips the insulation off of the wire, presses it down into the connector, and cuts off the excess at the end. A wire stripper simplifies the task of preparing the cable for the connection process. A crimper is used only for attaching connectors to patch cables. Pigtail splicers and fusion splicers are used only on fiber-optic networks.

153. A. An optical power meter measures the signal strength on fiber-optic cables to locate breaks and measure signal degradation as part of an optical loss test set (OLTS); it can only be used on fiber-optic cables. Toner and probe tools are used in copper-based cabling installations, not fiber-optic cabling. A protocol analyzer is a tool that captures network packets for the purpose of analyzing their contents. A visual fault locator is a laser light source used to locate breaks in fiber-optic cables, not signal degradation.

154. B. You can use a cable certifier to identify a variety of cable performance characteristics, typically including cabling lengths, signal attenuation, crosstalk, propagation delay, delay skew, and return loss. The other tools listed are dedicated to a single testing modality and do not test for crosstalk.

155. A, C. Cable certifiers can detect all of the faults that toners and probes can detect, and they can do a great deal more, such as specify whether a cable run meets the performance specifications defined in a cable standard. When testing a new cable type, the specifications defined in the cable standard must be added to the device. Cable certifiers are far more expensive than most other cable testing solutions. Cable certifiers are available that support various cable media, including copper and fiber-optic.

156. B, D. A crimper is a device used for attaching connectors to patch cables. A wire stripper, while not essential to the process, can simplify the task of preparing the cable. A punchdown tool is used for attaching keystone connectors to cable ends, for use in wall plates and patch panels. A standard set of pliers is not used in the process of attaching connectors.

157. B. A cable certifier is a complex electronic device that can perform a battery of tests on a cable run, confirm that the cable conforms to the required wiring standards, and maintains records of the testing procedure. Cable certifiers are by far the most expensive of the devices listed. Crimpers and punchdown tools are relatively simple and inexpensive mechanical devices that cable installers use to connect bulk cable to connectors. A toner and probe is an electronic device for cable testing, but it is still relatively simple.

158. B. The device shown in the figure is a punchdown tool, used to connect unshielded twisted-pair cable ends to the keystone connectors used in modular wall plates and patch panels. After lining up the individual wires in the cable with the connector, you use the tool to press each wire into its slot. The tool also cuts the wire sheath to make an electrical contact and trims the end of the wire. This tool is not capable of performing any of the tasks described in the other options.

159. A. The device shown in the figure is a toner and probe, used to test unshielded twisted-pair wiring and detect certain basic wiring faults. This tool is not capable of performing any of the tasks described in the other options.

160. B. The device shown in the figure is a crimper, which is used to create patch cables by attaching connectors to both ends of a relatively short length of bulk cable. This tool is not capable of performing any of the tasks described in the other options.

161. A. The failure to detect a tone on a wire indicates that there is either a break in the wire somewhere inside the cable or a bad connection with the pin in one or both connectors. This condition is called an open circuit. A short is when a wire is connected to two or more pins at one end of the cable. A split pair is a connection in which two wires are incorrectly mapped in exactly the same way on both ends of the cable. Crosstalk is a type of interference caused by signals on one wire bleeding over to other wires.

162. B. A short is when a wire is connected to two or more pins at one end of the cable or when the conductors of two or more wires are touching inside the cable. This would cause a tone applied to a single pin at one end to be heard on multiple pins at the other end. An open circuit would manifest as a failure to detect a tone on a wire, indicating that there is either a break in the wire somewhere inside the cable or a bad connection with the pin in one or both connectors. A split pair is a connection in which two wires are incorrectly mapped in exactly the same way on both ends of the cable. Crosstalk is a type of interference caused by signals on one wire bleeding over to other wires.

163. C. A split pair is a connection in which two wires are incorrectly mapped in exactly the same way on both ends of the cable. Each pin on one end of the cable is correctly wired to the corresponding pin at the other end, but the wires inside the cable used to make the connections are incorrect. In a properly wired connection, each twisted pair should contain a signal wire and a ground wire. In a split pair, it is possible to have two signal wires twisted together as a pair. This can generate excessive amounts of crosstalk, corrupting both of the signals involved. Because all of the pins are connected properly, a toner and probe cannot detect this fault. An open circuit would manifest as a failure to detect a tone on a wire, indicating that there is either a break in the wire somewhere inside the cable or a bad connection with the pin in one or both connectors. A short is when a wire is connected to two or more pins at one end of the cable or when the conductors of two or more wires are touching inside the cable. Transposed pairs is a fault in which both of the wires in a pair are connected to the wrong pins at one end of the cable. All three of these faults are detectable with a toner and probe.

164. D. A split pair is a connection in which two wires are incorrectly mapped in exactly the same way on both ends of the cable. Each pin on one end of the cable is correctly wired to the corresponding pin at the other end, but the wires inside the cable used to make the connections are incorrect. In a properly wired connection, each twisted pair should contain a signal wire and a ground wire. In a split pair, it is possible to have two signal wires twisted together as a pair. This can generate excessive amounts of crosstalk, corrupting both of the signals involved. Because all of the pins are connected properly, a toner and probe cannot detect this fault, and neither can a multimeter. A visual fault locator is a laser light source used to locate breaks in fiber-optic cables. However, a cable certifier is a highly sophisticated electronic device that can detect all types of cable faults, including split pairs, as well as measure cable performance characteristics.

165. D. A time-domain reflectometer (TDR) is a device that determines the length of a cable by transmitting a signal at one end and measuring how long it takes for a reflection of the signal to return from the other end. Using this information and the cable's nominal velocity of propagation (NVP)—a specification supplied by the cable manufacturer—the device can calculate the length of a cable run. In a cable with a break in its length, a TDR calculates the length of the cable up to the break.

Cable certifiers typically have time-domain reflectometry capabilities integrated into the unit, which determines the location of a break by transmitting a signal at one end and measuring how long it takes for a reflection of the signal to return from the break. A toner and probe or a multimeter cannot locate a cable break. A visual fault locator is a laser light source used to locate cable breaks, but only in fiber-optic cables.

166. B. An optical loss test set (OLTS) is the term for the combination of an optical light source and an optical power meter. The optical power meter by itself cannot be used to test the cable runs when there are no devices connected to them. A spectrum analyzer is a device for measuring the amplitudes and frequencies of wireless signals. A multimeter is a device for measuring the electric current on a copper cable.

167. B, E. One possible cause of the problem is that the DNS process on the remote server is corrupted or not running. Another possible cause is that there is a firewall blocking access to the server's UDP port 53. Both of these would render the port unreachable. The TCP/IP client on the server is operating, as verified by the `ping` utility. This means that the IP host configurations on Ralph's computer and on the DNS server are both functioning. The router does not need to be running DNS to forward datagrams.

168. D. The Windows `tracert` tool transmits a series of ICMP messages with incrementing time-to-live (TTL) values, which identify each router on the path the packets take through the network. `Ping` uses ICMP, but it does not manipulate TTL values. `Netstat`, `route`, and `nslookup` do not use ICMP messages, nor do they manipulate TTL values when performing their normal functions.

169. B. If Alice suspects that a DNS server is not resolving hostnames, she should try connecting to a remote host using the IP address instead of the name. If she can connect, she knows that all internal local area network (LAN) components and the Internet gateway are functioning, and the remote host is functioning. The problem most likely lies within the DNS server itself. If Alice cannot connect to a remote host using the IP address, the problem is not the DNS server. She would need to do more testing to isolate the problem device and the affected area. `Ipconfig` is a workstation command that enables you to verify the local IP configuration; it is not used to test a DNS server's functionality. Using the `ping` command will only tell you whether the computer hosting the DNS service is functioning at the Network layer of the Open Systems Interconnection (OSI) model; it will not test the DNS service functionality. The `tracert` (or `traceroute`) command is used to identify the hop-by-hop path taken to reach a destination; it does not allow you to test functionality above the Network layer of the OSI model.

170. B, E. `Nslookup` and `dig` are both command-line utilities that you can direct to a specific DNS server and then generate queries that display resource record information the program retrieves from the server. `Netstat` displays information about networking protocols, whereas `nbtstat` displays information derived from the system's NetBIOS over TCP/IP implementation. `Arp` is a tool that you can use to display and manage a system's ARP table entries. `Netstat`, `nbtstat`, and `arp` are not able to display resource record information.

171. D. Running the `arp` utility with the `-a` parameter on a Windows system displays the contents of the Address Resolution Protocol (ARP) cache. The cache contains records of the IP addresses on the network that `arp` has resolved into MAC addresses. The `ping`, `tracert`, `netstat`, and `hostname` utilities are not capable of producing this output.

172. B. The Windows `tracert` utility functions by transmitting a series of Internet Control Message Protocol (ICMP) Echo Request messages to a specified destination with incrementing time-to-live (TTL) values. Each successive message reaches one hop farther on the route to the destination before timing out. Therefore, the `tracert` display lists the names and addresses of the routers that packets must traverse to reach the destination. The `ping`, `netstat`, `arp`, and `hostname` utilities are not capable of producing this output.

173. A. The Windows `ping` utility functions by transmitting a series of Internet Control Message Protocol (ICMP) Echo Request messages to a specified destination. The destination system responds with ICMP Echo Reply messages that are listed in the output display. The `tracert`, `netstat`, `arp`, and `hostname` utilities are not capable of producing this output.

174. C. Running the Windows `netstat` utility with no parameters generates a list of the workstation's active connections. The `ping`, `tracert`, `arp`, and `hostname` utilities are not capable of producing this output.

175. B. Like `traceroute` and `tracert`, `pathping` is capable of generating a list of the routers that packets pass through on the way to a specific destination system. `Pathping` also displays the percentage of lost packets for each hop, which `traceroute` and `tracert` cannot do. The `ping`, `netstat`, and `route` utilities are not capable of displaying route traces.

176. C. The `traceroute` (or `tracert`) utility can locate a malfunctioning router by using an Echo Request messages with incrementing TTL values. `Ifconfig` is a network configuration utility for Unix and Linux systems; `ping` can test connectivity to another TCP/IP system, but it cannot locate a malfunctioning router; and `netstat` displays information about network connections and traffic but cannot locate a malfunctioning router.

177. E. All Windows ping transactions use ICMP messages. ICMP messages are encapsulated directly within IP datagrams; they do not use Transport layer protocols, such as UDP

and TCP. Ping transactions to destinations on the local network are encapsulated within Ethernet frames. On Unix and Linux, ping uses UDP, which is also encapsulated in IP datagrams.

178. B. The netstat utility can display the routing table, along with other types of network traffic and port information. The arp utility is for adding addresses to the ARP cache; it cannot display the routing table. The ifconfig command displays TCP/IP configuration information on Unix and Linux systems; it cannot display the routing table. Telnet is a terminal emulation program; it cannot display the routing table. Show route is a router console command that does nothing on the local computer.

179. C. Running ping with the -l parameter enables you to specify the size of the messages sent to the target—in this case, 2,048 bytes. The -n parameter enables you to specify the number of messages the ping tool should transmit—in this case, 11. Combining these two parameters generates the output in the figure. The -t parameter causes the ping tool to transmit messages until manually halted.

180. C. The arp -a command displays the entries in the ARP table stored in its cache. The arp -d command is for deleting entries, and the arp -s command is for adding entries. The arp -c command is not a valid option.

181. B. The nslookup tool enables you to generate DNS request messages from the command line and send them to a specific DNS server. The other options listed are not DNS utilities.

182. A. On a Unix or Linux host, the ifconfig command displays the system's current IP configuration settings and parameters. Ipconfig is a Windows command-line utility that performs the same basic function. The other options are command-line utilities that do not display IP configuration information.

183. B. Running the ping tool with the -t parameter causes it to send messages to the target continuously until it is manually stopped. The -n parameter specifies the number of messages the ping tool should transmit. The -i parameter specifies the time-to-live (TTL) value of the messages ping transmits. The -a parameter resolves the IP address specified as the target to a hostname.

184. B. The arp -d command is for deleting cache entries, and by running it with the asterisk wildcard, the command deletes all of the entries in the cache. The arp -a command displays the entries in the ARP table stored in its cache, and the arp -s command is for adding entries. The arp -c * command is not a valid option. Show arp is a console command used on switches, not in Windows.

185. D. The nmap utility is capable of scanning a system for open ports that might be a security hazard. The tcpdump, dig, iptables, and iperf utilities cannot do this.

186. C, D. Ping and tracert are both utilities that test Network layer characteristics using ICMP messages. Ping tests the Network layer functionality of the host, and traceroute displays the path to the host through the internetwork. Ipconfig and netstat do not use ICMP messages.

187. C. Running the ping tool with the -i parameter specifies the time-to-live (TTL) value of the messages ping transmits. The -t parameter causes the ping tool to send messages to the target continuously until it is manually stopped. The -n parameter specifies the number of messages the ping tool should transmit. The -a parameter resolves an IP address specified as the target to a hostname.

188. B. Ralph wants to store and view only the traffic relating to the hosts that are experiencing problems. The best way to do this is to set a capture filter. Capture filters determine what is stored in the buffer. Display filters only determine what is displayed from the contents of the buffer. You do not set a trap on an analyzer—you set traps on Simple Network Management Protocol (SNMP) agents. Also, there is no need to configure both a capture filter and a display filter. If you set a capture filter that blocks all other traffic from entering the buffer, the display filter would be redundant.

189. A, D. Ralph can use the ping and traceroute tools to verify the Network layer functionality of the application server and the router. The ping tool tests the Network layer through the exchange of Internet Control Message Protocol (ICMP) Echo and Echo Reply messages. The traceroute tool can verify that there is a functioning path between the users' workstations and the application server. The route tool is used to administer the routing table on the local machine. The arp tool is used to view a computer's Internet Protocol to Media Access Control (IP to MAC) address resolution table stored in memory.

190. A, B, C, D. Of the utilities listed, tcpdump, dig, iptables, and ifconfig are all tools that run on Unix/Linux systems only. The route utility runs on both Unix/Linux and Windows. Show is a console command that runs on switches and routers with a syntax such as show interface, show vlan, or show power.

191. A. Nslookup is a command-line utility that generates DNS resource record requests and sends them to a specific DNS server. The output shown here specifies first the name and address of the DNS server to which the request was sent and then the response to the request, containing the name to be resolved and the IP addresses contained in the server's resource record for that name. The pathping, netstat, and route utilities cannot perform DNS queries.

192. A. Running the ping tool with the -n parameter specifies the number of messages the ping tool should transmit with each execution. The -t parameter causes the ping tool to send messages to the target continuously until manually stopped. The -i parameter specifies the time-to-live (TTL) value of the messages ping transmits. The -a parameter resolves an IP address specified as the target to a hostname.

193. A, E. The ping and nslookup utilities can both run on Windows or Unix/Linux systems. The traceroute command runs only on Unix/Linux, although there is a Windows version called tracert. The ifconfig and iptables commands exist only on Unix and Linux systems.

194. D. The ifconfig command runs only on Unix and Linux systems. The ping and netstat utilities run on both Windows and Unix/Linux systems. The ipconfig and tracert commands run only on Windows, although there is a Unix/Linux version of tracert called traceroute.

195. B. The `ipconfig` command runs only on Windows, although there is a similar Unix/Linux-only command called `ifconfig`. The `ping` and `netstat` utilities run on both Windows and Unix/Linux systems. The `traceroute` utility runs only on Unix/Linux systems, although there is a Windows version called `tracert`.

196. B, D. Both Linux and the Cisco IOS operating systems have the `traceroute` utility. Windows has a version of the utility, but it is called `tracert`. The CSU/DSU cannot run a `traceroute` command.

197. B. The `netstat -s` command displays packet counts and other traffic statistics for the IPv6, IPv4, ICMP, TCP, and UDP protocols. The `netstat -a` command displays all of a workstation's current connections and ports on which it is listening. The `netstat -e` command displays Ethernet statistics, such as the number of bytes and packets sent and received. The `netstat -r` command displays the computer's routing table.

198. A. Running `netstat` with the `-e` parameter on a Windows workstation displays Ethernet statistics, including the number of bytes and packets the workstation has sent and received. The `ipconfig` command displays TCP/IP configuration data; it does not display network traffic statistics. The `tcpdump` and `iptables` commands both run only on Unix and Linux workstations. `Show mac-address-table` is a console command used on switches, not Windows workstations.

199. A, B, D. Windows, Linux, and the Cisco IOS operating systems all include the `ping` utility. The CSU/DSU cannot run a `ping` command.

200. B. The IP address 127.0.0.1 is a dedicated loopback address that directs outgoing IP traffic directly into the incoming IP traffic buffer. A successful ping test using that address indicates that the computer's TCP/IP stack is functioning properly, but the traffic never reaches the network adapter or the network, so the test does not confirm that the adapter is functioning or that the computer has a correct IP address for the network.

201. B, C. The IP address 127.0.0.1 is a dedicated loopback address that directs outgoing IP traffic directly into the incoming IP traffic buffer. The hostname localhost resolves to the 127.0.0.1 address on every TCP/IP system. Ed can therefore ping either the hostname or the IP address to test that his TCP/IP stack is functional. Loopback is not a hostname for the loopback address, and 127.0.0.0 is a network address, not a host address, so it will not work in this situation.

202. B. `Ipconfig` is a Windows command that displays a computer's current IP address and TCP/IP configuration settings, including whether the computer has obtained its address from a DHCP server. The `ifconfig` command displays the same information for Unix and Linux systems. `Msinfo32` is a Windows program that generates a graphical display of the computer's hardware and software configuration, but not its IP address and TCP/IP settings. The `tracert` command in Windows displays the path that packets take through the internetwork to reach a specified destination, but it does not display DHCP information.

203. B, C, D. When you run the `netstat` command without any switch options, it displays the computer's active connections. Running `netstat -e` displays the computer's interface statistics. Running `netstat -r` displays the routing table. There is no `netstat` switch that displays the computer's connection state.

204. B. The `route print` command displays both the IPv4 and IPv6 routing tables. To display only the IPv6 routing table, you add the `-6` parameter to the `route print` command. `Route list` and `route list -6` are not valid commands.

205. C. Running the Windows `netstat` command with the `-e` parameter displays Ethernet statistics, including the number of bytes and packets that have been transmitted and received. The `ping`, `tracert`, and `arp` utilities are not capable of producing this output.

206. B. Running the `arp -e` command on a Linux system displays the contents of the ARP cache in the format shown here. The `arp -a` command displays the cache using an alternative format. The `arp -d` command is for deleting cache entries, and the `arp -s` command is for creating cache entries.

207. D. The `arp -s` command enables you to create a cache record specifying the MAC address and its associated IP address. The `arp -N` command enables you to display the ARP cache entries for a specified network interface. The `arp -d` command is for deleting cache entries. The `arp -a` command displays the entries in the ARP table stored in its cache.

208. C. The `tcpdump` utility is a command-line tool that captures network packets and displays their contents. The `iptables`, nmap, and `pathping` utilities cannot capture and analyze packets. `Iptables` manages Unix/Linux kernel firewall rules; nmap is a port scanner; and `pathping` is a Windows `route` tracing tool.

209. C. A NetFlow analyzer is a tool that can collect network traffic data and analyze how bandwidth is being used and who is using it. A protocol analyzer is also a tool that captures network packets, but for the purpose of analyzing their contents. A bandwidth speed tester measures a networks Internet access speed. An IP scanner lists the IP addresses that are in use on a network. A cable tester measures the properties of the network medium, but not the traffic passing over it.

210. B. The destination system is the last one listed in the trace. By averaging the response times of 99, 106, and 108 ms, you can calculate the average response time: 104.33 ms.

211. B. The `dig` utility in Linux can display the authoritative DNS servers for a particular domain when you specify the domain name and the ns (name server) parameter. The `netstat`, nslookup, and `route` commands cannot generate this particular output.

212. D. On Unix and Linux systems, the `traceroute` utility tests TCP/IP connectivity by transmitting User Datagram Protocol (UDP) messages. This is unlike the `tracert` utility on Windows systems, which uses Internet Control Message Protocol (ICMP) messages. Neither version uses the Transmission Control Protocol (TCP), the Hypertext Transfer Protocol Secure (HTTPS), or the Link Layer Discovery Protocol (LLDP).

213. D. A protocol analyzer is a tool that enables a user to view the contents of packets captured from a network. In Ed's case, if IPsec is properly implemented, he should be able to see that the data in packets captured from his workstation is encrypted. A packet sniffer is a tool that captures packets for the purpose of traffic analysis but cannot view their contents. In practice, however, packet sniffer and protocol analyzer capabilities are usually integrated into a single tool. A port scanner examines a system, looking for open TCP and UDP ports, and a multimeter is a tool that reads voltages on electrical circuits. An IP scanner queries the network for the IP addresses currently in use and gathers information about the devices using them. None of these tools can examine packet contents.

214. A. A packet sniffer is a tool that captures packets for the purpose of traffic analysis but cannot display their contents. A protocol analyzer is a tool that enables a user to view the contents of packets captured from a network. In practice, however, packet sniffer and protocol analyzer capabilities are often integrated into a single tool. Both tools can function in promiscuous mode to capture packets from an entire network.

215. B, E. The `ipconfig /release` command terminates the current DHCP address lease. Then, the `ipconfig /renew` command causes the client to begin the process of negotiating a new lease, this time with an authorized DHCP server. Dump, `lease`, and `discard` are not valid `ipconfig` parameters.

216. C. Port scanning identifies port states on a single computer, such as open ports, whereas port sweeping scans multiple computers for a single open port. War driving and bluejacking are methods of attacking wireless networks.

217. D. Microsoft Windows operating systems do not include a protocol analyzer. A protocol analyzer, such as Microsoft Network Monitor 3, enables administrators to capture network frames, display their contents, and analyze the network data they contain, including the header fields created by the protocols at the various OSI model layers. Administrators can use a protocol analyzer to troubleshoot network conditions and communications between systems. However, in order to interpret the exchanges between the computers on the network, you must be familiar with the protocols and how they operate. Protocol analyzers are useful tools in the hands of experienced network administrators, but they can also be used for malicious purposes, such as displaying unencrypted passwords and other confidential information in the captured packets. The difference between analyzers and sniffers is that analyzers read the internal contents of the packets they capture, parse the individual data units, and display information about each of the protocols involved in the creation of the packet, whereas sniffers look for trends and patterns in the network traffic without examining the contents of each packet.

218. A, B. Nmap is a command-line utility that scans a range of IP addresses, runs a series of scripts against each device it finds, and displays a list of the open ports it finds on each one. Nessus is similar to `nmap` in that it also scans a range of IP addresses to find open ports, but it then proceeds to mount attacks against those ports, to ascertain their vulnerability. Network Monitor is a packet sniffer and protocol analyzer, which is a program that captures network traffic samples and analyzes them. It is not a port scanner. Performance Monitor is a program that displays statistics for specific system and network performance criteria. It is not a port scanner.

219. B. The `top` utility displays performance information about the currently running processes on a Unix/Linux system. `Netstat` is a tool that enables you to view active network connections and TCP/IP traffic statistics; it does not measure system performance. There are no Unix/Linux tools called `monitor` or `cpustat`.

220. B. Protocol analyzers report the total number of frames seen compared to the number of frames that were accepted. If a capture filter is in place, there will be a discrepancy between these two values. Only frames that meet the capture criteria will be accepted by the analyzer and placed in the buffer for later display. Protocol analyzers place good and bad frames into the buffer as long as they meet the capture criteria. If only good frames were placed in the buffer, there would be no way to identify problems.

221. C. A protocol analyzer is capable of looking at the data inside packets, which in the case of packets generated by Telnet and FTP, can contain passwords in cleartext. Packet sniffers analyze traffic patterns, vulnerability scanners search for open ports, Trivial File Transfer Protocol (TFTP) servers transfer boot files to DHCP client workstations, and network taps monitor and copy network traffic. None of these can actually parse and display the data inside the packets. Telnet is itself a terminal emulator and does not display packet contents.

222. A. Protocol analyzers capture packets from the network and interpret their contents, which includes displaying the Application layer payload, which can include confidential information. Protocol analyzers can display the IP addresses of systems on the network, but this is not as great a security threat. Protocol analyzers cannot decrypt the protected information they find in captured packets. Vulnerability scanners detect open ports and launch attacks against them; protocol analyzers do not do this.

223. B. A spectrum analyzer is a device for measuring the amplitudes and frequencies of wireless signals. A visual fault locator is a tool for testing fiber-optic cables. Neither of these have vulnerability scanning capabilities. Nessus and `nmap` are tools that include vulnerability scanning but that have other capabilities as well.

224. D. Port scanning, the process of looking for open TCP and UDP ports that are exploitable by attackers, is one of the many functions that qualify as a type of vulnerability scanning. Network mapping, the remediation of vulnerabilities, and penetration testing, which is the process of deliberately performing a planned attack, are not considered vulnerability scanning techniques.

225. A. Once the frames are in the buffer, Alice can configure a display filter to block the unwanted frames from view. This does not delete them from the buffer. Since the capture was already performed, there is no need to restart the capture. Configuring a capture filter will not meet the requirements, because the filter will eliminate the other frames completely from the buffer. It is not possible to delete specific frames from an analyzer buffer.

226. D. Internet Group Management Protocol (IGMP) snooping is a switching technique that prevents network hosts from receiving multicast packets when they are not members of the multicast group. The multicast traffic will still appear on the network, but only the members of the multicast group will process the packets. Asymmetric routing and multipathing all affect the route that the packets take through the network, and flow control only affects the speed at which transmitting systems send packets. None of these can control which hosts process the incoming packets.

227. C. If someone on the network is spoofing the MAC address of Ed's workstation, the MAC address table in the switch handing the network traffic might be continually changing as packets from each computer reach the switch. This could cause some of the response packets to be forwarded to Ed's workstation and some to the spoofer's workstation. Duplicate IP addresses would not cause this problem, because they would be detected by the operating system. Blocked ports, incorrect firewall settings, or a flood of multicast transmissions could prevent Ed from receiving responses, but they would not be sent to another workstation.

228. B, D. The `route` print tool displays the contents of the routing table on a Windows computer. So does the `netstat -r` command. The `nbtstat` and `nslookup` tools cannot display the routing table.

229. D. To access the Internet, the workstation's routing table must include a default gateway entry. To create a default gateway entry in the routing table, you use the `route add` command with a Network Destination value of 0.0.0.0, a `MASK` value of 0.0.0.0, and the address of a router on the local network (in this case, 192.168.2.99). The entry must also have a `METRIC` value that is lower than the other entries in the table so that it will be used first.

230. A, B. Both Telnet and FTP are protocols that include command-line client applications, with Telnet providing terminal emulation and FTP file transfer functionality. SNMP and DNS are both Application layer protocols, but neither one includes a program. Nslookup has a command-line interface, but it executes commands on the local system, not a remote one.

231. C. The `netstat` utility can display the incoming and outgoing packets for a specific network interface, as well as other statistics, depending on the operating system. Top and `ifconfig` are Unix/Linux utilities, and `nbtstat` is a Windows tool.

232. B. NetFlow is a network traffic monitoring feature first introduced in Cisco routers in 1996. Netmon, `netstat`, and `nbtstat` are all operating system utilities, not router features.

233. A. A crimper or crimping tool is a jawed device that has a set of dies in it. Installers use a crimper to squeeze the two halves of an RJ-45 or RJ-11 connector together, with the wires inside securing the connector to the cable. Installers use a splicing tool to splice two cable segments together. There is no tool called a pigtail or a patch.

234. B. The router interface uses the `show` command to display various types of configuration data. The `show route` command displays the contents of the router's routing table. None of the other options are router interface commands.

Chapter 6: Practice Test 1

1. **A, C, D.** The three-tier hierarchical architecture for datacenters consists of core, distribution, and access layers. The access layer in a datacenter contains servers; the distribution layer contains redundant switch connections; and the core layer provides high-speed transport between the switches. There is no intermediate layer in the architecture.

2. **B.** An acceptable use policy (AUP) specifies whether and how employees can use company-owned hardware and software resources. AUPs typically specify what personal work employees can perform while on the job, what hardware and software they can install, and what levels of privacy they are permitted when using company equipment. This is the document that will most likely include the information you seek. A service-level agreement (SLA) is a contract between a provider and a subscriber. A nondisclosure agreement (NDA) specifies what company information employees are permitted to discuss outside the company. A bring your own device (BYOD) policy specifies how employees can connect their personal devices to the company network.

3. **A.** There are many possible causes for the problem that are more likely than a router configuration error, so this is not something you should check first. Asking if the user can access the local network attempts to isolate the problem. If she cannot, the problem could be in her computer; if she can, then the problem lies somewhere in the Internet access infrastructure. If other users are experiencing the problem, then the issue should receive a higher priority, and you will know for sure that the problem does not lie in the user's computer. While the user's job title might not be the first thing you check, it is a political reality that higher ranking users get preferential treatment.

4. **B.** Biometric scans, identification badges, and key fobs are all mechanisms that are designed to distinguish authorized from unauthorized personnel. Motion detection cannot make this distinction and is therefore not a means of preventing unauthorized access.

5. **C.** The problem is most likely the result of a duplex mismatch. There should be no collisions at all on a full-duplex network, so the problem is clearly related to the duplexing of the communications. A twisted-pair Ethernet adapter, running in its original half-duplex mode, detects collisions by looking for data on both the transmit and receive pins at the same time. In full-duplex mode, however, data is supposed to be transmitted and received at the same time. When one side of a connection is configured to use full duplex, as the new computers are, and the other end is configured to use half duplex (as the network switches must be), the full-duplex communications on the one side look like collisions to the half-duplex side. The half-duplex adapter transmits a jam signal as a result of each collision, which causes the full-duplex side to receive an incomplete frame. Both sides then start to retransmit frames in a continuing cycle, causing network performance to diminish alarmingly. The ping tests do not detect a problem because ping transmits only a small amount of data in one direction at a time. All of the other options would likely cause the ping tests to fail. The solution to the problem is to configure the new computers to autonegotiate their speed and duplex modes.

6. B. An ad hoc topology (also known as an independent basic service set) is one in which wireless computers communicate directly with one another without the need for an access point. A wireless access point is a device with a wireless transceiver that also connects to a standard cabled network. Wireless computers communicate with the access point, which forwards their transmissions over the network cable. This is called an infrastructure topology. Star and bus topologies are not used by wireless networks; they require the computers to be physically connected to the network cable.

7. C. A multilayer switch is a network connectivity device that functions at both layer 2 and layer 3 of the Open Systems Interconnection (OSI) model. At layer 2, the Data link layer, the device functions like a normal switch, providing an individual collision domain to each connected node and enabling you to create multiple VLANs. At layer 3, the Network layer, the device also provides routing capabilities by forwarding packets between the VLANs. Virtual routers, load balancers, and broadband routers are strictly layer 3 devices that can route traffic but cannot create VLANs.

8. B, C, D. *Data at rest* is a data loss prevention (DLP) term that describes data that is currently in storage while not in use. *Data in transit* is the term used to describe network traffic. *Data in use* describes endpoint actions. Data online is not one of the standard data loss prevention terms.

9. D. Wi-Fi Protected Access (WPA) is the wireless security protocol that was designed to replace the increasingly vulnerable Wired Equivalent Privacy (WEP) protocol. WPA added an encryption algorithm called Temporal Key Integrity Protocol (TKIP) that was more difficult to penetrate. Over time, however, TKIP too became vulnerable, and WPA2 was introduced, which replaced TKIP with the Advanced Encryption Standard algorithm (AES).

10. A. The device shown in the figure is a toner and probe, which you can use to test twisted-pair wiring and detect certain basic wiring faults. By connecting the toner to each wire in turn and touching the probe to the other end, you can determine whether each wire is attached to the appropriate pin in the connector. This tool is not capable of performing any of the tasks described in the other options.

11. C. The term *something you have* refers to a physical possession that identifies a user, such as a smartcard. This type of authentication is nearly always used as part of a multifactor authentication (MFA) procedure because it is possible for a smartcard or other physical possession to be lost or stolen. A fingerprint would be considered something you are, a password something you know, and a finger gesture something you do.

12. A. Port number 1433 is used by SQL Server. The port number 3389 is used by the Remote Desktop Protocol (RDP), 443 by Hypertext Transfer Protocol Secure (HTTPS), and 5060 by the Session Initiation Protocol (SIP), none of which are involved in SQL communications.

13. D. Wireless LAN equipment built to the 802.11ac standard can only use the 5 GHz frequency band. However, the 802.11n access point is configured to use only the 2.4 GHz frequency band. Therefore, the network adapters cannot be made to connect to your access point.

14. A. A hot site is the most expensive to implement because it has all of the necessary hardware already installed, configured, and ready to go in the event of a disaster. A warm site has hardware in place, but it is not yet installed and configured, which makes it less expensive than a hot site. A cold site is just a space at a remote location. The hardware and software must be procured and installed before the network can be restored. Therefore, it is the least expensive of the hardware-based options and takes the most time. A cloud site is a virtual facility maintained with a cloud service provider. The cloud site does not require physical space or physical hardware, so it is the least expensive.

15. A, C, E. The 2.4 GHz band used by wireless LANs (WLANs) consists of channels that are 20 (or 22) MHz wide. However, the channels are only 5 MHz apart, so it is possible for channel overlap to occur between the access points, which can result in interference. Channels 1, 6, and 11 are the only channels that are far enough apart from each other to avoid any overlap with the adjacent channels. Channels 4 and 8 are susceptible to overlap.

16. B, C, D. Disabling services and ports that are not in use is a server hardening technique that reduces the attack surface of a server. Creating privileged user accounts that are only used for tasks that require those privileges reduces the chance that the administrative accounts will be compromised. Therefore, these are all forms of server hardening. Installing additional memory, while a benefit in other ways, is not considered to be server hardening technique.

17. C. The Default Gateway setting should contain the address of a router on the workstation's local network that provides access to other networks, such as the Internet. In this case, therefore, the Default Gateway address should be on the 192.168.23.0 network, but it contains an address on the 192.168.216.0 network, which is not local. So, the user can only access systems on the 192.168.23.0/24 network. The Subnet Mask setting must be correct; otherwise, the user would not be able to access any other systems. Unlike the default gateway, the DNS server does not have to be on the workstation's local network, so the address shown can be correct. DHCP does not have to be enabled for the computer to access the Internet; the computer could have a manually configured static address.

18. C, D, E. A smartphone app that can adjust your thermostat, a remotely monitored cardiac pacemaker, and a camera-equipped refrigerator are all examples of IoT devices because they all have IP addresses and use the Internet to communicate with a controller or monitoring station. Key fobs that unlock cars and TV remote controls are typically short-range radio or infrared devices that do not use the Internet for their communications.

19. B. In most cases, it is a Remote Authentication Dial-In User Service (RADIUS) server that performs the authentication server role in an 802.1X transaction by verifying the identity of the client. The authenticator is a switch or access point to which the supplicant is requesting access, and the supplicant is the client attempting to connect to the network. There is no accountant role in an 802.1X transaction.

20. C, D. The solution requires you to create a VLAN on the ADSL router that matches the VLAN the network switch port is using. Therefore, you should create a VLAN4 on the router's switch module and assign an Ethernet port to it, which will be the port you use to connect the ADSL router to the network switch. There is no need to create a VLAN1 on the network switch, because all switches already have a default VLAN called VLAN1. Modifying the VLAN assignments on the network switch is not a good idea, because it might interfere with the existing VLAN strategy in place.

21. A, C. Tailgating refers to the practice of closely following an authorized individual through a physical security barrier, such as a locked door. Security cameras can successfully prevent tailgating by identifying individuals attempting to gain unauthorized access to a protected facility, and access control vestibules (or mantraps) prevent tailgating by admitting only one entrant at a time. Badge readers are the security mechanisms that tailgating is intended to defeat, and motion detectors cannot distinguish authorized from unauthorized entrants.

22. A, D. Infrastructure as a service (IaaS) provides consumers with processing, storage, and networking resources that they can use to install and run operating systems and other software of their choice. In the public cloud model, one organization functions as the provider, and another organization—in this case, you—consumes the services of the provider. Platform as a service (PaaS) provides consumers with the ability to install applications of their choice on a server furnished by the provider. Software as a service (SaaS) provides consumers with access to a specific application running on the provider's servers, but the consumers have no control over the operating system, the servers, or the underlying resources. In a private cloud, the same organization that uses the cloud services is also the sole owner of the infrastructure that provides those services. A hybrid cloud is a combination of public and private infrastructure so that the consumer organization is only a partial owner of the infrastructure.

23. D. The plier-like device is a crimper, which cable installers use to attach RJ-45 connectors, like those in the bag, to lengths of bulk cable. This is the process of creating patch cables, which are used to connect computers to wall plates and patch panel ports to switches. Your boss is telling you to start making patch cables in 5- and 10-foot lengths. You do not use a crimper to attach keystone connectors, and the boss has not given you the tools and components needed to pull cable runs or install a patch panel.

24. B. The default port for the Post Office Protocol 3 (POP3) is 110, but that is used for incoming mail. Outgoing mail uses the Simple Mail Transfer Protocol (SMTP), which uses the well-known port number 25 by default. Port number 143 is the default port for the Internet Message Access Protocol (IMAP), a different email mailbox protocol that clients never use with POP3. Port number 80 is the default port for the Hypertext Transfer Protocol (HTTP), which is not used by email clients.

25. B. The cable connector used for thin Ethernet segments is called a Bayonet Neill-Concelman (BNC) connector. Straight Tip (ST) and Multi-fiber Push-On (MPO) connectors are for fiber-optic cables. RJ-45 is a type of connector used with twisted-pair cabling for data networks. RJ-11 is a connector type used with twisted-pair cabling for telecommunications networks.

26. A. A rollover cable is a type of null modem cable, usually flat and light blue in color, with the pinouts reversed on either end, to enable a terminal to communicate with a router or switch through the device's dedicated console port. It cannot connect a workstation to the network. A straight-through cable is the standard network cable used to connect a workstation or other device to an Ethernet network. A crossover cable is designed to connect network adapters to each other directly, creating a two-node network. A plenum cable is a type of cable intended for use within air spaces that has an outer sheath that does not produce toxic fumes when it burns. A shielded cable is intended to protect signals from electromagnetic interference. Both plenum and shielded cables can connect a workstation to a network.

27. A. Authentication Header (AH) is a protocol in the TCP/IP suite that provides digital integrity services, in the form of a digital signature, which ensures that an incoming packet actually originated from its stated source. Encapsulating Security Protocol (ESP) provides encryption services for IPsec. Secure Sockets Layer (SSL) is a security protocol that provides encrypted communications between web browsers and servers. Remote Desktop Protocol (RDP) is a component of Remote Desktop Services, a Windows mechanism that enables a client program to connect to a server and control it remotely.

28. B. VLANs are virtual layer 2 (Data link layer) LANs defined within switches. As with physical LANs, only devices in the same VLAN can communicate with each other until a layer 3 device, such as a router or a layer 3 switch, is added to the network. Re-creating and reconfiguring the VLANs will not correct the problem. Traffic filters are usually implemented on routers, not switches. Once a router is in place, VLANs do not have to use the same data link protocol to communicate with each other.

29. A, C. The term for an IPv4 address and port number in combination, which identifies an application running on a specific host, is *socket*. A media access control (MAC) address is an address hard-coded into a network adapter; it is not a TCP/IP element. A subnet mask is not needed to identify a host or an application running on it.

30. A, B, C, D. A cable modem must function as a broadband router to provide access to the cable provider's network. Many cable modems are also wireless access points, enabling users to construct a LAN without a cable installation. Many cable modems have switched Ethernet ports for connections to wired devices, such as printers and computers. Most cable modems use DHCP to assign IP addresses to devices on the home network. Cable modems for home use typically do not function as proxy servers or Remote Authentication Dial-In User Service (RADIUS) servers, which are devices generally used on large networks.

31. A. Like A and AAAA records, which are used for forward name resolution, pointer (PTR) records contain hostnames and IP addresses. However, PTR records are used only for reverse name resolution—that is, resolving IP addresses into hostnames. A mail exchange (MX) record specifies the mail server that the domain should use. Canonical name (CNAME) records specify aliases for a given hostname. An AAAA resource record maps a hostname to an IPv6 address for name resolution purposes. All of these records except PTR are used for forward name resolution.

32. C, D. Protocol analyzers capture packets from the network and interpret their contents, which can include displaying the Application layer payload. Depending on the application, the payload can conceivably include confidential information, such as passwords. Protocol analyzers also display the IP addresses of the systems involved in packet transmissions. Although this in itself might not be a great security threat, intruders might use the IP address information to launch other types of attacks. Protocol analyzers cannot decrypt the protected information they find in captured packets. Vulnerability scanners detect open ports and launch attacks against them; protocol analyzers do not do this.

33. B, D, E. A Remote Authentication Dial-In User Service (RADIUS) server, also known as an AAA server, provides centralized authentication, authorization, and accounting for other network services. Attenuation and assistance are not functions provided by RADIUS or AAA servers.

34. C. Only Domain Name System (DNS) servers perform FQDN resolutions, so that is likely to be the source of the problem. It is possible to successfully ping a device on the local network using its computer name without the use of DNS. Dynamic Host Configuration Protocol (DHCP) cannot be the problem; if it were, you would not be able to ping the server at all. Electromagnetic interference (EMI) would inhibit all network communication, and access control lists (ACLs) are an authorization mechanism that has no effect on ping tests.

35. B. Proxy servers provide network users with access to Internet services, and the unregistered IP addresses on the client computers protect them from unauthorized access by users on the Internet, which satisfies the primary objective. The proxy servers also make it possible for network administrators to monitor and regulate users' access to the Internet, which satisfies one of the two secondary objectives. However, proxy servers are not capable of assigning IP addresses to the client computers, and the proposal makes no mention of a Dynamic Host Configuration Protocol (DHCP) server or any another automatic TCP/IP configuration mechanism. Therefore, the proposal does not satisfy the other secondary objective.

36. C. Software as a service (SaaS) provides the least amount of control. Consumers receive access to a specific application running on the provider's servers, but they have no control over the operating system, the servers, or the underlying resources. The infrastructure as a service (IaaS) model provides the consumers with the most control, as the provider furnishes processing, storage, and networking resources that the consumer can use as needed. Platform as a service (PaaS) provides consumers with the ability to install applications of their choice on a server furnished by the provider, but they have only limited control over the server and no control over the underlying resources.

37. A. Ethernet uses jumbo frames at the Data link layer to transfer large amounts of data more efficiently. Ethernet typically restricts frame size to 1,500 bytes, but jumbo frames enable Ethernet systems to create frames up to 9,000 bytes. PPP does not support the use of jumbo frames. Frames are protocol data units (PDUs) associated only with the Data link layer, so they do not apply to IP and TCP, which operate at the Network and Transport layers, respectively.

38. C. The first step in the troubleshooting methodology involves identifying the problem by questioning the user and creating a trouble ticket. You complete the other steps in the troubleshooting methodology after the trouble ticket has been created and prioritized.

39. C. The user has experienced a ransomware attack. Ransomware is a type of attack in which a user's access to his or her data is blocked unless a certain amount of money is paid to the attacker. The blockages can vary from simple screen locks to data encryption. Denial-of-service is a type of attack that overwhelms a computer with traffic, preventing it from functioning properly. Social engineering refers to various methods attackers can use to gain access to secured resources by manipulating authorized users, either physically or digitally. ARP poisoning is the deliberate insertion of fraudulent information into the ARP cache stored on computers and switches.

40. B, D. BPDU guard and root guard are both mechanisms that protect the Spanning Tree Protocol against infiltration by attackers. Bridge protocol data units (BPDUs) are messages that switches running the Spanning Tree Protocol (STP) exchange to learn about the available paths through a switched network. Switches should receive BPDUs only through ports connected to other switches. BPDU guard is a feature that prevents BPDU messages from arriving through ports connected to end systems, such as computers. A root guard affects the behavior of the STP by enforcing the selection of root bridge ports on a switched network. Without root guards, there is no way for administrators to enforce the topology of a network with a redundant switching fabric. Geofencing is a wireless technology that uses radio frequency identification (RFID) or GPS coordinates to define a geographic perimeter for a network. DHCP snooping is a security feature that prevents unauthorized DHCP servers from accessing the network.

41. B, C. A large enterprise network will—at minimum—have demarcation points for telephone services and a connection to an Internet service provider's network. In many cases, these services enter the building in the same equipment room that houses the backbone switch, which enables all the devices on the network to access those resources. This room is then called the main distribution frame (MDF). An intermediate distribution frame (IDF) is a place where localized telecommunications equipment, such as the interface between the horizontal cabling and the backbone, is located. For example, an enterprise network housed in a single building might have its MDF in the basement and an IDF on each floor. Mean time between failures (MTBF) and Remote Desktop Protocol (RDP) are not network cabling locations.

42. B. A plenum space is an area of a building that provides air circulation as part of its ventilation system, such as a heating or air-conditioning duct. Plenum cables have a sheath made of a fire-retardant material that does not outgas toxic fumes when it burns. When network cables are installed in plenum spaces, many local building codes require that installers use plenum-rated cables conforming to specific standards. Plenum cables provide no benefit when installed near other cables, or EMI sources, or when they exceed specified lengths.

43. D. Clustering refers to the combination of multiple servers—not network adapters—into a single unit to enhance performance and provide fault tolerance. Bonding, link aggregation, port aggregation, and NIC teaming are all terms for the same basic technology, in which the bandwidth of multiple network adapter connections is joined to speed up transmissions. The technology also enables the network communication to continue if one of the adapters fails or is disconnected.

44. C, D. Secure Shell (SSH) and Telnet are both remote terminal programs, but Telnet clients pass instructions (including passwords) to the target server in cleartext, whereas SSH uses encrypted transmissions. In the same way, Hypertext Transfer Protocol Secure (HTTPS) is the encrypted version of HTTP. In both of these cases, the substitute is more secure and should be suggested to the director. However, Temporal Key Integrity Protocol (TKIP) provides encryption that is less secure than Advanced Encryption Standard (AES), and Wired Equivalent Protocol (WEP) is less secure than Wi-Fi Protected Access 2 (WPA2).

45. A. A management information base (MIB) is the database on an SNMP agent in which information about the properties of the managed device is stored. The other three options do not perform this function. A trap is an alert message that SNMP agents send to the network management console when an exceptional event occurs. Syslog is a standard for message logging components. Security information and event management (SIEM) is a combination tool that uses information gathered from logs and network devices to provide a real-time analysis of the network's security condition.

46. A, D. Secure Sockets Layer (SSL) is a now-deprecated security protocol that formerly provided encrypted communications between web browsers and servers. Transport Layer Security (TLS) is an updated security protocol that is designed to replace SSL. Datagram Transport Layer Security (DTLS) is a security protocol that provides the same basic functions as TLS but for User Datagram Protocol traffic instead of TCP. Secure Shell (SSH) is a character-based tool that enables users to execute commands on remote computers; it does not provide web server/browser security.

47. B. Another term for a screened subnet is a DMZ, or demilitarized zone. They are also known as perimeter networks. A virtual LAN (VLAN) is a logical network segment created within a switch. Protected Extensible Authentication Protocol (PEAP) is an authentication protocol, and Temporal Key Integrity Protocol (TKIP) is an encryption algorithm. These three options are not terms for a screened subnet.

48. D. RDP is a component of Remote Desktop Services, a Windows mechanism that enables a client program to connect to a server and control it remotely. RDP does not carry actual application data; it just transfers keystrokes, mouse movements, and graphic display information.

49. B, D. Of the options shown, only the 802.11n and 802.11ax standards define wireless LAN devices that can support both the 2.4 GHz and 5 GHz frequencies. The 802.11ac standard supports only 5 GHz, and the 802.11g standard supports only 2.4 GHz.

50. B. Multitenancy does not call for tenants to have individual virtual machines. Multitenancy is a software architecture in which multiple tenants share a single instance of an application running in the cloud. Because tenants share a single application, there is a chance that data could be compromised. Because a single application instance is running in the cloud, the operational overhead is reduced compared to the use of individual virtual machines. Tenants share a finite amount of bandwidth, so the possibility exists for competition to occur, such as when one tenant is the target of a denial-of-service attack.

51. E. On a wireless network, an extended service set identifier (ESSID) is used to identify a configuration in which there is a single SSID using multiple access points. A basic service set (BSS) refers to the wireless network itself, consisting of a single AP and a number of clients. An extended service set (ESS) consists of two or more BSSs, using multiple APs. The service set identifier (SSID) is the name that you use when connecting to a wireless network. The basic service set identifier (BSSID) is the MAC address of the access point associated with a BSS.

52. B. Least privilege is the practice of only providing users with the permissions they need to perform their designated tasks and no more. For her standard activities, Alice is given an account that does not have administrative permissions, because she does not need those permissions to perform standard tasks. The administrative account has the additional permissions needed for Alice to perform administrative tasks. The intention is for Alice to use that account only for those administrative tasks. Zero day is a type of vulnerability; multifactor authentication (or MFA) calls for users to supply two identifying factors; defense in depth refers to the use of multiple security mechanisms to provide additional protection. None of these other three options refers to the use of multiple user accounts.

53. E. After you have established a theory of probable cause, you can try to test the theory by replacing hardware components one by one until you find the faulty device. All of the other options are steps that come either earlier or later in the troubleshooting process.

54. A. While it is not definitive evidence, an IP address assignment from the wrong subnet could be an indication that there is a rogue (unauthorized and unknown) Dynamic Host Configuration Protocol (DHCP) server on the network. A workstation with an IP address from the wrong subnet cannot access any network resources, local or Internet. The DHCP Enabled setting would be Yes if a workstation had gotten its IP address from a rogue DHCP server. An address on the 169.254.0.0/16 subnet indicates that the workstation was unable to obtain an IP address from any DHCP server.

55. D. All of these occurrences are malfunctions on a full-duplex Ethernet network, but collisions are normal and expected on a half-duplex network. Runt frames occur when a network interface generates packets that are smaller than the 64-byte minimum allowable length. Giants occur when frames are larger than the 1,518-byte maximum allowable length. Late collisions occur when network cables are too long, and frames collide after leaving the sending system.

56. B. The Unix/Linux `tcpdump` utility is a protocol analyzer. It is a command-line tool that captures network packets and displays their contents. The `iptables`, `nmap`, and `pathping` utilities cannot capture and analyze packets. `Iptables` manages Unix/Linux kernel firewall rules, `nmap` is a port scanner, and `pathping` is a Windows route tracing tool.

57. A, B. NAS devices are self-contained file servers that connect directly to a standard IP network. A NAS device provides file-level access to its storage devices, and it includes an operating system and a filesystem. NAS devices are typically not iSCSI targets. SANs provide block-level storage and typically function as iSCSI targets, but they do not include an operating system or filesystem.

58. C. Penetration testing is a type of network security evaluation in which a client engages an outside consultant who attempts to penetrate the network's security and gain access to protected network resources without authorization. Testing by an internal administrator familiar with the security barriers would not be a valid test. Although having a consultant examine the network's security from within can be useful, it is not a penetration test. Computers or networks that are alluring targets for intruders are called honeypots or honeynets. Implementation of a new security protocol can only come after the current security situation has been evaluated.

59. C. All of the mechanisms listed are designed to make any attempts to tamper with or physically compromise the hardware devices immediately evident. Therefore, these mechanisms are various forms of tamper detection. Asset tracking is for locating and identifying hardware. Geofencing is a wireless networking technique for limiting access to a network. Port security refers to protection of network switch ports.

60. A, B. A visual fault locator is a laser light source used to locate breaks in fiber-optic cables. An optical power meter measures the signal strength on fiber-optic cables to locate breaks and measure signal degradation as part of an optical loss test set (OLTS). These two tools can only be used on fiber-optic cables. A protocol analyzer is a tool that captures network packets for the purpose of analyzing their contents. It can function on a network of any cable type. Toner and probe tools are used in copper-based cabling installations, not fiber-optic cabling.

61. A, B, C. Virtual private networks (VPNs), IPsec, and Generic Routing Encapsulation (GRE) are all mechanisms that encapsulate packets in an encrypted form within another protocol to secure their contents. Network address translation (NAT) enables workstations on private networks to access the Internet by substituting a public IP address in packets generated with private addresses. NAT does not use tunneling.

62. C. To create a network with 8 subnets and 30 hosts per subnet, you must allocate 3 of the 8 bits in the last octet for use as a subnet identifier. This results in a binary value of 11100000 for the last octet in the subnet mask, which converts to a decimal value of 224. Therefore, the correct subnet mask value is 255.255.255.224. Values for the last octet that are lower than 224 would not enable you to create 8 subnets. Values higher than 224 would not enable you to create 30 host addresses.

63. B. MAC filtering takes the form of an access control list (ACL) on the wireless network's access points, listing the MAC addresses of all the devices that are permitted to access the network. If the MAC address of your laptop is not included in the ACL, you will be unable to connect to the network. Geofencing is intended to prevent users outside the office from accessing the network. You are inside, so this should not be the problem. You have been given the passphrase for the network, so you should be able to configure the WPA3 protocol on your laptop. You have been given the SSID of the network, so you should be able to connect by manually entering it, even if the access points are not broadcasting the SSID.

64. D. In order for the link pulse LED on the switch port to light up, there must be an active connection between the switch and a functioning network device at the other end. Plugging a running computer into the wall plate will enable the Ethernet adapters at both end of the connection to communicate, causing the LED to light. None of the other options will cause the LED to light.

65. B. The Ethernet (or IEEE 802.3) protocol at the Data link layer uses MAC addresses to identify computers on the local network. Media access control (MAC) addresses are coded into the firmware of physical network interface adapters by the manufacturer. The Physical layer deals with signals and is not involved in addressing. The IP protocol at the Network layer has its own addressing system. The Transport layer protocols are not involved in addressing.

66. C, D. The Internet Protocol (IP) in both of its versions (IPv4 and IPv6) includes a Time to Live (TTL) field in its message header that specifies how many times a packet can be routed. Each router processing the packet reduces the TTL value by one until it reaches zero, after which it is discarded. The Internet Control Message Protocol (ICMP) and the Internet Group Management Protocol (IGMP) do not have TTL fields.

67. B, D. By inserting modified entries into a device's ARP cache, an attacker can cause traffic to be diverted from the correct destination to a system controlled by the attacker. This can enable the attacker to intercept traffic intended for another destination. In an on-path attack (also known as a man-in-the-middle attack), the attacker can read the intercepted traffic and even modify it before sending it on to the correct destination. In a session hijacking attack, the attacker can use the intercepted traffic to obtain authentication information, including passwords. Neither of the other two options is facilitated by ARP poisoning. An evil twin is a fraudulent access point on a wireless network. Social engineering is a form of attack in which an innocent user is persuaded by an attacker to provide sensitive information via email or telephone.

68. D. A honeypot is a computer configured to function as bait for attackers, causing them to waste their time penetrating a resource that provides no significant access. This is also a technique that enables the target to gather information about the attackers. A demilitarized zone (DMZ), also known as a screened subnet or perimeter network, is a network segment on which administrators locate servers that must be accessible from the Internet but that are separated from the internal network by a firewall. A root guard provides protection to switch ports. Spoofing is an attack technique in which an intruder modifies packets to assume the appearance of another user or computer.

69. C. A switch is a type of bridge that receives data through any one of its multiple ports and then retransmits the data out through the one port connected to the data's designated recipient. A repeater is a Physical layer device that regenerates incoming signals and retransmits them. A hub is a type of repeater that receives data through any one of its multiple ports and retransmits the data out through all of its other ports. Bridges and switches are Data link layer devices, and routers are Network layer devices.

70. D. A port scanner examines a system for open ports or endpoints that are accessible from the network using the TCP or UDP protocol, which intruders can conceivably exploit to gain access to the system. Port scanners do not list user processes, hardware ports, numbers of packets, or IP addresses.

71. A, D. A storage area network (SAN) is a network that is dedicated to carrying traffic between servers and storage devices. SANs can use specialized network protocols, such as Fibre Channel in this case, or standard Gigabit Ethernet. A local area network (LAN) is a connected group of computers, usually inside a single room or building. In this case, the cluster has one LAN connecting the nodes together and another providing other users with access to the cluster. A wide area network (WAN) is a network that connects devices or networks at different geographic locations. A metropolitan area network (MAN) is a type of WAN that connects devices within a limited geographic area. The cluster is not connected to a WAN or MAN.

72. C. Since only one user is reporting the problem and he has admitted to making changes to his IP configuration, you should start by checking the workstation configuration using the ipconfig command. If the routers, the switches, or the DNS server were causing the problem, more than one user would be affected, and there would be additional users calling the help desk.

73. C. Because your colleague can connect to WebServ1 successfully, the problem is not an unresponsive service or blocked ports on the server. The problem is not a name resolution failure, because you can successfully ping WebServ1 by name. Therefore, of the options listed, the only possible problem must be that the firewall on your workstation is configured to block the remote desktop client's traffic.

74. C. The device shown in the figure is a punchdown tool, which you use to connect unshielded twisted-pair cable ends to the keystone connectors used in modular wall plates and patch panels. After lining up the individual wires in the cable with the connector, you use the tool to press each wire into its slot. The tool also cuts the wire sheath to make an electrical contact and trims the end of the wire. This tool is not capable of performing any of the tasks described in the other options.

75. A, B, C. The 5 GHz frequency has 23 channels available in the United States, whereas the 2.4 GHz frequency has only 11. Many household devices, such as cordless telephones, use the 2.4 GHz frequency band, but relatively few devices use the 5 GHz band. Higher frequencies typically support faster transmission speeds because with all other conditions equal, they can carry more data in the same amount of time. The 5 GHz frequency typically has a shorter range than 2.4 GHz because it is less able to penetrate barriers.

76. D. The standard unit height for IT equipment racks is 1.75 inches, which is the equivalent of one unit. Therefore, six units would be 10.5 inches.

77. A. The File Transfer Protocol (FTP) uses two port numbers. It uses the first, port 21, for a control connection that remains open during the entire client-server session. The second port, 20, is for a data connection that opens only when the protocol is actually transferring a file between the client and the server. Simple Network Management Protocol (SNMP), Network Time Protocol (NTP), and Hypertext Transfer Protocol (HTTP) all use a single port on the server.

78. A. The 13-bit prefix indicated in the network address will result in a mask with 13 ones followed by 19 zeroes. Broken into 8-bit blocks, the binary mask value is as follows:

11111111 11111000 00000000 00000000

Converted into decimal values, this results in a subnet mask value of 255.248.0.0.

79. B. The failure to detect a tone on the eighth wire indicates that there is either a break in the wire somewhere inside the cable or a bad pin connection in one or both connectors. This type of fault is called an open circuit. None of the other three options are faults that manifest as described. A short circuit is when a wire is connected to two or more pins at one end of the cable. A split pair is a connection in which two wires are incorrectly mapped in exactly the same way on both ends of the cable. Crosstalk is a type of interference caused by signals on one wire bleeding over to other wires.

80. B, D. The Session layer is responsible for creating and maintaining a dialog between end systems. This dialog can be a two-way alternate dialog that requires end systems to take turns transmitting, or it can be a two-way simultaneous dialog in which either end system can transmit at will. The Session layer functions are called dialog control and dialog separation. Data encryption is performed at the Presentation layer, and datagram routing occurs at the Network layer.

81. A. When individual packets in a data stream are delayed, due to network congestion, different routing, or queuing problems, the resulting connectivity problem is called jitter. While this condition might not cause problems for asynchronous applications, real-time communications, such as VoIP or streaming video, can suffer interruptions from which the phenomenon gets its name. Latency describes a generalized delay in network transmissions, not individual packet delays. Attenuation is the weakening of a signal as it travels through a network medium. A bottleneck is a condition in which all traffic is delayed, due to a faulty or inadequate component. None of these three options would account for the problems reported by the users.

82. D. The 802.11ax standard defines a wireless LAN running at speeds of up to 9.6 gigabits per second (Gbps). The 802.11ac standard supports speeds of up to 6.9 Gbps. None of the other ratified 802.11 standards define networks running at speeds beyond the 600 Mbps of 802.11n.

83. B, D. Network address translation (NAT) is a Network layer service, typically integrated into a router, that converts the private IP addresses in all of a client's Internet transmissions to a registered IP address. Therefore, NAT works for all applications. A proxy server is an Application layer device that performs the same type of conversion but only for specific applications. A Remote Authentication Dial-In User Service (RADIUS) server can provide authentication, authorization, and accounting services for remote access servers, but it does not convert IP addresses. A unified threat management (UTM) appliance typically performs virtual private network (VPN), firewall, and antivirus functions. It does not convert IP addresses.

84. A, B. 1.1.1.0 and 9.34.0.0 are both valid IPv4 network addresses. IPv4 addresses with first byte values from 224 to 239 are Class D addresses, which are reserved for use as multicast addresses. Therefore, the user cannot use 229.6.87.0 for his network. 103.256.77.0 is an invalid address because the value 256 cannot be represented by an 8-bit binary value.

85. B. Distance vector protocols rely on hop counts—that is, the number of routers between a source and a destination—to evaluate the efficiency of routes. Link state protocols use a different type of calculation, usually based on Dijkstra's algorithm. The terms *interior gateway protocol* and *edge gateway protocol* do not refer to the method of calculating routing efficiency.

86. A, C. Any type of fiber-optic cable will satisfy the client's requirements. Fiber-optic cable supports the required 1,000 Mbps data rate and can connect networks that are 500 meters apart. Fiber-optic cable is also immune to EMI. Although both multimode and single-mode fiber would meet the corporation's general needs, multimode is substantially less expensive than single-mode fiber. Twisted-pair wiring (STP or UTP) can meet the data rate requirement, but it does not support connections longer than 100 meters. Thin coaxial cable does not support the data rate or distances longer than 185 meters.

87. C, D. An incorrect frequency, SSID, or WPA3 passphrase would prevent the user's laptop from ever connecting to the network, so these cannot be the cause of the problem. Greater distance from the access point or interference from intervening walls can both cause a weakening of wireless signals, which can result in the intermittent connectivity that the user is experiencing.

88. A, C, E. Static routes are not automatically added to the routing table by routing protocols and do not automatically adapt to changes in the network. Therefore, they are not recommended for large internetworks with redundant paths between networks. Administrators must manually add, modify, or delete static routes when a change in a network occurs. For this reason, static routes are recommended only for use in small networks without multiple paths to each destination.

89. C. Network layer protocols specify logical addresses, such as IP addresses, for end system communication. They also use those addresses to route packets to destinations on other networks. The Physical layer defines standards for physical and mechanical characteristics of a network. The Data link layer uses media access control (MAC) or hardware addresses, not logical addresses. The Transport layer uses port numbers, not logical addresses. Session layer protocols create and maintain a dialog between end systems. Presentation layer protocols are responsible for the formatting, translation, and presentation of information. The Application layer provides an entry point for applications to access the protocol stack and prepare information for transmission across a network.

90. C. The use of an incorrect wireless security protocol is a well-known source of errorless connection failures, so checking this will most likely enable you to discover the source of the problem. Channel overlap is a problem that you would check and resolve at the access point, not at the users' workstations. It is not possible to change the frequency on the access point, because the 802.11ac standard only supports the 5 GHz frequency. Although signal interference could conceivably be the cause for a connection failure, the users can see the network's SSID, so this is not likely to be the problem.

91. A, B, C. iSCSI does not include its own flow control mechanism, so option D is incorrect. It runs over a TCP connection, which is the protocol responsible for flow control. Fibre Channel requires a dedicated network using fiber-optic cable. iSCSI traffic can coexist with standard LAN traffic on a single network, although some type of quality of service (QoS) mechanism is frequently recommended. Because it runs on any IP network, iSCSI traffic is routable, and it is far less expensive to implement than Fibre Channel.

92. B, C, E. The client's DNS server uses iterative queries when sending name resolution requests to root domain servers and to the authoritative servers for the com and `adatum.com` domains. In an iterative query, the server replies immediately with the best information it possesses, and the transaction ends. When a client sends a name resolution query to its DNS server, it uses a recursive request so that the server will assume the responsibility for resolving the name. The only other use of recursive requests is in the case of a forwarder, which is configured to pass that responsibility on to another DNS server.

93. D. To access the Internet, the workstation's routing table must include a default gateway entry. The default gateway is a router on the local network that provides access to other networks, such as the Internet. To manually create a default gateway entry in the routing table, you use the `route add` command with a Network Destination value of 0.0.0.0, a MASK value of 0.0.0.0, and the address of a router on the local network (in this case 192.168.2.99). The entry must also have a METRIC value that is lower than the other entries in the table so that it will be used first.

94. A, B, D. Thin Ethernet networks use Bayonet Neill-Concelman (BNC) connectors. Thick Ethernet networks use N-type connectors. All unshielded twisted-pair (UTP) Ethernet networks use RJ-45 connectors. You will not need F-type or DB-9 connectors. F-type connectors are used with coaxial cable but are typically used for cable television installations. DB-9 connectors are commonly used for serial communications ports.

95. A. Geofencing is the generic term for a technology that limits access to a network or other resource based on the client's location. Therefore, it is best described as somewhere you are. A finger gesture would be considered something you do, a password something you know, and a smartcard something you have.

96. A. Hot, warm, and cold backup sites differ in the hardware and software they have installed. A cold site is just a space at a remote location. The hardware and software must be procured and installed before the network can be restored. Therefore, it is the least expensive and takes the most time. A warm site has hardware in place, but it still must be installed and configured. A hot site has all of the necessary hardware already installed and configured. A warm site is more expensive than a cold site, and a hot site is the most expensive of all and takes the shortest amount of time to be made operational.

97. A. A host-to-site VPN is a remote access solution, enabling users to access the corporate network from home or while traveling. A site-to-site VPN enables one network to connect to another, enabling users on both networks to access resources on the other one. This is usually a more economical solution for branch office connections than a wide area network (WAN) link. A host-to-host VPN enables two individual users to establish a protected connection to each other. An extranet VPN is designed to provide clients, vendors, and other outside partners with the ability to connect to your corporate network with limited access.

98. B, C, D. The leaf and spine topology uses a full mesh topology in its two layers of switches. This is more expensive than the three-tier topology, but it reduces latency by requiring the same number of hops in the path between any two routers. The use of software defined networking provides adaptive path determination without the use of the Spanning Tree Protocol (STP) for layer 2 port blocking.

99. D. Performance Monitor is a Windows application that can create logs of specific system and network performance statistics over extended periods of time. Such a log created on a new computer can function as a baseline for future troubleshooting. Event Viewer is a Windows application for displaying system log files; it cannot create a performance baseline. Syslog is a log compilation program originally created for Unix systems; it does not create performance baselines. Network Monitor is a protocol analyzer. Although it can capture a traffic sample that can function as a reference for future troubleshooting efforts, this cannot be called a performance baseline.

100. C. Although a DoS attack typically involves traffic flooding, any attack that prevents a server from functioning can be called a DoS attack. A permanent DoS attack is one in which the attacker actually damages the target system and prevents it from functioning. This can be a physical attack that actually damages the server hardware, or the attacker can disable the server by altering its software or configuration settings. Flood-based attacks include the distributed denial-of-service (DDoS) attack, in which the attacker uses hundreds or thousands of computers, controlled by malware and called bots or zombies, to send traffic to a single server or website in an attempt to overwhelm it and prevent it from functioning. An amplified DoS attack is one in which the messages sent by the attacker require an extended amount of processing by the target servers, increasing the burden on them more than simpler messages would. A reflective DoS attack is one in which the attacker sends requests containing the target server's IP address to legitimate servers on the Internet, such as DNS servers, causing them to send a flood of responses that overwhelm the target.

Chapter 7: Practice Test 2

1. B. A firewall is a network device—either hardware or software—that functions as a filter that can prevent dangerous traffic originating on one network from passing through to another network. A device that connects two networks together and forwards traffic between them is a router, not a firewall. A device that caches Internet data is a proxy server or caching engine, not a firewall. A device that enables Internet network clients with private IP addresses to access the Internet is a description of a network address translation (NAT) router or a proxy server, not a firewall.

2. C. All half-duplex port connections on a switch represent a different collision domain. Therefore, each of the nine connected computers forms its own collision domain. Full-duplex connections are not subject to collisions, so they do not define separate collision domains.

3. D. A Remote Authentication Dial-In User Service (RADIUS) server can provide authentication, authorization, and accounting services for remote access servers. Network attached storage (NAS) devices, intrusion detection systems (IDSs), and next-generation firewalls (NGFWs) do not provide this type of authentication service.

4. B. A multilayer switch is a network connectivity device that functions at both the Data link layer (layer 2) and the Network layer (layer 3) of the Open Systems Interconnection (OSI) reference model. At layer 2, the device functions like a normal switch, creating an individual collision domain for each connected node and enabling administrators to create multiple VLANs. At layer 3, the device also provides routing capabilities by forwarding packets between the VLANs. Virtual routers, broadband routers, and load balancers are strictly layer 3 devices that can route traffic but cannot create VLANs.

5. C. The value after the slash in a classless inter-domain routing (CIDR) address specifies the number of bits in the network identifier. An IPv4 address has 32 bits, so if 19 bits are allocated to the network identifier, 13 bits are left for the host identifier.

6. D. On a TCP/IP network, the Internet Protocol (IP) at the Network layer is the protocol responsible for the delivery of data to its final destination, using IP addresses that can be routed through an internetwork. Data link layer protocols are only concerned with communication between devices on a local area network (LAN) or between two points connected by a wide area network (WAN). The Transport, Session, and Application layers are not involved in the actual delivery of data over the internetwork.

7. **C, D.** The iSCSI protocol runs on a standard IP network, and the Fibre Channel over Ethernet (FCoE) variant runs on a standard Ethernet network. Both of these protocols can share a network with LAN traffic, although the use of a quality of service (QoS) mechanism is usually recommended to prioritize traffic. The original Fibre Channel implementation and InfiniBand both require a dedicated network medium that does not support LAN traffic.

8. **B, D.** SMTP and DNS are both Application layer protocols, but neither one includes a character-based program. Both Telnet and FTP are protocols that include command-line client applications, with Telnet providing terminal emulation and FTP file transfer functionality.

9. **A, B.** Switches are Data link layer devices that amplify and repeat incoming signals only through the port to which the data is destined, not through all ports. Switches typically provide an internal crossover circuit connection, and uplink ports are sometimes used to extend the distance of a star/hub and spoke network, forming a hierarchical star. Switches are used to physically connect end systems to a star/hub and spoke topology. Switches use MAC addresses, not IP addresses, to identify the devices connected to specific ports.

10. **D, E, F.** DHCP servers use well-known port numbers 67 and 68. TFTP uses port number 69. Neither protocol uses port 64, 65, or 66.

11. **C, D.** The change management team is usually not responsible for tasks directly involved in the implementation of the changes they approve. Therefore, they would not be the ones to notify users exactly when the change will take place or document the procedure afterward. They would, however, be responsible for providing a maintenance window, during which the change must occur, and authorizing any downtime that would be needed.

12. **C.** A server with dual power supplies can run in one of two modes: redundant or combined. In redundant mode, each of the power supplies is capable of providing 100 percent of the power needed by the server. Therefore, the server can continue to run if one power supply fails, making it fault tolerant. In combined mode, both power supplies are needed to provide the server's needs, so a failure of one power supply will bring the server down. Individual mode and hot backup mode are not terms used for this purpose.

13. **B.** The word paris is the name of the bottommost domain in the given FQDN. Paris is a subdomain within mydomain, and mydomain is a second-level domain registered by a particular organization. The topmost layer in the DNS hierarchy is represented by org, which is a top-level domain. In this FQDN, www is not the name of a domain; it is the name of a particular host in the paris.mydomain.org domain.

14. **B, C.** The two main connectionless protocols in the TCP/IP suite are the Internet Protocol (IP) and the User Datagram Protocol (UDP), both of which use the term *datagram* for their protocol data units. Ethernet uses the term *frame,* and Transmission Control Protocol (TCP) uses the term *segment.*

15. **A.** The confidentiality element of the CIA triad prevents data from being viewed by unauthorized users. Integrity is protection against unauthorized modification of data. Availability provides users with access to the data they need.

16. B. A patch is a relatively small update that is designed to address a specific issue, often a security exploit or vulnerability. Patches do not add features or new capabilities; they are fixes targeted at a specific area of the operating system. Updates, upgrades, and service packs are larger packages that might include new features and/or many different fixes.

17. A, D. The twisted wire pairs inside twisted-pair cable prevent the signals on the different wires from interfering with each other (which is called crosstalk). The twists also provide resistance to outside electromagnetic interference (EMI). The twists have no effect on collisions. The twists do nothing to facilitate the attachment of connectors. Twists have nothing to do with the bend radius allowance for the cable.

18. D. The `top` utility displays performance information about the currently running processes on a Unix/Linux system. The other options are tools that do not display running processes. `Netstat` is a tool that enables you to view active network connections and TCP/IP traffic statistics; it does not measure system performance. The `dig` tool generates Domain Name System (DNS) queries. `Perfmon` is a Windows performance monitoring tool; there is no Unix/Linux tool by that name.

19. B. The software as a service (SaaS) model provides consumers with access to a specific application, such as email, running on the provider's servers. Infrastructure as a service (IaaS) provides the consumers with processing, storage, and networking resources that they can use to install and run operating systems and other software of their choice. Platform as a service (PaaS) provides consumers with the ability to install applications of their choice on a server installed by the provider.

20. D. In SIEM, forensic analysis is a process of searching logs on multiple computers for specific information based on set criteria and time periods. The other three options specify other SIEM functions. Data aggregation is a process of consolidating log information from multiple sources. Correlation is the process of linking logged events with common attributes together. Retention is the long-term storage of log data.

21. A. DHCP clients use broadcasts to transmit DHCPDISCOVER messages on the local network. DHCP servers are then required to respond to the broadcasts. DHCP clients cannot use unicast, multicast, or anycast messages to initiate contact with DHCP servers, because the clients have no way of learning the addresses of the DHCP servers.

22. E. VPN typically enables remote users to connect to a VPN router at a central site, much like the star/hub and spoke topology of a local area network, in which computers are all connected to a central switch. A clientless VPN creates an encrypted tunnel to a server using a browser, without the need to install additional client software. Dynamic multipoint virtual private network (DMVPN) is a technology that creates a mesh topology between the remote VPN sites, enabling the remote sites to connect directly to each other, rather than to the central VPN server. A virtual private network (VPN) concentrator is a type of router that enables multiple client systems to access a network from remote locations. A Session Initiation Protocol (SIP) trunk provides a connection between the private and public domains of a unified communications network. Multiprotocol Label Switching (MPLS) is a data transfer mechanism that assigns labels to individual packets, and then routes the packets based on those labels.

23. C, D. IEEE 802.11b, 802.11g, and 802.11n networks all can use the 2.4 GHz frequency band for their transmissions, which can experience interference from a wireless telephone using the same frequency. IEEE 802.11a and IEEE 802.11ac, however, use the 5 GHz band, which will not experience interference from a 2.4 GHz phone.

24. C. A switch is a Data link layer device that essentially performs the function of a bridge for each device connected to one of its ports. Therefore, it can be described as a multiport bridge. Multiport repeater is another term for a hub, and multihomed router is a redundancy, as all routers are by definition multihomed—that is, connected to multiple networks. There is no such device as a multicast hub.

25. D. The term *out-of-band* describes any type of management access to a device that does not go through the production network. Plugging a laptop into the console port avoids the network, so it is considered to be an example of out-of-band management. In-band management describes an access method that does go through the production network. Client-to-site is a type of VPN connection, and bring your own device (BYOD) is a policy defining whether and how users are permitted to connect their personal devices to the network.

26. B. Single sign-on (SSO) uses one set of credentials and requires the user to supply them only once to gain access to multiple resources. Same sign-on also uses a single set of credentials, with one password, but the user must perform individual logons for each resource. Neither single sign-on nor same sign-on calls for multifactor authentication.

27. B. The technology that uses human physical characteristics to authenticate users is called biometrics. Biometric devices can identify users based on fingerprints, retinal patterns, voice prints, and other characteristics.

28. B, C, D. Option B contains a *p*, which is a nonhexadecimal digit. Option C contains blocks larger than 16 bits. Option D contains only seven 16-bit blocks (and no double colon) instead of the eight required for a 128-bit IPv6 address. The address fe00::c955:c944:acdd:3fcb in Option A is correctly formatted for IPv6, with the double colon replacing three blocks of zeroes. Uncompressed, the address would appear as follows: fe00:0000:0000:0000:c955:c944:acdd:3fcb.

29. A. The terms *fail close* and *fail open* refer to the default position of an electric or electronic door lock when there is a power failure. Physical security is often a trade-off with safety, and in the event that an emergency occurs that results in a power outage, whether secured doors are permanently locked or left permanently open is a critical factor. The terms *fail closed* and *fail open* do not apply to motion detectors or video cameras. A honeypot is a computer, application, or website configured to lure potential attackers; it is not a physical security mechanism.

30. B. The IT director's concern is that the disgruntled senior associate might take advantage of his access to devices and facilities to sabotage the network. When an individual takes advantage of information gathered during their employment, it is called an internal (or insider) threat. An external threat is one originating from a non-employee. Social engineering is a form of attack in which an innocent user is persuaded by an attacker to provide sensitive information via email or telephone. A logic bomb is a code insert placed into a legitimate software product that triggers a malicious event when specific conditions are met. Rogue devices are unauthorized components, such as wireless access points or DHCP servers, planted on a network with nefarious intent.

31. C. The IP address 127.0.0.1 is a dedicated loopback address that directs outgoing IP traffic directly into the incoming IP traffic buffer. A successful ping test using that address indicates that the computer's TCP/IP stack is functioning properly, but the traffic never reaches the network adapter or the network, so the test does not confirm that the adapter is functioning or that the computer has a correct IP address for the network.

32. B, C. Multifactor authentication (MFA) combines two or more authentication methods and reduces the likelihood that an intruder would be able to successfully impersonate a user during the authentication process. A password and a retinal scan is an example of a multifactor authentication system. A smartcard and a PIN, which is the equivalent of a password, is an example of multifactor authentication because it requires users to supply something they know and something they have. Multifactor authentication refers to the proofs of identity a system requires, not the number of servers used to implement the system. Therefore, the use of a RADIUS server does not make for an example of multifactor authentication. A system that requires two passwords is not an example of multifactor authentication, because an attacker can compromise two passwords as easily as one. A multifactor authentication system requires two different forms of authentication.

33. C. To access the Internet, the workstation's routing table must include a default gateway entry, which would have a Network Destination value of 0.0.0.0. A workstation's routing table does not have to specify the address of a DNS server. The loopback (127.0.0.1) and multicast (224.0.0.0) addresses are normal routing table entries that do not affect Internet access.

34. A, D. Multimode cables use an LED light source and have a smaller bend radius than single-mode cables. Single-mode cables have a smaller core filament and can span longer distances than multimode cables. Fiber-optic cables are not conductors of electricity, so they do not require a ground.

35. D. Authentication is the process of confirming a user's identity. Smartcards and passwords are two of the authentication factors commonly used by network devices. Authorization defines the type of access granted to authenticated users. Accounting and auditing are both methods of tracking and recording a user's activities on a network, such as when a user logged on and how long they remained connected.

36. B, D. Ethernet has never used a ring or mesh topology. The first Ethernet networks used a Physical layer implementation commonly known as Thick Ethernet or 10Base5. The network used coaxial cable in a bus topology. Later Ethernet standards use twisted-pair or fiber-optic cables in a star/hub and spoke topology.

37. C, D. Disabling SSID broadcasting prevents a wireless network from appearing to clients. The clients must specify the SSID to which they want to connect. MAC address filtering is a form of access control list (ACL) that is maintained in the access point and that contains the addresses of devices that are to be permitted to access the network. Both of these mechanisms make it more difficult for unauthorized devices to connect to the access point. The other two options will not help to prevent unauthorized access. Remote Authentication Dial-In User Service (RADIUS) is a server that can provide authentication, authorization, and accounting services for remote access servers. Relocating the access point to a screened subnet (or perimeter network) will not resolve the problem.

38. B. First Hop Redundancy Protocol (FHRP) is a fault tolerance mechanism that enables other routers on a LAN to use the IP address of the network's designated default gateway router in the event that the default router should fail. The other three options do not provide default gateway fault tolerance. Open Shortest Path First (OSPF) is a routing protocol. Spanning Tree Protocol (STP) protects the network against switching loops. Network address translation (NAT) is a routing technology that enables hosts with private IP addresses to access the Internet using a shared public IP address.

39. E, F. The primary function of a network switch is to process packets based on their media access control (MAC) addresses, which makes it a Data link layer device. However, multiprotocol switches are devices that can also perform routing functions based on IP addresses, which operate at the Network layer. Switches are not typically associated directly with the other layers of the OSI model.

40. B. An SSID that is not being broadcasted does not appear in the list of available networks, so you must type it in manually. Security protocols are also not detectable, so you must select the WPA3 protocol from the list of options provided on the laptop.

41. C. The IEEE 802.11ac standard, like all of the wireless LAN standards in the 802.11 working group, uses CSMA/CA for media access control. The 802.1X standard defines an authentication mechanism and does not require a media access control mechanism. The IEEE 802.3 (Ethernet) standard uses a different mechanism for media access control: Carrier Sense Multiple Access with Collision Detection (CSMA/CD).

42. D. The place containing the demarcation points and the backbone switch is called the main distribution frame (MDF). An intermediate distribution frame (IDF) is the location of localized telecommunications equipment such as the interface between the horizontal cabling and the backbone. Mean time between failures (MTBF) and Remote Desktop Protocol (RDP) are not network wiring locations.

43. A. Geofencing is the generic term for a technology that limits access to a network or other resource based on the client's location. In wireless networking, geofencing is intended to prevent unauthorized clients outside the facility from connecting to the network. By allowing only users with strong signals to connect, you help to prevent access to outside users. Local authentication is an application or service that triggers an authentication request to which the user must respond before access is granted. Port security is a method for protecting access to switch ports. Motion detection is a system designed to trigger a notification or alarm when an individual trespasses in a protected area. None of these other options are related to signal strength.

44. C. Social engineering is the practice of obtaining sensitive data by contacting users and pretending to be someone with a legitimate need for that data. No software or hardware solution can prevent it; the only way is to educate users of the potential dangers and establish policies that inform users what to do when they experience a social engineering attempt.

Social engineering is not a virus or other form of malware, so an antivirus product has no effect against it. Social engineering is not implemented in network traffic, so a firewall cannot filter it and IPsec cannot protect against it.

45. C. A Class B address uses the first two octets as the network identifier, which yields a binary subnet mask of 11111111 11111111 00000000 00000000. In decimal form, the subnet mask is 255.255.0.0. The 255.0.0.0 mask is for Class A addresses, and the 255.255.255.0 mask is for Class C addresses. 255.255.255.255 is the broadcast address for the current network.

46. B. All the mechanisms that Alice has implemented are designed to make any attempts to tamper with or physically compromise the network hardware devices immediately evident. Therefore, this is a form of tamper detection. Asset tracking is for locating and identifying specific hardware components. Geofencing is a wireless networking technique for limiting access to a network based on signal strength. Port security refers to the protection of network switch ports from unauthorized access.

47. A. Because the administrative site is encrypted, you must use the HTTPS:// prefix to access it. Because the administrative site uses the nondefault port number 12354, you must append that number to the server name after a colon.

48. C. Disabling SSID broadcasts is a way of hiding the presence of a wireless network, but if an intruder knows that a network is there, it is a relatively simple matter to capture packets transmitted by the wireless devices and read the SSID from them. The other options do not explain the weakness of suppressing SSID broadcasts. It is not possible to connect to a wireless network without the SSID. SSIDs are set by the administrator of the access point; they are not printed on the device's label. SSIDs can be discovered relatively easily, but guessing them is no easier than guessing a password.

49. A. In a private cloud, the same organization that uses the cloud services is also the sole owner of the infrastructure that provides those services. In the public cloud model, one organization functions as the provider, and another organization consumes the services of the provider. A hybrid cloud is a combination of public and private infrastructure so that the consumer organization is only a partial owner of the infrastructure. There is no such thing as an ad hoc cloud model.

50. B. On-boarding and off-boarding are identity management processes in which users are added or removed from an organization's identity and access management (IAM) system. This grants new users the privileges they need to use the network, modifies their privileges if they change positions, and revokes privileges when they leave the company. On-boarding and off-boarding are not data loss prevention, incident response, or inventory management processes.

51. B, D. A standard VPN typically uses full tunneling, in which all of the system's network traffic is encapsulated and encrypted for transmission. Split tunneling is a variation of this method in which only part of the system's traffic uses the VPN connection; the rest is transmitted over the network in the normal manner. Administrators can select which applications and devices use the VPN. Split tunneling can conserve the Internet bandwidth used by the VPN and provide access to local network services without the need for encapsulation. Split tunneling does not provide additional data integrity protection or improved performance through multiplexing.

52. B, C. If there is no way for unauthorized people to access the datacenter, then there is no danger of someone plugging a device into a port that is left enabled. If the switch uses an access control list (ACL) that specifies the MAC addresses of systems permitted to connect to it, then there is no need to disable unused ports, because any unknown devices plugged into open ports will not be granted access to the network. The other two options are not valid reasons. Ports that are not patched in can still be compromised at the switch location. Enabling ports is not difficult for authorized administrators, so accommodating new users is not a valid reason for leaving the ports enabled.

53. A. A honeypot or honeynet is a computer or network configured to function as deceptive bait for potential attackers, causing them to waste their time and effort penetrating a resource that provides no significant access or advantage. The other three options are not deception technologies. A root guard provides protection to switch ports by affecting the behavior of the Spanning Tree Protocol (STP) to enforce the selection of root bridge ports on a switched network. A screened subnet (also called a perimeter network) is the part of a network where administrators locate servers that must be accessible from the Internet, such as email and web servers. Geofencing is a security mechanism that prevents unauthorized clients outside the facility from connecting to the network.

54. A, B, C, E. ACLs restrict access to network devices by filtering user names, MAC addresses, IP addresses, or other criteria. Routers, servers, switches, and wireless access points all can use ACLs to control access to them. Hubs are purely Physical layer devices that relay electrical or optical signals. They have no access control mechanisms.

55. A. Administrative distance is a Network layer value that enables routers to select the most reliable routing protocol to use when multiple protocols supply routes to the same destination. The other three options are all associated with the Data link layer. Ethernet uses jumbo frames at the Data link layer to transfer large amounts of data more efficiently. The maximum transmission unit (MTU) value of a Data link layer frame specifies its maximum size. Switches use the Spanning Tree Protocol (STP) at the Data link layer to prevent redundant switches from causing traffic loops on the network. Ethernet typically restricts the size of Data link layer frames to 1,500 bytes, but jumbo frames enable Ethernet systems to create frames up to 9,000 bytes.

56. A, C, D. DHCP snooping is a feature found in some network switches that prevents rogue DHCP servers from assigning IP addresses to clients. It can also detect when DHCP release or decline messages arrive over a port other than the one on which the DHCP transaction originated. Although DHCP snooping can prevent DHCP clients from being assigned an incorrect IP address, it does not directly prevent the poisoning of DNS server caches with erroneous information.

57. D. In this scenario, only one user is reporting a problem. Therefore, the likeliest next step is to perform the same task on another computer attached to the same segment. If you can perform the task successfully, the problem most likely lies within the user's computer or the connection to the switch. Since no other users are reporting the same problem, the server and switches on the network are probably up and functioning. Checking the router is not necessary, because the user and server are on the same network.

58. C. A captive portal is a web page displayed to a user attempting to access a public wireless network. The user typically must supply identification, submit credentials, provide payment, or accept an end-user agreement before access is granted. A captive portal does not refer to a switch port, a secured entryway to a room, or a type of extortionate computer attack.

59. B. After identifying the problem, the next step is to establish a theory for the probable cause of the problem. After that, you can test your theory, establish a plan of action, implement a solution, verify the functionality of the system, and document the entire process.

60. B, D. The well-known port for HTTPS is 443. The port for unsecured HTTP is 80. Neither of the other options are ports used by HTTP or HTTPS by default. Port 25 is used for the Simple Mail Transfer Protocol (SMTP), and port 110 is used for the Post Office Protocol (POP3).

61. A, C, D. A load balancing router typically works by processing incoming traffic based on rules set by an administrator. The rules can distribute traffic among a group of servers using various criteria, such as each server's current load or response time or which server is next in a given rotation. Load balancers generally do not use the hardware configuration of the servers to direct traffic, as this is a factor that does not change over time.

62. D. Since only one user is reporting difficulty, the problem is most likely to be in the user's computer and its configuration. A DNS server, proxy server, or router problem would affect more than one user.

63. A. VLAN hopping is a method for sending false commands to switches to transfer a port from one VLAN to another. This can enable the attacker to connect his or her device to a potentially sensitive VLAN. VLAN hopping does not modify the switch's patch panel connections, only its VLAN assignments. It is not possible to rename a switch's default VLAN. VLAN hopping does not enable an attacker to change a switch's native VLAN.

64. A. A problem that affects the entire network should be given highest priority. This includes the issue with the mission-critical backbone router. Problems that affect multiple LANs or an entire department are generally given the next highest priority. A problem that affects a shared application server on a LAN should be given the next highest priority. Barring other seniority factors, a problem with a single user's computer should be given the lowest priority, compared to the other problems that have been reported.

65. C, D. One possible cause of the problem is that the DNS process on the remote server is corrupted or not running. Another possible cause is that there is a firewall blocking access to the DNS server's UDP port 53. Both of these would render the port unreachable. The TCP/IP client on the server is operating, as verified by the `ping` utility. This means that the IP host settings on your computer and on the DNS server are both configured properly and functioning. A router does not need to be running DNS to forward datagrams.

66. D. Store-and-forward switches take in the entire frame and verify its contents by performing a CRC calculation before forwarding it. Cut-through switches are faster because they look at only the first 6 bytes (the destination media access control, or MAC, address) when forwarding a frame; they do not perform a CRC on the entire frame. Source route is a bridging technique in which the source host, not the switch, determines the path a frame will take through a network to reach a destination. Packet filtering is a technique used by firewalls. Neither of these is a type of switch.

67. A. A logic bomb is a code insert placed into a legitimate software product that triggers a malicious event when specific conditions are met. Therefore, it can affect both wired and wireless clients. The other options are all attacks directed at wireless networks. Deauthentication is a type of denial-of-service attack in which the attacker targets a wireless client by sending a deauthentication frame that causes the client to be disconnected from the network. The object of the attack is often to compel the client to connect to a rogue access point called an evil twin. An evil twin is a fraudulent access point on a wireless network that mimics the SSID of a legitimate access point, in the hope of luring in users. A rogue AP is a wireless access point that has been connected to a network by an intruder in the hope of luring users into connecting to it.

68. B. Configuring the devices to use the 5 GHz band will provide many more channels to choose from and will avoid the interference from the surrounding 2.4 GHz networks. The other options will not resolve the problem. The type of encryption that a wireless network uses has no bearing on the ability of the devices to avoid the interference generated by surrounding networks. Suppressing SSID broadcasts will not help the devices to connect to the network. Upgrading the firmware on the devices is not likely to have any effect on the connection problems when they are the result of interference from other networks.

69. A. Running the arp utility with the -a parameter on a Windows system displays the contents of the Address Resolution Protocol (ARP) cache, as shown here. The cache contains records of the IP addresses on the network that ARP has resolved into MAC addresses. The ping, tracert, and netstat utilities are not capable of producing this output.

70. C. The device shown in the figure is a crimper, which is used to create patch cables by attaching connectors to both ends of a relatively short length of bulk cable. This tool is not capable of placing telephone calls, generating a tone on a wire, or measuring electric current.

71. B. The device shown in the figure is a punchdown tool, used to connect unshielded twisted-pair cable ends to the keystone connectors used in modular wall plates and patch panels. After lining up the individual wires in the cable with the connector, you use the tool to press each wire into its slot. The tool also cuts the wire sheath to make an electrical contact and trims the end of the wire. The tool shown is not a crimper, a butt set, or a toner and probe.

72. E. IEEE 802.11n supports transmission speeds up to 600 Mbps, and it is backward compatible with 802.11g equipment. IEEE 802.11ac is faster than 802.11g, but it is not backward compatible with 802.11g, because it can only use the 5 GHz band. Bluetooth is not compatible with any of the IEEE 802.11 standards. IEEE 802.11 and 802.11a cannot exceed the speed of 802.11n. 802.11a is also limited to the 5 GHz band and is not backward compatible with 802.11g.

73. A, B. Both Linux and the Cisco IOS operating systems include the traceroute utility. Windows has its own version of the utility, but it is called tracert. The CSU/DSU cannot run a traceroute command.

74. C, E. WLANs can use the ad hoc topology, in which devices communicate directly with each other, or the infrastructure topology, in which the wireless devices connect to an access point. The bus and star/hub and spoke topologies are used by wired networks only. Spine and leaf is a datacenter topology used for switches.

75. C. SNMP version 1 (SNMPv1), SNMP version 2 (SNMPv2), and SNMP version 2c (SNMPv2c) all rely on unencrypted community strings that are sent with GET requests as a security mechanism. However, SNMPv2c uses two separate community strings, one for read-write and one for read-only access. SNMP version 3 (SNMPv3) uses fully encrypted transmissions for more advanced security and does not use a community string.

76. C. The customer's IP address, subnet mask, and default gateway values are appropriate for her home network. There is nothing wrong with having a zero in the network address. Therefore, of the options presented, the only logical choice is that the workstation's network cable is damaged or unplugged.

77. D. The Spanning Tree Protocol (STP) prevents packets from endlessly looping from switch to switch due to redundant links. Creating redundant links is a good preventive measure against switch failure, but packets transmitted over multiple links can circulate from switch to switch infinitely. STP creates a database of switching links and shuts down the redundant ones until they are needed. None of the other three protocols listed can perform this function. Network address translation (NAT) is a routing method that enables private networks to share registered IP addresses. Routing Information Protocol (RIP) propagates routing table information to other routers. A virtual local area network (VLAN) is an organizational tool that operates within switches by creating multiple broadcast domains.

78. C. In this scenario, only the users on one LAN are experiencing problems connecting to the Internet and the other internal LANs. This isolates the problem to a component within that LAN only. Since users can connect successfully to local resources, the problem does not lie within the individual computers, the switch that connects the users to the network, or the backbone network cable. Therefore, the likeliest problem is in the router connecting the problem LAN to the backbone network. Since users on the other internal LANs are not reporting problems connecting to the Internet, the problem most likely does not involve the Internet router.

79. B. The agreed upon 99.9 percent guaranteed availability will be part of a service-level agreement (SLA), which is a contract between a provider and a subscriber that specifies the percentage of time that the contracted services are available. None of the other three options contain the guaranteed reliability language. Acceptable use policies (AUP) specify whether and how employees can use company-owned hardware and software resources. A nondisclosure agreement (NDA) specifies what company information employees are permitted to discuss outside the company. A bring your own device (BYOD) policy specifies the personal electronics that employees are permitted to use on the company network and documents the procedures for connecting and securing them.

80. A, B. A switch creates a separate collision domain for each port. A bridge can split a single network into two collision domains because it forwards only the packets that are destined for the other side of the bridge. Both bridges and switches forward all broadcast packets, so they maintain a single broadcast domain for the entire network. A firewall does not affect the collision and broadcast domain configuration of the network. A router creates two collision domains, but it does not forward broadcasts, so it creates two broadcast domains as well.

81. A. MAC addresses are hard-coded into network interface adapters and are not easily change-able. There is also no need to change them for this purpose. First, you will have to change IP addresses of the web servers. This is because the computers on the other side of the router, on the screened subnet, must use an IP network address that is different from the internal network's address. Next, you will have to change the default gateway address setting on the internal network computers to the address of the router on the internal network so that traffic can be forwarded to the screened subnet. Finally, you will have to update the resource records on your DNS server to reflect the IP address changes.

82. C. A short is when a wire is connected to two or more pins at one end of the cable or when the conductors of two or more wires are touching inside the cable. This would cause a tone applied to a single pin at one end to be heard on multiple pins at the other end. The other three options would not cause this to occur. An open circuit would manifest as a failure to detect a tone on a wire, indicating that there is either a break in the wire somewhere inside the cable or a bad connection with the pin in one or both connectors. A split pair is a con-nection in which two wires are incorrectly mapped in exactly the same way on both ends of the cable. Crosstalk is a type of interference caused by signals on one wire bleeding over to other wires.

83. B. Elevator machinery, fluorescent light fixtures, and other electrical devices in an office envi-ronment can generate magnetic fields, resulting in electromagnetic interference (EMI). When copper-based cables are located too near to such a device, the magnetic fields can generate an electric current on the cable that interferes with the signals exchanged by network devices. If the network users experience a problem every time the elevator machinery switches on, EMI is a likely cause of the problem. Crosstalk and attenuation can both cause intermittent network communication problems, but they cannot be caused by elevator machinery. Latency describes a generalized delay in network transmissions, not intermittent packet delays.

84. B, D. In an active-active configuration, servers can balance the incoming client load between them. Because the active servers are all servicing clients, the overall performance of the cluster is increased. Both active-active and active-passive configurations provide fault toler-ance. Data encapsulation is not a factor in either configuration.

85. D. It is possible that the wireless access point has been configured not to broadcast the network's SSID as a security measure, so you should first attempt to access it by typing the SSID in manually. You cannot type in the WPA3 passphrase until you are in the process of connecting to the SSID. Moving the laptop closer to the access point or away from possible sources of electromagnetic interference might be solutions to the problem, but they should not be the first things you try in this case.

86. D. The 802.11g standard does not support 5 GHz communications, only the 2.4 GHz band. Configuring the access point to support 2.4 GHz is the only way for the 802.11g computers to connect to the network. The 5 GHz band does support automatic channel selection, so there is no need to configure the channel on each laptop manually. The 5 GHz band does support MIMO, and the 802.11n laptops should be able to connect.

87. D. The name server (NS) resource record identifies the authoritative servers for a particular DNS zone. Pointer (PTR) resource records are used to resolve IP addresses into hostnames.

Mail exchange (MX) records identify the mail servers for a particular domain. Service locator (SRV) records identify the designated servers for a particular application. None of these other options identify the authoritative servers for a zone.

88. B. The 2.4 GHz band used by wireless LANs (WLANs) consists of channels that are 20 (or 22) MHz wide. However, the channels are only 5 MHz apart, so there is channel overlap that can result in interference. Channels 1, 6, and 11 are the only channels that are far enough apart from each other to avoid any overlap with the adjacent channels. This is why they are often recommended. However, in this scenario, these channels are too crowded with other networks. So, you should use a channel that is as far as possible from the crowded ones. Channels 2, 5, and 10 are all immediately adjacent to a crowded channel, but channel 9 is at least two channels away from the nearest crowded channel. Therefore, you should configure your equipment to use channel 9.

89. A. Material safety data sheets (MSDSs) are documents created by manufacturers of chemical, electrical, and mechanical products that specify the potential risks and dangers associated with them, particularly in regard to flammability and the possibility of toxic outgassing. A properly documented network should have MSDS documents on file for all of the chemical and hardware products used to build and maintain it. MSDSs can be obtained from manufacturers or the Environmental Protection Agency (EPA). Electrostatic discharges (ESDs), nondisclosure agreements (NDAs), and bring your own device (BYOD) policies are not concerned with the dangers inherent in building contents.

90. C. The Alternative B PoE variant can use the spare wire pair in a 100Base-TX cable to supply power to connected devices. The Alternative A and 4PPoE variants cannot use the spare wire pair in this manner; they supply power using the wire pairs that carry data at the same time. For Gigabit Ethernet or faster installations, Alternative B is also capable of using the data wire pairs.

91. B, D. A storage area network (SAN) is a separate network dedicated to shared storage devices, while NAS devices are self-contained file servers that connect directly to a standard IP network NAS devices are typically not iSCSI targets. A NAS device provides file-level access to its storage devices and includes an operating system and a filesystem. SAN devices typically do not have operating systems.

92. C. WPA has been found to be vulnerable, and WPA3 was designed to address those vulnerabilities, so you should use WPA3 instead of WPA. Suppressing SSID broadcasts does not prevent users from connecting to the network, and MAC filtering strengthens security without exposing MAC addresses to undue risk.

93. B, D, E. Subscriber Connector (SC), Multi-fiber Push On (MPO), and Straight Tip (ST) are all types of fiber-optic connectors. DB-9 is a D-shell connector used for serial ports. Bayonet Neill-Concelman (BNC) is a type of connector used with coaxial cable. RJ-11 is used with twisted-pair cable for telephone connections.

94. E. The IoT consists of devices that are ordinarily passive but which have been made intelligent by installing a network client configuring them to participate on an IP network. All of the devices listed are available as "smart" devices that enable remote users to interact with them over the Internet.

95. D. The Physical layer defines the mechanical and electrical characteristics of the cables used to build a network. The Data link layer defines specific network (LAN or WAN) topologies and their characteristics. The Physical layer specification you will implement is dependent on the Data link layer protocol you select. The Network, Transport, and Application layers are not concerned with cables and topologies.

96. D. The 169.254.203.42 address assigned to the workstation is from the 169.254.0.0/16 network address assigned to Automatic Private IP Addressing (APIPA), a standard for the assignment of IP addresses to DHCP clients when they cannot obtain an address from a DHCP server. The workstation's DHCP client is activated, and since no one else is experiencing a problem, you can assume that the DHCP server is functioning. The Subnet Mask value is correct for an APIPA address, and APIPA does not provide Default Gateway or DNS server addresses. Therefore, an exhausted DHCP scope is the only one of the explanations provided that could be the cause of the problem.

97. C. Operating systems detect duplicate IP addresses immediately and display error messages or notifications on the computers involved. Therefore, the user with the problem would have been informed immediately if another system were using her IP address. All of the other options are possible causes of the problem that are more difficult to troubleshoot.

98. C, D. The `ipconfig /release` command terminates the current DHCP address lease. Then, the `ipconfig /renew` command causes the client to begin the process of negotiating a new lease, this time with the authorized DHCP server. Dump, `lease`, and `discard` are not valid `ipconfig` parameters.

99. C. East-west traffic describes traffic flow within the datacenter, while north-south is traffic between devices inside the datacenter and outside devices. The terms *east-west* and *north-south* do not pertain to the OSI model layers or to the specific devices used.

100. D. Running the Windows `netstat` utility with no parameters generates a list of the workstation's active connections, as shown here. The `arp`, `ping`, `tracert`, and `hostname` utilities are not capable of producing this output.

Index

R